THE ZONDERVAN
PASTOR'S
ANNUAL

AN IDEA & RESOURCE BOOK

T. T. CRABTREE

ZONDERVAN®

ZONDERVAN.com/
AUTHOR**TRACKER**
follow your favorite authors

ZONDERVAN

The Zondervan 2010 Pastor's Annual
Copyright © 1968, 1988, 2009 by Zondervan

Requests for information should be addressed to:

Zondervan, *Grand Rapids, Michigan 49530*

Much of the content of this book was previously published in *Pastor's Annual 1969* and *Pastor's Annual 1989.*

ISBN 978-0-310-27589-3 (softcover)

09 10 11 12 13 14 15 16 17 18 19 · 24 23 22 21 20 19 18 17 16 15 14 13 12 11 10 9 8 7 6 5 4 3 2 1

CONTENTS

SERMONS

MISCELLANEOUS HELPS

Messages on the Lord's Supper

INDEXES

CONTRIBUTING AUTHORS

Bill Causey   A.M.: November 28
                                  December 5, 12, 19, 26

H. C. Chiles   A.M.: August 1, 8, 15, 22, 29

T. T. Crabtree   All sermons not attributed to others

R. B. Culbreth   P.M.: March 7, 14, 21, 28
                                  April 4, 11, 18, 25

William T. Flynt   A.M.: February 7, 14, 21, 28
                                  July 18, 25

J. M. Gaskin   A.M.: July 4
                                  October 31
                                  November 14

James G. Harris   A.M.: May 16, 30
                                  June 6, 13, 20

David G. Hause   P.M.: May 2, 9, 16, 23

David L. Jenkins   A.M.: January 31

R. Furman Kenney   A.M.: January 3, 10, 17, 24

Howard S. Kolb   P.M.: October 3, 10, 17, 24, 31

Jerold R. McBride   P.M.: January 3, 10, 17, 24, 31
                                  February 7, 14, 21, 28

R. Trevis Otey   P.M.: July 7, 14, 21, 28
                                  August 4, 11, 18, 25

E. Warren Rust   A.M.: September 5, 12, 19, 26
                                  October 3, 17, 24

Fred H. Willhoite   P.M.: December 1, 8, 15, 22

PREFACE

During my service of ordination to the ministry, Dr. Cal Guy quoted the words of Jesus to Peter: "Feed my lambs"; "Feed my sheep"; "Feed my sheep." He then summarized by saying that this does not mean "warmed-over mutton three times a day." He emphasized that one must not only study the Bible and pray, but also love and know the needs of the sheep if he is to feed them.

As a seminary student, I was introduced to the books of Andrew W. Blackwood, professor of homiletics at Princeton. His book *Planning a Year's Pulpit Work* made a significant impact on my thinking as I began to give serious consideration to the task of being a "feeder of the sheep" over which the Good Shepherd had made me an undershepherd.

It dawned upon my mind that the Holy Spirit did not have to wait until Friday night or even Saturday night to impress upon my heart what the Lord intended for the sheep to receive on Sunday. As this truth became a conviction, I became convinced that the sheep would probably receive a greater variety and much better quality of messages if the "shepherd" did some looking ahead rather than just waiting for the agonizing "inspiration of the hour" that might not come on Saturday night.

A prayerfully prepared program of preaching helped to organize my study habits and made significant some events, articles, or truths that otherwise would have escaped my notice. It is easier to accumulate fresh illustrations when one has a good idea of what he or she will be speaking on for the next few weeks.

With a planned program of preaching, it is possible to have greater assurance that the specific spiritual needs of the congregation are being met. Dr. J. B. Weatherspoon taught that every sermon should have one central aim and that the aim is determined after a need has been discovered and defined. As pastors get better acquainted with their congregations by personal visitation and counseling, and as they study the conditions in their communities with an awareness of the world conditions that affect us all, there is no limit to the spiritual and moral needs that they should seek to meet. As good mothers work to provide balanced diets for their families, good pastors should give careful attention to the spiritual diets they are "dishing out" to their congregations Sunday after Sunday.

Each sermon a pastor preaches should be born out of a personal experience with God as he or she seeks to meet the needs of the congregation. These abbreviated manuscripts and outlines are only to be used as a guide. If the manuscripts in this volume can be of assistance, we will thank the Father and rejoice in each pastor being a better undershepherd of the Great Shepherd who encouraged us to feed his sheep.

— T. T. Crabtree, formerly pastor
First Baptist Church
Springfield, Missouri

JANUARY

■ **Sunday Mornings**

The theme for the first Sunday mornings of the year is "Christian Living in the New Year." The sermons encourage faith, surrender, trust, prayer, and worship as proper responses to God.

■ **Sunday Evenings**

The theme for Sunday evenings is "Great Night Scenes of the Bible."

■ **Wednesday Evenings**

On Wednesday evenings study the epistle of James. The lessons emphasize that the practice of the Word of God and of genuine religion in daily life is necessary for a Christian witness.

SUNDAY MORNING, JANUARY 3

Title: The Pattern of Life

Text: "For I through the law am dead to the law, that I might live unto God. I am crucified with Christ: nevertheless I live; yet not I, but Christ liveth in me: and the life which I now live in the flesh I live by the faith of the Son of God, who loved me, and gave himself for me" **(Gal. 2:19–20).**

Scripture Reading: Galatians 2:15–21

Hymns:　"Holy Ghost, with Light Divine," Reed

"O for a Closer Walk," Cowper

"When We Walk with the Lord," Sammis

"Take My Life, and Let It Be," Havergal

Offertory Prayer: Heavenly Father, we finite beings of your creation realize keenly our total dependence on you. We are ever aware that all that we have comes from you, that you are ever the Provider of our time, our talents, our health, and our strength. We come before you in an act of dedication, presenting to you not only our tithes and offerings but also ourselves in useful service. On the first Sunday of this new year, we make a vow to you of honesty and faithfulness. We long to see your kingdom grow and prosper in all parts of the world, and we earnestly desire to have a part in that growth. Therefore we now place before you our tithes and offerings even as in our hearts we have already dedicated ourselves afresh to you. In the name of Christ we pray. Amen.

Introduction

People seldom begin a vacation without carefully plotting an intended course of travel. Unfortunately, too many people do not consider life as an adventure to be carefully mapped out prior to takeoff. As Christians we need to ask ourselves what we expect to receive from life for the coming year and, more important, what we expect to give to life during the months ahead.

No two people look upon life in exactly the same fashion. Some see it as pessimistically, as did Macbeth in William Shakespeare's play by that name when he cried out, "Life ... is a tale told by an idiot, full of sound and fury, signifying nothing." Somewhat less pessimistic but in much the same vein are the words of the great Seneca, philosopher, dramatist, and statesman of ancient Rome: "Life is neither a good nor an evil; it is simply the place where good and evil exist." A more optimistic concept of life was presented in Athens some 425 years prior to Christ's birth by the great Greek philosopher Socrates, who taught that "the end of life is to be like God, and the soul following God will be like him." It remained for Paul, however, in the words of our text, to present the thoroughly Christian teaching of what life for the believer is all about: "I live; yet not I, but Christ liveth in me: and the life which I now live in the flesh I live by the faith of the Son of God, who loved me, and gave himself for me" (Gal. 2:20).

As we begin this new year, we need to be much aware that there is before us a journey of twelve months, the pathway of which will be woven into a pattern interlaced with opportunities, tragedies, and victories.

I. Life's pattern will contain opportunities.

Among the joys of facing a new year of life is the joy of knowing that opportunities for growth and service lie before us.

    A. *Opportunities for growth.* When we stop growing in some fashion, we begin to decay. Therefore, during the new year we should seize the opportunity for growth.

        1. Mentally. When Christians have stopped studying and have stopped cultivating their mental capacities, they begin to atrophy; their God-given mental abilities "dry up." We are stewards of our intellect, and we are responsible to God for the cultivation and enlargement of that capacity. Too many people are satisfied with mental mediocrity. Albert Einstein once remarked about his time in history, "We live in a time of perfect mediocrity and confused ends." As Christians we need to be much aware that, in the words of Richard C. Raines, "It does not take a great mind to be a Christian, but it takes all the mind a man has."

        2. Spiritually. During one summer vacation from college, I worked at going from one small church to another conducting vacation Bible schools and teaching study courses. In one community I encountered a pitiful sight; I saw through the window of the dining room where we sat at a beautifully set table something that made an indelible impression on my mind and heart. Being led across the back lawn by a nurse was

a person who was stumbling along and jabbering, a person somewhat dwarfed and quite odd in appearance. My gracious hostess, detecting my startled expression, turned to me and said sadly, "What you see out there is the sorrow of our hearts. Our child, now in her late twenties, has the mind of an infant." Pitiful? Yes, quite pitiful, but there is something more pitiful than that. That to which I refer is the Christian now old in years since conversion but still no more spiritually mature than a newborn Christian. Let us determine that during the coming year we will grow in grace and in the knowledge of our Lord Jesus Christ.

B. *Opportunities for service.* We as Christians need to remind ourselves constantly that we have been saved to serve and not to sit in the kingdom of our Christ. During this coming year we need to serve our Master through:

1. Meaningful Christian service. Jesus taught simply one of life's greatest principles of service to him: "Inasmuch as ye have done it unto one of the least of these my brethren, ye have done it unto me" (Matt. 25:40). During this year we need to come out of our cocoon of self-centeredness and avail ourselves of the opportunities of ministering to the sick, the shut-ins, the physically needy, the imprisoned, and the troubled in the name of our Savior, witnessing for him as we serve.

2. Soul winning. The greatest of all of life's opportunities is the opportunity for person-to-person witnessing with the sole intent of winning a lost person to a saving knowledge of Christ. The joy in soul winning cannot be overestimated. As George W. Truett, the "silver-throated orator" of the pulpit of an earlier generation, expressed it, "The bringing of a soul to Jesus is the highest achievement possible to human life."

So hungry for souls was Deacon George W. Chipman of Tremont Temple in Boston that each Sunday morning he would walk along the wharves looking for waifs and runaways. He would take these unfortunate boys to his church with him. On one such morning he found an eleven-year-old runaway in a barrel, where he had probably slept the preceding night. Chipman took the lad to Tremont Temple, where he found Christ. This worthy servant of God could not possibly know that in later years that little runaway lad would become the founder of Grace Baptist Temple in Philadelphia, Temple University, and two hospitals in that city. Nor could he visualize the hosts of people who would gather to hear his famous lecture "Acres of Diamonds." You see, the little waif George Chipman pulled out of the barrel and witnessed to was none other than Russell H. Conwell.

II. Life's pattern will contain tragedies.

As much as we would like to avoid the tragedies or heartaches that will probably be woven into the pattern of our lives for the coming year, we need to realize that they are the goads that thrust us along in our Christian growth. As Kirby Page has expressed it, "Tragedy crushes and tragedy ennobles, and you had better find out the difference between that which flattens and that which upbuilds." Some of the heartaches or tragedies for which we ought to prepare ourselves are:

A. *Loss of business and wealth.* To lose all of one's material possessions may be a blessing in a strange disguise. I heard of a man who lost his business, his home, and all of his possessions. He went to the Salvation Army for food and for a place to lay his head. Of all things for the Salvation Army worker to confront him with in an attempt to meet his needs was the subject of tithing! Certainly that was hardly appropriate, considering that the man did not have a penny to share with the Lord. He did, however, accept the principle of tithing. Later he migrated to Oklahoma and "struck it rich" in the oil business. True to his newfound principle, he became a partner with the Lord and found life to be much more meaningful than ever before.

B. *Loss of health.* Paul's "thorn in the flesh" has been the subject of much conjecture through the years. I agree with those who hold that it was a physical disability. Paul prayed for its removal. Though this request was not answered in the way he desired, Paul received sufficient grace to bear it. He even saw that the Lord could bring glory to himself through this infirmity. Paul heard the Master saying, "My grace is sufficient for thee: for my strength is made perfect in weakness" (2 Cor. 12:9).

C. *Loss of loved ones.* I recently listened to a man as he stood beside the grave of his beautiful little daughter and said, "God spoke to me through this experience; now I am going to accept the Lord as my Savior." Even out of this catastrophe of life God can bring a great blessing.

III. Life's pattern will contain victories.

Every person experiences some measure of success along life's journey.

A. *For the Christian.* Those of us who have the joy of salvation in our hearts should experience:

1. The victory of growth in grace. At the beginning of this calendar year every Christian should be able to say, "How much better I know my Savior now than I did at the beginning of last year!" The warmth of close fellowship with Christ is reward and victory enough for any Christian.

2. The victory of leading someone to Christ. Every Christian ought to make one New Year's resolution, and that is to endeavor to win at least one soul to Christ each month during the coming year. Undergirding this goal must be earnest prayer for a specific lost person and a personal explanation of the biblical way of salvation to him or her. When the Holy Spirit has done his work of convicting and convincing, you will experience great joy in that person's coming to accept Christ as Savior and Lord.

B. *For the sinner.* Some of you sitting here this morning have felt a remorse over your spiritual condition, realizing that you are in God's sight crooked, perverse, and rebellious against his love. You desire to have a peace of heart and mind that is not yet yours. Accept Christ today as your Savior and Lord and experience the happiness, joy, and peace you crave. For you this will be the greatest of life's victories—the victory of surrender to the King of Kings, Christ Jesus.

Conclusion

Are you ready to face another year of living? Are you spiritually strong enough to seize every opportunity available this year to magnify Christ in your personal life and in your efforts to win souls for him? If you are not yet a follower of Christ, won't you in this first service of the year accept him as your Savior and Lord? Won't you bring Christ into the pattern of your life: "This is the victory that overcometh the world, even our faith" (1 John 5:4).

SUNDAY EVENING, JANUARY 3

Title: A Night of Mystery

Text: "There was a man of the Pharisees, named Nicodemus, a ruler of the Jews: The same came to Jesus by night, and said unto him, Rabbi, we know that thou art a teacher come from God: for no man can do these miracles that thou doest, except God be with him" **(John 3:1–2)**.

Scripture Reading: John 3:1–16

Introduction

In a time when people are eagerly probing into hidden secrets of the universe, we still remain surrounded by one mystery after another. Apparently the solution of one mystery only reveals the existence of countless others.

The bewilderment of our finite minds in the face of some unknown truth is often satisfied by a theory or hypothesis that allegedly explains it. But there is no theory or hypothesis that can lay bare the mystery of salvation. That marvelous transition through which a depraved, sinful person becomes a sanctified child of God remains a mystery to us even as it did to Nicodemus on that night he came to Christ.

Although we have no hope this side of heaven of ever fully understanding this mystery, we can learn enough about it to experience it and share it with others.

I. The mystery of human need.

Our text speaks of the mystery of human need. Nicodemus is identified as "a man of the Pharisees." The Pharisees were distinguished by the orthodox creed and strict observance of the Jewish laws. Paul speaks of them as "the straightest sect of our religion" (Acts 26:5). Nicodemus is further identified as "a ruler of the Jews." This title is reserved for members of the Sanhedrin. Therefore, Nicodemus represented the religious learned class of his nation.

We can understand why Bartimaeus, the Samaritan woman, and the lepers came to Christ, but why would a man of Nicodemus's high moral stature need to come to Christ? This is the mystery of human need!

15

A. *The need for salvation is universal.*
 1. Because all people have sinned, the need for salvation is universal (1 John 1:8).
 2. Because all people are accountable, the need for salvation is universal (Rom. 14:11 – 12). Daniel Webster, when asked about the greatest thought that had ever passed through his mind, answered, "My accountability to God."
B. *Urgency may have been the reason Nicodemus came to Christ "by night."* Some suggest that Nicodemus came to Christ at night because he desired to have a lengthy conversation with Christ and his own schedule or Christ's busy days wouldn't allow enough time during the day. Others say it was because of his fear of the Jews. But a natural reason would be that he came to Christ at night because he was deeply convicted of his need and felt the urgency to take that need to Christ even if it was at night. He could not wait until the next day.
 1. Nicodemus did not know when another choice opportunity to talk with Christ might come, for Christ taught from town to town, and Nicodemus was also a busy man. No one can be certain that he or she will have an opportunity to turn to Christ beyond that present opportunity which is his. "Seek ye the LORD *while* he may be found, call ye upon him *while* he is near" (Isa. 55:6, italics mine).
 2. Because of the seriousness of sin, our need is urgent. Isaiah says that sin is so serious that it separates people from God (59:2). The psalmist also takes sin seriously: "The wicked shall be turned into hell, and all the nations that forget God" (9:17).
C. *Our need is met only in God.* Surely Nicodemus was aware of this fact as he came to Jesus acknowledging that Jesus was "a teacher come from God" (John 3:2b). Nicodemus learned that his deep need for inner peace and a certainty of forgiveness of sins could not be met in himself, in biblical knowledge, or in faithful obedience to lofty religious ideals. The mystery he discovered was that in God alone can a person's real needs be met.
 1. Because of our inability to meet our own need, it can be met only in God. The three great forces operating in the time of Nicodemus — the Roman, Greek, and Hebrew cultures — demonstrate this truth. The Roman world sought to meet human needs by developing a strong and stern government. The Greek world sought to meet human needs by perfecting his personality through art and culture. The Hebrew world sought to meet human needs by changing people through rituals, rules, and regulations.
    But neither Roman government, Greek art, nor Hebrew ritual met people's real needs. Everywhere people were depraved, and concepts of morality and honesty were almost nonexistent.
 2. Because of God's unique provision for people's needs, they can be met only in God. Into this disillusioned world Jesus came proclaiming God's unique provision for humankind's eternal need — "a new birth."

II. The mystery of new life.

Nicodemus's question in verse 4 concerning this mystery is honest and profound. He asks, "Can a full-grown man be squeezed back into his mother's womb? If this cannot be done with the physical, how can it be done with that part of man that is more difficult to change, namely, his spiritual nature?" This indeed is a mystery!

A. *The mystery of new life is experienced through a new birth (John 3:3–7).* Jesus is saying, "If you want new life, Nicodemus, you must experience a new birth."

  1. The new birth ushers a person into the kingdom of God (John 3:3). Christ is saying that without the new birth you cannot even see, let alone enter, the kingdom of God.

  2. The new birth follows your physical birth (John 3:4–6). In these verses Jesus uses the symbolism of being born "of water" to signify physical birth in contrast with the spiritual birth of being "born of the spirit." Your birth to Christian parents no more bestows salvation on you than your birth to college graduate parents bestows a bachelor of arts degree on you. *You* must be born again!

B. *The mystery of new life is illustrated by the wind (John 3:8).* Christ frequently chose nature to illustrate profound spiritual truths. He spoke of the birds of the air, the lilies of the field, the grass of the field, the fields ready for harvest, and the soil.

  1. The wind is mysterious even as the new birth. Jesus points out that although you cannot see the wind or take a handful of it and study it, nevertheless, you can neither deny its existence nor ignore its presence. It is free to move wherever it desires (John 3:8).

  2. The wind, even as the new birth, is known by its effects (John 3:8). You can feel the wind, you can see its effects, but you cannot see the wind itself. Neither can you see the active agent in salvation, the Holy Spirit. Nevertheless, you can feel his presence and see his effects, which he brings into the lives of those who submit to the salvation he imparts.

C. *The new birth is incomprehensible to human reason (John 3:9–13).* The experience of the new birth is necessary to understand the new life that Christ expects us to live. This is why evangelical Christianity declares that it is useless to attempt to teach the world the ethics of Jesus when the world lacks the ability to understand it. In order to have a clear vision of the social implications of the gospel, one must have a vivid experience of the salvation proclaimed by the gospel.

  1. Because the new life is experiential and not rational, it remains incomprehensible to human reason. That we do not need to understand everything we experience is illustrated by the fact that we experience our natural birth without understanding it at the moment it is occurring.

  2. Because a person's intellect bears the effects of the fall, the new birth is incomprehensible to human reason. We must remember that the *totality*

of each person was affected by the fall, and the human mind has never fully recovered. It, too, is depraved and thus is limited in what it can comprehend, and a depraved mind can never fully comprehend the truths of God (Rom. 11:33–34).

III. The mystery of God's love.

The greatest mystery of all time is to be found neither in the complexities of physics nor in the vastness of our universe but in the simple fact that God loves us (John 3:14–16).

A. *The mystery of God's love is that it is offered to undeserving humans (John 3:14).* The Israelites were undeserving of God's love. They had rebelled against him and transgressed his law. Yet God loved them and provided a way out for them. Need we say any more to see ourselves in the same undeserving position?

1. Undeserving people who rebel against God's claims are offered the love of God.

2. Undeserving people who are responsible for the death of God's Son are offered his forgiving love.

B. *The mystery of God's love is that it moves God to unbelievable acts.*

1. God's love moved him to sacrifice his only Son for our sins (John 3:16). This verse is called the epitome of the whole gospel. God's love is no sentimental matter. It was a demanding, sacrificial, and costly love.

2. God's love prompted him to offer himself in Christ on the cross (John 3:14). When in this verse Jesus used the word "must," he was not speaking of an unwelcomed necessity. Rather, he was saying that he must die because he willed to save those he loved.

C. *The mystery of God's love is that it imparts unending life (John 3:16).* In the search for perpetual youth, some people have asked, "How can I live forever?" The answer is found in Christ, through whom God's mysterious love provides unending life. This is a blessed state that begins on earth and continues through eternity.

1. Unending life comes to all believers, for Jesus simply says that whoever *believes* shall have this eternal life.

2. Unending life preserves us for all ages to come. The person who believes will not perish but presently *has* everlasting life.

Conclusion

The mystery of humankind's need is that it is universal and urgent and is met only in God. The mystery of new life is experienced through new birth, is illustrated by the wind, and is incomprehensible to human reason. The greatest mystery of all, the mystery of God's love, is offered to undeserving people, moves God to extraordinary acts, and imparts unending life. You have the opportunity today to respond to the mystery of God's love, experience the mystery of the new birth, and enter into the mystery of a new life.

WEDNESDAY EVENING, JANUARY 6

Title: Prayers for 2010

Text: "Go to now, ye that say, Today or tomorrow we will go into such a city, and continue there a year, and buy and sell, and get gain; whereas ye know not what shall be on the morrow. For what is your life? It is even a vapour, that appeareth for a little time, and then vanisheth away. For that ye ought to say, If the Lord will, we shall live, and do this, or that" **(James 4:13–15)**.

Introduction

With excitement we should begin the journey through this new year with a strong faith in God. Life during this year will be a task. It should be a mission. It may be a contest. It probably will involve battle.

As we come together for prayer, let us unite together in singing our prayers to the Lord.

While some hymns take the form of a personal testimony or a proclamation concerning the nature of God, there are other hymns that take the form of a personal address to God. In reality they are prayers set to music. We do violence to these hymns if we sing them without recognizing that they are prayers addressed to God. Appropriate prayer hymns have been selected for our use tonight as we unite in prayer.

I. Let us pray for proper motivation.

Our motives are those desires or needs that drive us to action. As followers of Christ, it is of supreme importance that we have proper motivation for all that we seek to do. The highest motive is love. Let us unite in praying for more love for Christ.

Let us now join together in singing "More Love to Thee, O Christ."

II. Let us pray for divine guidance.

As we face the journey of the new year, we should recognize that there are some dangers involved in every journey. If we are to walk through this year confidently and in a manner that glorifies God, we need divine guidance.

Let us again unite our hearts in prayer together as we sing "Savior, Like a Shepherd Lead Us."

III. Let us pray for proper purpose.

The controlling purpose of one's life is of tremendous importance. Some people never achieve anything of real significance because they have a low purpose. The Bible teaches that God blesses his people in order that they might be a blessing to others. It is appropriate that we join together in praying that God will help us to be a blessing to others.

Let us sing together our prayer "Make Me a Blessing."

IV. Let us join together in praying for an unsaved world.

Christians are not as compassionate as they should be. The vast multitude of unsaved people about us does not bother us as it should. We should join together in praying that God will bestow upon each of us the blessing of a burdened heart for those who do not yet know our Savior. As we let God place a burden of compassion on our hearts, we will be more inclined to share the good news of what Christ can do if we will trust him.

Let us join together in singing and praying "Send the Light!"

V. Let us pray for the homes of our congregation.

The home is of supreme importance both to the church and to the purposes of God in this world. The well-being of our homes is of tremendous importance to each of us personally. Our witness for Christ in the world can rise no higher than the quality of our Christian life at home.

Let us join together in singing and praying that our homes might be Christian. Let us sing "God Give Us Christian Homes!"

VI. Let us pray a prayer of personal dedication.

Life is made up of decisions. The Christian life, if it is genuine and fruitful, is made of a continuous series of decisions that bring us closer and closer to God's purpose.

If we can mean it with all of our heart, let us join together in singing and praying "I'll Go Where You Want Me to Go."

Other appropriate hymns may be selected if those suggested are not in your hymnal.

SUNDAY MORNING, JANUARY 10

Title: What Is Delightful?

Text: "I delight to do thy will, O my God: yea, thy law is within my heart" (**Ps. 40:8**).

Scripture Reading: Psalm 40:4–11

Hymns: "All Hail the Power of Jesus' Name," Perronet

"Thy Word Have I Hid in My Heart," adapted by E. O. Sellers

"How Firm a Foundation," Keith

"Softly and Tenderly," Thompson

Offertory Prayer: Our Father, in humility we bow before you in these sacred moments. We come before your throne of grace in a spirit of thanksgiving, being fully mindful that "every good gift and every perfect gift is from above, and cometh down from the Father of lights." We seize upon this opportunity to make manifest our thankfulness to you for your gracious generosity to us, blessing each of us beyond measure. We pray that you will accept our tithes and offerings as tokens of our sincere appreciation for your material and spiritual kindnesses extended day by day to each of us. Magnify our gifts in your kingdom's service, through Christ our Lord. Amen.

Introduction

Psalm 40 contains an intimate and colorful description of the psalmist's experience of God's grace. As pastor and author M. Kyle Yates Sr. so beautifully expresses it: "It is a clear picture of what happened when he (the psalmist) found himself utterly helpless, in danger and in imminent peril. He called loudly unto God for mercy and deliverance.... Now he knows what it is to be saved. He is mightily stirred, and he is happy to have the privilege of telling what happened when the Lord took over" (*Preaching from the Psalms* [Nashville: Broadman, 1953], 84).

Thus, the background of this psalm seems to be that the author has suffered, has been graciously relieved, and now has responded in worshipful praise and grateful obedience. He does not show his gratitude simply by observing the mere externals of worship but more especially by his delighting to do God's will, by having God's law in his heart, and by proclaiming God's glorious attributes and gracious dealings as set forth in the first ten verses of this psalm.

As Christians we need to realize that

> the Church has no right to be a little "Pleasant Sunday Afternoon" gathering of people living in an ivory tower. It has no business to separate itself from the sins and sufferings, the pain and wants of the world. Jesus lived out his ministry going about "doing good," healing all manner of sickness, and ministering to the poor. If we regard ourselves as a privileged community, engaged primarily in religious activities on Sunday, we are denying the belief in the Word made flesh. (Canon Raven, quoted by Murdo Ewen Macdonald, The Need to Believe [New York: Scribner, 1959], 79–80)

The keen delight in "doing" God's will as expressed by the psalmist ought to speak to our hearts today. As we look toward the following months of this new year, we need to resolve that during the days ahead we will delight to do the will of Almighty God.

The following sure points need to be stressed for "doing the will of God."

I. What is the will of God?

I would suggest to you three distinct senses in which this term "God's will" is used.

A. *The will of purpose.* This type of God's will is always done, for what he purposes he performs. His will is at work in the world to perform that which is necessary to conform to his good conscience for the needs of humankind. As Daniel expressed it in the Old Testament era, "He doeth according to his will in the army of heaven, and among the inhabitants of the earth" (Dan. 4:35). Paul in the Christian era expressed it in much the same way:

"...being predestinated according to the purpose of him who worketh all things after the counsel of his own will" (Eph. 1:11).

B. *The will of desire or wish.* This type of God's will is not always done, because he permits human beings to be free agents to act counter to his wishes for them. When God created humans, he gave these unique creatures the ability to make decisions. As a result, people may choose to do either the will of God or the will of Satan. Jesus expressed great anguish over the people's choice of ignoring him when he cried out, "O Jerusalem, Jerusalem ... how often I have longed to gather your children together, as a hen gathers her chicks under her wings, but you were not willing" (Matt. 23:37 NIV).

C. *The will of command.* It is our duty to obey every command of God, but we do not always do so. Our heavenly Father gave to the Israelites, during their spiritual kindergarten days when they were wandering in the wilderness at the foot of Mount Sinai, certain laws that began, "Thou shalt not ...," laws that serve even to this day as marvelous guides to humankind's mode of conduct as outlined by divine wisdom. How tragic that Christians today do not realize that to break these commandments is to break the express commands of the will of a righteous God. Though we live in the Christian era, not one of these laws has been set aside or nullified, for Jesus clearly pointed out to his followers that he did not come to change them but to fill them full of meaning (Matt. 5:17).

II. The fulfillment of God's will.

God's will is going to be done in this world whether we like it or not.

A. *God's purpose is not dependent on us for accomplishment.* He may overrule us, or he may simply find others through whom to carry out his will. To accomplish his judgments by one stroke of nature is pointed out in his dealings with Sodom and Gomorrah (Gen. 19:24).

B. *God is perfectly capable of raising up a heathen nation to be a whip in his hand to bring his own into submission, just as during many decades his permissive will allowed Babylon to be a devouring fire over Judah.*

C. *God can bring about the fulfillment of his will by breaking down our stubborn and rebellious wills.* The story is told of St. Francis, the founder of an order of monks, who strictly adhered to the observance of the grand rule of the order—implicit submission to the superior. One day a monk proved refractory. His stubborn will had to be subdued. St. Francis gave an order that a grave be dug sufficiently deep in which a man could be buried while standing upright. The monk was put into it; his brothers began to shovel in the dirt while their superior stood by with his countenance as stern as death. When the dirt had reached the knees of the rebellious monk, St. Francis asked, "Are you dead yet? Is your will dead? Do you yield?" There was no answer to this question, for down in that grave there seemed to be a man with a will of iron. The burial continued. Seemingly dead to pity and to all the weaknesses of humanity, St. Francis stood ready to give the signal

22

that should finish the burial. Finally, the stubborn will of the recalcitrant monk was bent and broken by the more determined will of St. Francis, and the funeral was stopped just in time.

III. We should always do God's will even if it does not bring delight.

How often we hear our children whine, "But I don't like it," when we insist that they eat a certain food. How often when our wives tactfully suggest that it is again time to paint the house do we men whine, "But I don't like to paint the house." Though we may have strong preferences against doing these things, our better judgment tells us that for the best interests of all concerned, we need to do these things, disagreeable though they be. As Christians it may not always be a profound pleasure to do the will of God, for it may not be compatible with out selfish interest. As Christians, however, we can find any number of reasons why we must do the will of almighty God.

   A. *We must do God's will from a sense of duty.* How many saints of the Lord, old and feeble of body, are heard to say, "I don't feel like going to prayer meeting tonight, but it is my duty to be there, and somehow I will muster up the strength to go." We need to realize that Jesus found it his duty to quaff the bitter dregs of the cup of sorrow in the Garden of Gethsemane and to partake of the awful brine of the wrath of a holy God against all the sins of humankind as heaped upon him on Calvary's cross.

   B. *Bearing God's will for our lives may have to be done with a sense of resignation.* Socrates, the renowned man of wisdom of ancient Greece, said on one occasion, "No evil can happen to a good man either in life or after death. His fortunes are not neglected by God." A devout layman of our state is hopelessly crippled and twisted of body, and his speech is far from distinct. Sunday by Sunday he endeavors to teach a Bible class in his church. His new pupils shudder at the sight and sound of him, but before the first class is over, they forget his disabilities as they are translated by his love for and knowledge of the Master into heavenly avenues of thought. This layman has long since resigned himself to the will of God for his life and is daily pushing ahead in service for Christ.

   C. *Bearing God's will for our lives may be done with fear and reluctance.* If we were to call before us our honest servicemen who have tasted of battle on the front lines—and notice that I said "honest"—and were to question them concerning their emotions when in the thick of the battle, each one of them would admit to great fear. Yet these same ones would admit that they had a duty to perform, and perform it they did. Often doing the will of the Master involves fear of criticism or of being "different," but the will of the Master must be obeyed.

IV. We should delight to do God's will—no holds barred!

The theology that we have in our hearts and minds is of no consequence unless shared. As the great European theologian Karl Barth expressed it:

"Theological existence does not swim alone in this world's seas, drifting with the waves or battling against them. It is not only shared with other human beings; it is also Christian existence inasmuch as it is existence in the community, called together and sustained by the witness of the Old and New Testaments to the Word of God" (*Evangelical Theology, An Introduction*, trans. Grover Foley [New York: Holt, Rinehart and Winston, 1963], 80).

A. *A sense of right.* Christians should never ask why when they know in their hearts that it is God's will to do a certain thing. His is to command; ours is to obey!

B. *By feelings of benevolence.* You will want to do the will of the heavenly Father for the sheer delight of joy flooding your soul when you have done a kind deed for another person. As Goldsmith expressed it, "Learn the luxury of doing good."

C. *By feelings of gratitude.* Gratitude to God should be reason enough for us to obey him in every aspect of life. Those who have been washed white in the blood of the Lamb of God should spend their days delighting to do the will of the heavenly Father.

Conclusion

Rearranging the words of our text, we who are Christians should be able to say in a swelling chorus this morning, "To do your will, O my God, is my delight!" Friends who do not know Christ through a personal experience of rebirth, I trust that this morning you may desire to have the law of God written in your hearts and that you may come to delight to do his will. Won't you be "washed in the blood of the Lamb"? Accept him now.

SUNDAY EVENING, JANUARY 10

Title: A Night of Eternal Darkness

Text: "He then having received the sop went immediately out: and it was night" (**John 13:30**).

Scripture Reading: John 13:29–30

Introduction

Of all the night scenes painted on the canvas of sacred Scripture, none is as bleak as the night of eternal darkness. Scan this scene as we may, we find in it no ray of hope, no promise of sunrise.

This melancholy portrait reminds us that buried within the heart of every human is something of the nature of a Judas. It tells us that for the person who refuses to accept Christ, the sunset of death is swiftly followed by the night of eternal darkness.

This tragic night in the life of Judas is not without meaning for us today. In it is contained three great lessons that, if learned well, will save a soul from the night of eternal darkness.

I. The warning of eternal darkness.

"Then Judas, which betrayed him, answered and said, Master, is it I? He said unto him, Thou hast said" (Matt. 26:25).

Midnight does not come unannounced. The setting of the sun, the appearing of the first stars, the darkening of the sky all warn that the midnight hour approaches. Judas's night of eternal darkness did not come unheralded. One warning sign after another came, but he did not heed them.

    A. *Christ's words are a warning sign of eternal darkness (John 13:21, 26).*

        1. Jesus speaks in a spirit of concern (John 13:21). As Christ turns toward Judas, who is still wearing the mask of hypocrisy that deceived his fellow disciples, he shows no hint of anger, hatred, or animosity, but rather there sweeps over him a sudden accession of sorrow, a great disturbance of soul, and a sincere concern for Judas. And because of his heart of concern, Christ may be speaking to you today and saying, "Be careful, you may betray me, too."

        2. Christ's words are intended to bring conviction (John 13:26). This was the last word that Judas could endure. So convicted was he that he either had to repent or flee Christ's presence. Jesus' intention was not to drive him away but to draw him near through the power of conviction.

    B. *The wrongs of your life are a warning sign of eternal darkness (John 12:4–6).* The New International Version translates John 12:6 in this manner: "He did not say this because he cared about the poor but because he was a thief; as keeper of the money bag, he used to help himself to what was put into it." Judas did not get into this destitute condition overnight. It came at the end of a long, long line of wrongs that must have warned him time and time again.

        1. You are fully aware of the wrongs of your life. David said, "My sin is ever before me" (Ps. 51:3). Judas was not unaware of his sins either. He knew of his wrongs long before any other man, yet he would not forsake them. The fact that others thought highly of Judas brought little sleep during his restless nights.

        2. The wrongs of your life condemn you (Ezra 9:6). The most terrifying condemnation of Judas was an inner condemnation brought on by his own wrongs. Thirty pieces of silver—no, not even thirty thousand pieces of silver—could calm the tempest that was raging within. And no one needs to point an accusing finger at you, for your own wrongs stand to condemn you before the judgment bar of your own conscience.

    C. *The woefulness of hell is a warning sign of eternal darkness (John 13:30).* With this verse the curtain closes on Judas's life. Not the slightest ray of hope is offered. This was the last earthly night he would ever see, for it was the prelude to that night of eternal darkness in which he abides to this very day!

        1. The woefulness of hell arises from the needlessness of hell. The most inexcusable error ever made by Judas was to die without Christ and to

enter his night of eternal darkness. He had heard the same message, seen the same miracles, felt the same Spirit, witnessed the same power of Christ as each of the other eleven disciples had, yet he made his exit from this life utterly unprepared.

2. The woefulness of hell arises from the hopelessness of hell. There is no hope for Judas. All of the prayers said, all of the money given, all of the candles burned, all of the rituals performed, and all of the sermons preached cannot spark so much as a flicker of hope.

II. The one responsible for eternal darkness.

"And he cast down the pieces of silver in the temple, and departed, and went out and hanged himself" (Matt. 27:5). Who ushered Judas unprepared into eternal darkness? Judas, and Judas alone, must be the answer! This was not murder; this was suicide! Circumstances may have had their influences, but it was Judas who had to tie that last knot; it was Judas who made the final decision to slip the noose over his head; it was Judas who chose to tie the rope to the overhanging tree; and it was Judas alone who determined that he would leap off the ledge and take his own life. He faced God with his own blood on his hands.

A. *The one who loves darkness is the one responsible for eternal darkness.* "And this is the condemnation, that light is come into the world, and men loved darkness rather than light, because their deeds were evil" (John 3:19). Those who have a depraved nature and distorted vision love darkness (Eph. 2:3; 1 John 5:9; 1 Cor. 1:18).

B. *The one who lives in darkness is the one responsible for eternal darkness.* Judas chose to live in the darkness of unbelief. At any moment he could have turned to the light of salvation in Christ, but he would not. Each person who makes the choice to live in darkness is responsible for eternal darkness in his or her own life (Deut. 30:19; Ezek. 18:20).

C. *The one who lingers in darkness is the one responsible for eternal darkness.* Up to the moment of the kiss of betrayal, Judas could have turned from his sin, but he chose to linger in the darkness of his own wrong.

1. Some linger in the darkness until death is experienced. This was Judas's choice, but Scripture records that "falling headlong, he burst asunder in the midst, and all his bowels gushed out" (Acts 1:18). We dare not gamble with time.

> *The clock of life is wound but once*
> *And no man has the power*
> *To tell just where the hands will stop*
> *At late or early hour.*
> *To lose one's wealth is sad indeed,*
> *To lose one's health is more,*
> *To lose one's soul is such a loss*
> *As no man can restore.*

26

> *So do not wait until tomorrow*
> *To do His blessed will,*
> *The clock of life may then be stopped—*
> *The hands may then be still.*
>
> *—Author Unknown*

2. Some linger in darkness until the Holy Spirit is withdrawn. The Lord warned us of this dreadful possibility early in sacred Scripture when he said, "My spirit shall not always strive with man" (Gen. 6:3).

III. The way out of eternal darkness.

Only moments after Judas had departed to complete his treacherous plot, Jesus spoke once again of his death, and the shadow of gloom hovered over his disciples. Thomas asked Christ to show him the way, and Jesus said, "I am the *way,* the truth and the life" (John 14:6, italics mine).

A. *The way of the cross is the way out of eternal darkness (John 3:13–14).*
1. On this cross Christ died in your place (Rom. 5:6).
2. The cross had the power to dispel the darkness of sin (John 8:12).

B. *The way of confession is the way out of eternal darkness.* "If thou shalt confess with thy mouth the Lord Jesus, and shalt believe in thine heart that God hath raised him from the dead, thou shalt be saved" (Rom. 10:9).
1. You must confess that you are a sinner, for the promise is made, "If we confess our sins, he is faithful and just to forgive us our sins and to cleanse us from all unrighteousness" (1 John 1:9).
2. You must confess that Christ is your Savior (Rom. 10:9).

C. *The way of committal is the way out of eternal darkness.* In Romans 10:9 the word "believe" underscores the need of committal. To say, "I believe in Jesus Christ," is to say, "I commit my life from this point on to Jesus Christ." It is like saying, "I do," as part of a wedding vow that commits you from that moment on to the one to whom you have made this sacred pledge.
1. Committal brings release from sin. Romans 10:9 says that if we believe, then we shall be saved.
2. Committal brings relief to oneself (Ps. 31:1, 3, 5).
3. Committal brings reliance on the Savior. "Commit thy way unto the LORD, trust also in him; and he shall bring it to pass. And he shall bring forth thy righteousness as the light, and thy judgment as the noonday" (Ps. 37:5–6). No more will there be a reliance on oneself to "hold out"; our reliance is on the Lord, who shall "bring it to pass."

Conclusion

Only five suicides are recorded in the entirety of the Bible, which covers numerous centuries and all kinds of people.

Ahithophel, David's chief military adviser turned traitor, defected to Absalom's side and ultimately hanged himself.

Saul, who was fatally wounded in Gilboa, took a sword and fell on it.

Saul's armor bearer fell on his sword and died by the side of his king.

Zimri, the one who became king by assassination, when seeing retribution closing in on him, burned his own house over his head.

Judas went out and hanged himself—and it was night!

All of these men had two things in common. First, they entered a night of eternal darkness. Second, they rejected the light offered by God's grace.

But you need not join this sad processional. The promise of Christ with all of its hope is made to you: "Whoever comes to me I will never drive away" (John 6:37 NIV).

WEDNESDAY EVENING, JANUARY 13

Title: How Pure Is Your Religion?

Text: "Pure religion and undefiled before God and the Father is this, to visit the fatherless and widows in their affliction, and to keep himself unspotted from the world" **(James 1:27)**.

Introduction

The writer of the book of James sets before us the various fruits and manifestations of a genuine relationship with God. James, the preacher of practical righteousness, urges people to prove their faith by a life of benevolent works. He boldly declares that the faith that does not produce works is dead. Faith, by its very nature, cannot exist and be fruitless.

James wrote to Christians scattered abroad and gave to them some practical tests by which it was possible to measure the genuineness and depth of their faith in God. In so doing, he presented to them a challenge to live a full Christian life.

In James 1 the readers are warned four times against the peril of being self-deceived about the quality of their faith. It is possible for one to consider himself to have a genuine faith and be mistaken. Jesus said, "Not every one that saith unto me, Lord, Lord, shall enter into the kingdom of heaven; but he that doeth the will of my Father which is in heaven" (Matt. 7:21). Numbered among the followers of Christ are many superficial believers who will be greatly surprised on the day of judgment to discover that they are excluded from heaven because of the lack of a faith that manifests itself in a life surrendered to the will of God and to the good of others.

By studying the book of James, we can discover the tests by which we can measure the quality of our faith. We can also discover the ideals toward which we should strive.

I. Pure religion has its origin in the heart of God.

A. *God is the source of every good and perfect gift (James 1:17).*

B. *Our faith, our religious service, and our worship are but responses to God's initiative.*

II. Pure religion requires that we be teachable in both mind and heart.

A. *James says that we should be "swift to hear."*

B. *A genuine faith in Christ will manifest itself by an eager desire to hear the truth of God concerning the issues and activities of life.*

C. *The book of James warns us against being mere auditors (James 1:22).*

III. Pure religion will put forth an earnest effort to control the use of the tongue.

A. *The inspired writer encourages us to be "slow to speak."* We should all remember that while the Creator has given us two ears and two eyes, he has given us only one mouth — one tongue. Evidently he meant for us to hear twice as much as we speak. When we hear something that is not good, especially about someone else, instead of letting it come through the mouth, we should let it go through the other ear.

B. *Compare James 3:3 – 10 for the devastating effects of the wrong use of the tongue.* Once a young man came to the philosopher Socrates to be instructed in oratory. The moment the young man was introduced, he began to talk and continued for some time. When Socrates could get in a word, he said, "Young man, I will have to charge you a double fee." "A double fee? Why?" The old sage replied, "I will have to teach you two sciences. First, how to hold your tongue and, then, how to use it."

IV. Pure religion involves a constant crusade to eliminate all evil from our hearts and lives.

A. *Even the Christian has a nature that would induce him to compromise with every possible type of sin.*

B. *We are challenged to put aside all filthiness, malice, and wickedness and to keep ourselves unstained by the world (James 1:27).* Every genuine Christian must have some great negatives in his or her life.

V. Pure religion reveals itself in the practice of compassionate acts of kindness.

A. *Pure religion is something more than ritual and ceremony.*

B. *Pure religion is infinitely more than attendance at the regular worship services.*

C. *Pure religion hears distress calls, sees needs, and with helping hands gives joyful assistance.*

Conclusion

As followers of Christ, it is possible for us to have pure religion. To do so we must bring our lives regularly under the searching, penetrating light of the life and teachings of our Lord.

Pure religion will produce joy in our own hearts. Pure religion is contagious. Many of the unsaved about us will become attracted to our Savior if they can see a living demonstration of what it means to be a Christian in our daily conduct.

SUNDAY MORNING, JANUARY 17

Title: When Trouble Comes

Text: "I lift up my eyes to the hills—where does my help come from? My help comes from the Lord, the Maker of heaven and earth. He will not let your foot slip—he who watches over you will not slumber; indeed, he who watches over Israel will neither slumber nor sleep" (**Ps. 121:1–2 NIV**).

Scripture Reading: Psalm 121

Hymns: "Holy, Holy, Holy," Heber

            "God Will Take Care of You," Martin

            "Be Still, My Soul," Schlegel

            "Have Thine Own Way, Lord," Pollard

Offertory Prayer: This morning, Father, we are reminded of the words of the psalmist who said, "Blessed is every one that feareth the LORD; that walketh in his ways." We express to you our awesome fear of your power, our reverence of your righteousness, and our gratitude for your unparalleled love. We are ever conscious of your divine love, which day by day expresses itself in so many ways toward us. For the privilege of bringing to you a representative portion of our total income—our tithes and offerings—we thank you. In laying on your altar this symbol of our Christian stewardship, we are made to feel honest toward you. Bless these tithes and offerings and multiply them for use in your kingdom's service, we pray. Amen.

Introduction

At the expense of offering up a note of pessimism so early in the year, we need to face the fact that during the coming months every person present this morning will likely encounter some difficulty along the way that may be spelled out as t-r-o-u-b-l-e. The author of Psalm 121 obviously speaks out of a vast experience of trouble of one sort or another.

This psalm belongs to a collection of psalms known as the "pilgrim collection." Scholars differ in their views as to the dialogue in Psalm 121. Some feel that it is a dialogue between a man and his soul; others say that it is liturgical chanting between a layman and a priest in the temple; still others insist that it is a dialogue between a group of pilgrims and their spiritual leader or leaders. Since it obviously belongs to the pilgrim collection, the latter view seems most logical.

It was probably sung in an antiphonal fashion by the pilgrims on their way to the holy city of Jerusalem to attend some solemn feast, a group of leaders at the front of the procession singing one stanza and the group of pilgrims at the rear singing the next stanza. At night the pilgrim-psalmist would look to the hills surrounding his campsite and see the sentries placed there to protect him and his fellow travelers against bands of robbers. Looking past these sentries on the hills, he saw, as it were, the Lord in the glory of the star-lit heavens. Here was true help

30

against greater troubles of life than mere robbers. With renewed courage he would then turn to his sleep, arising on the morrow to face any trouble that might present itself. Thus he could answer his own question concerning the origin of his help: "My help cometh from the LORD, which made heaven and earth" (Ps. 121:2).

In achieving serenity of life in the face of troubles, a person must take the following steps:

I. Gain a proper perspective of his difficulties or troubles.

It has often been said that a person needs on occasion to remove himself many miles from his usual scene of activity in order to truly get an objective view of his situation there. Certainly we need to look away from our troubles to the Source of all help before turning back to face them squarely.

A. *There is a danger of confusion by proximity — we can't see the forest for the trees.* The psalmist took a long look at the distant hills and at the Lord of the hills; then he turned back to analyze his problems. Somehow, as he looked at his troubles with eyes of faith, the whole perspective changed; each problem seemed to fall into its proper place.

B. *There is a danger of magnifying our trials by brooding over them.* As a minister, it is my privilege to visit day in and day out in the hospitals of our city. Through this continuous visitation of the sick, I have gleaned a comparative value of patient reaction to sickness. Some of the patients brood over their illness to the point of gloating over it. Even when their bodies have responded adequately to surgery and subsequent convalescence, they continue to be obsessed with the idea of sickness and cannot seem to snap out of their illness. On the other hand, many patients, though quite ill, maintain their sense of humor and continue to look at themselves objectively, refusing to brood over their illness but rather looking on it as but a valley between the sun-lit mountain ranges of life. They look to the Great Physician, who "now is near, the sympathizing Jesus."

II. See his troubles as opportunities.

The passing of the years has a way of teaching us that things are not always what they appear at first to be. There have been events along life's way that have at first appeared to be the greatest of catastrophes but in reality have turned out to be — or were converted into — the greatest of life's opportunities. In looking over biblical history and world history, we are able to cite many examples where this was so. Joseph, son of Jacob and victim of sibling rivalry, suffered the catastrophe of being sold into slavery in Egypt. Instead of sitting and sighing over his great misfortune, he addressed himself to the situation as he found it, taking advantage of each avenue of service opened up to him by God. In due time, he rose to the second greatest place of power in Egypt (Gen. 37–50). In the history of social reform, William Wilberforce, enslaved in a twisted and shriveled body, fought in the English Parliament during the latter part of the eighteenth century and the early part of the next for the abolition of slavery.

III. Allow his troubles to call forth strength from within.

Marcus Aurelius said eighteen hundred years ago, "Man must be arched and buttressed from within, else the temple wavers to dust." Paul said, "I have learned in whatsoever state I am, therewith to be content" (Phil. 4:11). Until a person has gone through the fiery trials of life, that person has not known the strength that comes from within. A person whose heart is bound in faith to the Master grows and develops day by day through the difficulties and troubles the Lord uses as stepping-stones for his growth in grace and in knowledge of him. A person of poise is one who has weathered by God's grace many storms of life.

IV. Look outside himself to the source of strength — the Lord.

The psalmist looked from his own little sphere of life out to the great hills and beyond them to the Lord of heaven and earth. Obviously he received strength from the Lord through the following:

A. *Prayer.* Jesus laid it on the line to his followers concerning prayer. He said, "Ask, and it shall be give you; seek, and ye shall find; knock, and it shall be opened unto you" (Matt. 7:7). And again he chided them concerning their lack of persistence in prayer when he said, "If ye then, being evil, know how to give good gifts unto your children, how much more shall your Father which is in heaven give good things to them that ask him?" (Matt. 7:11). Inner strength and calmness come over us when we pray effectively. In the words of Horatius Bonar:

> *Calm me, my God, and keep me calm,*
> *While these hot breezes blow;*
> *Be like the night-dew's healing balm,*
> *Upon the earth's fevered brow.*

B. *Bible study.* The psalmist's prayer was always that God's Word might be hidden in his heart that he might not sin against the Lord (Ps. 119:11). In the twelfth century AD, there arose in the inaccessible valleys of the Alps a hardy group of believers known as the Waldensians. The Bible was their buttress and shield, and for their faith they suffered the burning of their villages and the massacre of their people. Waldensian preachers, disguised as silk and jewel merchants, gained entrance into the homes of nobility, displaying their wares. When asked if they had anything more to sell, they would reply, "Yes, we have something more precious than anything you have seen." Then they would tenderly unwrap a package and disclose a Bible and explain God's saving grace. An individual Christian's growth in grace and in knowledge of the Lord can be in the "go position" only when that growth is promoted through in-depth Bible study.

C. *Exercising faith.* The substance of faith is that by which all humans live daily. We reach out in faith to toggle the light switch so that we may see at night; we turn the ignition switch with confidence, expecting our automobiles to start so that we may go to our daily work. Christians live each day fully dependent on the leadership of their Master. As we endeavor day by day to live to our maximum for the Master, we do so in faith, believing that the Master will give us strength for that day. As we witness to each lost soul, we do so in faith believing that God's Spirit can work in and through our feeble efforts to complete the task. Faith, then, expresses itself in daily exercise, proving its reality in deeds of love.

> *Workless faith God never regards,*
> *Faithless work God never rewards.*

With such a faith there is no room in a person's heart for pessimism such as that expressed by Bertrand Russell when he said, "Life ... is a temporary accident in a universe where it cannot happen again."

D. *Exercising trust.* There is a point in every person's life when he or she must exercise complete trust in Christ. If you have never done that, now is the time to examine your hearts and lives and see yourselves as the Lord sees you. Under the leadership of the Holy Spirit, there should come sweeping into your heart a heavy burden of remorse over your sinfulness and an earnest desire to turn from sin to salvation. It is a matter of trusting Jesus alone to save you. Trust is literally faith in action. This morning you may have a great intellectual belief that Jesus died to save you, but until you have acted on that belief by saying to the Master, "Lord Jesus, here and now I am trusting my eternal soul into your care and keeping, and depending on you alone to cleanse me of my sins and to save me to the uttermost," you have not come to the point of trusting him.

Conclusion

When life falls in on you, as it were, and seems impossible for you to bear, turn your eyes upon the Lord from whence cometh your help. Look to him in faith believing that he has the power to undergird you and to strengthen you to face life. To the non-Christian—won't you this morning turn to the Lord and let him have his way with you? Trust him now.

SUNDAY EVENING, JANUARY 17

Title: A Night of Anxiety

Text: "And Jacob was left alone; and there wrestled a man with him until the breaking of the day" (**Gen. 32:24**).

Scripture Reading: Genesis 32:24–30

Introduction

What does your anxiety do? It does not rid tomorrow of its sorrow; it robs today of its strength. Anxiety does not keep you from experiencing evil; it makes you incapable of coping with it when it comes. Anxiety does not bless tomorrow; it curses today.

Our Lord grants us power to bear all the burdens of his making, but he does not grant us the power to bear the burdens of our own making that anxiety most assuredly brings on us.

Jacob spent a night of anxiety from which we may gain both an insight into this problem and a knowledge of how to escape it.

I. The reasons for anxiety.

Why do people torture themselves with the vicious tool of anxiety? Why do they subject themselves to such senseless tension and inner turmoil? The experience of Jacob reveals four reasons.

A. *Loneliness.* "And Jacob was left alone" (Gen. 32:24). Although Jacob was already disturbed, it was only after being left alone that the cruel, cold grip of anxiety lay hold of him. Anxiety has an affinity for loneliness.

1. Loneliness is contrary to God's intention as expressed in Genesis 2:18: "It is not good for the man to be alone. I will make a helper suitable for him" (NIV). Sociologists testify that married people live longer, are more emotionally stable, and lead happier lives than single people. Loneliness seldom breeds happiness, but rather it provides fertile soil for anxiety.

2. Loneliness renders us incompetent for life's great tasks. Moses was aware of this fact, for he said, "I am not able to bear all this people alone, because it is too heavy for me" (Num. 11:14). God's solution was that Moses surround himself with seventy elders to help him.

3. Loneliness removes us from a source of encouragement and strength. "If one falls down, his friend can help him up. But pity the man who falls and has no one to help him up!" (Eccl. 4:10 NIV).

4. Loneliness develops a spirit of self-pity that intensifies anxiety. Even a man as great as Elijah was guilty of inflicting such anxiety on himself.

   And he came thither unto a cave, and lodged there; and, behold, the word of the LORD came to him, and he said unto him, What doest thou here, Elijah? And he said, I have been very jealous for the LORD God of hosts: for the children of Israel have forsaken thy covenant, thrown down thine altars, and slain thy prophets with the sword; and I, even I only, am left; and they seek my life, to take it away: And he said, Go forth, and stand upon the mount before the LORD. (1 Kings 19:9–11)

   God's call was for Elijah to come out of his cave of self-pity and withdrawal and as a spokesman of the Lord to thrust himself into the midst of the masses who desperately needed the message of God.

B. *Some past transgression.* Jacob could never forget the underhanded manner in which he took advantage of his brother, Esau (Gen. 25:29–33; 27:18–24, 34–35). This past transgression plagued his conscience day and night.

   Our past sins have a way of haunting our consciences and bringing a fear of exposure. That person is to be pitied who will not forgive himself of some past wrong done.

34

C. *The threat of judgment.* When the messenger returned and reported that Esau was coming to meet Jacob with four hundred men, he was actually afraid (Gen. 32:6–8). As the offender of his brother, Jacob knew he deserved the severest judgment of Esau. Living beneath the threat of judgment strikes fear in any person.

D. *The fear of the unknown.* Jacob spent a sleepless night because he feared what tomorrow might bring upon him. Ninety-five percent of our worries are either about past events that we cannot change or future events that never materialize.

II. The results of anxiety.

A. *Needless worry.* "Jacob was greatly afraid and distressed" (Gen. 32:7). The events of the next day proved all of Jacob's worry to be needless; the worst did not come.

 1. Worry only complicates life's problems. The problem was relatively simple, that of gaining reconciliation with and making amends to a brother whom Jacob had wronged. But by the time Jacob worried for a day and a night, it appeared to be an unsolvable problem. Someone has wisely said, "Worry is interest paid on trouble before it is due."

 2. Worry is unbecoming to a Christian. "Cast thy burden upon the LORD, and he shall sustain thee" (Ps. 55:22).

B. *Feverish works.* Genesis 32:4–5 relates how Jacob spent much time and vast sums of money unnecessarily to appease an already forgiving brother.

 1. Often our works unmask our faithless hearts. If we, unlike Jacob, would pray and trust God, we would not feel compelled to try to buy off God by our good works.

 2. Sometimes our works are an attempt to escape facing the real issue involved. As long as we can keep our hands busy, we can manage to avoid the problems in our lives. The need is seldom for more to be done but rather for our inner spiritual condition to be changed.

C. *Division of God's people.* "And he divided the people that was with him" (Gen. 32:7). In this case, division was a precautionary action. Nevertheless, there is a lesson here to be learned—anxiety often divides God's people, and this to their own harm.

D. *Sleepless nights.* "Jacob was left alone; and there wrestled a man with him until the breaking of the day" (Gen. 32:24). Each of us could testify of how anxiety has robbed from us the sleep God intended night to bring because of the disturbing memories of the past and the fearful anticipation of the future.

III. The remedy for anxiety.

A. *Confession.* "I am not worthy of the least of all the mercies ...," Jacob confessed (Gen. 32:10). So we must confess both our unworthiness and our need if we are to feel the divine hand lift from us the unbearable burden of anxiety.

B. *Petition.* After sending numerous messengers and countless gifts to Esau, Jacob still was a captive of anxiety. He now turned to the only real remedy for anxiety—a prayerful petition to God (Gen. 32:11–12).
   1. Prayerful petition pleads for deliverance from harm. "Deliver me, I pray thee, from the hand of my brother" (Gen. 32:11).
   2. The promises of God are claimed through petition. Jacob recalled and reclaimed a precious promise that God had made (Gen. 32:12).
   3. Prayerful petition leads to an abandonment of sin. Jacob had no intention of continuing as the "supplanter."
C. *Persistent faith.* The experience of Jacob's wrestling with the angel (Gen. 32:24–30) is a candid portrayal of persistent faith. From this we learn that we must hold on no matter how tough the battle may become.

Such faith is rewarded with the promise of a brighter tomorrow (Gen. 32:27–29). No longer was Jacob to be a "deceiver" but rather "God's fighter," with no fear or cowardice.

Persistent faith imparts deep confidence in God's protective power (Gen. 32:30). Like Jacob, we can be confident of God's protection in advance of experiencing it.

Conclusion

> *If the world from you withhold*
> > *Of its silver and gold,*
> *And you have to get along with meager fare,*
> > *Just remember, in His Word,*
> *How He feeds the little bird—*
> > *Take your burden to the Lord*
> *And leave it there.*
> *If your body suffers pain*
> > *And your health you can't regain,*
> *And your soul is almost sinking in despair,*
> > *Jesus knows the pain you feel.*
> *He can save and He can heal—*
> > *Take your burden to the Lord*
> *And leave it there.*
> *When your enemies assail*
> > *And your heart begins to fail,*
> *Don't forget that God in heaven answers prayer;*
> > *He will make a way for you*
> *And will lead you safely through;*
> > *Take your burden to the Lord*
> *And leave it there.*
> *When your youthful days are gone*
> > *And old age is stealing on,*

And your body bends beneath the weight of care,
He will never leave you then,
He'll go with you to the end —
Take your burden to the Lord
And leave it there.

—Charles Albert Tindley

WEDNESDAY EVENING, JANUARY 20

Title: The Faith That Saves

Text: "What doth it profit, my brethren, though a man say he hath faith, and have not works? Can faith save him?" (**James 2:14**).

Introduction

The book of Romans strongly emphasizes that salvation comes to an individual who makes a faith response to the grace of God in Christ Jesus.

The book of James emphasizes that genuine faith manifests itself in a transformed life that issues in service to God and man. Our text raises the question, "Can [that] faith save him?" James raises the practical question concerning whether a faith that does not produce a changed life can be considered genuine. He concludes that faith that does not produce works is dead, "being alone" (James 2:17).

I. The faith that saves is more than intellectual assent (James 2:19).

The demons give intellectual assent to the existence of God but do not repent and trust him for redemption. One can believe everything that the Bible says about God and yet not have genuine faith.

II. The faith that saves responds positively to the good news of the gospel (Rom. 1:16).

This response of faith involves the surrender of the human will to the good will of a loving God who has revealed himself in the life and death of Jesus Christ.

Paul not only responded to the good news of God's love but also manifested that response in the question, "Lord, what wilt thou have me to do?" (Acts 9:6).

III. The faith that saves leads to a separation from pagan habits.

When Matthew trusted Jesus, he arose from the seat of custom and followed him (Matt. 9:9).

Paul described the actions of the converts in Thessalonica in terms of their turning from idols to serving the living and true God (1 Thess. 1:9). He insisted that as converts who had been the slaves of sin, they were now to be the servants of righteousness (Rom. 6:18).

37

IV. The faith that saves is a faith that leads to service.

One of the major emphases of James 2 is that of a faith that brings us into a transforming experience with Jesus Christ and that will create within us compassion for the poor and unfortunate. James would encourage us to examine carefully the quality of our faith so that we might be certain we have the genuine article rather than a counterfeit.

V. Saving faith analyzed.

Charles Haddon Spurgeon said that there were three vital elements to the faith that saves — knowledge, assent, and trust. One must have some knowledge about God as he has revealed himself in Jesus Christ. However, one can have complete knowledge as far as information is concerned and still not have the faith that saves. One can give the full assent of his or her mind to the truthfulness of what the Bible has to say about God and still not have the faith that saves. Faith becomes genuine when we act on the knowledge we have received about God's grace and power and his purpose to redeem those who will make Jesus Christ the Lord of life. Knowledge and assent to the truth of that knowledge are but two of the ingredients that can make it possible for you to have genuine faith. Genuine faith expresses itself in trust, confidence, and commitment.

SUNDAY MORNING, JANUARY 24

Title: The Perfect Prayer

Text: "O my Father, if it be possible, let this cup pass from me: nevertheless not as I will, but as thou wilt" (**Matt. 26:39**).

Scripture Reading: Matthew 26:36–46

Hymns: " 'Tis the Blessed Hour of Prayer," Crosby

"Purer in Heart, O God," Davison

"Near to the Heart of God," McAfee

Offertory Prayer: Our Father, we are mindful that our Savior was willing to offer up to you his all on the cross of Calvary. Help us this morning to be willing to offer up to you our sacrificial gifts in adoration and heartfelt love. We pray that you will take these tokens of our love and stewardship and bathe them in your compassion for the spiritually lost and straying, causing these gifts to be effective messengers of salvation here on the local church field, in our state, our beloved nation, and throughout the world. In these moments we consecrate our hearts anew to the divine task of witnessing to others of the power of the gospel in our hearts and lives. Through Jesus Christ our Lord. Amen.

Introduction

What do knees have to do with consecrated Christian living? Can there be any relationship between our knee joints and Christ? Can he have any claim

38

upon them? It is true that they are not named among our "members" when Paul is pleading for coordination among constituent elements, the members of the Corinthian church (1 Cor. 12:20–25). But our knees are worthy agents in an "All for Christ" program, and he does have a buyer's right to them. "Bow the knee!" cries the glory and majesty of the Creator; and all around the earth in the darkness of ignorance and in the light of revelation, on the blind side of God's high altar stairs and also on that one side where is the Way, the Truth, and the Life, human beings have knelt and are now kneeling.

Strangely enough, those who bow down in fear and superstition have thicker calluses than many of us who are at rest in the sure knowledge of God through Christ Jesus. What makes the difference between dark and light, between fear and calm? For Christ it was being on his knees. "He was withdrawn from them about a stone's cast, and kneeled down, and prayed, saying, Father, if thou be willing, remove this cup from me: nevertheless not my will, but thine, be done" (Luke 22:41–42).

Spiritual rheumatism is one of the most troublesome afflictions in Christendom today. With some, especially among those who are occupied with this world, the trouble has progressed until it is a crippling arthritis when it comes to falling on our knees and confessing our sins before the righteous heavenly Father. We have in our modern churches stiff knees that will not bend to allow the wise, the wealthy, the honored, the bemedaled to bow side by side with the lowly while together their hearts sing, "In my hand no price I bring; simply to Thy cross I cling." How we need to bow the knee of our spirits and humble our hearts before our God in prayer! In our day we hear so much about what prayer is and what prayer is not that the less informed of our people find doubts arising. There is a tendency today to worship and pray for selfish reasons; subconsciously we ask, "What will they give me in net results?" We ministers may be somewhat responsible for this in that we present God as a means to an end. Prayer must never be understood as simply a means of receiving favors from God; it is rather the most important phase of the whole experience of worship. It is the two-way communication between God and humans, the by-product of which is gratitude, submissive humility, and joyous hope.

For a true understanding of prayer, we need to examine the prayer of our Lord in the Garden of Gethsemane. An analysis of his prayer in that moment of crisis in his life reveals to us the vital elements of the perfect prayer.

I. Recognition of the Fatherhood of God.

The salutation with which Jesus began his prayer of anguish, "O my Father" Matt 26:39), was reminiscent of the salutation "Our Father" (Matt. 6:9), which he taught his disciples in the Model Prayer. The very word *Father* has certain connotations for us.

A. *Symbol of protection.* In our prayers we recognize God as our omnipotent protector, one who has all power to protect his own from harm. In the words of the psalmist, "Thy rod and thy staff, they comfort me" (Ps. 23:4), we are able to express our own confidence in his protective power.

B. *Symbol of love.* The love for an earthly father as expressed by an understanding child is a love, respect for, and dependence on one who proved himself to the child. How much greater is the Christian's respect for and dependence on the heavenly Father! Every time Christians use the term *Father* in their prayers, there radiates from their hearts upward to God's throne of grace a love that is unique among all the emotions felt in the human breast.

C. *Symbol of providential love.* In his great sermon on the mountainside, Jesus pointed out the providential care of God for even the lesser creatures of his creation. "Look at the birds of the air; they do not sow or reap or store away in barns, and yet your heavenly Father feeds them. Are you not much more valuable than they?" (Matt. 6:26 NIV). In his great teaching on the pointlessness of anxiety, he drew a beautiful picture of the great providential love expressed to all.

II. Recognition of God's plan for the ages: "If it be possible."

In that moment of anguish, there was no question in Jesus' mind and heart that his heavenly Father had the power to swoop out of heaven and completely destroy the Roman soldiers now approaching, to lay waste the holy city of Jerusalem, to dry up the brook Kidron, to erase the Mount of Olives, and to blast the hill of Golgotha out of existence. "Thinkest thou that I cannot now pray to my Father, and he shall presently give me more than twelve legions of angels?" (Matt. 26:53). Yes, it was possible for God to do that, speaking from the viewpoint of his ability and power. Yet was it possible for him to do that and still be able to carry out his plan for the ages that had been so carefully mapped out in the Law and the Prophets? "But how then shall the scriptures be fulfilled, that thus it must be?" (Matt. 26:54). Jesus fully recognized the fact that God did have a great plan; he desired to fit fully into that plan even at the expense of his own suffering and death.

If our prayer would be perfect—complete—we must pray earnestly that God will reveal to us his plan for our individual lives.

III. Admission of human frailty: "Let his cup pass from me."

When people come to the point where they admit to God that they are, after all, only frail human beings and therefore subject to the weaknesses of the flesh, they are then ready to enter into the relationship of true splendor—the holiness and righteousness of God the Father and his perfect love. "Woe is me! for I am undone; because I am a man of unclean lips, and I dwell in the midst of a people of unclean lips: for mine eyes have seen the King, the Lord of hosts," cried Isaiah when he recognized his frailty before his God (Isa. 6:5).

"Let this cup pass from me" (Matt. 26:39) is a precious phrase to us, for it reveals to our thinking that though Jesus was all God, very God, he was at the same time all man, very man—the "Son of man." It teaches us that he experienced the fears and doubts of man and that now as our Mediator he is able to understand and to sympathize with us in our fears and doubts.

IV. A spirit of submission.

"Nevertheless not as I will, but as thou wilt." As we come to this part of our Lord's prayer of anguish, we discover that the spirit of human fear has now been superseded by a calm and peaceful submission to the divine will of God. He is at rest in God. He has prayed "the perfect prayer." He has laid his case before the heavenly Father; he has rested the burden of his proof before the throne of grace. Now he is perfectly confident that all is well and that his Father's will shall be done.

As Christians we need to continue on our knees in prayer until we have become completely submissive to the will of our heavenly Father. When we have come to that point, we will be able to sing with meaning:

> *Perfect submission, perfect delight,*
> *Visions of rapture now burst on my sight;*
> *Angels descending bring from above*
> *Echoes of mercy, whispers of love.*
> *Perfect submission, all is at rest,*
> *I in my Savior am happy and blest;*
> *Watching and waiting, looking above,*
> *Filled with His goodness, lost in His love.*

If Christians are to imitate the example of the Savior's "perfect prayer," they must pray until the sense of perfect submission enshrouds their entire beings.

Conclusion

In this prayer of our Lord in the Garden of Gethsemane, we are made aware of his great agony as he gained submissiveness of self to the great plan of God for the salvation of lost humankind. In these quiet moments, we need to pay undivided attention to the matter at hand. Sinners should pray the prayer of anguish, "Have mercy upon me, O God, according to your unfailing love; according to your great compassion blot out my transgressions" (Ps. 51:1 NIV). Christians should fervently pray, "Restore to me the joy of your salvation and grant me a willing spirit, to sustain me. Then I will teach transgressors your ways, and sinners will turn back to you" (Ps. 51:12–13 NIV). Let us in these moments yield to the loving call of God's Holy Spirit to accept Christ as Savior. If you have not already done so, pray the perfect prayer and submit yourself completely to him.

SUNDAY EVENING, JANUARY 24

Title: A Night of Tears

Text: "And all the congregation lifted up their voice, and cried; and the people wept that night" **(Num. 14:1)**.

Scripture Reading: Numbers 14:1–10

Introduction

One of the saddest nights in Israel's history is recalled in our text. "And all the congregation lifted up their voice, and cried; and the people wept that night." Within this pitiful experience is found at least a partial answer to the question, "Why do people shed tears?"

I. Because of despair.

The appalling description of Canaan given in Numbers 13:32–33 had such a depressing influence on the congregation that they were thrown into utter despair and wept the whole night long (Num. 14:1).

    A. *Despair arises from a seemingly insoluble problem.* "But the men that went up with him said, We be not able to go up against the people; for they are stronger than we" (Num. 13:31). Verses 32 and 33 of this same chapter continue to paint a gloomy picture of the Promised Land with the clear implication that to conquer it would be impossible. Therefore, all the congregation wept that night.

        What possible solution could be found to this overwhelming problem? After all, they were only "grasshoppers" in the face of "giants."

      1. When we approach our problems with such an attitude, we often expand them out of proportion (Num. 13:33). The problem could not possibly be as bad as verse 33 indicates. Their conclusion that this was an insoluble problem was built on misinformation.

      2. Like pessimistic Israel, we too are often guilty of complicating our problems of faithfulness (Num. 13:31). Faithlessness in the face of difficulty has the magnifying effect of powerful binoculars on a molehill.

    B. *Despair gives vent to irresponsible accusations (Num. 14:2–3).* Because the lack of courage blinds their eyes to the answer to their problem, the congregation turns on Moses and Aaron and murmurs against them and their God. Despair is the mother of irresponsible accusations.

      1. In Numbers 14:2 we learn that one who suffers from despair, like a wounded animal, often turns on those whom he loves. Despair accounts for many irresponsible accusations made against one's fellowman.

        When the chief priests realized that they had no satisfactory answer to the teachings of Christ and no effective tool for holding back the multitudes from following him, they were overwhelmed with despair and thus "accused him of many things" (Mark 15:3).

      2. Despair often gives vent to irresponsible accusations against God (Num. 14:3). These people were actually accusing God of going to all the trouble of raising up Moses, bringing devastating plagues on Pharaoh, miraculously opening up the Red Sea, destroying the Egyptian army, providing manna from heaven and water from dry places, and granting victories over superior armies all so they would at last be destroyed by the sword hundreds of miles from their land of captivity! How ridiculous and irresponsible

could they be? And yet often we have expressed the same ugly spirit in our spoken and unspoken accusations against God in times of despair.

C. *Despair proposes no workable solutions.* "And they said one to another, Let us make a captain, and let us return into Egypt" (Num. 14:4). This was an unworkable solution, because every one of them would want to be "captain," and to return to Egypt would be to return to the fierce anger of a nation upon whom they had brought devastation, death, and national defeat! As long as you choose to live in the depths of despair, you will never find any workable solution to life's problems.

II. Because of disillusionment (Num. 14:5).

Because of murmuring, now growing into open rebellion, Moses and Aaron fell upon their faces before the whole congregation and tearfully poured out their hearts to God. Theirs were tears of disillusionment—they had given the best years of their lives to these people, had prayerfully followed divine leadership, had loved them and often stood between them and the judgment of God—and this is the thanks they received!

A. *Disillusionment is often created by unbecoming conduct (Num. 14:1).* The conduct of the whimpering coward is hardly a becoming attribute for God's chosen people.

Sometimes our conduct is contrary to the name that we bear. Israel was to be "God's fighters," for this was what their name signified, but instead they cried in the face of difficulty like whimpering cowards. How often do we bear the name "Christian" when our conduct is hardly "Christlike"? At other times some unbecoming deed places a question mark around all prior conduct. Why had these people been following Moses and Aaron anyway? Was it simply to leave the hardships of Egypt? Was it only to receive the milk and honey of the Promised Land? Had they all along been guided by mercenary motives? Was there no real desire to conquer the land for God and make his people strong? Their unbecoming attitude now placed a question mark around all of their prior conduct.

B. *An unexpected attitude may bring disillusionment to some soul (Num. 14:2).* As long as things went well, the people loved and complimented Moses. But when the last great challenge confronted them and apparent difficulty came near, they adopted a strange and unexpected attitude of murmuring.

III. Because of difficulty (Num. 14:6–10).

Joshua and Caleb, who had gone with the others to explore the land, tore their clothing as a sign of their discouragement and disappointment at the rebellious attitude of the people.

Difficulty often serves to sift our lives. Through its coarse mesh, little ambitions, feeble hopes, and selfish endeavors are sifted out relentlessly. Those things that are big enough not to sift through are not in the least affected by difficulty.

Big things like hope, love, faith, kindness, and courage cannot be hurt by difficulty. Rather, difficulty discloses new charm and beauty and power in them.

Few experiences bring tears to the eyes of a sensitive soul quite like difficulty in getting others to believe his or her testimony. Joshua and Caleb were honest men whose word had always been believed. But now Israel turned a deaf ear to them and refused to believe their testimony (Num. 14:7).

Joshua and Caleb had *seen* this land, and they believed that Israel should take it. A Christian has *experienced* the salvation of which he bears testimony. To meet the rebuff of unbelief brings tears to any compassionate child of God.

If only Israel would believe these men and enter the Promised Land, all their needs would be met and their pressing problems would be solved. To see Israel so near to the Promised Land yet not to enter because of unbelief in their testimony broke the hearts of Joshua and Caleb. To see a soul so close to the kingdom of God and yet not enter moves the hearts of concerned Christians to tears of compassion.

A. *At other times tears are shed because of the difficulty in leading others to claim the promises of God (Num. 14:8).* God had promised Israel the land of Canaan. These men had worked hard to lead the people to act upon God's promises and claim the land, but they refused to claim the promises of God.

B. *The difficulty involved in persuading others to cease from spiritual rebellion not only brought tears to Joshua and Caleb but also brings tears to those today who seek to lead others from rebellion into salvation.* Joshua and Caleb tried to persuade Israel not to rebel against God's will for them by telling them of the goodness and glory of the land and of the presence of God, but they failed to persuade Israel to cease their rebellion (Num. 14:9–10).

1. Rebellion insists on one's own way. Israel would have none of God's way; rather, they would insist on their own foolish pattern of life.

2. Rebellion always ends in sorrow and tragedy (Jer. 20:16). Rebellion brings hurt to others (Num. 14:10).

IV. Because of deliverance.

Such tears are tears of joy (Num. 14:19–21). When Moses had prayed and was assured of the deliverance of Israel, tears of joy streamed down his face.

A. *Deliverance from the just condemnation of sin may bring tears of joy (Num. 14:11–12).* This condemnation would have been just, for God had offered his mercy again and again only to see it trampled underfoot. As the thief on the cross, indeed we all must say, "And we indeed justly; for we receive the due reward of our deeds" (Luke 23:41).

B. *Deliverance through the intercessory prayers of God's people inevitably results in joy, and often it is joy accompanied by tears (Num. 14:19).* Surely Monica, the godly mother of Augustine, experienced such joy when, after years of intercessory prayer for her wayward son, Augustine came to know Christ as his Savior.

C. *Deliverance for the glory of God may move a soul to tears of joy (Num. 14:20–21).* The deliverance of Israel was irrefutable evidence of God's mighty power and inexplicable mercy. Israel's deliverance brought glory to God and, at the same time, tears of joy to Moses.

Conclusion

Jesus also spent a night of tears for you! In the Garden of Gethsemane on the night before his crucifixion, he prayed and shed tears for your sins. Don't let the tears of Jesus be shed in vain; find in him the deliverance he so readily offers today.

WEDNESDAY EVENING, JANUARY 27

Title: The Power of the Tongue

Text: "But the tongue can no man tame; it is an unruly evil, full of deadly poison" **(James 3:8)**.

Introduction

When a patient goes to the doctor, one of the first things that the physician requests is, "Let me see your tongue." To diagnose spiritual health, a good look at the use of the tongue can be a most reliable procedure. Words have a way of revealing character. Someone has truthfully said:

> *A careless word may kindle strife;*
> *A cruel word may wreck a life;*
> *A bitter word may hate instill;*
> *A brutal word may smite and kill;*
> *A gracious word may smooth the way;*
> *A joyous word may lift the day;*
> *A timely word may lessen stress;*
> *A living word may heal and bless.*

I. The importance of the tongue.

James points out the importance of the tongue in three figures.

A. *The tongue is a wild, untamed creature (James 3:8).* The tongue cannot be domesticated, like some wild animals can, to become harmless. While it cannot be domesticated, it should be bridled and regulated (vv. 2–3). Unless the tongue is bridled, it will be the doom of the soul.

B. *The tongue is like a quickly kindled fire reaching out of hell (James 3:5–6).* A word can quickly start a panic on its way. Once a rumor is started, it is impossible to stop it.

C. *The tongue is like a rudder.* The rudder is very small but very significant. The speech of an able speaker can serve as a rudder to turn multitudes of people either to the good or to the bad. The Holy Spirit, rather than clever words, should be what serves as the rudder of the Christian.

45

II. The wrong use of the tongue.

Satan has no more effective instrument for producing evil than an unbridled tongue.

A. *With the tongue one can sow discord.* By an unbridled tongue one can upset the harmony of an intimate fellowship. Friendships have been destroyed by the tale-bearing of another who was sowing discord. Chaos ensues in the church when people begin to say untrue or unkind things about those in leadership. In many instances, people who sow discord are unaware that they are being used by Satan to defeat God's work.

B. *By the tongue one can pass along gossip.* There are very few who take pride in being carriers of gossip. However, there are many who have been the means of communicating untruth by listening to gossip and then reporting what they have heard. One can encourage gossip by merely being curious and expressing a desire to know the facts. Sometimes it is much better for us to remain in ignorance.

C. *With the tongue we can give expression to condemnation.* It seems that we have an inborn tendency to be critical of others. Humans seem to be natural-born faultfinders. When we use the tongue to give expression to criticism, we not only harm others but also cause others to distrust us. It would be profitable for all of us if we would follow the "Four-Way Test" of the things we think, say, and do of Rotary International:

1. Is it the truth?
2. Is it fair to all concerned?
3. Will it build goodwill and better friendships?
4. Will it be beneficial to all concerned?

If you cannot answer yes to all four of these questions, it is best to remain silent.

III. The proper use of the tongue.

The Scriptures suggest many ways by which the tongue may be used more profitably.

A. *We should confess our faith (Rom. 10:9–10).* A public confession of our faith is a vital part of the salvation experience. With our tongue we are to express the deep emotions of our hearts as the result of making Jesus Christ the Lord of our lives. Jesus emphasized this by saying, "Whosoever therefore shall confess me before men, him will I confess also before my Father which is in heaven. But whosoever shall deny me before men, him will I also deny before my Father which is in heaven" (Matt. 10:32–33).

B. *We should continue to confess our sins (1 John 1:9).* While our Lord encouraged us to live a life of perfect unity and loyalty, he also taught us to confess our sins (Matt. 6:12). James encourages us also to make confession of our faults to others and particularly to those to whom we have done wrong (James 5:16).

C. *We should use our tongue to calm hostility (Prov. 15:1).* By controlling the use of our tongues and replying with a soft answer, we can turn away wrath and promote harmonious relationships with others and between others.

D. *We should use our tongue to encourage others.* There are times when all of us need encouragement. One of the most valuable contributions that can be made to others is to provide encouragement when they are depressed or in need of the strength a word of cheer can bring.

E. *We should use our tongue to declare our Christian testimony.* It is not enough for us just to live a good life. We must give a verbal witness concerning the goodness of God as he has revealed himself in Jesus Christ. We should do more than just tell of the death, burial, and resurrection of Christ. We should give a verbal testimony concerning our daily companionship with the living Christ. We should use our tongue in this manner so as to persuade others to put their faith and confidence in the Christ who never disappoints and who always meets the deepest needs of those who trust and obey him.

Conclusion

Use your tongue to praise God. Use your tongue to bless others. Use your tongue as an instrument for God.

SUNDAY MORNING, JANUARY 31

Title: The Nature of True Worship

Text: "God is spirit, and his worshipers must worship in spirit and in truth" (**John 4:24 NIV**).

Scripture Reading: John 4:21–24

Hymns: "Come, Thou Fount of Every Blessing," Wyeth

"Praise to the Lord, the Almighty," Gesangbuch

"Great Redeemer, We Adore Thee," Conte

Offertory Prayer: Our Father, in giving to humankind the greatest gift of all, your own dear Son, you have demonstrated to us the true spirit of giving. We recognize our inherent selfishness, Father, and we ask your forgiveness. Purify our gifts this morning. May they bring honor and glory to your name and promote the progress and growth of your kingdom's work on this earth. In Jesus' name we pray. Amen.

Introduction

The conversation between Jesus and the Samaritan woman at Jacob's well is one of the high points of John's gospel. Included in this conversation is a priceless revelation concerning true worship. Note that this encounter did not take place in a hushed, sacred setting, but in Samaria of all places, and to a woman whose life was jaded with moral sin! But then this is the glory and beauty of God's truth: it knows no limit of time, place, or person. It is revealed to those who are ready to receive it, whoever they are and wherever they are. So by God's Spirit the truth was revealed to this Samaritan woman. Actually, she tried to change the subject as Jesus began to probe deeply into her life. The popular evasive question in her day seemed to have been, "Where is the proper place to worship—in Jerusalem or on this sacred mountain in Samaria?" Jesus did not ignore the question. He used it as a springboard from which to reveal to her the classic Christian definition of worship, the pattern for all true worship.

I. First of all, Jesus talks about manmade worship.

A. *Three basic weaknesses of manmade worship are revealed in Jesus' words to the woman.* First, manmade worship is contrived. It is the result of people adding a little here and taking away a little there until they have turned the Scriptures into a monstrosity. This is what the Samaritans had done in their insistence that true worship must be conducted on Mount Gerizim. They had adjusted history to suit themselves by insisting that it was on this mountain that Abraham had been willing to sacrifice Isaac, and that it was here that Abraham had paid tithes to Melchizedek. Furthermore, they tampered with the Scriptures themselves when they taught that it was on this mountain that Moses first built an altar and sacrificed to God in preparation for the entry of the Israelites into the Promised Land. Deuteronomy 27:4 clearly states that it was Mount Ebal, not Mount Gerizim. Every cult has done this same thing in twisting and distorting the Scriptures. A contrived gospel is a false gospel and will lead people to destruction.

B. *Not only is manmade worship contrived; it is also ignorant of the truth.* Jesus said to this woman, "You Samaritans worship what you do not now; we worship what we do know" (John 4:22 NIV). The Samaritans accepted only the Pentateuch. They rejected all of the great messages of the prophets and all of the beauty and inspiration of the Psalms. They had a partial revelation of the truth, and a fuller revelation was available to them, but they would not accept it. They chose to remain in spiritual darkness. There is no excuse today for believers in the Lord Jesus Christ to be ignorant of what they believe or of the basic teachings of God's Word. There was a time when people were ignorant of spiritual things because they did not have the full revelation of God. But that time is no more; Jesus has come and has revealed God's true nature to us. We have the completed Word of God with the ministry of the Holy Spirit available to interpret it to us.

C. *Manmade worship is also superstitious.* The Samaritans had adulterated the pure worship of Jehovah by recognizing the pagan gods of the foreigners who had come to dwell among them. They had mixed in with their worship of Jehovah all of the superstitions of the pagans. Many Christians have allowed superstition to become a basic part of their worship. Some will attend church not out of a genuine sense of need, nor out of any real desire to meet God in a worship experience, but because they are afraid not to! They feel that if they do not go through the motions of worship, something bad will happen to them. They may even contribute to the church and pay tithes because they are afraid some calamity will befall them if they don't. This is worship out of fear (not reverential fear), and such an attitude is synonymous with superstition. A true worship experience is motivated by love for God and by gratitude for what God has done in one's life and family.

II. Then Jesus told the woman about a God-centered worship.

In telling the Samaritan woman about a God-centered worship, Jesus gave her the eternal formula for true worship: "But the hour cometh, and now is, when the true worshippers shall worship the Father in spirit and in truth: for the Father seeketh such to worship him. God is a Spirit: and they that worship him must worship him in spirit and in truth" (John 4:23–24).

   A. *The first thing Jesus said about worship is that it is God-initiated.* God makes the first move toward people in establishing a true worship experience. People do not have to seek after God or beg and plead with him to meet them in worship. This is what the prophets of Baal did on Mount Carmel in that famous contest with Elijah. They begged and cried and worked themselves up into a hysterical state – finally cutting themselves and shedding their own blood in their fanatical frenzy — trying to attract and coerce Baal to hear them and answer their call. But what did Jesus say? "The Father seeketh such [those who worship him in spirit and in truth] to worship him." People do not seek God; God seeks people. In other words, when we come apart privately or when we come together in our worship assemblies, God is waiting, eager to meet us! He is seeking us in order to enter into the worship experience with us.

   B. *Besides being initiated by God, worship is a spiritual experience.* "God is a Spirit," said Jesus, "and they that worship him must worship him in spirit and in truth" (John 4:24). What do we mean when we say that "God is a spirit"? Is he a vague, impersonal, ethereal being, indescribable to man? Not at all! Rather, because he is Spirit, he is free; he is not confined to any one place or time. For thirty-three years, in a mystical union humans cannot comprehend, God entered human flesh in the person of his sinless Son, the Lord Jesus Christ. Then, in an even greater miracle, God died in the person of his Son and rose again the third day. But even during that amazing time of identification with man, God was still omnipotent, omniscient, and omnipresent.

   Because God is spirit, his omnipresence makes it possible for me to worship him anytime, anywhere. In the privacy of my room, I can worship God; in the midst of the mundane affairs of the everyday world, I can worship God. I can anticipate the blessed privilege of assembling together with my brothers and sisters in Christ at the appointed times, as we are exhorted to do in the Scriptures, and enter into an experience of corporate worship. In the midst of the rarest fellowship in the world—the *koinonia* of the people of God—I can blend my voice both audibly and silently in the midst of the congregation! Yes, God-centered worship is a spiritual experience that is expressed both privately and within the blessed togetherness of God's people.

C. *We are to worship God not only in spirit, but also in truth.* In his great high-priestly prayer, Jesus invoked the Father on our behalf, and he prayed: "Sanctify them through thy truth: thy word is truth" (John 17:17). I cannot read God's Word properly without having a worship experience every time I do. For as I tune my heart to read his Holy Book, the Holy Spirit begins to open my understanding. God's Word, which is the truth of God, is the compass of the church. It keeps both the individual Christian and the church as a whole in the pathway of righteousness, always attuned to the leadership of its head, the Lord Jesus Christ. And not only this, but when I neglect God's Word, I find that I grope through my days, stumbling here and faltering there, unsure at this point, blundering at that decision. Only as I make my way back to the Book and to the altar of prayer in sincere worship do I find my life once more on an even keel.

Conclusion

What is the worship of the church? If it is man-made worship, it is bathed in ignorance of the true message of God's Word, and it is permeated with all kinds of false ideas and superstitions. But if it is God-centered worship, then it is always initiated by God. He is ever seeking his children to enter into a worship experience with them. The worship of the church is spiritual experience that transcends the earthly, the mundane, the worldly; and it is Bible-centered, because God's Word is truth. Worship is genuine when God's people find a friendship and an intimacy with him, who ever seeks us and longs to have fellowship with his redeemed people.

SUNDAY EVENING, JANUARY 31

Title: A Night of Fear

Text: "And when the disciples saw him walking on the sea, they were troubled, saying, It is a spirit; and they cried out for fear. But straightway Jesus spoke unto them, saying, Be of good cheer; it is I; be not afraid" (**Matt. 14:26–27**).

Scripture Reading: Matthew 14:22–33

Introduction

Students of animal behavior contend that fear is both a universal emotion and the first of the emotions to be developed in humans and beasts. All of creation lies beneath the terror of fear.

Have you ever caught a little bird and, holding it in your hand, felt the terrified, rapid beating of its little heart? The bird had neither experience nor acquaintance with you or any other person. It had no reason to fear you except that of instinctive reaction. Although we may be higher in the animal kingdom than the bird, yet there beats in the breast of each of us that dreadful emotion of fear. Perhaps we can learn how better to cope with this problem as we discover within our text the answer to three great questions concerning fear.

I. When does fear usually arise?

Verse 24 of our text says, "But the ship was now in the midst of the sea, tossed with waves: for the wind was contrary." Fear usually arises in the midst of life's storms. As long as the disciples were close to Christ, they did not fear. It was not until the disciples were "on their own" in the midst of the sea tossed by the waves that fear struck.

A. *Life's storms may rest within God's will.* "And straightway Jesus constrained his disciples to get into a ship" (Matt. 14:22). The disciples did not get themselves into this difficulty. Christ clearly "constrained" them to get into the ship and go before him to the other side of the sea.

1. Surely one reason that life's storms may well rest in God's will is because they may serve to strengthen our own faith. Mark tells us that Jesus *saw* them harassed but for a time did not go to them. Previously when they were in a storm at sea, Christ was with them, and they needed only to awake him. This time he wanted them to face the storm with only their faith, so he remained ashore. Thus their faith was more severely tried and strengthened.

2. Another reason that life's storms may rest within God's will is that they may be unavoidable in accomplishing God's purpose. Christ had told the disciples to cross the lake and dock on the west side. If they were to accomplish this purpose, they had to sail immediately, even if it meant sailing in the face of a storm. Nevertheless, they did launch out knowing full well the risk they were running. For you to become what God wants you to be may necessitate your going through life's storms.

B. *Life's storms may be intensified by prayerlessness.* After sending the disciples away, Jesus went into a mountain to pray. At this same time the ship was in the midst of the sea tossed with the waves (Matt. 14:23–24). Simply because the disciples were instructed to cross the sea did not mean that they had no need or time for prayer. They became busy doing Christ's bidding without having made proper spiritual preparation.

1. Prayerlessness makes knowledge of God's will difficult and consequently intensifies the storms of life. Matthew Henry says, "The boldest spirits must wait for a call to hazardous enterprises, and we must not rashly and presumptuously thrust ourselves upon them."

2. Life's storms are often intensified by prayerlessness because prayerlessness robs from us any inner spiritual power. The disciples' boat was not a

sailboat but rather a rowboat. These were strong and experienced men of the sea, but all their physical strength was no match for the storm. Theirs was a need not for physical power but for inner spiritual power. The storm was more inward than outward. And prayerlessness had robbed them of the inner spiritual reserve that could have been theirs.

II. Why does fear arise?

Having seen *when* fear arises, we now ask *why* does it arise in the Christian's life? Why can't the Christian sail through the storms of life with faith unfaltering and emotions undisturbed? There is only one answer—because of his failure to perceive the presence of Christ (Matt. 14:25–26).

    A. *The presence of Christ may come in an unexpected manner and thus may not be recognized.* "And in the fourth watch of the night Jesus went unto them, walking on the sea" (Matt. 14:25). Christ's "walking on the sea" was a most unexpected manner in which to reveal his presence.

        1. The manner in which Christ chooses to reveal his presence does not always conform to our expectations. Perhaps the disciples expected to meet Christ on the other side but certainly not at 4:00 A.M., three and one-half miles from the shore out in the open sea! It is not likely that you would expect Christ's presence to be felt at the bedside of a critically ill child or in the midst of family strife or in the depths of financial reversals, but often the presence of Christ is felt even there.

        2. Whatever manner Christ may choose to reveal his presence is intended to meet your own specific need. Verse 25 says that Jesus went to them. The disciples were in trouble, and the coming of Christ in this unexpected manner was intended to meet their immediate need.

    B. *The presence of Christ may be misinterpreted.* The New International Version translates verse 26: "When the disciples saw him walking on the lake, they were terrified. 'It's a ghost,' they said, and cried out in fear." The disciples, like the Greeks and most Jews (except the Sadducees), believed in apparitions or ghosts. They misinterpreted the presence of Christ as a ghost.

        The presence of Christ has been interpreted at times as something to fear and at other times as one's own imagination. But it is neither of these, and to so interpret the presence of Christ is to miss the blessings intended.

III. What can dispel fear?

None of us likes to live beneath the dark shadow of fear. But what can dispel this most contagious of all human emotions?

    A. *Christian courage can dispel fear.* "But straightway Jesus spake unto them, saying, Be of good cheer; it is I; be not afraid" (Matt. 14:27). Jesus gives the answer in his first words, "Take courage—be of good cheer!"

        1. Christian courage is grounded in Christ. Jesus said, "It is I." He did not say, "Trust in yourselves" or "Trust in the strength of your ship."

During World War I a group of British soldiers who had been on furlough were being led back to the front. Their country was torn with war, and cold rain was falling. The men were aware that they were returning to battle, blood, and the threat of death. Despondently they marched along, no words spoken and no songs sung. As they marched past the ruins of a church, their officer happened to see the figure of Christ high above the altar. This brought to him new strength and courage, a new sense of security. He then gave the command, "Eyes right! March!" The eyes of the anxious and despondent soldiers fell upon that object of worship that their officer had seen. In the form of the agonizing and yet victorious Christ, they found their courage renewed. Standing erect with hearts filled with new courage, they marched on like victors! Their courage was grounded in Christ.

2. Christian courage accepts the word of Christ. These disciples asked for no signs or omens. They simply accepted the word of their Savior and acted on it.

B. *Response to the call of faith can dispel fear (Matt. 14:28–29).* "Lord, if it be thou" implies that Peter takes for granted that this is indeed the Lord. When his Lord said, "Come," Peter responded to this call of faith and stepped out upon the water.

1. Response to the call of faith must be made in the face of the severest tests. If Peter's faith were ever severely tested, it was at this time. No sheer profession would keep him from sinking into the stormy sea. No mere desire to demonstrate his superior faith could make him walk on the water. Faith alone was required for this task, and the response would soon reveal his faith.

2. Response to the call of faith must be made to the most unusual request. Should Christ ask you, can you walk on the sea? Almost anyone can walk on the land, but you are called to walk on the sea. What is your particular sea? It may be the sea of sickness or the sea of loneliness or the sea of sorrow, pain, disillusionment, or temptation. By God's grace and with your faith, you *can* walk on your sea.

3. A proper response to the call of faith serves to confirm your faith (Matt. 14:29).

C. *The rescuing hand of Christ can dispel fear (Matt. 14:30–31).* Under a sudden impulse of confidence in Christ mingled with his own self-confidence, Peter proposed and undertook to walk on the water himself. But his faith failed just when his task was almost finished. Yet the rescuing hand of Christ was extended.

1. The rescuing hand of Christ is extended even when our faith fails (Matt. 14:30).

2. The rescuing hand of Christ is readily offered when we acknowledge our need (Matt. 14:30b–31).

3. The rescuing hand of Christ is all-sufficient, for the Scripture says, "And immediately Jesus stretched forth his hand, and caught him" (Matt. 14:31).

D. *The indwelling presence of Christ can dispel fear.*

1. The presence of Christ imparts peace and security, for "when they [Christ and Peter] were come unto the ship, the wind ceased" (Matt. 14:32).

2. The indwelling presence of Christ brings the response of joy and adoration to those who will receive it (Matt. 14:33).

Conclusion

> *Maker of the mighty deep*
> *Whereon our vessels fare,*
> *Above our life's adventure, keep*
> *Thy faithful watch and care.*
> *In Thee we trust whate'er befall;*
> *Thy sea is great, our boats are small.*
> *We know not where the secret tides*
> *Will help us or delay,*
> *Nor where the lurking tempest hides,*
> *Nor where the fogs are gray.*
> *We trust in Thee, whate'er befall:*
> *Thy sea is great, our boats are small.*
> *When outward bound we boldly sail*
> *And leave the friendly shore,*
> *Let not our hearts in courage fail*
> *Until the voyage is o'er.*
> *We trust in Thee, whate'er befall:*
> *Thy sea is great, our boats are small.*
> *Beyond the circle of the sea*
> *When voyaging is past,*
> *We seek our final port in Thee.*
> *Oh, bring us home at last!*
> *In Thee we trust, whate'er befall:*
> *Thy sea is great, our boats are small.*
>   —*Author Unknown*

FEBRUARY

■ **Sunday Mornings**

"The Christian and the Church in Today's World" is the suggested theme for Sunday mornings in February.

■ **Sunday Evenings**

Continue the series "Great Night Scenes of the Bible."

■ **Wednesday Evenings**

Continue with messages that emphasize the practice of genuine religion in daily life from the epistle of James.

WEDNESDAY EVENING, FEBRUARY 3

Title: Spiritual Poverty and the Neglect of Prayer

Text: "Ye have not, because ye ask not" (**James 4:2**).

Introduction

One of the major emphases of the epistle of James concerns our privilege and responsibility in prayer. In the first chapter we are encouraged to pray for wisdom (v. 5). In the last chapter we are encouraged to pray for the sick and for the forgiveness of sin (5:14–16). Elijah is used as an illustration of the powerful results that can come about as a result of sincere, earnest, believing prayer to God (vv. 17–18).

In the words of our text, James declares that to neglect the privilege of prayer is to bring spiritual poverty into one's life. He who neglects to pray is guilty of self-robbery. He who neglects to pray refuses to let God bestow the blessings that come as a result of the spiritual dialogue of prayer. James was insisting that God is a prayer-hearing and prayer-answering God. He was encouraging his readers to give themselves to prayer.

How long has it been since you really prayed? How long has it been since you really talked with God? How long has it been since you let God talk with you? Is it possible that the spiritual poverty of your soul is due primarily to your neglect of the privilege of communicating with God through the avenue of prayer? The story is told of a woman who dreamed that she died and went to heaven. In her dream she was led by an angel to the place where she was to dwell. After arriving she discovered a large pile of beautifully wrapped presents. She inquired concerning the owner of the presents. The angel who conducted her thus far replied, "These are blessings that the heavenly Father had for you, but you never did make request for them."

The Bible clearly teaches that the heavenly Father is more eager to bestow his blessings on us than we are to receive them.

In the verse that follows our text, James emphasizes that God is under no obligation to answer a prayer that is motivated by selfishness. Prayer was never intended as a means whereby selfish persons could requisition from God things that would contribute to their selfish advantage. Prayer is the divinely ordained channel through which we are to receive the blessings from God that are needed for the living of a victorious Christian life of devoted service to others. The Bible gives us some specific things for which we are to pray, and when we pray for these, we can know that we are praying in accordance with the will of God (1 John 5:14–15).

I. Everyone should pray for salvation (Rom. 10:13).

All of us must personally invite Jesus Christ to come into our hearts as Lord and Savior if we want to receive the salvation that God offers to those who are willing to trust him. Like the unworthy publican (Luke 18:13–14), each one should call upon God for the mercy that he offers to sinners. To sincerely and earnestly do so is to receive the gift of eternal life.

II. Everyone should pray for wisdom (James 1:5).

Life has always been difficult. People have always been perplexed by the alternatives that life offers. People have always been in need of guidance. Wisdom is something more than knowledge. Wisdom is a divinely bestowed insight that enables us to choose between the good and the evil or between the better and the best. Wisdom is needed in our home relationships and in our business relationships. Wisdom is greatly needed if we would bear a winning witness concerning the love of God for sinners.

III. Everyone should pray for grace (Heb. 4:16).

The child of God kneels before a throne of grace when he or she addresses the heavenly Father in prayer. Because of our sympathetic High Priest, Jesus Christ, who has entered into heaven to intercede for us, we are to boldly come for grace and mercy to help in every time of need. God's grace is God in action on behalf of needy sinners. He saves us and sustains us by his grace. He will make us sufficient by his grace (2 Cor. 12:9).

IV. Everyone should pray for the power of the Holy Spirit (Luke 11:13).

The Holy Spirit enters the heart of the convert at the moment when the new birth takes place. The Holy Spirit enters the heart in order to reproduce the character of Christ in the lives of God's children. It is not necessary that we pray for him to come. He has already arrived (1 Cor. 3:16). In the experience of prayer, we open up our own hearts and minds to the fullness of the work of the Spirit. As we pray for him to take charge of our lives, we experience his presence in a richer and fuller manner. When we neglect to pray, we restrict him and deprive him of the privilege of working both in us and through us.

Conclusion

It is impossible to list all of the blessings that come as a result of earnest, sincere, believing prayer. James would have each of us recognize that much of the spiritual poverty of our lives is due to our neglect to enter into the closet of prayer where the rich rewards and blessings of God are bestowed on those who enter the closet for dialogue with the heavenly Father (Matt. 6:6).

Paul challenged his dear friends at Philippi to bring their every need before God's throne of grace, and he assured them that if they would do so, the peace of God would stand as a sentinel or guard over their hearts and minds. The Bible from beginning to end encourages us to give ourselves to prayer. May God help us to cease being neglectful of this privilege and responsibility.

SUNDAY MORNING, FEBRUARY 7

Title: God Becomes Real

Text: "Blessed are the pure in heart, for they will see God" (**Matt. 5:8 NIV**).

Scripture Reading: Genesis 28:16; Exodus 33:18–23; Matthew 5:1–8

Hymns: "Sun of My Soul, Thou Saviour Dear," Keble

"God of Grace and God of Glory," Fosdick

"Since Jesus Came into My Heart," McDaniel

Offertory Prayer: Through the blessings of good health and gainful employment, you enable us, O God, to come into possession of money with which to purchase the things we need. We thank you and bless your name for your sustaining power with which we are energized. May we make such use of those things that are passing in order that we may possess those things that abide. Through Jesus Christ, our Lord. Amen.

Introduction

On the American scene in recent decades churches have been in big business. One ingredient of affluence "à la the American way" is to be respectable, churchgoing people. At least this is still true in many communities. A sore conscience requires that the Saturday golf or goofing-off or partying and the Sunday afternoon and night television watching be soothed by Sunday morning churchgoing. It is doubtful that we adults are fooling ourselves, but it is certain that we are not fooling our young people.

People who think just a little now and then are quite capable of detecting superficiality, insincerity, and hypocrisy in our religious exercises. Young people will not perpetuate empty forms in order to keep alive what they consider to be counterfeit religion. They know whether we are people of God or people of the cash register.

Many adults, too, suffer from a sense of unreality about God, the church, and Christian living. How many people could say, "I have been in the church for years. I believe in God and try to serve him, yet to be perfectly candid, God isn't real to me. What can I do?" The most real thing about the faith of some folks is its nebulous quality.

I. God became real to Moses.

Moses wanted to see God more clearly, following the crisis of his fellow Hebrews at the foot of the mountain where they had made the golden calf. He would go into the tent of meeting pitched outside the camp and converse with God. While, in the language of the Exodus account, their communication with each other was very clear, Moses wanted a firmer hold on his sense of reality.

God told Moses that it would be fatal for anyone to see him face-to-face. He instructed Moses to hide in the cleft of a rock, and "while my glory passes by I will … cover thee with my hand while I pass by: And I will take away mine hand, and thou shalt see my back parts: but my face shall not be seen" (Ex. 33:22–23).

God spoke to Moses' need, and he speaks to ours. Through Moses' obedience and patience, God became real. Note in the larger Scripture passage that obedience was to wait. Trust issues in patience. This is not to suggest that Moses folded his hands and lived in a vacuum. He had to get on with the day-to-day details of leading the Hebrew people. But he came through the confusion and uncertainty with a keen sense of God's living reality. His experiences following indicate that he could have said, as Jacob said on one occasion: "Surely the LORD is in this place; and I knew it not" (Gen. 28:16).

II. God became real to Jesus of Nazareth.

Jesus once said, "Blessed are the pure in heart, for they shall see God." This does not contradict or change the truth as expressed to Moses, but it is to say that to the pure in heart the divine shall be vitally real. This beatitude opens a window into the Master's own experience. Jesus was a teacher of ethics and a prophet of social righteousness, a religious reformer and a specialist in human friendship — much more besides. But all such things were like space capsules orbiting around a central fact of utmost importance, for God was real to him. From the time when as a boy in the temple he said to his parents, "Don't you know that I must be about my Father's business?" until on the cross he said, "Father, into thy hands I commend my spirit," God was real to him. Whatever other explanations may be given — and a lifetime is too short and human limitations too pronounced to explain Jesus — this central fact should not be forgotten. Here was the one to whom the loving heavenly Father was vividly real.

III. God becomes real to us.

Every person possesses, or may come to possess, an "organ" whereby it is possible to see God — in the sense that Jesus meant it. Examine briefly the beatitude "Blessed are the pure in heart, for they shall see God." The Greek word for "pure" has a variety of usages, all of which have something to add to the meaning of this beatitude for the Christian life.

58

Originally it meant simply "clean" and could be used, for instance, of dirty clothes that had been washed clean. It was used of grain that had been winnowed or cleansed of chaff and of an army that had been purged of all discontented, cowardly, unwilling, and inefficient soldiers, thus making it a first-class fighting force. This word for "pure" was used of wine or milk undiluted and of metal that had no foreign substance. When used of glass it means clear glass.

The word "heart" in the Bible usually means the whole personality.

This beatitude is demanding. It tells us that the Christian whose motives are unmixed shall see God. What about our churchgoing, our money contributions, our prayers, and a dozen other things—are they motivated by love and service, or are we trying to gain God's good favor? Or maybe our prestige and respectability are at stake?

We see what we are prepared to see. The average person looks into the sky on a clear night and sees a host of pinpoints of light. This is what he is equipped to see. The astronomer will call the stars and planets by their familiar names, and he will move among them as among friends. The average person walks across the meadow and woodland and sees trees, grass, weeds, and wild flowers—maybe. The trained botanist sees things and calls them by name. He knows their use. He may even find something of value and rarity because he is equipped to see.

Only the pure in heart see God, said Jesus. The organ whereby we may see God is not the physical eye nor the brain. It is a heart that is pure, a life that has single aim or vision—to please God. Those who with singleness of mind try to do God's will come to new awareness of God's presence and love. God becomes real. Tennyson left instruction that his "Crossing the Bar" was always to be placed at the end of his published works. It closes:

> *For tho' from out our bourne of Time and Place*
> *The flood may bear me far,*
> *I hope to see my Pilot face to face*
> *When I have crossed the bar.*

IV. God becomes real when in our relation to him we meet the conditions that the laws of friendship demand.

Dr. John A. Redhead, in his book *Getting to Know God*, suggests that religion is friendship with God. Then he talks about two laws of friendship—association and expression.

All of us have had friends of past years. We did things together; we shared certain interests, joys, and problems; we enjoyed being in each other's company. Then one or both of us moved to other parts of the country, separated by great distance. For the friendship to continue through the years in any meaningful way, we had to stay associated through correspondence and occasional visits. Friendship feeds on expression. This is sometimes in word, sometimes in deed. God never moves away. If we spend time seeking him, we will maintain our friendship with him.

Conclusion

The church asks its members to pledge their support—finances, attendance, loyalty, prayer, and so on. The church must have this support and can do little or nothing worthwhile without it. But the other side is not to be underestimated. Individual church members need to express love and friendship for God, and one of the best ways is to serve through the church to meet the needs of humanity outside its doors. This is Christlikeness, and Jesus said, "He that hath seen me hath seen the father" (John 14:9).

SUNDAY EVENING, FEBRUARY 7

Title: A Night of Denial

Text: " 'I tell you the truth,' Jesus answered, 'this very night, before the rooster crows, you will disown me three times' " **(Matt. 26:34 NIV)**.

Scripture Reading: Matthew 26:34–35, 69–75

Introduction

John Calvin said, "The fall of Peter is a mirror of human infirmity and a memorial example of God's goodness and compassion." Reflected in Peter's denial is our own weakness in temptation and the danger that at any moment we too may deny our Lord just when he needs us most. In a hundred different ways each day, Jesus continues to be denied by the very people who bear his name. And that denial hurts the one who denies as well as the one denied.

We do not come to the point of denial without having seen in our own lives one warning sign after another.

I. The warning signs of denial.

Jesus was fair with Peter, for he clearly warned him that a moment of denial would soon approach. But Peter, like many of us, would not believe that he could ever be guilty of such an act (Matt. 26:34–35).

    A. *Prayerlessness is a warning sign of denial.* Jesus said to Peter, "What, could ye not watch with me one hour? Watch and pray, that ye enter not into temptation: the spirit indeed is willing, but the flesh is weak" (Matt. 26:40b–41). Why did Christ direct these words to Peter? Because Christ anticipated the denial of Peter and wanted him through prayer to prepare himself for a night of trial.

        1. Prayerlessness cuts the heart out of our convictions. A few weeks earlier at Caesarea Philippi, Peter had made a marvelous confession of his deep conviction about Christ. "Thou art the Christ, the Son of the living God" (Matt. 16:16). But prayerlessness now had cut the heart out of this conviction. Peter discovered that he lacked the power to stand before nonbelievers and proclaim once again that Jesus is the Christ, the Son of the living God.

60

2. Prayerlessness removes the fear of sin (Matt. 26:43). Why should Peter fear Christ's opponents? He had battled them for more than three years and had not been swayed by them. He had neither fear of tomorrow nor fear of the pressures it might bring. He was a strong soul! Therefore he had no need of prayer. He could sleep on, for he no longer had a fear of sin.

B. *Indifference is a warning sign of denial (Matt. 26:40–41).* "Watch" refers primarily to keeping awake but also suggests mental alertness. The disciples were soon to fall prey to Satan's snare because of their indifference.

   1. Indifference results in a failure to make adequate preparation. In only a few minutes, the chief priest and elders would invade the garden and take Christ captive (Matt. 26:26–47), yet Peter and the other disciples slept on! Despite Jesus' warning through the parable of the five foolish bridesmaids that indifference results in a failure to make adequate preparation, the disciples squandered these final moments in sleep.

   2. Indifference makes us unaware of Satan's approach. Peter and the other disciples were not aware of the close proximity of their enemies until Jesus told them of their presence.

C. *Self-confidence is a warning sign of denial.* "Peter answered and said unto him, Though all men shall be offended because of thee, yet will I never be offended" (Matt. 26:33). And again Peter said, "Though I should die with thee, yet will I not deny thee" (Matt. 26:35). Here is the beginning of that self-confidence that led step by step to Peter's dreadful denial.

   1. Self-confidence often casts aspersions on others (Matt. 26:33). The peculiar Greek construction (two indicative futures) implies that all other disciples will be offended. And so the pattern continues today that those who are the most self-confident are usually those who look down on others, questioning their spiritual sincerity.

   2. Self-confidence has a detrimental influence on others. Matthew says that after Peter had made his boast of his loyalty to Christ, "likewise also said all the disciples" (Matt. 26:35). Encouraged by Peter's ardor and positivity, the other disciples made a similar claim. Through our own self-confidence, we may lead another to think more highly of himself than he ought and thus contribute to his own denial and spiritual defeat.

D. *Spiritual aloofness is a warning sign of denial (Matt. 26:58).*

   1. There is a tendency for a Christian to become spiritually aloof when he is fearful of becoming too "involved" in times of stress. This doubtlessly is why Peter "followed [Jesus] afar off." These were treacherous times. For Peter to become too involved in Jesus' conflict might well cost him his life. To follow Jesus at a distance was far safer.

   2. Spiritual aloofness leads to association with Christ's enemies. After following Jesus afar off, Peter went into the high priest's palace and sat down with the servants. Not much time lapses between the moment

when one becomes spiritually withdrawn from others and the moment one begins to gravitate toward the enemies of Christ.

3. Spiritual aloofness tries to maintain a spectator's perspective. Having sat down with servants of the high priest, it is said that Peter's intention was "to see the end" (Matt. 26:58). Peter could not maintain this detached approach to Jesus' trial for long. Whatever involves Christ equally involves his followers. There is no neutral ground on the spiritual battlefield of life.

II. The wrongs of denials.

One might ask, "When the pressures of life are brought to bear so heavily on one as they were on Peter, is there really much wrong with giving in for a moment? What possible serious harm can be done by an innocent word of denial?" The wrongs of denial are spelled out in verses 69–74.

A. *Denial strengthens the position of Satan (Matt. 26:60–61).* Every moment of Peter's silence brought Christ's false conviction closer. Peter might have spoken in Christ's defense, but instead he spoke a word of denial!

1. Denial helps the cause of Satan because it provides ammunition to be used against the cause of Christ. Later people could say, "Surely you don't believe in Christ! His most outspoken follower, Simon Peter, denied him openly!" How many have seen you this week deny Christ either in what you said, what you did, where you went, or what you failed to do?

2. Denial assists the cause of Satan because it allows the claims and charges of Satan to go unchallenged. All of the lies being made against Christ went unchallenged when one who could refute them stood so nearby but said nothing.

B. *Denial weakens one's testimony (Matt. 26:70–72, 74).*

1. Because one can never quite outlive its hurt, denial weakens one's testimony. You say, "But look at how Peter was used at Pentecost!" Yes, but how many more might have believed if they could only have erased from their memory that vehement denial uttered by the same lips that now call them to believe in this one whom he had formerly denied?

2. Because denial leads a person to revert to his old ways, it weakens his testimony (Matt. 26:74). The Jews were much given to careless use of oaths. Under the excitement of the hour, Peter reverted to an early habit that he had abandoned through the Savior's teaching—the habit of cursing. The pattern continues to be true that whenever we begin to deny our Savior we begin to slip back into our old ways of life.

C. *Denial becomes a future stumbling block.* Once Peter had denied his Lord, he doubtlessly found that the temptation to deny him again was always present in difficult hours. Once a person has established the pattern of denial, he will discover that there is an ever-growing tendency to repeat this pattern when similar problems arise.

D. *Denial brings grief to Christ.* "Just as he was speaking, the rooster crowed. The Lord turned and looked straight at Peter" (Luke 22:60–61 NIV).

1. Because of all that Christ has done for you, his heart is grieved at your denial.
2. Because denial reflects upon Christ's regenerating power, grief comes to his heart. We have claimed that we have become new creatures in Christ Jesus, yet we find in these moments of weakness we give reason to nonbelievers to question the regenerating power of our Savior.

III. The way out of denial.

"Immediately a rooster crowed. Then Peter remembered the word Jesus had spoken: 'Before the rooster crows, you will disown me three times.' And he went outside and wept bitterly" (Matt. 26:74–75 NIV). Once Peter had denied Christ, he became a victim of his own falsehood and sought to create a way out by additional denials. He learned that there is no human way out of denial.

A. *A way out of denial is made possible by Christ's intercession.* "I have prayed for thee, that thy faith fail not: and when thou art converted, strengthen thy brethren" (Luke 22:32).

Even as Christ's intercession for Peter made possible a way of escape, so his intercession for us makes possible a way out of denial.

B. *The way out of denial is entered through repentance.* Matthew 26:75 reveals that Peter acknowledged the wrong of his denial. Luke tells us that one look from Jesus cut deeply into Peter's heart. Peter was convicted of the awfulness of his denial and repented because of it. Sincere repentance part of man is always met by loving forgiveness on the part of God.

C. *The way out of denial ushers in a new kind of life.* "And when thou art *converted*, strengthen thy brethren" (Luke 22:32, italics mine). This crisis was the pivotal point in Peter's life. He was a new man after this experience. What could have destroyed him actually made him. On the other side of this experience, Peter emerged a man of courage, faith, and loyalty. When threatened and commanded never to preach again, Peter said, "We cannot but speak the things which we have seen and heard (Acts 4:20).

Conclusion

The Meaning of the Look

I think that look of Christ might seem to say —
"Thou Peter! art thou then a common stone
Which I at last must break my heart upon,
For all God's charge to his high angels may
Guard my foot better? Did I yesterday
Wash thy feet, my beloved, that they should run
Quick to deny me 'neath the morning sun?

And do thy kisses, like the rest, betray?
The cock crows coldly. — Go, and manifest
A late contrition, but no bootless fear!
For when thy final need is dreariest,
Thou shalt not be denied, for I am here;
My voice to God and angels shall attest,
Because I know this man, let him be clear."

—Elizabeth Barrett Browning

WEDNESDAY EVENING, FEBRUARY 10

Title: Victory Over the Devil

Text: "Submit yourselves therefore to God. Resist the devil, and he will flee from you" **(James 4:7)**.

Introduction

We must recognize the reality of the existence of the devil. To fail to do so and to fail to take proper steps of precaution is to expose ourselves to the possibility of being greatly hindered from doing God's good will.

Paul described the devil as "the god of this world" (2 Cor. 4:4). He also described the work of the devil in terms that should speak a word of warning to all of us: "For such are false apostles, deceitful workers, transforming themselves into the apostles of Christ. And no marvel; for Satan himself is transformed into an angel of light" (2 Cor. 11:13–14).

Peter described the devil as a roaring lion who walks about seeking whom he may devour (1 Peter 5:8).

Jesus described the devil as the Evil One, the Wicked One, a murderer, a liar, the father of lies, and the prince of this world.

I. Christ overcame the devil: therefore victory is possible for us.

A. *Jesus relied on the Scriptures for help (Matt. 4:4, 7, 10).*
B. *Jesus was completely surrendered to the leadership of the Holy Spirit (Luke 4:1).* Because Christ conquered Satan, it is possible for his disciples, in the strength that he makes available to them, to overcome the Evil One (cf. 1 John 2:13).

II. A word of warning from the apostle Peter.

The apostle Peter had had a lot of experience with the devil. The devil had gotten control of both his mind and his tongue to the extent that on one occasion he sought to thwart Jesus from his redemptive mission. Jesus explained to his disciples the nature and the necessity of his death on the cross (Matt. 16:21), but Peter immediately sought to persuade him to do otherwise (v. 22). Our Lord

64

turned to Peter and spoke words of compassion and stinging rebuke at the same time (v. 23). If Satan could capture the mind of the apostle Peter, then you and I should be modest enough to admit that it is possible for him to infiltrate our thinking and to use our faculties to dissuade others from doing God's will.

Peter's advice to us is: "Be sober, be vigilant; because your adversary the devil, as a roaring lion, walketh about, seeking whom he may devour" (1 Peter 5:8). By virtue of the warning, Peter encourages us to believe that it is possible to overcome this adversary who waits to attack us as we walk the road of life.

III. The way to victory over the devil.

James emphasizes the practice of pure religion in his epistle. He encourages us to practice the teachings of God's Holy Word as words of divine truth. The words of the text provide both positive and negative suggestions concerning our conflict with the devil. Positively, we are to submit ourselves completely to the will of God. At the same time, we are to resist and to strive against every effort of the devil to lead us astray.

A. *Some neither submit themselves to the Lord nor resist the devil.*

B. *Some submit themselves to God but do not resist the devil.*

C. *Some resist the devil but do not submit themselves to God.*

D. *Submissiveness to God and resistance against the devil should be simultaneous.*

    1. The devil is older, wiser, cleverer, and stronger than we are (Eph. 6:10–18).

    2. We should gladly submit ourselves to our loving heavenly Father because he knows our foe and he knows us.

    3. We need God's wisdom, grace, and power to live a victorious Christian life.

Conclusion

By hiding the Word of God in our heart, by keeping contact with God through prayer, and by yielding to the loving will of God, we can overcome our adversary, the devil.

SUNDAY MORNING, FEBRUARY 14

Title: Equality in Christ

Text: "Then Peter began to speak: 'I now realize how true it is that God does not show favoritism but accepts men from every nation who fear him and do what is right'" (**Acts 10:34–35 NIV**).

Scripture Reading: Acts 10:24–43; Galatians 3:26–28

Hymns: "God, Our Father, We Adore Thee," Frazer

              "In Christ There Is No East or West," Oxenham

              "Rise Up, O Men of God," Merrill

Offertory Prayer: O God, who through Jesus of Nazareth has given us an example, receive these offerings that we bring in response to your love. As you have identified with us in our need, so may we identify through our gifts with the need of others to hear the Good News. In Christ's name we pray. Amen.

Introduction

Imagine a sensitive soul looking out over the universe centuries ago. He must have been puzzled as he looked day after night and year after month at the sun, moon, and stars. Admiring the sky and the land, the sea and the mountains, and fearing the great monsters that stalked the earth and other unseen forces, he wondered about many things. "In the beginning God created the heavens and the earth," he was inspired to say in an attempt to explain these marvelous things.

In one sweep of the centuries, and increasingly in our generation, science has explained many things. But science has never contradicted or improved the simple expression in Genesis 1:1: "In the beginning God...." The Christian church declares that the universe and humans came from God. Our existence on the earth is not accidental, and the universe is not the result of blind chance. Neither does the church take the position that we are on the earth all dressed up with no place to go. Our origin is in God, and our destiny rests with God. A biblical faith centers in the conviction that God *is* and that he has created humans for wholesome purposes.

God's purposes include the whole person and all persons. To the extent that one is Christian, he or she must seek to be Christian in relationships with others. This may be seen more clearly in light of the following principles.

I. Dependence on God.

    A. *People are dependent on God.* This could be illustrated in many different ways—for example, life after death. Christians, believing in a kind of God revealed in Jesus Christ, accept his promises of life after death. At death we move into an area over which we have absolutely no control. Science has lengthened our days on the earth, but still somewhere in our earthly existence we come up against the inescapable event that we call death. We reach the point where the things on which we depend for life—food, air, sunshine, water, technology, wealth, learning, and friends—no longer sustain us. Breath leaves our body, and there is nothing that the pooled might and resources of the whole world can do about it.

    B. *Tomorrow's world is dependent on God.* Humans are dependent on God for the kind of world that only he can build. Just as there are scientific and physical laws by which the universe is governed and by which people must abide, there are ethical and moral laws by which people must regulate their lives. For example, all high school students should be familiar with the simple chemical formula H_2O. They know that this proportion of hydrogen and oxygen will yield the same result the world over. The chemist discovered the formula, but he did not create the fact that the combination of the proper parts gives us water. Likewise, in the area of human relations, true friendship between one person and another produces a happy relationship—assuming the other essential ingredients are present. Hatred between the two leads to estrangement and unhappiness. The fact that love binds two people together and hatred tears them apart may be discovered, but it cannot be created or destroyed.

We cannot build a good world if we disregard the moral and ethical laws established by God and revealed through the Hebrew prophets of old. There are forces at work in the universe concerning our relation to others that are beyond our control.

People search for something on which they can completely rely. They rely on the God of the Christian faith, the god of some other religion, or a kind of private god of their own construction, that is, some scale or method of values by which their loyalties are determined. The God of the Scriptures is a universal God of justice, mercy, and love. He is not a god of a class or race or nation. The light of this truth broke on Peter with tradition-shattering consequences in his experience at Cornelius's house, and he exclaimed: "You are well aware that it is against our law for a Jew to associate with a Gentile or visit him. But God has shown me that I should not call any man impure or unclean.... I now realize how true it is that God does not show favoritism but accepts men from every nation who fear him and do what is right" (Acts 10:28, 34–35 NIV; cf. Gal. 3:26–28).

The Christian sees people first as human beings, children of one God (potentially, at least) and only secondarily as members of a particular race or nation. An Asian, Latin-American, African-American, Indian, or Anglo-Saxon is first of all a human being and only secondarily, or incidentally, something else.

II. A person's love of God and love of others are inseparable.

We can demonstrate our love for God by demonstrating our love for others in concrete ways. One "loves his neighbor as himself" when he is willing to do—and does—all he can to respond in a helpful way to meet the needs of another. This means that we will not seek special privileges for ourselves at others' expense. We forgive them the wrongs done to us, taking the initiative to restore a broken fellowship.

Jesus showed us that love of God is not isolated from our everyday activities. When Jesus showed his love for people—particularly people in trouble—he got into trouble (cf. Matt. 23). Jesus' life was governed by what he understood to be God's will. When his behavior in obedience to God's command began to be observed, his own family said that he was out of his mind. The Pharisees, Sadducees, Zealots, and Roman officials were disturbed too. His belief in and love of man could not be separated from his belief in and love of God, and he paid for it with his life. The author of 1 John states it clearly when he says, "If anyone says, 'I love God,' yet hates his brother, he is a liar. For anyone who does not love his brother, whom he has seen, cannot love God, whom he has not seen" (4:20 NIV).

III. Prejudice has no place among God's people.

Prejudice is premature judgment; it is to form an opinion, usually unfavorably, before the examination of the facts. Erection of religious, political, economic, and social barriers between one group and another makes it impossible for members of the two groups fully to know, appreciate, and understand each other.

Conclusion

The church is a unique institution. It has a divine origin, and its allegiance is not to man, government, or tradition, but to God. The church is made up of all people who have accepted Jesus Christ as Lord and Savior, being adopted by God the Father as joint heirs with his Son.

SUNDAY EVENING, FEBRUARY 14

Title: A Night of Accounting

Text: "But God said unto him, Thou fool, this night thy soul shall be required of thee: then whose shall these things be, which thou hast provided?" **(Luke 12:20)**.

Scripture Reading: Luke 12:13–21

Introduction

The most sobering truth of the Christian faith is that one day we will give an account of our lives to God. Regardless of the circumstances that surround us and the influences that are brought to bear upon us, we are accountable! Jesus tells us of one man who refused to face this fact and thus entered his night of accounting unprepared. The Christ whom we one day will face would have us to know that we too are accountable.

I. We are accountable for life's priorities (Luke 12:13–15).

Luke tells us that on one occasion a man came to Christ and said, "Master, speak to my brother, that he divide the inheritance with me" (Luke 12:13). Christ quickly detected the real priority of this man's life. He saw through this man's scheme to use his position and ability as a respected religious teacher for his own worldly interest so that his brother might be pressured into sharing the inheritance with him. In response Christ pointed out that people are accountable for the priorities of their lives and that they must choose with care that to which they give primary allegiance.

    A. *Our personal interests reveal our priorities (Luke 12:13).*

        1. We invest heavily in the things that we love most. This is what Jesus meant when he said, "For where your treasure is, there will your heart be also" (Luke 12:34). Have you ever taken your canceled checks at the end of the

68

year and placed your gifts to God's work in one stack and your purchases in another? This is only one of many possible illustrations. You may study the way you spend your time or your efforts or your talents.

2. The attention we give a matter places our evaluation on it. This man who came to Jesus was devoting all of his attention to obtaining a part of the inheritance that had fallen to his brother. The amount of attention that he was giving to it revealed that to him nothing else really mattered. I ask you, what matters most in your life?

B. *Life's priorities may rest outside God's will (Luke 12:14).* This man asked Christ to help him obtain his heart's desire—a portion of his brother's inheritance. But Christ refused because the granting of this request was not within his divine will.

1. Because of the personal harm life's priorities may bring, they may rest outside God's will. Perhaps like many of us this man could not stand the blessing of prosperity. It was denied him because of the harm it would bring.

2. Because God has something better in store, our life's priorities may rest outside God's will. Had Christ answered this man's request and secured for him part of his brother's inheritance, doubtlessly the man would thank him and go his way, ending his relation with Christ forever. But Christ had something better in store for him. Rather than an earthly inheritance, Christ would have him remain and learn of and receive a heavenly inheritance.

C. *Life's priorities can be deceiving (Luke 12:15).* In essence, this man was saying, "My only desire is that justice be done." Christ properly labeled his priority as "covetousness." This man had deceived himself into believing that he was a champion for justice when in fact he was only a grasper after that which belonged to another.

Either because of a wrong evaluation placed upon life's priorities by the world or because of their transient value, they may prove in time to be most deceiving.

II. We are accountable for life's blessings (Luke 12:16–19).

To help this man rise above the spirit of covetousness, Christ tells a parable that asserts that people are accountable for all of life's blessings—however great or small.

A. *Life's blessings come from God, for "the ground of a certain rich man brought forth plentifully" (Luke 12:16).* The rich man could only plant the seed, but God alone could put the forces of nature into operation that would cause the seed to germinate, sprout, and grow.

1. We are indebted to this God from whom life's blessings come. The man in the parable is not a bad man; he does no direct harm; he does no harm to anyone; he simply prospers without a thought of obligation to

God or of generosity to others. And our Lord reminds us, "Unto whomsoever much is given, of him shall be much required" (Luke 12:48).

2. God tries to speak to us through life's blessings. That this man's land brought forth "plentifully" surely means that God was trying to speak to this man. Could it have been that God was saying to him, "I love you and want you for my own"? But like so many he could not hear the voice of God in the pleasant things of life. It is strange but true that some can hear the voice of God only in the storms of adversity.

B. *Life's blessings may be misinterpreted (Luke 12:17–18).* Throughout all of this man's conversation with himself, there runs a gross misinterpretation of the blessings God had given him.

1. We may misinterpret life's blessings as a result of our own ability. God warns in Deuteronomy 8:17–18 against such a misinterpretation.

2. We may misinterpret life's blessings as evidence of our own personal merit. Perhaps the rich man felt that he was just a little above the average person.

C. *Life's blessings may be misappropriated (Luke 12:19).* This man not only misinterprets the blessings of God, but he also plans to misappropriate them. He plans to squander them on ease, eating, drinking, and merry-making.

You will do well to ask yourself this question: "Why has God given me the income I have?" The obvious answer is that he has given you this for a definite purpose. To refuse to use it for that noble purpose is, in God's sight, a misappropriation of funds.

1. We may misappropriate life's blessings by ignoring total Christian stewardship. The man in the parable felt that he owed God nothing! He would use all for self. We may acknowledge God's claim on the tenth but be guilty of misappropriating the nine-tenths. Total Christian stewardship includes the proper use of position, education, influence, and the entirety of life.

2. We may misappropriate life's blessings by serving Christ halfheartedly. Have you ever been guilty of saying, "Well, if you can't get someone else, put me down and I'll do it." Paul reminds us, "And whatsoever ye do, do it heartily, as to the Lord, and not unto men" (Col. 3:23).

III. We are accountable for life's decisions (Luke 12:20–21).

The rich man had the right and the freedom to make his own life's decisions, but he was also accountable for these decisions.

A. *Life decisions may make a fool of us.* "But God said unto him, Thou fool" (Luke 12:20). The world would acclaim him as wise, thrifty, or shrewd, but God calls him a "fool."

1. Life's decisions may make a fool of us because of a blind obsession for material gain.

Tolstoi had a powerful tale of a young Russian who fell heir to his father's small farm. He was no sooner in possession of this land than he began to dream eagerly of how he could

70

add to it. One morning a stranger, evidently a person of power and authority, came to him and told him, as they were standing near the old homestead, that he could have, for nothing, all the land he could walk over in one day—but at sundown he must be back at the very place from which he started. Pointing to the grave of the young man's father, the stranger said, "This is the point to which you must return."

His first plan was to cover a tract of ground six miles square; but when he had walked the six he decided to make it nine, then twelve, and then fifteen—which would give him sixty miles to walk before sundown!

By noon he had covered two sides of this square, or thirty miles. But eager to get on and compass the whole distance, he did not stop for food. An hour later he saw an old man drinking at a spring, but in his hunger for land he brushed aside the cup which the old man offered him and rushed on in his eager quest for possession of land. When he was a few miles from the goal he was worn down with fatigue.

A few hundred yards from the line, he saw the sun approaching the horizon and knew he had but a few minutes left. Hurrying on and ready to faint, he summoned all his energies for one last effort—and managed to stagger across the line just as the sun was sinking. But as he crossed the line he saw a cruel, cynical smile on the face of the stranger who had promised the land, and who was waiting for him there at his father's grave. Just as he crossed the line the youth fell dead upon the ground which he had coveted.

The stranger then said to the servants, "I offered him all the land he could cover. Now you see what that is: 6' long and 2' wide; and I thought he would like to have the land close to his father's grave, rather than to have it anywhere else."

With that, the stranger, who was Death, vanished, saying as he did so, "I have kept my pledge." The youth had made his decision and it made of him a fool (Clarence Edward MacCartney, MacCartney's Illustrations [New York: Abingdon, 1945], 26–27).

2. Life's decisions may make a fool of us because of a loss of the respect of those about us. A man may become so concerned in the abundance of things he possesses that in the accumulation of his wealth or position or public recognition he loses the respect of those who know him best.

B. *Life's decisions will be faced at a definite time.* "But God said unto him, Thou fool, *this night* thy soul shall be required of thee" (Luke 12:20, italics mine). This man had repeatedly put off thinking seriously about the direction in which his decisions were leading him. But the night came when he was compelled to face them. Whenever this time comes in your life, you can rest assured that you will be dealt with justly and that the verdict will be determined by your own decision. Our Savior says, "Whosoever therefore shall confess me before men, him will I confess also before my Father which is in heaven. But whosoever shall deny me before men, him will I also deny before my Father which is in heaven" (Matt. 10:32–33).

C. *Our life's decisions may cause us to meet eternity with only temporal preparation (Luke 12:20–21).* The rich fool had made adequate preparation for this life but none for the life to come. He had prepared for old age, famine, drought, depression, family security—for everything except death, which would strip him of it all.

1. We may not even live to enjoy what little temporal security we may be able to accumulate. The Bible reminds us, "He heapeth up riches, and knoweth not who shall gather them" (Ps. 39:6). And again, "Wise men die ... and leave their wealth to others" (Ps. 49:10).
2. Temporal preparation will be of no benefit in eternity (Luke 12:21). Paul asserts, "We brought nothing into this world, and it is certain we can carry nothing out" (1 Tim. 6:7).

Conclusion

We are accountable and we know it! One day we will give an account of the life we lived here on earth, of the faith we placed or refused to place in Jesus Christ, and of our willingness to follow him as Lord and Savior. May God grant that through faith in Jesus Christ you may lay up treasures for yourself in heaven and thus be rich toward God.

WEDNESDAY EVENING, FEBRUARY 17

Title: Draw Near to God

Text: "Draw nigh to God, and he will draw nigh to you" (**James 4:8**).

Introduction

The Bible opens and closes with God and humans enjoying perfect harmony and fellowship with each other. Humans began their existence in a garden with God. The Bible closes in Revelation 22 with the redeemed in the city of God where the River of Life flows, where the Tree of Life bears its fruit.

People are always at their best and happiest when they are close to God. God has always been eager for people to enjoy his divine blessings. When people refuse to believe in and to live for the Lord, they destroy themselves and bring harm into their lives as well as into the lives of others.

How close to God do you live? How often do you communicate with him? How often do you seek to be still so that you can hear God communicating with you? Do you feel accepted, comfortable, and at ease in the divine presence? Is God the source of your delight and inspiration? Or do you consider God as a disturber? A restrainer? An irritant?

James would encourage us to trust in the loving grace of God and to abide always in the center of his loving will.

I. Living close to God brings rich rewards.

A. *The highest possible happiness: "Thou wilt shew me the path of life: in thy presence is fulness of joy; at thy right hand there are pleasures for evermore" (Ps. 16:11).*

B. *The conquest of fear (Ps. 23:4).* The psalmist was greatly encouraged in times of crisis by an awareness of the nearness of God. The comfort to which he refers is the courage that one needs for the living of life under difficult circumstances.

C. *Necessary spiritual energy.* The source of spiritual vitality is to be found in daily fellowship with God. We need to put forth the effort necessary to draw near to the God who is seeking continually to draw near to us.

II. James wrote to those who were living at a distance from God.

A. *They were living under the control of their passions and desire for pleasure (4:1–2).*

B. *They were totally self-centered even when they prayed (4:3).*

C. *They were completely compatible with the world, which is in rebellion against God (4:4).*

D. *They had grown proud and were indifferent toward God (4:6).*

E. *Evidently they were rebellious against God (4:7).* Have you drifted away from God without being aware of it?

> *It is easy to drift with the current swift,*
> *Just lie in your boat and dream;*
> *But in nature's plan, it takes a real man*
> *To paddle the boat upstream.*

Could it be that we have drifted away from God as far as those to whom James wrote? Is it possible that our greatest need is that of drawing close to God?

III. Do you want to live close to God?

A. *Try to believe that the living God loves you and is eager to bless you (Heb. 11:6).*

B. *Believe that the living Lord who conquered death draws near with purposes of love (Luke 24:15).*

C. *Confess and forsake all known sin in your life (1 John 1:8–10).*

D. *Fully follow the known will of God for your life.*

E. *Respond positively to the inward leading of the Holy Spirit of God (Eph. 5:18–21).*

Conclusion

The living Lord comes again and again and stands at the door seeking entrance into our minds, our hearts, and our lives (Rev. 3:20). He has drawn near to us. Let us draw near to him.

SUNDAY MORNING, FEBRUARY 21

Title: Going into All the World

Text: "Go ye into all the world, and preach the gospel to every creature" (**Mark 16:15**).

Scripture Reading: Matthew 28:16–20; Acts 1:1–8

Hymns: "All Creatures of Our God and King," Saint Francis of Assisi

"We've a Story to Tell to the Nations," Sterne

"Hark, the Voice of Jesus Calling," March

Offertory Prayer: Enable us, O Lord, to have an awareness of the people, institutions, and righteous causes needing the affection of our hearts and the gifts of our hands. Strengthen our wills with a stronger determination to open our lives and our purses in Christlike concern, we beseech, in his name. Amen.

Introduction

Jesus said to the Eleven before his ascension, "Go ye into all the world, and preach the gospel to every creature" (Mark 16:15). In Matthew's account the disciples were to "teach all nations" (28:19). In the Acts account Jesus' followers were to "receive power" and were to be Jesus' "witnesses . . . both in Jerusalem, and in all Judaea, and in Samaria, and unto the uttermost part of the earth" (1:8).

We usually interpret these commands in an exclusively geographical sense. There is no inhabited spot on the globe that we should purposely neglect. The good news that God was in Christ needs to be shouted from the housetops. But are we to think of "going into all the world" only in a geographical sense? These orders from our Commander are a mandate to minister to the many worlds about us.

I. The many worlds.

In our big world there are many little worlds, each existing separately from the others and demanding a ministry peculiar to its own needs. There is the world of the church, and within it there are the "countries" of worship—Bible study, finance, evangelistic outreach, and so on. There is the business world; the working person's world; the domestic world; the academic world; the scientific world; the military and civilian government worlds; the rich and poor people's worlds; and so on.

The boundaries of many of these worlds overlap. For example, the world of the church (the arena of the church's responsibility and involvement) is not something separate and apart from the other worlds of human society. But each world needs to be reached with the gospel of Jesus Christ.

II. A needed confession.

Among the greatest heresies of our generation are the concepts that a church, in the fuller sense of the term, is on a certain street corner or country road and that the ministry of the church is the responsibility of a paid professional staff. Too long the minister has wanted to play exclusively on his (or her) own court; he wants to dribble the ball—the statistics game—not realizing that he cannot depend on the bounce; he wants to play by his own rules, that is, his regularly organized church programs at their regularly assigned time and place; he wants to prescribe the church's orthodoxy; and so on.

More and more ministers need to realize what some members have known for a long time—that they have neither the time, training, nor talent to minister effectively and concurrently in all the worlds about them. This thought has some discomforting aspects about it, to be sure, and some would rather pull the curtains of fellowship around themselves and let the worlds go by.

III. The nature of our task.

Most churches have within their membership individuals who try to be different people depending on which world they are in on a given day. For example, a man may be one kind of person in church on Sunday and another when he is at the place where he earns his living on Monday and still another when he is "out with the boys" or alone in a distant city. He may have one set of beliefs in Sunday school when studying from the book of Genesis and another in a biology class when studying the origins of life. How much better off he would be if he saw himself as one person, not two, three, or four. As a person surrendered and loyal to his Creator and loving heavenly Father, he can establish beachheads for Christ in these worlds of which he is a part. He can be the salt that flavors or preserves; he can be the light that penetrates—as Jesus said his people are to be.

IV. Christ, our example.

Jesus saw life as it was. We may assume that as a growing boy in Nazareth he saw the traders traveling the caravan route that came up across the Plain of Esdraelon and crossed at his front doorsteps. The traders haggled and cheated. The rich and powerful had many miseries to go along with their arrogance and greed. The poverty-stricken had no hopes of improvement of their lot in life. He saw the whole picture of human life, and he was wise enough to see that beyond his little town it was the same everywhere.

Jesus made a declaration of his ambition, and that was to fit himself into the will and purpose of God and do for humankind the things that he was convinced must be done. "The spirit of the LORD is upon me," he read from Isaiah 61:1–2, "because he hath anointed me to preach good tidings to the meek; he hath sent me to ... proclaim liberty to the captives, and recovery of sight to the blind, to set at liberty those who are oppressed, to proclaim the acceptable year of the LORD." He went into the worlds of need in Palestine.

Conclusion

Our day demands that we share the concerns and goals of Christ. To the extent that we are true to him, we will be willing to alter the traditional when necessary to meet the pressing needs of humankind. We cannot help to meet these needs by living a cloistered existence or by allowing ourselves to be saturated in the sins of the world. "Going into *all* the world" demands both an attitude of separation from the world in its sins and identification with the world and its needs.

SUNDAY EVENING, FEBRUARY 21

Title: A Night of Unprofitable Toil

Text: "Simon Peter saith unto them, I go a-fishing. They say unto him, We also go with thee. They went forth, and entered into a ship immediately; and that night they caught nothing" **(John 21:3)**.

Scripture Reading: John 21:1–14

Introduction

The final chapter of 1 Kings relates that at Ezion-geber, on the Red Sea, Jehoshaphat built his ships. Long and at last his fleet was prepared. With the sound of trumpets, the unfurling of banners, and the benediction of royalty, the anchors were lifted, the sails were set, and the fleet sailed out of Ezion-geber, down the Red Sea, bound for far-off Ophir in quest of wealth.

But the ships did not sail! A storm arose, driving them onto the treacherous rocks and banks of the Red Sea. When the night had passed and the morning dawned, the proud fleet lay broken and scattered on the rocks—a tangled mass of wood and rigging. And those who had proudly sailed on the ships a day before rested buried in the depths of the sea. The Scripture simply says, "They went not; for the ships were broken at Ezion-geber" (1 Kings 22:48).

Many hopes and strenuous efforts find their epitaph in this saying. Too often this is the final sentence in the story of a soul's adventure. The keels are laid, the ships constructed, the seas charted, the anchors lifted, and the sails unfurled, but the ships do not sail! Unprofitable toil ends in utter futility.

Such was the experience of the disciples during that night of unprofitable toil on the Sea of Galilee.

I. Unprofitable toil follows a reversion to your former life (John 21:3–4).

Even after Peter had seen the risen Lord, he seemed ready enough to return to the way of life that he had known before, so he said, "I go a-fishing."

A. *A reversion to your former life influences others.* Peter's impulse to resume his former life for a night did not fail to influence others to follow him, for they said, "We also go with thee."

    1. Others look to you for guidance, yet your influence on them may have a detrimental effect. Peter was a natural-born leader, and the other disciples looked to him for guidance from the day he joined them. But here he betrayed the sacred trust they had placed in him and led them to go fishing when he should have led them to go witnessing of the resurrected Lord.

    2. You are responsible for others whom you influence. Who was to blame for this night of unprofitable toil? The obvious answer is Peter, since he had influenced others to join him.

B. *A reversion to your former life results in empty hands.* The Scripture says, "And that night they caught nothing" (John 21:3). As once before, the disciples toiled all the night long and caught nothing. Because night was the best time for fishing, failure to catch anything was disturbing to accomplished fishermen such as James, John, and Peter.

1. Sometimes we discover that a reversion to our former ways results in empty hands because the old ways no longer bring joy. A wayward Christian who returns to his old life will discover that those things that once satisfied and thrilled no longer thrill but leave hands empty and heart remorseful.
2. Because God has a nobler purpose for you, you may well discover that a reversion to some old pattern in your life results in empty hands.
3. Because God cannot grant spiritual victories to wayward Christians, you will always discover that your hands are empty and your life is meaningless whenever you revert to former sins.

C. *A reversion to your former life makes you insensitive to the presence of Christ (John 21:4).*
1. Because of preoccupation with other things, you may become insensitive to the presence of Christ. These disciples were so busy steering their ship, lowering and lifting their nets, and arranging their gear that they did not even recognize Christ as he stood on the shore.
2. Because of the numbing effect of sin, you may become insensitive to the presence of Christ. Few tragedies equal that moment when a man like Samson, once mighty in the Lord, awakens to the fact that his reversion to his former life has left him weak and so calloused that he is unaware whether his Lord's presence is near or far away.

II. Unprofitable toil finds its solution in Christ (John 21:5–6).

The night was dark, the disciples downcast, and their nets empty *until* Jesus entered the scene and spoke from the shore. They were soon to find in Jesus Christ the solution to their night of unprofitable toil.

A. *Christ expresses a concern in our moments of unprofitable toil.* "Then Jesus saith unto them, Children, have ye any meat? They answered him, No" (John 21:5). Even though we may revert to our former ways and drift aimlessly upon the sea of barren toil, Christ still is concerned about us.
1. Because Christ's will is that you bear much fruit, he is concerned. "Herein is my Father glorified, that ye bear much fruit" (John 15:8).
2. Because the progress of Christ's kingdom depends on your fruitfulness, he expresses a concern. "I have chosen you, and ordained you, that ye should go and bring forth fruit" (John 15:16).

B. *Christ issues a command.* "Cast the net on the right side of the ship, and ye shall find" (John 21:6a).
1. The command of Christ may call for the unusual. The disciples' net was usually let down on the left side of the ship. The command to lower it on the right side called for unusual action. "Anyway," they could have reasoned, "we have been lowering the net not far from the place where

77

you have commanded that we lower it now, so why should lowering it again make any real difference?"

2. Christ's command provides needed guidance. With all their knowledge of the sea, the disciples were in need of divine guidance in order to fish with any degree of success. We may know the "sea" well, we may have the finest nets made, we may have years of experience, but still we need divine guidance in the work of our Lord.

C. *Christ makes possible life's great accomplishments.* "They cast therefore, and now they were not able to draw it for the multitude of fishes" (John 21:6).

1. When Christ's commands are obeyed, life's accomplishments begin to be realized. Notice that they did not catch the fish until they cast their net into the sea in obedience to the command of their Lord.

2. Accomplishments made possible by Christ surpass our fondest expectation. These disciples were not able to draw the net full of fishes into the boat. They drew it in the water to the shore. After hours of catching nothing, the most they were hoping for was a small catch of fish. But to their utter amazement they caught so many fish that they could not care for them in their usual manner.

III. Unprofitable toil affords some worthy lessons (John 21:7–14).

What a waste to go through the whole night of unprofitable toil and not learn some valuable lessons from it! These disciples would long remember this night and profit from the lessons that it had afforded them, and so must we profit from our own personal nights of unprofitable toil.

A. *A lesson on the watchful care of Christ may be learned from our nights of unprofitable toil (John 21:7).* No matter how far on the sea these men drifted, they were never beyond the watchful eyes of Christ.

1. Some are more aware of the watchful care of Christ than others, for John was the first to exclaim, "It is the Lord!"

2. Some respond more quickly than others to the watchful care of Christ. Although John was the first to recognize Christ, Peter was the first to respond. Recognizing at once the truth of John's remark, Peter drew his outer garment about him and plunged into the sea to reach the shore and the Lord as quickly as possible.

B. *A lesson on the abundant blessings from God may be learned from our nights of unprofitable toil (John 21:11).*

1. The abundant blessings of God underscore our dependence on God. Verse 11 indicates that these men caught nothing by themselves, but they caught 153 fish with Christ's help. Here is a lesson for all of us. The time will never come when we will be able to conquer the world without Christ. Likewise, the day will never dawn when directed by him we spend our strength for naught.

2. The abundant blessings of God are not intended to be wasted. There were 153 fish of great size, yet the net did not break, for Christ had not

given these fish to be wasted. Neither does God grant blessings to you and me for us to squander.

C. *A lesson on the gracious invitation of Christ to humans may be learned from our nights of unprofitable toil (John 21:12–13).* The sweetest words these fatigued disciples had heard since they last had seen their resurrected Lord were, "Come and dine" (John 21:12).

   1. The gracious invitation of Christ to man is impartial. Jesus did not say, "John, you were the first to recognize me, so you only may come." Nor did he say, "Peter, you were the only one who cared enough to rush to greet me, so only you may come." Rather, his invitation was impartially extended to all. And it is equally extended to all today (Rev. 22:17).

   2. The gracious invitation of Christ offers to meet your deepest need. The disciples had fasted all the night long as they lifted and lowered their heavy nets and rowed their boat. They were famished and exhausted. The most pressing need of the moment was for nourishment, and Christ invited them to partake of the food he had prepared. Christ also invites you to "come and dine." The bread of this world leaves unsatisfied the inner hunger of the soul. This is why Jesus said, "I am the living bread which came down from heaven: if any man eat of this bread, he shall live for ever" (John 6:51).

   3. The gracious invitation of Christ to humans is still extended. Christ told the parable of the man who prepared a great supper and invited many to come. He sent his servants out into the streets and lanes to invite the poor, the maimed, the lame, and the blind. After having gathered a great number of guests, the servant said, "Lord, it is done as thou hast commanded, and *yet there is room*" (Luke 14:22).

Conclusion

Thank God, though many have partaken, yet there is room. Christ still says to you, "Come and dine."

WEDNESDAY EVENING, FEBRUARY 24

Title: Needed: Personal Evangelists

Text: "Brethren, if any of you do err from the truth, and one convert him; Let him know, that he which converteth the sinner from the error of his way, shall save a soul from death, and shall hide a multitude of sins" (**James 5:19–20**).

Introduction

What does our church need most? Better buildings? A bigger budget? A larger congregation?

What does our community need most? Better streets? Better parks or schools?

What does God need most from us? Would we agree that God desires from us the end result of the practice of true religion? Is it possible that James has been writing with a view to persuade his readers to become personal evangelists? He concludes his epistle by emphasizing the need for personal evangelists.

I. Our task as a church and as individuals.

A. *The Great Commission (Matt. 28:18–20).* Instead of limiting the Great Commission to the foreign mission enterprise, we should recognize that our Lord was speaking not only to the disciples who were with him but also to each of his followers in the present. He was urging upon them and upon us that in our going about from place to place we are to make disciples. This is not an option; it is an obligation — the mandate of the Master.

B. *Acts 1:8.* In this statement of his redemptive program, our Lord emphasized that his disciples were to begin right where they were. As Christians moved out into other areas, they were to give their Christian testimony concerning the good news of God's love as it had been revealed in the life, death, resurrection, and continuing presence of the living Lord.

II. Facing our responsibility to be evangelists.

A. *The responsibility of a prophet (Ezek. 33:7–9).* God held the prophet Ezekiel responsible for warning the people in the time of peril. The greatest peril that people can face is the peril of entering into eternity without God. If the people of ancient Israel held the watchman responsible for issuing a warning when the city was in peril, and if God held the prophet responsible for warning people concerning the peril of living in sin, then we can be sure that God holds us responsible when we neglect to encourage the unsaved about us to forsake the way of sin and unbelief.

B. *The responsibility of Christians (John 20:23).* Either the living Christ was endowing the apostles with the authority to forgive sin, as Roman Catholics believe, or he was speaking to them as representatives of all and informing them that they could be the means whereby sins could be forgiven. The only way by which the disciples could retain the unsaved in their sins would be by a refusal or a neglect to share with them the way of salvation. Evangelical Christians believe that Jesus was not speaking to an official priesthood but rather that he was speaking to all Christians, urging them to recognize their responsibility to communicate the good news of God's love to the lost and needy world.

C. *The sin of neglect (James 4:17).* James declares that to be guilty of neglecting to do the good is to fall into sin. Perhaps the sin of which we are guiltiest is the sin of neglecting to communicate the message of God's grace to those about us as well as through our church to a needy world.

III. The challenge of a great opportunity.

James speaks to his readers concerning the blessings and the rewards that come to those who convert a sinner from the error of his or her way. There are many reasons why each of us should be busy at the task of serving as personal evangelists.

80

A. *We can be the means of saving a soul from death.*

B. *We can be the means of covering a multitude of sins.*

C. *We can be the one who brings the gift of eternal life to those who receive Jesus as Lord and Savior.*

D. *We can be the channel through which the blessing of peace of mind and heart can come to a new convert.*

E. *We can help the individual overcome his fear of death and impart to him the assurance of eternal life.*

F. *By winning a soul to Christ, we render a patriotic service to our country in that the convert will be a better citizen.*

G. *To win a convert is to render some family, possibly several families, a tremendous service.*

H. *To win a soul to Christ is to render that particular individual life's greatest favor.*

Conclusion

Use any worthy method of communicating God's love, mercy, and grace. Make a personal approach to a friend, relative, neighbor, or even a stranger if the Holy Spirit creates the proper situation and opportunity. Be persuasive as you talk in terms of what the Lord Jesus Christ has done and what he continues to mean to you. By all means, let us be persistent. We must continue to pray and continue to present Christ as the answer to the deepest problems of life to those about us.

Let us trust the Holy Spirit for divine guidance and help. Let us move out to bear our witness in the faith that the Savior who promised to always accompany us will bless us with his presence and with his power to save.

SUNDAY MORNING, FEBRUARY 28

Title: Get Out of the Church

Text: "For God so loved the world that he gave his one and only Son, that whoever believes in him shall not perish but have eternal life" (**John 3:16 NIV**).

Scripture Reading: Matthew 5:13–24

Hymns: "The Spacious Firmament," Addison

"He Leadeth Me! O Blessed Thought," Gilmore

"Take the Name of Jesus with You," Baxter

Offertory Prayer: Eternal God, who has brought yourself to us in so many ways and places, we pause to consider our responses. We bring to you the moments of this church service, asking that our entire use of them may find favor in your sight. We bring to you our lives as expressed in our activities during the days past, asking your forgiveness of wrongs done and your continuing strength to enable us to do the right more perfectly. We bring to you our houses of thought, asking for foundations of rock that they might withstand the storms of doubt and the winds of controversy. We bring to you, too, our tithes and offerings,

81

asking that these may be accepted as portions of our total selves in dedication to your work in the world. In Jesus' name we bring our offerings and make our prayer. Amen.

Introduction

C. W. Edwards has told a parable of the missing who were not missed, as follows:

Man-of-the-church: *A strange thing happened in church Sunday: our pastor fell asleep while preaching.*

Man-of-the-world: *That is strange!*

Man-of-the-church: *No, that is not strange, but he fell asleep in the pulpit, and no one in the congregation noticed it.*

Man-of-the-world: *That certainly is strange.*

Man-of-the-church: *No, that is not strange either. What is strange is that we didn't realize what happened and continued the service until Wednesday, but when we got home we found that no one in town had even missed us.*

Man-of-the-world: *That's not strange at all. (*The Pulpit, *October 1961, 12)*

There is enough truth in the parable to make it sting those of us who love the church. Yet there is some validity to its conclusion: so much of our church life is ingrown and self-centered that the world on the outside, where the masses of people live and die, never misses us when we fail to show up.

This exhortation to "get out of the church" is not meant to suggest that the church is to be done away with or that its services are to be curtailed. There is a sense in which the real need of the day is to get people into the church not out of it. The exhortation does suggest that we need to get the good news that "God was in Christ reconciling the world unto himself" out of the church buildings, out of the sanctuary and Sunday school rooms, out of the steady preoccupation with its own machinery and interests. God expects the church in each generation to get out of the harbor and sail on the open seas of human needs, to get out of the briefing room and head for the battlefield, to give up its place on the sidelines and get in the game.

I. The exhortation to get out of the church makes sense when we understand what the church is.

The church idea has its roots in the Old Testament religion, but Jesus brought a new conception to it, a new community, a new Israel, based on personal loyalty to him as God's Messiah. All through the Gospels we see Christ at work creating this new *ecclesia*, or community. He summoned people to repent and believe the good news.

After Jesus' days in the flesh, his followers used different expressions to talk about this community of believers. Consider Paul's familiar picture of the church as Christ's body (1 Cor. 12:12–30; Eph. 4:15). The body is a wonderful instrument, with many different parts designed for their particular functions. Its unity and significance is dependent on the personality that dwells within it. So it is with the church. At its best it is the most amazing community, made up of people who have been made new by his redeeming grace. However much the members may bring to this community, its life — the mind, the heart, the soul of the church — is Christ who holds it together and uses it to express his purposes and grace to the world. It is his presence that makes the church, not a certain label or a particular set of doctrines or programs, as important as these may be in their proper places.

The apostle Paul never merely says that the church is "a body." The words "of Christ" are always added. His thought may thus be phrased: "The church is Christ in the body, that is, it is God acting in history — today, now — in visible, solid form."

II. The exhortation to get out of the church makes sense when we understand what the world is.

Most of us have known John 3:16 by heart for a long time: "For God so loved the world that he gave his one and only Son, that whoever believes in him shall not perish but have eternal life." (NIV). The Bible is an enormous, sweeping love story. God's love for the world can be seen from many standpoints. The drama of suspense comes from the fact that the world turns on its divine Lover over and over again. We break with him and throw him over for some other affection.

We too often overlook, not the fact that God loves, but what or whom he loves. We think it is just *us* that he loves: men, women, children, spirits, souls, as we say. But there is more. Theodore A. Gill has written:

> He made us flesh and blood ... whole men, real live, bony, bloody, glandular, hairy human beings, and he put us in a real live, earthy, rocky, watery, substantial world, and he set us to making real live, structural, institutional, political, economic history, and it is all that that he loves. All of that is in that word in the New Testament. All of this is the world which he loves. All of that is what he lived in. All of that is what he died for. All of that is what he wants back. All of that is what he expects us to reclaim for him. (*The Pulpit*, October 1961, 5)

Christian life and action are initiated, envisioned, and inspired in the church. But they count most in God's economy outside the church, in the world. There is where the great decisions are made that determine the plight of the masses — in the board rooms and committee meetings, in the schools and marketplaces, in the homes and offices and factories. It is exceedingly important that something happen to us and in us when we are in a church service. But being Christian is not merely a matter of letting our spirits go all atwitter in the occasional hush of a church service. This is my Father's world. "God did not send his Son into the world to condemn the world, but to save the world through him" (John 3:17 NIV). The incarnation was God getting right into the thick of things.

Conclusion

The church is being true to its mission when it takes seriously the injunction to go beyond the walls of the church building and take the message of God's redeeming love into the world where people live and work and fight and suffer and die. Revelation 21:22, describing John's vision of the new Jerusalem, says, "And I saw no temple in it." This suggests that the church is transitional, provisional. It is here to do a job, and the job is in the world. Not the church for the church: that is sinful. The church is for the world.

SUNDAY EVENING, FEBRUARY 28

Title: A Night That Never Shall Be

Text: "And the city had no need of the sun, neither of the moon, to shine in it: for the glory of God did lighten it, and the Lamb is the light thereof. And the nations of them which are saved shall walk in the light of it: and the kings of the earth do bring their glory and honour into it. And the gates of it shall not be shut at all by day: for there shall be no night there" **(Rev. 21:23–25).**

Scripture Reading: Revelation 21:23–22:5

Introduction

The bright and final hope of the Christian faith is that beyond the nights of anxiety, tears, and fear; beyond the nights of denial, accounting, and mystery; and beyond the nights of unprofitable toil and eternal darkness, there rests a place of which God's Word says, "And there shall be no night there." This is the night that never shall be.

Thus in the midst of all the clouds and darkness, the mysteries and disappointments, we pause and lift our eyes toward this ultimate place where there is no need of candle nor light of the sun.

I. There will never be a night of darkness in heaven (Rev. 21:23–27).

    A. *Because of the radiance of God there will never be a night of darkness in heaven.*

        1. The radiance of God illuminates all of heaven (21:23; 22:5). The light of the sun and moon will no longer be needed. The immediate presence of God radiates heaven and thus provides light for all.

        2. The radiance of God eliminates all fear of harm (21:25). The gates along the walls of ancient cities were shut at night and in times of danger. This would keep out the enemy and those who would destroy. Jesus tells John that in heaven, because of the radiance of God, there will never be a night of darkness or fear of harm, and thus "the gates of it shall not be shut."

    B. *Because of the redemption of humans there will never be a night of darkness in heaven (21:24, 27).* There will be no reason for darkness. The redeemed

84

are people who no longer love darkness but rather light. They "shall walk in the light of it."

1. Redemption is received from God's grace. "And the nations of them that are saved shall walk in the light of it" (21:24). "For by grace are ye saved through faith; and that not of yourselves: it is the gift of God" (Eph. 2:8).
2. Redemption is revealed by God's light (21:24). "But he that doeth truth cometh to the light, that his deeds may be made manifest, that they are wrought in God" (John 3:21). "But if we walk in the light, as he is in the light, we have fellowship one with another, and the blood of Jesus Christ his Son cleanseth us from all sin" (1 John 1:7).
3. The redemption of human beings is recorded in God's book. Scripture says that only those will enter into heaven whose names "are written in the Lamb's book of life" (Rev. 21:27). Why is this book called "the Lamb's book of life"? Because it is by the blood of the "Lamb of God" that our names are indelibly written on the record of eternal life.

II. There will never be a night of death in heaven (Rev. 21:4; 22:1–2).

There are three basic things necessary for death never to be experienced—water, food, and health. The picture in 22:1–2 symbolizes provision of all three—the water of life, the perpetual fruit of the tree of life, and the leaves of the tree that provide healing powers. The question is asked, "How can people live eternally?" The answer is found in these verses.

A. *Because of the provision of water, there will never be a night of death in heaven (22:1).* This is no ordinary water; it is "the water of life."
   1. This water comes from God, for this verse describes it as "proceeding out of the throne of God." No more expressive symbol of eternal life could be imagined than that of the flowing river with its waters shining brightly and its source inexhaustible and its stream full while on either side bloom trees with abundant fruit.
   2. This water quenches spiritual thirst forever. This is "a river" of water; it is not a reservoir that can be replenished but rather a river that eternally flows.

      In John 4:10–15 we read of a woman who had drunk from Jacob's well repeatedly but found it necessary to return. She had also drunk deeply from the wells of sinful indulgences but at last discovered that they too failed to quench her inner thirst. Now she accepted Christ's provision of living water never to thirst again.

B. *Because of the production of food, there will never be a night of death in heaven (22:2).* The picture painted here is that of a river bordered with trees on either side bearing fruit abundantly.
   1. This food sustains life, for it is called "the tree of *life*." Unlike the "tree of knowledge of good and evil" that brought death into the Garden of Eden, this tree sustains life eternally in the paradise of heaven.

85

2. This food is abundantly provided for all, for it bare "twelve crops of fruit, yielding its fruit every month" (22:2 NIV). The "twelve crops of fruit" is a symbolic way of speaking of an abundant supply of food for all. None will ever want spiritual food in heaven, for the harvest is every month. Hundreds of years earlier, Ezekiel had foreseen this garden of eternal life (Ezek. 47:7–9).

C. *Because of the prevention of disease, there will never be a night of death in heaven.* "The leaves of the tree are for the healing of the nations" (22:2 NIV).

"Healing" is more correctly translated by an obsolete word, but one that we find in Old English literature — *healthing. Healthing* means preventing sickness, whereas "healing" may mean restoration to health from sickness. The idea, therefore, is that in the city of God, provision will be made for the continuation of perfect health. This truth was also foreseen by Ezekiel (Ezek. 47:12).

1. Disease is barred from heaven (Rev. 21:4).
2. Disease results from sin, and since there is no sin in heaven, there is no disease in heaven (Rom. 5:12).

III. There will never be a night of damnation in heaven (Rev. 22:3–5).

There will be no curse in heaven as there was in the Garden of Eden.

A. *Because of the protection of God, there will never be a night of damnation in heaven.* "And there shall be no more curse: but the throne of God and of the Lamb shall be in it" (Rev. 22:3).

1. God's presence assures his protection, "for the Lamb of God shall be in it." "When thou passeth through the waters, I will be with thee; and through the rivers, they shall not overflow thee" (Isa. 43:2).
2. God's promise asserts his protection. Our Lord has said, "I will preserve thee,... to inherit the desolate heritages" (Isa. 49:8). Our Savior said, "Verily, verily, I say unto you, He that heareth my word, and believeth on him that sent me, hath everlasting life, and shall not come into condemnation; but is passed from death unto life" (John 5:24).
3. God's power provides his protection. "Thy right hand, O LORD, is become glorious in power" (Ex. 15:6).

B. *Because of the performance of the saints, there will never be a night of damnation in heaven, for "his servants shall serve him" (Rev. 22:3).*

1. The performance of the saints gives no cause for condemnation in heaven. There they shall walk not after the flesh but after the Spirit (Rom. 8:1).
2. The performance of the saints manifests their redeemed nature (Rom. 6:16–18).

C. *Because of the permanence of salvation, there will never be a night of damnation in heaven (Rev. 22:4–5).*

1. The permanence of salvation is evidenced by the intimacy of communion. "And they shall see his face" (Rev. 22:4). This implies the intimacy of personal fellowship that Paul anticipates (1 Cor. 13:12).

2. The permanence of salvation is confirmed by the identification of divine ownership. "And his name shall be in their foreheads" (Rev. 22:4). This signifies how entirely the redeemed belong to him who has redeemed them. They are his own and are so identified! No one else can ever claim them.

3. The permanence of salvation is established by the tenure of the reign of the redeemed. The Scripture says, "And they shall reign for ever and ever" (Rev. 22:5).

Conclusion

There Is No Night in Heaven

There is no night in heaven,
The Lamb of God is there;
There is no time of sorrow
Nor is there dark despair.
The gates of it shall not be shut
Tho' it be day or night,
The light of God removes all fear
And thoughts that conjure fright.
There is no death in heaven,
The waters and the tree
Provide for every Christian
A life eternally.
The light of heaven brightly shines,
Inviting every man
To enter through the door of faith
And gain the Promised Land.

MARCH

■ Sunday Mornings

Using "The Christ Who Confronts Us," emphasize the abiding presence of the Christ and the implications of a proper response to him.

■ Sunday Evenings

The suggested theme for Sunday evenings is "Pictures of Jesus in the Gospel of John." The adequacy of Jesus to meet the deepest needs of life is the recurring emphasis.

■ Wednesday Evenings

For the next three months the suggested theme is "The Call of God and Our Response." The experiences in which God called his servants will be examined for insight and assistance for understanding and responding to God's call in the present.

WEDNESDAY EVENING, MARCH 3

Title: The Call of Abraham

Text: "Now the LORD had said unto Abram, Get thee out of thy country, and from thy kindred, and from thy father's house, unto a land that I will shew thee" **(Gen. 12:1).**

Scripture Reading: Genesis 12:1–4

Introduction

Some people labor under the mistaken idea that the Great Commission of our Lord was enunciated only once and that this took place following his resurrection. The truth is that the redemptive purpose of God has been clearly revealed since the call of Abraham.

If we would find the biblical background for the great commission of our Lord, we need to go to Genesis 12 and read carefully God's call to Abraham. This purpose was repeated to the patriarchs and declared to Israel by Moses. It is repeated again and again in the Psalms and Prophets.

We can learn something about God's purpose for us today by studying the record of God's call of Abraham.

I. The sovereign purpose of God.

With the call of Abraham in Genesis 12, God begins to form a family through whom he will reveal his purpose of redemption to the world.

The God of Abraham reveals his purpose and determination to redeem the race that he had created from the ruin of sin by the choice of his grace and love. God chose Abraham as the medium through whom he would begin to reveal this purpose of redemption.

Some have wondered why God chose Abraham rather than someone else. We cannot know for certain. Perhaps it was because Abraham was the most usable person available. God comes to those today who are willing to listen and respond.

II. The implications of God's call to Abraham.

A. *God's call involved separation.* To be God's man it was necessary that Abraham separate himself from his country, his kindred, and his relatives. It was necessary that he not only separate himself "from" but that he also separate himself "to."

It was necessary that Abraham recognize the sovereignty of God and make a proper response to that sovereignty.

B. *God's call involved obedience.* Abraham's God communicated with him and issued a call for loving obedience. In response to God's call to "get thee out ... unto a land that I will shew thee," "Abram departed" (Gen. 12:1, 4). Abraham's obedience to the known will of God was the proof of the genuineness of his faith in the God who was calling him. He obeyed and went out not knowing where he was going.

Obedience to the revealed will of God is the mother of spiritual success. Disobedience is an insult to the graciousness of God. It is an act and attitude that deprives us of walking the highway of spiritual achievement.

There is no substitute for obedience (1 Sam. 15:22–23).

III. God's commission to Abraham.

"Thou shalt be a blessing" (Gen. 12:2). These words are more than just a statement of fact. They are an imperative. God was calling upon Abraham to conduct himself in such a manner as to be a blessing not only to his contemporaries but also to his posterity. God did not tell Abraham that he would be a blessing merely because he had been chosen to be a redemptive instrument. Abraham was called to respond in a manner to God's purpose that would enable him to be a blessing to all people. It can be said to Abraham's credit that he responded with a glad obedience that lifted him to a position of usefulness and that enabled him to be a blessing to all people.

IV. God's promise to Abraham.

God promised to make of Abraham a great nation. He promised to give him a great name, and he promised to bless the peoples of the earth through Abraham. He promised to bless those who blessed Abraham and to curse those who cursed him.

The principle in this promise still applies to the people of God. Those who with malicious purpose try to stand in the way of God's work will sooner or later experience the wrath of God. Persons or nations who look with favor upon the work of God will experience the blessings of God.

Conclusion

God called Abraham for a redemptive purpose. He did not call him merely to pour out his blessings upon him. God called him so that in blessing him he might bless all the people of the earth.

Every blessing that comes from the hand of God to us comes with a redemptive purpose for others. We are blessed that we might be a blessing. If we forget this truth, we do so to our own peril as well as to the detriment of others.

God has called each of us to participate and cooperate with him in his continuing work of redemption.

SUNDAY MORNING, MARCH 7

Title: Christ at the Door

Text: "Behold, I stand at the door, and knock: if any man hear my voice, and open the door, I will come in to him, and will sup with him, and he with me" (**Rev. 3:20**).

Scripture Reading: Luke 24:15–31

Hymns: "He Lives," Ackley

"Thou, My Everlasting Portion," Crosby

"Abide with Me," Lyte

Offertory Prayer: Holy Father, today we offer to you the gratitude of our hearts and the praise of our lips. We dedicate our bodies as living sacrifices to be used for your glory in service to others. Today, because of gratitude and compassion, we come bringing tithes and offerings. We give them to you that the work that Jesus began might be continued. Receive these expressions of our worship and bless them in the advancing of your kingdom on earth, through Jesus Christ our Lord. Amen.

Introduction

The conviction that Christ Jesus had conquered death and that he was alive was the basis of the faith that motivated the early church. Those who loved him and were captivated by the challenge of his mission in the world discovered in personal experience that he was closer to them following his resurrection than he had been before his death on the cross.

In the days immediately following Jesus' resurrection, he manifested himself to those of faith by many infallible proofs. They suddenly realized that what he had been he continued to be. They were convinced that what he was he would continue to be. They would not feel forsaken. They knew that he had come to be with them in a real way by the Spirit. They were overwhelmed with excitement as they recognized that he took the initiative in coming to them. With great delight, as well as awesome fear at times, they experienced his presence on life's highway.

The living Christ takes the initiative in coming to us with purposes of love and ministries of mercy. We should not be surprised by this. God took the initiative in creation. The universe did not come into being by accident. God called it into being. God took the initiative in revelation. The Bible is not a book that contains human speculation about God; instead, it is the inspired record of God's activity of revealing himself to people through patriarch, prophet, psalmist, and supremely through the Messiah. God has taken the initiative in our salvation. Humans did not suddenly decide that they needed salvation. God came in the person of Jesus Christ on a rescue mission. The Holy Spirit reveals to humans our need for the salvation of God and works this salvation into their hearts and lives as they respond by the faith that expresses itself in faithfulness.

The divine initiative is pictured most beautifully in the words of our text: "Behold, I stand at the door, and knock: if any man hear my voice, and open the door, I will come in to him, and will sup with him, and he with me." These words dramatically reveal the divine initiative of the Lord. To limit this visit to a once and for all experience of conversion is to miss its beauty and the fullness of its meaning for each of us.

I. Christ is at the door.

The words of our text come from a letter that was addressed by the living and glorified Lord to the church of the Laodiceans. It was not addressed to the unsaved world as such, even though it does picture the Christ's concern for a lost world. Christ was revealing his personal program and policy for the future as his presence and power might be needed. As individuals and as a congregation, we need to recognize and respond to the Christ who comes again and again to the front door.

A. *Jesus comes and stands at the door.* He comes without invitation. He comes not because of our merits or achievements or because he is paid to come. As the sun rises silently but steadily every morning, so Christ comes to stand at the door of our lives.

B. *Jesus is speaking and knocking at the door.* The living Christ not only stands at the door, he also knocks, and he speaks desiring entrance. Politely and patiently he stands. Gently he knocks and knocks. Lovingly and tenderly he speaks with a still, small voice to those who have ears to hear. Because of divine compassion he comes. Because of our deep and personal needs he comes.

II. Christ wants to come in the door.

A. *Jesus stands at the front door of the church.* Could it be that you have shut the door of the Bible class or of the worship services of your church to the Christ who wants to come in? By a lack of faith in his promise to always be present when believers come together in his name, you can shut him out

(Matt. 18:20). By a lack of reverence and humility, you can make it impossible to hear his still, small voice seeking entrance into the services. By a preoccupation of your mind with careless or critical thoughts, you can rob yourself of his blessed presence.

B. *Jesus stands at the front door of your home.* On one occasion Jesus visited the city of Jericho and was bold and gracious enough as to invite himself to the home of Zacchaeus the publican. The wisest decision that Zacchaeus ever made was to let Jesus come into his house, for that decision led to his permitting Jesus to come into his heart. What a difference Christ could make in your marriage! What a change he could bring about between husband and wife and parents and children! He wants to help you experience the abundant life, which is more wonderful than the affluent life (John 10:10).

C. *Jesus stands at the front door of your vocation.* Previous to the beginning of his public ministry, our Lord worked at the carpenter's trade. He knew what it was to have calluses on his hands. He knew what it meant to earn a living by the sweat of his brow. Even in a computerized age the living Christ who is our contemporary is concerned about the manner in which we earn our daily bread. He would be our Counselor and Helper. He would warn us against the peril of living on the level of the material only. He would lead us to labor not just for the bread that perishes but also for the values that endure for eternity.

D. *Jesus stands at the front door of your heart.* You are the only one who can let him come in. The door of the heart can be opened only from the inside. On the banks of the Cumberland River in downtown Nashville, Tennessee, there is a reproduction of Fort Nashborough, which was built originally in 1870. The buildings were constructed of rocks, and the massive doors were locked from the inside by means of a heavy bar and latch. A rope is attached to the latch and is passed through a hole and permitted to hang outside. In times of danger, the pioneers would pull the latch string inside for safety. After the population had increased and law and order had been established, the latch string was permitted to hang outside at all times. When extending an invitation to potential guests, the pioneer would often say, "The latch string always hangs on the outside at our house." Such cannot be said concerning the human heart. It can be opened only from the inside. Christ will not enter unless he is invited.

III. Christ will continue to come to the door.

The picture presented in our text is not that of a once-in-a-lifetime visit. It pictures the Savior as one who has come, and he continues to stand; he continues to knock.

A. *Jesus will be there when you have decisions to make and need divine guidance and wisdom.*

B. *Jesus will be there when you have burdens to bear.* The responsibilities of life can often be oppressive. Everyone has a burden that would crush him or her sooner or later. The apostle Peter counseled his leaders to cast their cares on the Lord because he cared for them (1 Peter 5:7). While affirming that every man must bear his own burden, he testified that Christ would be available to help with the cares that have the capacity to crush those without inward spiritual resources.

C. *Jesus will be there when sorrow would crush your heart.* The pale horse, whose rider is death, will some day stop at the front door of every home. Some loved one will be ushered into eternity. It will seem that the earth has collapsed and that the heavens have caved in when this sad day arises. Those who have trusted Christ and walked with him in daily fellowship will discover his precious presence on that day. With authoritative promises he can and will give comfort to your heart and assure you that death is a defeated foe, and the grave shall have no final victory over your beloved one. In a real way, you will discover how significant was the event that called for the celebration of Easter. Eternity will become real!

Conclusion

The hand that knocks at the door of your heart is a nail-scarred hand. It belongs to the one who loved you so much that he died for your sins. The nail-scarred hand knocks in order that he might offer to you the forgiveness of sins and the gift of new life. He would bestow upon you the blessing of a life-transforming friendship. Hear him today. Join your heart to him today. Open your heart to him every day.

SUNDAY EVENING, MARCH 7

Title: Jesus the Lamb of God

Text: "Behold the Lamb of God, which taketh away the sin of the world" (**John 1:29**).

Scripture Reading: John 1:29–42

Introduction

The gospel of John differs from the Synoptics in several ways. It was written later, about AD 85, and is more of an interpretation of Christ and his great spiritual truths. John's gospel is not merely historical but also interpretive. In John the vineyard on the Galilean hillside has become a symbol of divine discipline and judgment. There are no pictures of sowing, reaping, and so on. There is no development in the recognition of Jesus. He is the divine Messiah from the first verse. In John there is no mention of Jesus' birth, baptism, temptations, transfiguration, or last supper. The agony of Gethsemane is not described. There is no parable in the gospel, unless the miracles, as some say, are acted parables. Each miracle is given for a definite purpose. They are key signs, and each gives a great spiritual truth that reveals the wonderful attributes of Jesus.

These spiritual truths that stand behind the miracles take place on the plane of history.

While John omits some things contained in the Synoptics, he introduces us to some things not contained in the Synoptics. The miracles at Cana, Nicodemus, the woman of Samaria, the paralytic at Bethesda, the raising of Lazarus, and the washing of the disciples' feet are all found in John only. The discourses in John are long. I point out these things not to say that they contradict each other but that they supplement each other. It seems that John knew what the Synoptics contained and did not care to repeat. He says that he selected his materials and wrote "that people may keep on believing that Jesus is the Christ and that they might have eternal life."

The humanity of Jesus is emphasized as well as his divinity. In John, Jesus is "wearied by the well," be becomes "hungry," and at one time he even "weeps" at the tomb of a friend. The writer was an eyewitness of the events recorded in the book.

John plunges immediately into the purpose of the gospel—to tell about Christ so that people might have everlasting life. He says that the "Word," which is Christ, was the very beginning. He was the source of life and of all things. He was the Light of humankind whom no darkness could overcome. The Baptist came as a witness to this Light. John testified that Jesus gives us all the grace we need. The ministry of John the Baptist is given prominence in the first chapter. People flocked to hear John, and many were puzzled as to who this fiery preacher was. They asked him if he was Elijah or a prophet. He told them that he was merely the voice that was sent to announce the coming of the Messiah. When John the Baptist saw Jesus, he said, "Behold the Lamb of God, which taketh away the sin of the world." This picture of the Lamb comes from Isaiah and is also found in Revelation.

I. The Lamb of God.

One is reminded of the words of Abraham when he was about to sacrifice Isaac: "God will provide himself a lamb" (Gen. 22:8). Jesus is not the Lamb of humankind but of God.

A. *One characteristic associated with the lamb in the Old Testament sacrifices was its innocence.* We speak of the innocence of children not in the sense that they are free from sin but in that they do not understand sin. As children emerge into adulthood, this innocence passes. Christ, however, never lost his innocence. He walked among the sins and temptations of life but remained pure and unsoiled.

B. *The second thing we can mention about a lamb is its gentleness.* It is the perfect type of meek, uncomplaining suffering. People are sometimes gentle because they must be. They say, "Well, we cannot help ourselves." Not so with Christ—he need only speak and legions of angels would be at his side.

C. *But the idea that our author would impress upon our minds is not so much the character of the lamb or its innocence and gentleness, but its death.* He connected

94

Christ with the sacrifices of the old dispensation. Christ is the fulfillment of all the sacrifices. The remarkable thing about the Lamb of God was that he went to his death voluntarily.

II. This Lamb takes away the sin of the world.

Some say that Jesus came to earth to heal, and they emphasize his healing ministry. He healed the blind, the crippled, the diseased, and even the dead. But Jesus' main purpose was to save people from their sins, which is greater than any bodily healing. Sin, the choice of evil instead of good, the perversion of the desires, the slavery of the will, the darkening of the mind, the deadly sickness of the heart—this is the fountain of all trouble, the cause of all disorder and wretchedness. This is the curse that destroys life's harmony and beauty. This is the obstacle that separates the soul in darkness and sorrow from God. The forms of religion, the voice of unceasing prayers, the smoke of endless burnt offerings, the blood of bulls and goats, the oblations of all that is most precious, cruel altars drenched with human gore, and flames consuming the offspring of woman's body—gifts, pleadings, sacrifices—bear witness to the deep and awful sense of sin that rests on the heart of the world. Thus John exultingly declares that Jesus "taketh away the sin of the world."

A. *The simplest meaning of the words "taketh away" is "to lift."* People unable to free themselves from the burden of sin feel it lifted from heart and conscience by the redeeming hand of God. The beginning of a person's salvation is to feel the need to cast one's infirmity and sin on the strength of God. People must realize that they cannot within themselves overcome sin and lift that burden but that they can safely leave it all with the boundless love and mercy of God.

B. *The second phase of the meaning of the word is "to bear."* The divine Savior who lifts the sin from our aching hearts bears it on his own.

C. *The last phrase of the meaning of the word is "to bear away."* The Savior *lifts* the sin of the world, he *bears* the sin of the world, he *bears away* the sin of the world. It can never return to condemn us. He has removed it across the measureless abysses of death and Hades and has hid it in the glory of his resurrection. This is the salvation of our God. It is completed in him. Won't you accept his death as a sacrifice for your sins? The Lamb of God takes away the sin of the world.

III. The invitation of the Lamb.

When Jesus turned around and saw two of John's disciples following him, he asked them what they were looking for. Suppose Jesus were to ask you that today. What would be your answer? What are you looking for in life? They answered, "Master, where do you live?" Jesus' answer is most significant: "Come and see." In our scientific age, it is customary in some circles to hear the statement that one cannot be scientific and spiritual at the same time. Such, of course, have overlooked the first invitation, "Come and see," explore, investigate, draw your own conclusions. Jesus issues an invitation to follow him.

Conclusion

The two disciples promptly accepted the invitation and spent two hours with Jesus. They became his followers. You can do the same today.

WEDNESDAY EVENING, MARCH 10

Title: The Call of Moses

Text: "And when the LORD saw that he turned aside to see, God called unto him out of the midst of the bush, and said, Moses, Moses. And he said, Here am I" (**Ex. 3:4**).

Scripture Reading: Exodus 3:1–10

Introduction

Sometimes God reveals himself and his purpose to man in the most unlikely places. He appeared to Moses at the back side of the desert "in a flame of fire out of the midst of a bush." It was in a desolate, lonely place that God came to him and made himself real to him. Moses' contribution was a curious mind that caused him to turn aside to see the bush that burned but was not consumed. This experience was both objective and subjective. We are dealing here with a divine communication with the mind and heart of a man who had eyes to see and ears to hear.

I. Whom God calls he prepares.

A. *Moses was born in a godly Hebrew home (Ex. 2:1–10).*

B. *Moses was reared and educated in the palace of Pharaoh (Acts 7:22).*

C. *Because of the training of his mother, Moses had a sympathetic heart toward the oppressed Israelites who were serving as slaves in Egypt.* The New Testament martyr Stephen implies that Moses felt an inward constraint to deliver these people from oppression even while he was still in Egypt (Acts 7:23–29).

D. *The university at the back side of the desert.* Because of the combination of faith and fear, Moses fled the palace of Pharaoh. He attended what someone has called "the university at the back side of the desert," and he had time to meditate. In the loneliness and desolation of the desert, he was in a place where God could speak to him.

At the same time, Moses had an opportunity to learn about roads, resources, climate, and the conditions of life in the desert. This information was to equip him for his role as a deliverer.

God had been at work preparing Moses for the task to which he was being called. In the home of his birth, his adoption, and his exile, God was at work equipping him.

II. The response of Moses to the divine call.

Although Moses was equipped by birth, training, and experience to do what God wanted him to do, we find him offering many excuses as to why he cannot achieve this task. In these excuses, Moses reveals his humanity rather than an attitude of humility. We can see ourselves in these excuses. We should recognize how foolish it is to refuse or to neglect to respond to God's call to our hearts.

A. *Moses first pled his own insignificance (Ex. 3:11).* He failed to recognize that one man plus God makes a majority. He seemingly was unaware that the authority of his God was a greater authority than that of Pharaoh. Like many people today, Moses looked only to himself rather than looking to the greatness of the God who had called him. God sought to encourage him by promising to go with him (Ex. 3:12).

B. *Moses then pled his ignorance.* He confessed that he did not know enough about the God of Abraham, Isaac, and Jacob (Ex. 3:13). In modern terminology, Moses was saying, "I have not been to a seminary. I do not have a degree in theology. I am not a theologian."

God revealed himself to Moses as the Eternal One, the "I AM," the one who was, is, and always will be.

C. *Moses then sought to excuse himself by declaring that the people would not listen to him (Ex. 4:1).*

God responded to this excuse by giving Moses three signs by which he could prove to them that the God of their fathers had called him and sent him to them. These signs were the sign of the rod that became a serpent, the hand that became leprous, and the water that turned into blood (Ex. 4:2–9).

D. *Moses then sought to evade the divine call by declaring that he was not an eloquent speaker.*

God answered this excuse by declaring that he would be with Moses' mouth and would teach him what he should speak (Ex. 4:11–12).

Conclusion

In an attitude of resignation, Moses finally yielded to the will of God, but only after God had become angry with him (Ex. 4:14). God had equipped Moses to be the deliverer. He had blessed him in order that he might be the deliverer. God had a right to be angry with Moses, for he refused to cooperate.

God has called us into his work so that we might be his redemptive instruments in delivering a sinful world from the slavery of sin. For us to make excuses as Moses did is to bring divine chastisement upon ourselves. God will make us adequate, in spite of our limitations, if we will respond by faith and obedience to his call. It is time for each of us to begin cooperating with him.

SUNDAY MORNING, MARCH 14

Title: How Are You Treating Him?

Text: "Behold, I stand at the door, and knock: if any man hear my voice, and open the door, I will come in to him, and will sup with him, and he with me" (**Rev. 3:20**).

Scripture Reading: John 1:10–14

Hymns: "I Surrender All," Van DeVenter

"Take My Life and Let It Be," Havergal

"Have Thine Own Way," Pollard

Offertory Prayer: Gracious heavenly Father, you have given most generously of your grace and mercy toward us. You have given us life with all of its joys and sorrows. You have granted to us the gift of faith. You have given to us the assurance of forgiveness and the joy of sonship. Today we give ourselves to you. We give of our substance that by means of this stored-up energy we may go and render ministries of mercy in your name where we cannot possibly go individually. Bless the poor, the unfortunate, the needy, the suffering, and the spiritually deprived by means of these tithes and offerings. Through Jesus Christ, your Son and our Savior. Amen.

Introduction

It is interesting to note the variety of manners in which Jesus was treated. Because he would not accommodate himself to the popular concepts of what the Messiah was to be like, he was rejected by the Jewish people. The people of the town in which he grew to manhood admired him at first and then threatened to cast him from a cliff because of what they considered to be his heretical beliefs. On one occasion an effort was put forth to compel him to assume the role of a king. In his triumphal entry into Jerusalem, he was treated as if he were going to be crowned as King. A short time after this, some shouted, "Crucify him, crucify him!"

The Christ who was crucified conquered death and the grave. He arose triumphant over humankind's last enemy—death. He revealed his living presence again and again to his disciples. He had promised never to leave them nor forsake them. They discovered in experience that he kept this promise. Because of the reality of a continuing companionship with this Christ, many faced death without fear and refused to renounce their faith to escape martyrdom.

The real question is not "How was Jesus treated then?" The real question is "How will you treat Jesus today?"

I. Will you treat Jesus as an intruder?

Do you look upon the Christ as one who would impose himself upon you as an unwelcomed guest? Do you believe that he would invite himself into a place where he is not wanted? If this is your understanding of Jesus, you need to have it corrected. He will never enter your life until you desire him to dwell in your innermost being.

II. Will you treat Jesus as if he were a thief?

In the parable of the good shepherd, Jesus spoke of the thieves and the robbers who came to destroy the flock. They had no love for the flock except as they could receive profit from them. Are you among those who have reached the conclusion that Christ would come in and steal something that is precious from you? Do you fear his presence? Would you be afraid to trust him completely? Instead of being a thief who would rob you, he comes to offer you the possibility of living the abundant life (John 10:10).

III. Will you treat Jesus as if he were a policeman looking for a fugitive?

Many people identify God with their own sense of guilt. Because of a violated conscience, they suffer inward torment. Having passed judgment on their own sins, they fear that punishment is inescapable. Some identify God with the pain and inner turmoil that guilt creates. Because of the destructive effects of unresolved guilt, they come to think of the Lord Jesus as a policeman who is searching for them in order that he might execute justice upon them.

The gospel is not good advice. It is good news that God loves the sinner and that Christ may be pursuing you, but it is in order that he might offer you a pardon instead of inflicting punishment. Consider for a moment how he prayed while on the cross: "Father, forgive them; for they know not what they do" (Luke 23:34).

IV. Will you treat Jesus as a beggar?

Has the devil deceived you into believing that Jesus wants something from you that you cannot afford to relinquish? He is a liar and a deceiver, and the truth is not in him. Jesus Christ, the King of Kings and Lord of Lords, is the Creator of all things. Do not degrade him to the level of a beggar with a cup who sits on the sidewalks. He doesn't have to have anything from you. The truth is, he wants to bestow rich gifts upon you. He would encourage you to try to give yourself away in unselfish service to others. The more you give, the more he will bestow upon you to give.

V. Will you treat Jesus as if he were a bully?

Christ has no selfish desire to be your boss. When the angels obey his every wish and the universe operates on a perfect time schedule according to his calculations, why should he be upset if you choose to shut him out of your life?

Christ wants to be the Lord of your life so that you might experience victory over the destructive evil that is within you and the corroding evil that is about you. To make him the Lord of your life will enable you to experience an inward harmony that will make happy living a present reality.

VI. Will you treat Jesus as a funeral director?

No one is eager to do business with a funeral director. Many labor under the mistaken impression that the only service that Jesus has to offer is that of receiving the soul in the moment of death and conveying it to some vague place in empty space. Because they associate him with a shroud and with dirges, they desire to avoid him.

Christ Jesus is the only one who can bring comfort in the time of sorrow. He is the only one who can transform a shroud into a garment of color. He is the only one who can enable a man to have victory over the tomb. Christ alone has conquered death and the grave and has revealed the reality of immortality. This is the good news of God's love for sinners.

Conclusion

May the Holy Spirit of God open your eyes and enable you to see Jesus Christ not as an intruder, thief, policeman, beggar, bully, or funeral director. May the Holy Spirit help you to see him as the expression of God's wonderful love for you. May you recognize today that he has a wonderful plan for your life. May God grant you the gift of faith in him that will enable you to work with him and to talk with him through the balance of your earthly journey. Do so; trust him and enable yourself to spend eternity in his wonderful presence. Do the right thing with Jesus today—and every day.

SUNDAY EVENING, MARCH 14

Title: Jesus, the Best and the Last

Text: "Everyone brings out the choice wine first and then the cheaper wine after the guests have had too much to drink; but you have saved the best till now" **(John 2:10 NIV)**.

Scripture Reading: John 2:1–11

Introduction

The occasion for Jesus' first miracle was a wedding in Cana of Galilee, not far from Jesus' home in Nazareth. Jesus and his disciples were invited and accepted the invitation. Mary, the mother of Jesus, was also present.

A rather embarrassing incident happened—the host ran out of wine for his guests. Some of you may have had situations where there weren't enough refreshments to go around, and you can sympathize with the host.

Mary apprised Jesus of the situation. We do not know what she expected him to do, but it seemed like the natural thing for a mother to turn to her unusual Son and tell him of the shortage.

The reply of Jesus, "Woman, what have I to do with thee? Mine hour is not yet come," was not disrespectful. The Greek word *gunai* translated "Woman" cannot be translated exactly. The New International Version has "Dear woman." Jesus and his mother had a close relationship, yet there was a part of his life that she could not enter. "What is that to you and me?" he asked. He was saying, "There has never been anything between us; don't make something now." She was not rebuffed. She simply turned and told the servants to do what he said.

"Mine hour is not yet come" is significant. It means that the time when Jesus would reveal himself and something of his wonderful nature had not yet come. His subsequent actions reveal that following the conversation he regarded his hour as having arrived. John tells us in verse 11 that in performing the miracle Jesus "manifested forth his glory; and his disciples believed on him."

Many people are disturbed that Jesus would have anything to do with wine. Many have tried to explain this wine by saying that it was not fermented. However, the Greek word used here is the word for fermented wine. Suffice it to say that no wine before or since has been made like this—from pure water, in a flash.

I. Jesus takes charge of the situation.

There were six stone jars that held from twenty to thirty gallons each and were used for the ceremonial purification of the Jews. Jesus had the servants fill them full from the water in the well. Then he told the servants to draw some out and take it to the master of the banquet.

II. The meaning of the miracle is found in the words of the master of ceremonies, "You have kept the good wine until now" (John 2:10).

A. *Jesus is the best that God has to offer humans.* God had given leaders, prophets, and the best from the human side already. The writer of Hebrews 1:1–2 confirms this truth: "God, who at sundry times and in divers manners spake in time past unto the fathers by the prophets, hath in these last days spoken unto us by his Son, whom he hath appointed heir of all things, by whom also he made the worlds."

B. *Jesus is God's last offer to man.* No Scripture leads us to believe otherwise. Jesus is the best and last that God has to offer to lost humanity.

C. *"Good wine until now."* Wine is the symbol of blood, blood is life, so the new wine is the new life that Jesus offers. This is the life-giving power of the new covenant. New life comes by the creative power of the Son of God.

Conclusion

This miracle in Cana was an introduction, or first sign (John 2:11). It "manifested [Jesus'] glory"—brought out his nature as Savior and Redeemer. God put his best foot forward in giving us the best he has—his Son.

"And his disciples believed on him" (John 2:11). We would do well to believe likewise.

WEDNESDAY EVENING, MARCH 17

Title: The Call of God to Israel

Text: "Now therefore, if ye will obey my voice indeed, and keep my covenant, then ye shall be a peculiar treasure unto me above all people: for all the earth is mine: And ye shall be unto me a kingdom of priests, and an holy nation" (**Ex. 19:5–6**).

Scripture Reading: Exodus 19:3–8

Introduction

Moses, God's servant, brought the children of Israel through the Red Sea and across the desert to the foot of Mount Sinai. Here God would enter into a covenant relationship with the people. Here God would give them the code upon which they would base their conduct. Here they would enter into a working relationship with God. And here God would give them the constitution for their new nation.

I. The covenant relationship was based on redemption (Ex. 19:4).

By many miraculous events God had delivered the Israelites from the power of Pharaoh. They had been delivered from slavery to a life of freedom within the will of God.

This redemption is described in terms of the care the mother eagle gives her eaglets. The mother eagle will tear up the nest when the baby eaglets are large enough to learn to fly. Then she will push them out of the nest or off the ledge and fly above them until they are ready to crash to the ground. She will then fly underneath them and let them grip her wings or back and fly them back up to a place of safety.

II. The covenant relationship required obedience of the people.

A. *God desired that Israel be a special treasure unto himself, a people for his own possession.* He wanted them to be his people in the world. This required obedience to his will.

B. *The Israelites were to be a kingdom of priests.* The function of the priest was to represent God to people and people to God; he was a mediator. He came to offer the blessings of God to the people. He entered into the presence of God to offer sacrifices for the sins of the people. He was the connecting link through which God was to reach the people and the people were to experience the presence of God. This was God's purpose for Israel.

C. *The Israelites were to be a holy nation.* This meant that they were to be utterly dedicated to God and available to him. They were to belong to him completely and exclusively.

III. The response of the people to the offer of the covenant relationship (Ex. 19:8).

The people of Israel responded positively to the offer of the covenant relationship. They agreed to be obedient to the will and word of God.

The history of the Old Testament is a record of Israel's unfaithfulness to the covenant relationship. God was extremely patient and merciful toward them. He sought to work with them and through them in every conceivable manner. Repeatedly they broke the covenant relationship.

Conclusion

How have you responded to the covenant relationship with God that we have through Jesus Christ? He died for our sins and has given us the privilege of being adopted as his children. He has bestowed upon us the gift of eternal life. He has placed within our heart the Holy Spirit. He would have us to be a special people for the glory of God. He would have us to serve a priestly function and be the means whereby God's grace touches the hearts and lives of others.

We must not repeat the record of Israel, which is a record of failure to keep the covenant relationship.

SUNDAY MORNING, MARCH 21

Title: God's Message to Us in Christ

Text: "God . . . hath in these last days spoken unto us by his Son" **(Heb. 1:1–2)**.

Scripture Reading: Hebrews 1:1–4

Hymns: "God, Our Father, We Adore Thee," Frazer

"Love Divine, All Loves Excelling," Wesley

"Tell Me the Story of Jesus," Crosby

Offertory Prayer: Our gracious and loving Father, we thank you for giving your Son for us. We thank you for giving your Spirit to dwell within our hearts. We thank you for giving us your Word to guide us, strengthen us, and help us. We thank you for allowing us to come into your presence in prayer in our time of need for grace and mercy. We also thank you today for the privilege of sharing the good news of your love and mercy with a needy world. We come now to bring tithes and offerings, asking that you would bless them in ministries of mercy here in this community and in the uttermost parts of the earth. Help us to give gladly and generously even as you have given so lavishly unto us through Jesus Christ, in whose name we pray. Amen.

Introduction

Through the ages God has been speaking to men and women who have ears to hear and hearts willing to respond to spiritual truths. God has spoken through the prophets. God has communicated his message to humans through angels. God has spoken in the hearts of all people through the wonders of nature: "The heavens declare the glory of God; the skies proclaim the work of his hands. Day after day they pour forth speech; night after night they display knowledge. There is no speech or language where their voice is not heard" (Ps. 19:1–3 NIV).

The words of the text declare that God has "in these last days spoken unto us by his Son." The author of the book of Hebrews was directing his message to Jewish Christians who were recent converts from Judaism. He seeks to point out that Christ was and continues to be superior to the angels who communicated God's message on occasion. He then focuses attention on the fact that Christ is and continues to be superior to Moses, the great lawgiver. He declares that Christ is superior to the prophets who foretold his coming. The climax of this book declares that Jesus Christ is superior to the Aaronic priesthood as a mediator between

103

sinful humankind and the holy God. Christ himself is the great High Priest, and at the same time, he is the sacrificial Lamb who gives his life as a sacrifice for the sins of man. As the holy High Priest, he enters into heaven itself to offer his blood as the atoning sacrifice for the sins of a guilty world.

If God has spoken in his Son, what is the unique message that he is seeking to communicate to the hearts and minds of people?

I. In Christ Jesus, God speaks to us concerning his unique nature.

From the beginning people have wondered about the nature and character of God. People have sought for an explanation for the origin of the universe and have sought to understand their unique nature as the highest of living creatures. Some have thought of God as being the all-powerful principle behind the universe. Some have thought of him as being a coldhearted mechanical engineer who operates the universe without concern for people. Others have thought of God as being the unloving one who dwells in the distant somewhere and is unmoved by the predicament of humans.

The Old Testament is a record of God's progressive self-revelation. He revealed himself continually as people were able to receive and respond to that revelation. God has always been limited by our willingness to receive and respond to the revelation of the divine will.

As we read the Old Testament, we discover God revealing more and more of himself to the prophets, the priests, and the psalmists. We must not fall into the fatal error of believing that Old Testament saints understood the nature and character of God in the same degree as New Testament saints. Their understanding was only partial, and consequently, their conduct in most instances is considerably below what we would consider Christian.

Through Jesus Christ, his Son, God desired to speak concerning his unique nature. On all occasions, Christ taught that God is good and that God is love, and he taught his disciples to think of God not as a king but as our heavenly Father. He pictures God as the Shepherd who goes in search of a lost sheep and as a father who longingly awaits with anxiety and eagerness for the return of a wayward son. He pictures God as a God who rejoices and welcomes the wayward son and immediately prepares a banquet.

To understand the nature of God, we need to examine the nature and character and motives of Jesus Christ. John records how that on one occasion Jesus said, "No one has ever seen God, but God the One and Only, who is at the Father's side, has made him known" (John 1:18 NIV). Later this same apostle quotes the conversation of Jesus with Philip:

"If you really knew me, you would know my Father as well. From now on, you do know him and have seen him."

Philip said, "Lord, show us the Father and that will be enough for us."

Jesus answered: "Don't you know me, Philip, even after I have been among you such a long time? Anyone who has seen me has seen the Father. How can you say, 'Show us the Father'?" (John 14:7–9 NIV)

104

II. In Christ, God clearly speaks concerning our need of salvation.

A. *Jesus defined his purpose for coming into the world in terms of meeting our need for salvation.* The angelic announcement to Joseph indicated that he was to save his people from their sins (Matt. 1:21). John the Baptist instructed his disciples to "Behold the Lamb of God, which taketh away the sins of the world" (John 1:29). On another occasion Jesus said, "For even the Son of man came not to be ministered unto, but to minister, and to give his life a ransom for many" (Mark 10:45). Paul declared that "Christ died for our sins" (1 Cor. 15:3).

B. *The sinfulness of our sin is dramatically revealed in the death of Christ on Calvary.* To see the awfulness of sin we need to see what sin did to Jesus Christ when he died on the cross for our sins. Some people ignore or minimize sin, but the wise man in the book of Proverbs points out that it is foolish to treat sin lightly.

Sin in its awful consequences is seen most vividly in what it wrought upon Jesus Christ as he died for our sins.

C. *The penalty of sin is revealed by the death of Christ on the cross (Rom. 6:23).* The death of Christ on the cross was a substitutionary death. The most terrible part of the suffering of Christ on the cross was his feeling of utter loneliness and isolation from the Father. Christ felt as if he were cut off from God because he had taken upon himself our sins.

III. In Christ, God reveals his inflexible justice.

It is paradoxical but true that the God of love and grace and mercy is also the God of justice. It is the law of God that the soul that sins shall die. It is not only a fact of nature but the truth of God that the wages of sin is death.

In a mysterious but miraculous way the God of justice has provided for our salvation by giving us a Savior, Jesus Christ. His death on the cross was a substitutionary death, for in a way the human mind cannot fully comprehend, God let Christ be our substitute. He paid the wages of our sins. "For he hath made him to be sin for us who knew no sin: that we might be made the righteousness of God in him" (2 Cor. 5:21). The prophet Isaiah declared, "All we like sheep have gone astray; ... and the LORD hath laid on him the iniquity of us all" (53:6).

The just law of God declares that sin results in death. The God of grace and mercy provided a Savior who died for our sin that we might be able to receive the gift of eternal life. In the cross God speaks concerning his desire and his determination to redeem people from the tyranny and penalty of sin. The holy God hates sin, but as a gracious God he loves the sinner, and he has made provision for his forgiveness and cleansing. That provision is through Jesus Christ. Through this Christ God speaks to us today.

IV. In Christ, on Calvary, God reveals his great love and concern for the unsaved.

It is the testimony of Scripture that "God sent not his Son into the world to condemn the world, but that the world through him might be saved" (John 3:17). Paul stood in amazement before the immeasurable and indescribable love of God for sinners and asked the question, "He that spared not his own Son, but delivered him up for us all, how shall he not with him also freely give us all things?" (Rom. 8:32).

To measure the love of God for us, we just go to Calvary where God gave his Son to die for us. There are many ways to speak—verbally, by means of a written message, by our expressions and actions, by means of a generous gift, etc.—but perhaps the most powerful way to speak is to suffer on behalf of the one who is loved. Our heavenly Father demonstrated his love for us by the suffering that his Son endured when he was crucified for our sins.

V. In Christ, on Calvary, God reveals his claim upon our lives.

Jesus Christ suffered and died on the cross to reveal the awfulness of sin and to redeem and to save us from sin in order that he might inspire and motivate us to act with God in his persistent quest to save all people from sin. Paul declared, "For the love of Christ constraineth us; because we thus judge, that if one died for all, then were all dead: And that he died for all, that they which live should not henceforth live unto themselves, but unto him which died for them, and rose again" (2 Cor. 5:14–15).

To visit Calvary and to behold the wonder of God's love for us is a life-transforming experience. This love not only bestows on us the blessings of God, but it also places us under a heavy debt of gratitude that should cause us to devote our lives to communicating to people the good news of God's love through Christ Jesus.

Conclusion

God has spoken through the lawgiver, through the prophets, through the priests, through angelic beings, and through the psalmist. God also speaks most powerfully through his Son. Have you heard him? Are you listening? Respond to his message to your own heart. Respond to him in such a manner as will cause you to become a communicator of this message that has come to us through Christ Jesus.

SUNDAY EVENING, MARCH 21

Title: Jesus, the Unlimited Savior

Text: "And the man believed the word that Jesus had spoken to him, and he went his way" (**John 4:50**).

Scripture Reading: John 4:46–54

Introduction

The following bit of conversation was heard on a street corner. "Why, son, you look more like your father every day." "Thank you, Mr. Jones. Do you really mean that?" "Yes, son, you are the spitting image of your father." "Oh, thank you, Mr.

Jones. I would rather be like my father than be a millionaire." With that prayer in my heart, I introduce to you the second miracle that Jesus performed as recorded in John's gospel. All of these messages are designed to help us to be like our Father and to love him more.

The first great introductory sign was at Cana, where Jesus changed the water into wine. That miracle revealed Jesus as the best and last that God has to offer to his highest creation—man. Following that miracle, we have the contrast between the old dispensation and the new demonstrated. In Jesus' cleansing of the temple (John 2:12–25), we have the deliverance from the old dispensation. The old was cleansed for the new. In John 3 Jesus deals with the highest of the old dispensation in the case of Nicodemus and contrasts it with entering into the kingdom. There he takes us into the great heart of God. Then he shows how John the Baptist stood between the old and the new, and his relation to both. The water and the Spirit also show the old and the new.

In John 4 we are introduced to the Samaritan woman at Jacob's well in Samaria. Jesus had to go through Samaria, for he had a task there—to break down the barriers between the Jews and the rest of the world. The Samaritans claimed Jacob for a father as the Jews claimed Abraham. The Assyrian kings were responsible for the presence of the Samaritans. They brought people from the East, and these people intermarried with the poorer Jews in the northern kingdom. From them came the race of Samaritans. The Samaritans claimed the five books of Moses but denied the oral law and the Prophets. They held to a belief in the coming Messiah from Deuteronomy 18:5.

The Samaritans were considered the lowest of the low by the Jews. The Jews would seek converts from among most of the Gentiles but not from among the Samaritans. The Samaritans considered the woman as the lowest of creation, and here the woman is a harlot, the lowest of women.

John tells us that after two days in Samaria Jesus and the disciples went back into Galilee. As a matter of fact, they went back to Cana, where he performed his first miracle, and it was there that the dramatic events of the second key sign took place. The scene opens with the following:

I. A father praying for his dying son.

"He besought Jesus that he would come down, and heal his son; for he was at the point of death" (John 4:47). This is an experience that touches the heartstrings of every parent.

    A. *This petitioner was a nobleman, perhaps a royal officer of the household of Herod Antipas.* He may have been Chuza, "Herod's steward," whose wife afterward supported Jesus out of her own means (Luke 8:3). Suffering is no respecter of persons.

    B. *It was affliction that brought the nobleman to Jesus.* Many people never think of Jesus until trouble comes. Nicodemus came because of a troubled soul. This man came because of a troubled son. Whatever the motive, the blessed fact is that he came.

107

C. *He not only came, but he came in faith.* Whether the man had ever met Jesus is not told us, but when "he heard that Jesus" was there, he came. Don't you wish that you had been the one who told him about Jesus? You never know what Jesus can and will do for a person who comes to him.

The name of the preacher who baptized Billy Graham is unknown by most people today. Frequently these people remain unknown to this world, but they shine as the stars in heaven.

It was another lawyer who grabbed the drunken attorney C. I. Scofield by the shoulders and said, "Why don't you quit your drinking and get right with God?" He did, and his version of the Bible has influenced thousands over the years. Someone told this nobleman about Jesus, and he came to see him.

II. What was Jesus' response to the father's coming?

He put him to a test with these words: "Except ye see signs and wonders, ye will not believe" (John 4:48). The words, though addressed to the nobleman, are really intended for the Jews who wished to see Jesus as a miracle worker. They desired to see miracles, not as the mere manifestations or signs of the invisible world, but as "wonders" calculated by their strangeness to arrest attention.

People today are seeking after signs. Billy Graham, in Jacksonville, Florida, in 1961, speaking at a luncheon, told of a wealthy man riding in his car near Tampa when he suddenly heard a voice say to him, "You can help Billy Graham." The man had never met Billy nor heard him preach, nor was he even a Christian. He tried to tell himself that he did not hear anything; people would think him crazy if he told them. Nevertheless, he could not dismiss it from his mind and did tell some of his friends about it. Finally, he said, "Lord, if you are talking to me, I want you to prove it. I'm going fishing Friday night, so let me catch the biggest fish on the boat. In fact, make it the biggest fish ever caught from a boat from Tampa, and let it be at 1:30 in the morning." Several other men went along. At 1:30 he caught the biggest shark ever caught there. He said as he played with that shark, which is the most worthless of fish, that the shark represented his worthless life. He later flew to North Carolina to see Billy, not knowing that he was in Florida, and talked to Dr. Bell, Billy's father-in-law. Upon his return, he looked up the pastor in Bradenton and made his decision and worked with Billy in the Florida crusade that year.

Jesus tested this man's sincerity. Many of us will pray in time of trouble and then forget all about our promises when trouble passes. But this man was in dead earnest.

III. The increasing urgency of the father's sorrow.

"Sir, come down before my child dies" (John 4:49 NIV). This father did not regard our Lord's words as a rejection of his prayer. His powerlessness led him to a more unreserved dependence on the Lord's power. The father said to Jesus,

"Come down and save him." The nobleman lived in Capernaum, a city at the north end of the Sea of Galilee. His earnest plea was for Jesus to go back to Capernaum with him and save his son. This is the mistake many of us make—telling Jesus how to do something for us. We must come to Jesus on his terms and let him work in our lives in the way he chooses. "Have thine own way, Lord! Have thine own way! Thou art the Potter, I am the clay; Mold me and make me after Thy will, while I am waiting, yielded and still."

IV. Our Lord's answer to his prayer: "Go thy way: thy son liveth" (John 4:50).

Jesus spoke the word of assurance. A word is enough, for divine power acts through a word. With a word the worlds were formed. God said, "Let there be light," and there was light (Gen. 1:3). "I do not have to go to Capernaum to heal your son. Go back home; he lives!" Jesus strengthened the faith of this royal officer by shifting his faith in the testimony of others to faith for himself in Jesus. It now rested on a better foundation.

V. We see next the triumph of faith.

The man did not stand and argue with Jesus about the impossibility of healing twenty-five miles away; rather, he "believed the word that Jesus had spoken unto him, and he went his way" (John 4:50). To believe as this man did is to know that it is so. Jesus told him that his son lived. Picture him as he walked or rode along the way back home. What a difference from the way he came—full of worry, anxiety, and fear. Now calmness, assurance, and complete peace flooded his soul. He was whistling and singing, the sun was shining, the birds were singing—everything was right with the world. A cloud of dust arose before them—someone was coming. "It's your servants," said the men with him. They rode up with the wonderful news, "Your son lives." "What hour did the fever leave him?" "At one o'clock, the seventh hour," they replied. "The same hour that Jesus spoke those words," said the nobleman.

Conclusion

This second sign shows that Jesus did not have to be present to heal. The spiritual power of Jesus was not limited by time and space. The result was immediate. The gospel is without time—it is for all people of all ages. Jesus is the unlimited Savior.

WEDNESDAY EVENING, MARCH 24

Title: The Call of God to Samuel

Text: "And the LORD came, and stood, and called as at other times, Samuel, Samuel. Then Samuel answered, Speak; for thy servant heareth" (**1 Sam. 3:10**).

Scripture Reading: 1 Samuel 3:1–10

Introduction

The dealings of God are always wonderful. They are both mysterious and miraculous.

God seeks to communicate with humans. Humans are spiritual receiving stations. They can receive communications from God if they are willing to listen and if they recognize the voice of God when they hear it. The experience of the boy Samuel is interesting and can be profitable for all of us at the point of responding to God's call to our lives.

I. Samuel was living away from his parents.

Samuel was a special child. He was a gift from God to Elkanah and Hannah, his wife (1 Sam. 1:22). He had been dedicated to the Lord and was living in the house of Eli, the high priest.

II. God spoke to Samuel while he was still a child (1 Sam. 3:1).

Some people think that God communicates only with adults. The case of Samuel would nullify that idea. God can and does speak to the minds and hearts of young people. Perhaps it is easier for children to hear the voice of God than it is for adults, since adults are more selfish and more preoccupied than children.

III. The voice of God came to Samuel in the silence of the night (1 Sam. 3:3).

A. *God always speaks softly.* He never raises his voice. We must somehow find a place and time of silence if we want to hear the still, small voice of God (Ps. 46:10).

B. *God always speaks personally.* He spoke to Samuel personally, and he will speak to us personally.

IV. Samuel did not recognize the voice of God at first (1 Sam. 3:5, 7).

God spoke to Samuel on four different occasions during the night. It was the fourth time when Samuel replied, as instructed by Eli, and said, "Speak; for thy servant heareth."

V. Samuel needed help to recognize and understand the voice of God.

A. *Parents can often help their children to recognize and understand the voice of God.*

B. *The pastor can help us hear the voice of God.*

C. *Teachers may help us understand the voice of God.*

D. *Christian friends may be used by God to speak to us.*

VI. God continues to speak to those who are willing to listen.

A. *God speaks through the Bible to the minds and hearts of those who read it reverently.*

B. *God speaks through the preaching of the gospel.*

C. *God speaks through the ministry of the Holy Spirit.*

D. *God speaks through the singing of the gospel.*

E. *God speaks with a still, small voice in the deepest zone of our being and in the highest part of our intellect.*

Conclusion

Each of us should respond to the Lord as Samuel did. We should say, "Speak, Lord; for thy servant heareth." God will speak to us of his love, of his plan for our lives, of the help that he will offer to us and to others, and of his need for our help. May God help each of us to hear and heed his voice.

SUNDAY MORNING, MARCH 28

Title: The Kingship of Jesus

Text: "And the multitudes that went before, and that followed, cried, saying, Hosanna to the son of David: Blessed is he that cometh in the name of the Lord; Hosanna in the highest" (**Matt. 21:9**).

Scripture Reading: Matthew 21:1–17

Hymns: "All Hail the Power of Jesus' Name," Perronet

"Come Thou Almighty King," Anonymous

"O Worship the King," Grant

Offertory Prayer: Today, our heavenly Father, we bow before him whom you have anointed to be our King. We worship him in spirit and in truth. We give to him the love and the loyalty of our hearts. We make ourselves obedient to his wishes. We dedicate ourselves to the doing of his good will. We come bringing tithes and offerings as an expression of our gratitude for your divine love and as a recognition of your divine authority over our lives. We pray that you would bless the use of these offerings to the relief of suffering and to the proclamation of the good news of your grace to the ends of the earth. In Jesus' name. Amen.

Introduction

The triumphant entry of our Lord into Jerusalem is celebrated each year on Palm Sunday. This is the beginning of Holy Week. Around the world the eyes and hearts of the devoted followers of Jesus Christ will be focused day by day on those events that took place during the last week of the earthly life of our Savior. His royal entry into Jerusalem was the beginning of that week. His triumphant resurrection from the tomb brought it to a grand conclusion.

The triumphant entry of Jesus was not much of a triumph if it is to be compared to the triumphant entry of a Roman king or a victorious general. When a Roman king made a triumphal procession into a city, he was preceded by the senate. This august body was followed by trumpeters, flute players, captives, spoils of war, and even oxen for sacrifices. The captives of war, particularly other kings and chieftains, were chained together and driven before him. Last in the procession would be the king, attired in the purple and gold of his majesty with the scepter of his kingdom in his hand.

In vivid contrast to this was the royal entry of the King of Kings into the holy city of Jerusalem. While earthly kings rode on gaudily draped war horses, our Lord rode on the foal of a donkey on which the garments of his admirers had been placed. While earthly kings were praised by the leaders of the kingdom, our Lord was praised by peasants and children. Our Lord was given the praise and the acclaim of a king. Again, in strange contrast to his former behavior, our Lord received and accepted this acclaim. He did not deny that he was entering the city as a king. Why this change in his attitude toward those who wanted to make him a king?

His royal entry was deliberate. It was part of his presentation of his messiahship to his disciples, to the people, and to the leaders of the nation. Jesus knew before his arrival in Jerusalem what was to take place. His every action was according to plan and purpose (Matt. 20:17–19). Prior arrangements had been made for the foal of a donkey upon which he was to ride. A password, "The Lord hath need of him," had been given to the owner of the donkey and her colt.

The royal entry of the Christ was a fulfillment of prophecy. Zechariah had foretold the royal entry: "Rejoice greatly, O Daughter of Zion! Shout, Daughter of Jerusalem! See, your king comes to you, righteous and having salvation, gentle and riding on a donkey, on a colt, the foal of a donkey.... He will proclaim peace to the nations. His rule will extend from sea to sea and from the River to the ends of the earth" (9:9–10 NIV).

Messianic prophecy in the Old Testament identified the coming Messiah under four major themes. First, he is portrayed as a prophet who will come with an authentic word from God concerning God. Second, he is pictured as both a priest who will offer a perfect sacrifice on behalf of man and as that sacrifice. He is to bring God down to people, and he is to lift people up to God. Third, the Messiah is also pictured as the Suffering Servant who is to die a substitutionary death on behalf of sinners. This is particularly the theme of Isaiah 53. And fourth, he is also pictured as a king.

As the centuries went by, Israel looked forward to the coming of the ideal king who would be their Messiah. In times of national crisis, the people earnestly longed for a king who would deliver them from the oppression of their enemies. This expectation was particularly uppermost during the earthly life of our Savior. There were times when it was necessary that Jesus suppress the efforts, even of his apostles, to force him into a position where he would have to assume kingship.

Not only was our Lord's royal entry a fulfillment of prophecy, but it was also an acted parable. Some of our Lord's parables were verbal. He told stories by which he communicated great truths. Others were in the form of pantomimes in which he was communicating with his actions. Such was the case with his royal entry.

I. Christ entered the city to offer himself as King.

    A. *He was born to be a king (Matt. 2:2).*

    B. *He was given the reverence due a king (Matt. 2:11).*

C. *He was feared by a rival king (Matt. 2:16).*

D. *He had been offered the kingdoms of the world by a usurper who claimed to have the authority to give him the kingdoms of the world (Matt. 4:8–10).*

E. *His disciples tried to force him to assert his royalty and assume the kingship (John 6:15).* They wanted him to reestablish the Davidic kingdom and throw off the dominion of the power of Rome. They would have been satisfied with a kingdom of military power and material glory.

F. *By his royal entry, our Lord was manifesting his kingship and demonstrating the authority of the kingdom of God.*

   1. As the divine King, he cleansed the temple by driving out the money changers (Matt. 21:12).

   2. He restored the temple to its divine purpose (Matt. 21:13; cf. Isa. 56:7).

   3. He healed the blind and the lame and thus exercised authority over disease.

   By Jesus' coming into the city in the manner in which he did, he was following in the tradition of David and the other kings of Israel. He was deliberately accepting the acclaim of the crowd as a king. He did not rebuke them when they gave him the applause and recognition of a king.

II. Christ entered the city to reveal the nature of his kingship.

On one occasion, our Lord denied that he had come in order to bring peace on earth: "Think not that I am come to send peace on earth: I came not to send peace, but a sword" (Matt. 10:34). There were certain situations that our Lord could not tolerate. He could not condone hypocrisy and injustice and unkindness. He could not give his approval to oppression whether it was social, political, or spiritual. He came into the world to call people to an undivided loyalty to the will of God. He recognized, as we should, that one cannot set out to set things straight without creating division and strife in some areas. Many believe that the only way by which some conditions in society can be changed is by violence, and there is a great amount of historical evidence that justifies their having this opinion.

Jesus Christ came not to create a peace of stagnation and indifference. He came not to condone the status quo and give approval to all that then existed. He challenged the status quo, and by the steel of a will completely surrendered to God, he challenged the corrupt religious and social system of his day. In that sense he created war instead of peace.

By Jesus' riding on the foal of a donkey instead of on a war charger, he was revealing that his kingship was based on love and grace and not on force and power.

A. *He came as King so that people might have peace with God.*

B. *He came as King so that people might have peace as they discover both the way and the power to live according to the divine will.*

C. *He came as King so that people of goodwill might enjoy peace with others.*

D. *As King he would rule by love rather than by force. He devoted himself to a life of humble self-giving service to others.*

III. Christ came into the city as King not to take the lives of Israel's enemies but to give his life for others.

The last six months of Jesus' ministry were spent in seclusion with his apostles. He gave himself to the task of teaching them the things concerning his kingdom. He sought to reveal to them that his kingdom was based on love, that it was inward and spiritual. With persistent effort, he sought to instill within them the concept of the kingdom of God as heaven's rule in the hearts of people. This was a strange concept to his disciples. They wanted a nationalistic king who would lead a revolt against the authority of Rome.

Jesus offered himself to Israel as the King who would rule by the principle of love, but Israel rejected the peace that he could have brought and instead chose destruction.

It was the public assumption of Jesus' kingship as Messiah that contributed greatly to his condemnation and crucifixion. Pilate inquired concerning whether Jesus was the King of the Jews (John 18:33). It was this charge that Pilate used as the basis for yielding to the request of the Jewish authorities that Jesus be put to death. The superscription placed above his cross read, "Jesus of Nazareth, the King of the Jews."

The Christ who was crucified on the cross was born to be a king. He lived a sinless life like a perfect king. He spoke with the authority of a king. There was something uniquely royal about the manner in which he died on the cross. It was as King over death that he arose triumphant and victorious on the resurrection day. It was with kingly authority that he commissioned his disciples to evangelize the world. One day he will return to earth as the King of Kings.

Conclusion

Have you made Jesus the King of your heart with control over your will? Are you willing today to recognize his kingship and grant him control of your economic life? It would be wise for you to make him King of your relationships with people. If you want to know the peace and power that comes from God, then you need to make him King of your loyalties. To know Jesus as the Prince of Peace, we must respond to him as Lord and King.

SUNDAY EVENING, MARCH 28

Title: Jesus, the Divine Healer

Text: "Immediately the man was made whole, and took up his bed, and walked: and on the same day was the sabbath" (**John 5:9**).

Scripture Reading: John 5:1–11

Introduction

The scene of the third key sign in John's gospel is Jerusalem. The first nine verses of John 5 give the facts of the sign. Verse 4 is not found in the oldest manuscripts and was probably written in as an attempt to explain the healing power of the water. The pool probably was a siphon spring with some sort of mineral in the water that soon dissipated after stirring. We have such springs as this in Warm Springs, Georgia, and Hot Springs, Arkansas.

I. Jesus is attracted by the misery.

There were many people around the pool who were miserable and needy. Jesus was also there. He was always found where he was most wanted and where he might do the most good. He was not found in places of luxury and ease but in the haunts of misery.

   A. *The misery was great.* There was presented to the eye of Jesus such pain and degradation, mental and moral, as could scarcely be described.
   B. *The misery was various.* It was confined to no one disease but embraced many classes—"the blind, the lame, the paralyzed" (John 5:3 NIV). Misery like this is found in many parts of the world today. A visitor to India tells of arriving in a certain city around 2:00 in the morning. While driving to the hotel from the airport, he noticed that the streets and sidewalks were white with people sleeping in the only clothes they had. Most of them never had had a square meal in their entire lives. Poverty abounds in wholesale lots in India. This is hard for us to understand, for our problem is not undereating but overeating.
   C. *The misery in Jerusalem was all around.* The porches were full, and doubtless many could not get close to the water. Physical suffering is the heritage of the human family and the special heritage of some. It is mercy that suffering is distributed. We know of one who bore all kinds of suffering, for "he was wounded for our transgressions, he was bruised for our iniquities: the chastisement of our peace was upon him; and with his stripes we are healed" (Isa. 53:5). All were waiting and struggling for the same blessing—restoration of health. With anxiety they would watch the moving of the waters, and with great effort they would try to be the first person in. Jesus was attracted to this place. The scene naturally aroused his wonderful compassion, and it stood forth as a picture to him of a more terrible and universal malady, that of sin, which he came to take away.

II. Jesus saw an individual among the masses.

Jesus was especially attracted to one individual. This man was probably a paralytic, thoroughly helpless and unable to plunge himself into the pool. Thirty-eight years he had been in this condition. We do not know how old he was, but the better part of his life was spent in this condition. He had enough life left to feel his pain and woe, but he was almost in the grip of utter despair. He had been at the pool for years and doubtless was the sport for the more fortunate and was the prey of despair. Still he mechanically dragged himself near every day, with an occasional glimmer of hope that some good chance would turn up. Listen as he tells his own sad story: "Sir, I have no one to help me into the pool when the water is stirred. While I am trying to get in, someone else goes down ahead of me" (John 5:7 NIV).

III. Jesus had compassion on him.

A. *Compassion means "to suffer with" someone in their sorrow.*

B. *Jesus asked the man a question that on the surface seems to be superfluous: "Do you want to get well?" (John 5:6 NIV).* Here we see the importance of the consent of the will in physical as well as spiritual recovery. Christ did not choose to help people against their will. The consent of the will is the first step toward help. This is Jesus' way of doing things.

C. *Christ was willing to help anyone who had the desire for it.* He is eager to encourage people to lay hold of help. "[God] is patient with you, not wanting anyone to perish, but everyone to come to repentance" (2 Peter 3:9 NIV).

D. *People struggle, even to running over another, to get into the water that will bring physical relief, but for the spiritual water of life they stand back.* Does it make sense? I have been touched by the concern church people have over the physical illness of a fellow church member. They gladly give flowers, visit, pray, and offer all sorts of help and comfort to a family. This is good, and I would not want to change it, but I would want us to develop a similar concern for lost persons that would cause us to act out our love by doing things to lead them to the Lord. For you see, a person without Christ is in far worse condition than the one without health but having Christ.

E. *The story of the man is a tale of human helplessness on the one side and human selfishness on the other.* The "will" to be helped was not entirely gone but was very weak. "Sir, I have no one" — "everyone for himself" was the rule. A picture of the "survival of the fittest" seems to be the law of nature under sin; but there is a law of grace by which the seemingly unfittest survive.

IV. Jesus gave an astounding command: "Rise."

A. *This man did not know Jesus, but perhaps Jesus was the first to show concern for him, and there was divine power in that command.* He had not risen in his own strength for thirty-eight years.

B. *This man could have said, "I can't," but he didn't.* He arose; he did that which could not be done.

C. *Jesus continued, "Take up thy bed."* You might as well tell the bed to take him up. Every human power had failed before. There is here a divine will and a divine right and power for immediate execution. There is no hesitancy, no timidity, but full and serene consciousness to carry out the command. Jesus had performed another miracle.

V. We can learn several things from the healing of this man.

A. *Jesus selected his own subject.* Many others needed help, but he selected the most miserable and helpless. Jesus often helps in a manner and degree that is least expected. This poor man never expected more than to be helped into the pool. But Christ made him completely whole by the power of his word. Love will do the big thing, if possible; if not, it will do the little thing well.

B. *Some people did not rejoice over the healing.* If this story could end with the man being made well, it would be beautiful, but the religious leaders saw the man carrying his bed on the Sabbath and censored him severely. They did not rejoice that the man was made whole. To heed the letter of the law was more important to them than for a fellow human being to be made well.

VI. This was the occasion for Jesus revealing himself to be the Son of God (John 5:17–47).

A. *Jesus said that he was the Son of God (John 5:18).*

B. *Jesus points out three witnesses for the fact.*

1. John the Baptist.
2. God the Father, who sanctioned his baptism with his presence.
3. The Word of God that the people had. He said, "You do err, not knowing the scriptures" (Matt. 22:29).

The story is told of an intellectual American visiting in Africa some time ago who came upon an African reading the Bible. He said to the African, "You mean to tell me that you read that silly old book? We in America have learned better." To which the African replied, "If you had come along thirty-five years before, your silly old body would be in that silly old pot, and I would have you for dinner, but this silly old book, as you call it, teaches me better."

Conclusion

What Christ did physically to this man he is ready and willing to do spiritually for the human race. Because of sin the human family is spiritually powerless, helpless. We need someone to help us to the healing powers of God. Christ, in the gospel of love and power, asks you, "Do you want to get well?" If you are willing to be healed, he is willing and able. The world is Bethesda, "house of mercy," because Christ the Healer has made it so.

Jesus not only heals physically but morally as well. A preacher friend told of an experience that he had concerning a fellow pastor whose wife, like Hosea's, went bad. She became a professional prostitute. An officer in the church came to my preacher friend and asked him to go with him to talk with her. They went, and she belligerently told them to mind their own business. My friend said, "I was ready to go. I felt that we had done all that was expected of us. I took the church officer by the arm to lead him back to the car, but instead the compassionate young man dropped to the floor of the house and began to pray as I never heard a man pray. I knelt with him, and soon there was the thump of other knees as this young wife knelt and, sobbing loudly, said, 'I lied when I said that I was happy. I am the most miserable person alive. Tell that good man that if he can forgive me I will come back and be the best wife possible.' She came back home, and today they are grandparents. She has never strayed since, and God has used both of them mightily."

Jesus is the Healer, even of sick morals.

WEDNESDAY EVENING, MARCH 31

Title: The Call of God to Amos

Text: "Then answered Amos, and said to Amaziah, I was no prophet, neither was I a prophet's son; but I was an herdman, and a gatherer of sycamore fruit: And the LORD took me as I followed the flock, and the LORD said unto me, Go, prophesy unto my people Israel" **(Amos 7:14–15)**.

Scripture Reading: Amos 3:7–8; 7:12–15

Introduction

The prophets were launched upon their prophetic careers by a definite call experience. Even as Israel moved forward because of a consciousness of a covenant relationship with God, so the true prophets entered the prophetic ministry because of the constraint of God's will. Amos, a herdsman from Tekoa, declared that he prophesied not out of personal choice but because God took him from following the flock and inducted him into the prophetic ministry. A prophet's call did not come to him in a vacuum. It was not an induction into an undefined ministry. Of necessity it was vitally connected with some particular occasion. The spiritual and the physical were inseparably connected in the Hebrews' experiences. God spoke to them in the experiences of life, and they were sensitive to learn.

I. Amos was a layman.

He says, "I was an herdman, and a gatherer of sycamore fruit" (Amos 7:14). Amos lived in Tekoa, the easternmost village of Judea. It was eight hundred feet above sea level. From Tekoa one could see the Mount of Olives in the distance. On the other side one could look down upon the Dead Sea. Tekoa was six miles south of Bethlehem and twelve miles from Jerusalem. It was a desolate place in which one would have to struggle for survival.

II. Amos was drafted to the prophetic office.

He declared, "I was no prophet, neither was I a prophet's son" (Amos 7:14). By this statement Amos was repudiating any relationship at all with the professional prophets of King Jeroboam. He was not a prophet by birth or because of personal choice. He did not come to Bethel to make a profit by proclaiming a word of judgment, as King Amaziah implied, saying, "O thou seer, go, flee thee away into the land of Judah, and there eat bread, and prophesy there" (Amos 7:12). Amaziah resented Amos's shocking message. Consequently, he demanded that Amos return to his home in the south and there earn his livelihood. By this commandment Amaziah was confessing that he was a hireling of the idolatrous King Jeroboam.

Amos declared, "The LORD took me as I followed the flock, and the LORD said unto me, Go, prophesy unto my people Israel" (Amos 7:15). Here he described the constraint of God's will upon his life. He declared that he was in Bethel proclaiming a message of judgment through no private choice of his own. He was God's spokesman by God's choice.

III. How did the call of God come to Amos?

We cannot be certain concerning the manner in which this sense of inward constraint gripped the mind and heart of Amos. Some people have surmised that as Amos meditated upon the moral nature of Israel's God and at the same time contemplated the immoral nature of the people, that he was guided to the conclusion that judgment must come upon the people. A holy God could not condone and perpetuate the idolatry, the immorality, the drunkenness, and the indifference of a people who had been so richly blessed. Amos knew the history of his nation. He knew the nature of his God and that judgment would come.

Perhaps one night while guarding his sheep Amos heard a lion roar as it pounced upon its prey. This became the occasion, or the vehicle, that convinced him that the God of justice was going to come in destruction upon the nation of Israel (Amos 3:8).

Conclusion

The Lord has always revealed his secrets unto his servants the prophets, and he has always warned his people before bringing destruction upon them. There have been times when repentance has averted disaster.

Have you heard the lion roar? Does God have a message of either warning or invitation that he wants you to communicate to someone? The New Testament teaches that all of God's children are to be God's servants. The Spirit of God has been poured out upon all.

God wants us to communicate his offer of forgiveness to sinners. He wants to use us to offer grace and salvation to those who are willing to trust his Son, Jesus Christ. Through us God wants to warn the unbelieving concerning the emptiness of life in the here and now and the awful consequences of an eternity without God. We must not be silent when God wants us to speak. "The lion hath roared, who will not fear? The LORD God hath spoken, who can but prophesy?" (Amos 3:8).

119

APRIL

■ **Sunday Mornings**

Continue with the theme "The Christ Who Confronts Us."

■ **Sunday Evenings**

Continue the series "Pictures of Jesus in the Gospel of John."

■ **Wednesday Evenings**

Continue the series "The Call of God and Our Response."

SUNDAY MORNING, APRIL 4

Title: Christ Is Risen

Text: "Christ has indeed been raised from the dead, the firstfruits of those who have fallen asleep" (**1 Cor. 15:20 NIV**).

Scripture Reading: 1 Corinthians 15:1–7

Hymns: "Hallelujah! Christ Is Risen," Wordsworth

"Christ the Lord Is Risen Today," Wesley

"He Lives," Ackley

Offertory Prayer: Holy heavenly Father, on this Easter morning we are reminded most forcefully of the greatness and generosity of your gifts to us through Jesus Christ your Son and our Savior. We thank you for the assurance that you have given us eternal life. We thank you for the companionship of this living Lord along the road of life. We thank you for the confidence that we have that death is a defeated foe and that heaven will be our home through Jesus Christ. Receive our tithes and offerings and bless them to the end that all people everywhere might hear the good news of your love, for in Jesus' name we pray. Amen.

Introduction

Easter Sunday is the most significant of all religious holidays—the day of days for Christians. On Easter Sunday many turn aside from their regular routine to attend a worship service. Why is this so? Why is it that many churches must have an extra worship service on Easter Sunday morning to accommodate the crowds that come?

Large crowds attend worship services on Easter because the resurrection of Jesus Christ is the ground of our salvation from sin and of our hope of victory over death. The resurrection of Jesus Christ is the guarantee of the final triumph of

God's kingdom on earth. Depression and despair would capture the citadel of the soul if there were no basis for hope for a better world. Henry H. Barstow tried to express it in his poem "If Easter Be Not True."

> *If Easter be not true,*
> *Then all the lilies low must lie;*
> *The Flanders poppies fade and die;*
> *The spring must lose her fairest bloom,*
> *For Christ were still within the tomb —*
> *If Easter be not true.*
> *If Easter be not true,*
> *Then faith must mount on broken wing;*
> *Then hope no more immortal spring;*
> *Then love must lose her mighty urge;*
> *Love prove a phantom, death a dirge —*
> *If Easter be not true.*
> *If Easter be not true,*
> *'Twere foolishness the cross to bear;*
> *He died in vain who suffered there;*
> *What matter though we laugh or cry,*
> *Be good or evil, live or die,*
> *If Easter be not true?*
> *If Easter be not true —*
> *But it is true, and Christ is risen!*
> *And mortal spirit from its prison*
> *Of sin and death with him may rise!*
> *Worthwhile the struggle, sure the prize,*
> *Since Easter, aye, is true!*

By many infallible proofs our Lord gave evidence of the fact that he had conquered death and the grave and that he was alive forevermore (Acts 1:3–4).

The resurrection of Jesus Christ had great significance for Christ himself, for his disciples, and for those of us who live today.

I. The significance of the resurrection for Christ himself.

    A. *The resurrection of Christ was a divine declaration concerning his unique sonship (Rom. 1:4).* On several different occasions our Lord assumed and claimed a unique relationship with God. He claimed to be the Son of God. He refused to deny that he was the Son of God when others declared him to be. It was the resurrection that provided the convincing evidence that indicated that he was indeed the God-man.

    B. *The resurrection of Christ lifted him to a position of unquestioned lordship in the eyes of his disciples (Acts 2:22–24, 36).*

    C. *The resurrection of Christ revealed him to be our eternal Judge (Acts 17:30–31).*

    D. *The resurrection of Christ affirmed that he is an all-sufficient Savior (Heb. 7:25).*

1. Christ came to save us from all past sin.
2. Christ came to save us from the power of sin in the present.
3. Christ lives in order to save us from the presence of sin in the future.

II. The significance of the resurrection for the disciples of our Lord.

The resurrection of Christ produced a transforming effect in the lives of his disciples. They had fled in fright and despair when he was seized, condemned, and crucified. Then they were shocked and surprised to learn that he had risen from the dead. Only after many proofs had been provided were they able to accept the reality of his resurrection.

A. *They came to understand his death in terms of an expression of God's great love for sinners.* At first they had seen it as only an indescribable tragedy, as a supreme political disappointment, and as the greatest sorrow of their lifetime. Because he met with them again and again and explained portions of the Old Testament that they had overlooked, they came to understand that in his death he was dealing with the penalty of their sin and expressing God's compassionate desire to deliver them from the tyranny of sin.

B. *By his resurrection, Christ gave his disciples the assurance of his continuing companionship.* He promised to bless them with his abiding presence and to go with them in all of their ways as they sought to carry out his command. As they shared their understanding of what God had done on Calvary and in the empty tomb, they discovered that he was as near to them as their breath and that his power rested on them and worked through them.

C. *They came to understand that death had been defeated and that immortality was a reality.* For them death had been a robber, an enemy, a despoiler of human hope and love. Death was the grim reaper that conquered the great, the strong, the wise, and the wealthy as well as the holy and the good. It was that grim reality that brought fear to the heart of even the strongest.

D. *By his resurrection from the dead, our Lord demonstrated that death was a defeated foe.*

E. *These great truths gripped the minds and captured the hearts of disciples of our Lord and thrust them out into a world with an enthusiasm that could be stopped only by death.*

III. The significance of the resurrection for the present.

A. *By raising Jesus Christ from the dead, God speaks to us today concerning the fact that people need not be alienated and estranged from Himself.* By his death, Jesus Christ suffered the penalty of the sin that separates people from God. Through faith in what Christ did on the cross and in the tomb, people can receive the remission of sins and the gift of eternal life.

B. *By raising Christ from the dead, God spoke concerning his desire for fellowship and friendship with people.* Christ came and lived and died as a substitute for the penalty of our sin, which is death. He conquered death and the grave in order to reveal to us that God's plan for us is life and not death. God's desire for us is fellowship and friendship, not alienation and estrangement.

C. *By raising Christ from the dead, God demonstrated the ultimate victory of good over evil.* Humans may crucify goodness on Friday, but God will raise up goodwill on Sunday.

D. *By raising Christ from the dead, God would assure us that we can trust him completely.* All of us desire to walk by sight. We would like to know what the future holds. We try to foresee how everything will turn out, but that is not always possible. This is true particularly when we give ourselves unreservedly in obedience to the commandments of God, which at the moment seem to be both unpleasant and unprofitable. On that black Friday, often called Good Friday, there was every appearance that the cause of Christ had entered into bankruptcy. His enemies were delighted. His friends were filled with utter despair. It seemed that Christ had gone down in complete defeat. The truth was that he had given himself completely by faith to the purpose of God. The triumphant resurrection would speak to each of us and encourage us to believe that God never disappoints those who give themselves completely to his purpose.

Conclusion

The Christ who conquered death and who is alive forevermore is present with us today. He is eager to replace the spiritual death in the hearts of people with spiritual life. He is capable of replacing fear with faith. He can displace grief with joy if a person is willing to respond to him in the faith that commits all to him. He loved you to the extent that he died for you. He is divine to the extent that he has conquered death and has walked through the corridors of time to this good day. B. B. McKinney speaks poetically and wisely to each of us:

> *Have you failed in your plan of your storm-tossed life?*
> *Place your hand in the nail-scarred hand.*
> *Are you weary and worn from its toil and strife?*
> *Place your hand in the nail-scarred hand.*
> *Place your hand in the nail-scarred hand;*
> *He will keep to the end; He's your dearest friend.*
> *Place your hand in the nail-scarred hand.*

SUNDAY EVENING, APRIL 4

Title: Jesus, the Source and Sustenance of Life

Text: "And Jesus said unto them, I am the bread of life: he that cometh to me shall never hunger; and he that believeth on me shall never thirst" (**John 6:35**).

Scripture Reading: John 6:22–40

Introduction

The feeding of the five thousand is recorded by all four of the gospel writers. The Synoptics refer to the miracle as an act of power, but John calls it a sign and gives the meaning of it. Apart from the gospel of John, it would be difficult to grasp the meaning of the miracle.

The site for the feeding of the five thousand was near the Sea of Galilee, close to Tiberias, the eastern side of the sea. The time was the Passover — spring. People were traveling toward Jerusalem in great numbers. Most of the Jews traveled the eastern side of Galilee on down through Perea to avoid crossing the territory of the despised Samaritans. A large crowd was following Jesus because they had seen the miracles that he performed for those who were sick. The people crowded Jesus so that he walked up the mountainside and sat down with his disciples.

The meaning of the Passover was important. A lamb was slain and eaten in remembrance of the night the death angel had passed over Egypt, slaying the firstborn of those who did not have their door frames marked with the blood of a lamb. The Lord had then led the Israelites out of Egypt. It is significant that they "ate of the lamb."

A great crowd of people drew near to Jesus, and he had compassion on them for they were as sheep without a shepherd. After speaking to them at length, Jesus turned to Philip and asked him where they were going to get bread to feed so many. There were five thousand men besides the women and children. This was to test Philip, for Jesus knew what he was going to do. He planned this miracle to teach them. Philip was a good mathematician. He quickly figured the amount needed — two hundred denarii (a denarius was a day's wage). If labor was five dollars per day, it would take a thousand dollars to buy the food.

I. The feeding of the five thousand.

    A. *Jesus had the multitude sit down in groups of fifty.* He arranged the people in an orderly manner so that it would be easier to serve them.

    B. *The disciples were passing up and down the aisles.* There were twelve disciples, twelve baskets, and twelve baskets of fragments left. Jesus was not wasteful. There was an inexhaustible supply from the five loaves and two fish.

II. The effect on the crowd.

    A. *When the people saw the miracle, they said, "This is truly the one we have been looking for."* He was the new Moses, who had come to lead them into the "promised land."

    B. *Then the people connected the new Moses with the Messiah.* That was their first reaction. The crowds were on their way to celebrate the Passover, the commemoration of the Israelites' exodus from Egypt.

    C. *Jesus perceived this crowd's intention.* He knew they were planning to make a concerted effort to make him King. It seemed to them that this was the right time. More crowds would be gathered at the feast than at any other time, and what more appropriate time was needed than for the Messiah King to set up his kingdom than at the great feast?

D. *The thing that Jesus had done declared to them that he had all power.* They could surely overcome all of their enemies. Jesus could heal any who got sick, he could restore life to any who may die, and he could provide at any time and in any place all the food and supplies necessary. No enemy could whip them! Victory was certain!

E. *The disciples were needling the crowd, saying, "Don't let him refuse."* This is the greatest day Israel ever saw. The excitement was intense! Judas could visualize himself as the secretary of the treasury, and Peter could see himself as secretary of state, and the other ten would have important jobs in this material, invincible kingdom!

III. The reaction of Jesus.

When Jesus saw the attitude and determination of the crowd, he knew that something must be done.

A. *Mark 6:45 tells us that Jesus had to compel the disciples to get into the boat.* He could not send the crowd away until the disciples were gone. Jesus was the Messiah but not the kind they expected.

It was only six or eight miles across the lake, and the time was about sundown when they got into their boat. They could have made it easily in about two hours, or 8:00. But in the fourth watch of the night, that is, 3:00 to 6:00 in the morning, they were still out there. A storm arose, and they tried to beat it.

B. *Jesus went into a nearby mountain to pray.* It is not the easiest thing to crush the fondest hopes of a crowd that wants a leader nor of the leader himself. Jesus had crushed those temptations once before when the devil led him to a high place on the mountain and offered him the kingdoms of the world. The disciples were now being used by Satan to tempt Jesus in the same way. That is why he went to the mount to pray. He was in the mount praying, and the disciples were in the boat fussing and fuming. When the storm arose, they settled down to business and tried to reach land. Jesus came walking on the water to them, but they did not recognize him until he identified himself. When Jesus entered the boat, "immediately they reached land" (John 6:21).

IV. The explanation of the sign.

A. *Verses 25–40 give us the explanation of the sign.* The crowd had seen the disciples leave, and there had been only one boat. But Jesus had not gotten into it, so they waited for him. Then they realized that he was gone, so they came around to the other side of Galilee and found him and his disciples.

B. *These people questioned Jesus, "Rabbi, how did you get here?"* He did not answer their question, for he knew what was behind it. Instead, he said, "Ye seek me, not because ye saw the miracles, but because ye did eat of the loaves, and were filled" (John 6:26). They saw that he had power to create bread, that he could do wonders, but they saw no meaning. He sustained the people physically, but they had no spiritual response.

C. *Jesus was leading up to the real interpretation.* Authority has been given to the Son to give the bread of eternal life. The disciples were in a real quandary, for they had not seen the sign's real meaning. Jesus told them that they could not believe God unless they believed his representative. Again they asked for a sign. They intimated that they wanted him to go on feeding them. They were hungry again. They referred to Moses, who fed the people from day to day. If Jesus did this, he would fulfill their ideas of the Messiah.

D. *Jesus told the people that Moses did not give the manna; God did.* And moreover, that manna was not the true bread. The true bread of God comes from heaven and gives eternal life to the world. The manna and quail would spoil, but not the true bread. It was only a symbol. They asked Jesus to give them this bread. "Give it to us for all time!" they said.

E. *Now we have the climax!* "I am the bread of life: he that cometh to me shall never hunger; and he that believeth on me shall never thirst." Jesus continued, "But I said unto you, That ye also have seen me, and believe not. All that the Father giveth me shall come to me; and him that cometh to me I will in no wise cast out. For I came down from heaven, not to do mine own will, but the will of him that sent me."

F. *Here we have the coming of God and of men.* We have to meet God's coming down. If we come to him, he does not cast us out but gives us eternal life.

V. The application of the sign.

A. *Verses 41–59 give the application of the sign.* The people still think in terms of the physical. Jesus continues to try to help them understand. He tells them that they are to "quit troubling." No one can come except the Father draw him. Jesus reminded the people that their fathers had eaten manna and died. The manna had nothing to do with the spiritual life; it sustained the physical. He said that he is the Living Bread who is capable of giving life (John 6:43–51).

B. *How could the people eat his flesh?* They dropped back to thinking about the physical, but Jesus told them that his life is the blood and flesh. The emphasis is on eating and drinking, which is a complete appropriation of life. Otherwise no life is possible. The one who will give his life will be raised up on the last day. He uses the analogy of the physical to get them to see the spiritual. Jesus lives because of the Father, and those accepting him shall live because of him. Jesus is the source and sustenance of life.

C. *Even the disciples said, "This is an hard saying; who can hear it?"* (John 6:60). What was hard? That Jesus had to give his life as the Lamb of God. They did not like it, for how could he be their earthly king if he was going to die?

Conclusion

Many of the crowd now left and "walked no more with [Jesus]" (John 6:66). He had reached the climax of his ministry. Jesus sensed the disciples wavering and said in effect, "Don't let this cause you to stumble. You cannot live unless I give up my life. A grain of wheat must die before it can bring forth new fruit." Jesus was hurt to think that so many were falling away. He said to his disciples, "Will ye also go away?" Peter answered for them, "Lord, to whom shall we go? thou hast the words of eternal life" (John 6:68).

Make Peter's words the words of your heart, and you, too, shall receive eternal life.

WEDNESDAY EVENING, APRIL 7

Title: The Call of Hosea

Text: "The beginning of the word of the LORD by Hosea. And the LORD said to Hosea, Go, take unto thee a wife of whoredoms and the children of whoredoms: for the land hath committed great whoredom, departing from the LORD" (**Hos. 1:2**).

Scripture Reading: Hosea 1

Introduction

The prophets' experience with God was always intensely personal, for they were very God-conscious. Out of a deeply personal experience with God, Hosea was granted insight into the spiritual need of his generation and was given a message for them.

Hosea was the prophet of the decline and fall of the northern kingdom. He ministered in a day of prosperity and power. Nominally the people paid homage to the God of Israel; in reality they worshiped the Baalim of the Canaanite religion. It was a time of moral degeneracy and spiritual adultery. Flagrant immorality, irreverence for the sacred, unfaithfulness, thievery, murder, and drunkenness were the order of the day.

Hosea was a younger contemporary of Amos. The conditions that Amos had described had only grown worse. It is possible that Hosea had heard Amos preach.

I. Fact or parable?

Hosea 1–3 has been exposed to a wide variety of interpretations. Some take the passage to be simply a literary device to illustrate a great truth. These interpreters consider Hosea 1–3 to be nothing more than a parable.

Most scholars believe that it is a description of the actual experience of Hosea. To the young man there came an impulse, which was later interpreted as the voice of God, to "Go, take unto thee a wife of whoredoms; and children of whoredom." To this command Hosea was obedient.

Most likely Hosea felt deeply compelled to marry a woman who was given to idolatry—an idolatry that was often associated with licentiousness. At first she was probably unchaste only in a spiritual sense. She bore her husband three children to whom symbolic names were given. Eventually idolatry brought forth its natural fruitage, and Hosea's wife became an unchaste woman in a real way. Whether she then deserted her husband or was divorced by him is not definitely stated in the record. At any rate, in obedience to the divine command, Hosea recovered his unfaithful wife and restored her to his home (Hos. 3:1–3).

II. The moment of the call.

Was Hosea's call to be a prophet simultaneous with the impulse to marry? Hosea 1:2, by itself, would certainly leave that impression. It is not necessary for us to believe that Hosea understood all of the implications of his marriage from the first. Hosea's taking Gomer as his wife was probably due to his own natural impulse. It was not until much later that he concluded that this impulse had been prompted by God. He later learned that this was the first step in his prophetic career. It was by a very painful discipline that he was prepared to be God's spokesman to a nation that was guilty of spiritual adultery.

Hosea continued with his prophetic career and gave symbolic names to each of the three children Gomer bore. The first was named Jezreel, symbolizing the overthrow of the dynasty of Jehu. The second was named Lo-ruhamah, indicating that God would have no mercy upon Israel. The third was named Lo-ammi, symbolizing the utter destruction of Israel. These names have prophetic significance for conditions existing in Israel as Hosea saw them.

III. A sad awakening.

As time went by, Hosea began to notice things that caused him to wonder and worry about Gomer. He had known from the first that she had tendencies toward idolatry (Hos. 1:2). Perhaps Hosea had hoped to win Gomer to the acceptance of the higher ethical religion of Israel. Before too long, Hosea realized that his effort was resulting in failure. We are probably safe in assuming that Hosea recognized that Gomer's second and third children were not his. This is implied in the phraseology of the story and even more clearly in the names that were given to them. Lo-ruhamah literally means "she that never knew a father's love." She was an orphan, not by death, but by her mother's sin. Lo-ammi literally means "no kin of mine."

The record does not describe the moment of Gomer's departure from the household of Hosea. It is impossible to know whether Hosea cast her out or whether she departed on her own accord. Most likely she became a sacred prostitute in one of the temples of Baal (Hos. 2:2, 7–13).

IV. The dawning of spiritual insight.

It is impossible for us to imagine the grief, disappointment, and shame that Hosea must have experienced during those days when the wife of his youth was "beloved of her friends."

It was while Hosea was groping for a solution to his problems that insight into the whole affair began to dawn upon his consciousness. He began to see that his experience with Gomer was but a picture of what had been happening between God and Israel for a long time. God had taken the initiative in establishing a union with Israel. He had delivered them out of Egypt. He had led them into the land that he had designated to be their own. God had shown the tenderest love for Israel, and he had expected a pure and undivided affection from them in return. Israel had been unfaithful to her Maker and spiritual husband and had sought other lovers and found them worshiping the Baalim. God had been forsaken by the people upon whom he had showered the abundance of his divine love.

As to whether Hosea continued to love the unfaithful Gomer and reasoned from this that God must still love Israel, or whether he recognized the persistent love of the Lord for adulterous Israel and reasoned that he should continue to love Gomer, one cannot be dogmatic. There is probably an element of truth in each of these alternatives. We can be sure that Hosea's private pain preceded his sympathy with God's pain. He learned of God's sorrow in his own sorrow. He learned to forgive and to redeem his wife only by hearing God forgive and redeem his people.

Conclusion

The command of Hosea 3:1 cannot be interpreted as something that was contrary to the wishes of Hosea. He went and bought Gomer because he wanted to deliver her from her shameful career. Because of his love for her, even though she was faithless, he purchased her at the price of a slave out of the depths of infamy into which she had fallen.

Hosea did not restore Gomer to her former position at once. Discipline was necessary for Gomer as well as for Israel (Hos. 3:3–4). The account is silent concerning what finally happened between Hosea and Gomer.

In the first three chapters of the book of Hosea, we find the veil lifted from the private life of a prophet just enough to reveal how Hosea came to his understanding of the suffering of the love of God. His power was in his wound. Because he suffered, he was equipped to preach of the suffering love of God.

SUNDAY MORNING, APRIL 11

Title: Christ Dwelling in the Heart

Text: "That Christ may dwell in your hearts by faith ..." (**Eph. 3:17**).

Scripture Reading: Ephesians 3:14–21

Hymns: "Jesus Saviour, Pilot Me," Hopper

        "Let Others See Jesus in You," McKinney

        "Let Him In," Atchinson

Offertory Prayer: Dear heavenly Father, you have blessed us in a lavish manner through Jesus Christ, your Son. You have given heaven's best to us and for us. No good thing have you withheld from us. We thank you for the privilege of being the channel through which your mercy and grace can flow into the hearts and lives of others. We come today bringing our tithes and offerings as symbols of our gratitude and as indications of our desire to make possible the proclamation of your grace to the entire world. Bless these gifts to ministries of mercy in and through the church and to the preaching of the gospel to the ends of the earth. In the name of our Lord we pray. Amen.

Introduction

Is Jesus Christ, the living Lord, real to you? Or is he a vague memory, a blur, a mere historical figure who walks through the pages of ancient history?

It is the witness of the New Testament, and it was the experience of the apostles, that Jesus Christ conquered death and made himself real to those who had faith. And it is through faith in the witness of the Holy Scriptures and in the testimony of those who have gone before us that we are able to experience his living presence in our hearts. By faith we open the door of our life to receive Christ as Savior and Lord and Friend. By faith we let him live in our hearts day by day and year by year.

Evidently the Laodicean church did not develop and cultivate their faith in the living presence of Jesus Christ, for it was to this church, and perhaps to the other six churches to which letters were addressed, that our Lord said, "Behold, I stand at the door, and knock: if any man hear my voice, and open the door, I will come in to him, and will sup with him, and he with me" (Rev. 3:20). When Christ is permitted to dwell in the heart, he produces some radical changes in our attitudes and actions. Zacchaeus is a case in point (Luke 19:1–10). He decided to let Jesus Christ come into his home. After the visit with Christ, Zacchaeus decided to let Christ come into his heart. This decision led to a tremendous change in his relationship to God, in his attitude toward others, and in his evaluation of things. Because he let Christ come into his heart, there was a change in his bank account, in his business affairs, and in his relationships with other people. He suddenly became very generous and was eager to make restitution for past wrongs.

The world will sit up and take notice when we let Christ dwell in our hearts, for he always produces a change when he is permitted to dwell there. The only assurance that we can have that he is in our hearts is to be able to see the transforming effects of his presence. Let us consider some of the changes that he seeks to bring about in those who permit him to dwell in their hearts.

I. Christ fills the heart with a new joy.

A. *The joy of forgiveness.* Jesus came to give his life as a ransom for many. He came to take our sins away on the cross. It is through faith in him that we receive the glad consciousness of forgiven sin (Acts 10:43).

B. *The joy of divine sonship.* Jesus came into the world that we might become the sons of God (John 1:11–12). John the apostle was amazed by the privilege of divine sonship (1 John 3:1–2).

C. *The joy of a continuing friendship.* Among the greatest joys that a person can experience is the joy of true friendship. The most wonderful Friend anyone can have is Jesus. "Ye are my friends, if ye do whatsoever I command you. Henceforth I call you not servants; for the servant knoweth not what his lord doeth: but I have called you friends; for all things that I have heard of my Father I have made known unto you" (John 15:14–15). This is an ever-enriching and transforming friendship.

II. Christ provides a new basis for security.

A. *Do you get your security from others?* Are you dependent on the people you know for security in financial relationships or job opportunities?

B. *Do you depend on yourself for security?* Self-confidence is a wonderful possession. One needs to be confident, not only in his vocation but also in relating properly to other people.

C. *Do you find your basis for security in the material things that you have been able to acquire?* It is a good thing to be successful in the business world, but there comes a time when material things cannot provide much security.

The only real security that we can have is that which comes to us through faith in the love, mercy, grace, and power of God. It is through Jesus Christ that we enter into this knowledge and experience of the security that can come only from God.

III. Christ would communicate to us a true estimation of our personal worth.

We live in a day in which human life is not considered very valuable in some parts of the world. There are times when each of us feels our insignificance as we recognize that we are but a very small part of a great nation. It is easy for a person to become depressed and to feel insignificant as he or she contemplates the immensity of the universe and the billions that make up the world's population.

A. *How do you arrive at an estimate of your personal worth?* Do you arrive at it by means of the salary you earn? Do you base your sense of personal worth on your savings and investments? Do you measure your significance in terms of the home in which you live and the automobile you drive?

B. *Each of us needs to face up to the fact that God considered us to be of infinite value to the extent that he was willing to give his Son Jesus Christ to die for us on the cross.* While others may consider us to be of very little value, the Bible tells us that God looks upon each of us as being of infinite value.

C. *When you are tempted to be depressed, stop for a moment and contemplate how love for you caused Jesus Christ to be willing to die on the cross for you.* Instead of thinking only in terms of the masses, let us remember that Jesus Christ loves each of us personally.

IV. Christ would deliver us from the folly of living in either the past or the future.

By faith we are to let Christ dwell in our hearts day by day.

A. *Yesterday is in the tomb.* The living Christ in our hearts would lead us out of yesterday. He would encourage us to cease looking to the past.

B. *Tomorrow is in the womb.* While tomorrow is important, it is still but a dream. He who waits until tomorrow is a procrastinator.

C. *Today is the only sure thing we have.* An awareness of the presence of the living Christ in our hearts would cause us to fully seize the opportunities and respond to the responsibilities of the present.

Too many of us live in either the past or the future. We need to come to grips with the present. The living Christ would impress upon us the supreme value of today.

V. Christ would encourage us to express Christian love spontaneously because he is the love of God in action.

Christ releases the love of God in the hearts of those who permit him to dwell there. He makes us capable of having a persistent unbreakable spirit of goodwill toward the unlovely as well as toward those who are lovable.

A. *Because Christ is God's love, he would use you as the channel through which that love can bless and lift the lives of others.*

B. *To let Christ truly dwell in your heart is to let God bless others through you.* When Christ dwells in our hearts, we see with the eyes of Christ, and we feel with the heart of Christ. Our feet carry us on missions of mercy in the name of Christ, and our hands perform the tasks that Christ would perform.

Christ does not come into our hearts merely to make us feel good and to give us a ticket to heaven. He comes into our hearts to use us for the glory of God and for the loving and lifting of a needy world to God.

Conclusion

With all of his heart, Jesus believed that it was more blessed to give than to receive. He lived to be a giver of life, light, hope, and love. He lived to give courage, strength, and energy to others. If you let him dwell in your heart by faith, you can be assured that through you he will continue his mission of redemption and mercy in the world today.

Decide now to let Jesus come into your heart, and decide also to give him the master key that will permit him to dwell in every area of your being. Let him transform your thoughts and attitudes. Let him give you direction concerning your ambitions and goals. Let the Lord of love be the Lord of your life.

SUNDAY EVENING, APRIL 11

Title: Jesus, the Light of the World

Text: "Then spake Jesus again unto them, saying, I am the light of the world: he that followeth me shall not walk in darkness, but shall have the light of life" (**John 8:12**).

Introduction

Jesus spoke these words in the temple at Jerusalem during the time of the Feast of Tabernacles when the temple court was crowded with people. The Feast of Tabernacles was to commemorate a chapter in the life of the Hebrew nation when the Israelites wandered for forty years in the wilderness. It was held at the close of the harvest season, and people from everywhere came to Jerusalem and made little booths to live in that week, recalling the lifestyle their fathers had lived in the Arabian desert.

Two characteristic features of the feast were:

1. Each morning water was brought in a golden vessel from the pool of Siloam and poured upon the altar of sacrifice. The water recalled to the people the supply drawn from the rock at Meribah and pointed forward to the spiritual water that men would draw "out of the wells of salvation."
2. In the evening there were in one of the courts of the temple two great lamps that are said to have cast their light over every quarter of the holy city. These recalled the pillar of fire that had guided the Israelites in the wilderness, and they pointed to the "Son of righteousness" who would arise with "healing in his wings." On such an occasion, and with sacred memories in the hearts of all the Jews, Jesus declared to them that he is the "light of the world" (John 8:12).

I. The facts of the sign.

John 9 points out the sign. Jesus gave a man born blind physical sight to point out the spiritual truth that he was and is the Light of the World. It is a familiar story.

A. *The man was born blind.* The disciples thought the man's blindness was caused from sin. Jesus explained that God's work was about to be shown because of this man. Again Jesus explained that he is the Light of the World and proceeded to give a demonstration. He spat on the ground and began to make some mud. He applied the mud to the man's eyes. When the man went and washed the mud from his eyes, he could see clearly. Whenever we wash the mud and filth from our eyes, we, too, can see more clearly. It is difficult to see the finer things in life as long as we look at the worldly.

B. *This miracle caused an uproar among the religious leaders.* They could hardly believe that the man now walking around was the one who had been blind.

They asked him about it, and he said, "A man that is called Jesus made clay, and anointed mine eyes, and said unto me, Go to the pool of Siloam, and wash: and I went and washed, and I received sight" (John 9:11).

C. *The man born blind was called before the Sanhedrin to give an account of what had happened.* They warned him that he had not been cured by God and asked him to deny the miracle, but the man could not deny it. He spoke from experience: "One thing I know, that, whereas I was blind, now I see" (John 9:25). The man's logic was too powerful for them, so they took the defeatest attitude and chased him out of the temple. Jesus found the man and asked him if he believed in the Son of God. The man did not know him and asked who he was. Jesus then revealed himself to him, and the man believed and worshiped Jesus as the Light of his spiritual life also.

II. Jesus, the Light of the World.

A. *These words of Jesus send us instantly abroad into the world of nature.* They set us on the hilltop watching the sunrise as it fills the east with glory. They show us the great flooded plains in the noonday sun. They hush and elevate us with the mystery and sweetness of the evening's glow.

B. *But Jesus' words go back to the pillar of fire that led the Hebrews through the wilderness, the light that assured them of God's presence.* Now Jesus is that Light and is in their midst. The guidance of that light was uninterrupted and unerring; it was never mistaken for an ordinary cloud, it never so altered its shape as to become unrecognizable. And each night the flame shot up and assured the people that they might rest in peace.

C. *There are two things that light does, and it seems that Jesus had both in mind.*

1. It enables people to see. The man born blind could see with the light Jesus gave him. Enter a dark room and you see nothing; switch on the light and you see everything in the room.

2. Light also guides us. The lights at the harbor's mouth are there to guide ships. The same is true of the lights at the airport and on your car. Christ is the Light of the World, for he enables people to see what is in the world—and because he is Light, he guides people through the world. Jesus also said that his followers are "lights." This means that Christ in us lights us up, and we are to help people to see and also offer them guidance.

III. Jesus enables people to see God.

A. *For centuries people had groped in the darkness in a vain attempt to find God.* Outside of Jesus, the picture of God had taken many forms and shapes. Very few had thought of God as having a capacity for loving his own. But God revealed himself to the Hebrews, and they came to know him as the loving God of Abraham, Isaac, and Jacob; as the covenant God who had led their fathers by the way of the wilderness into the Promised Land; as a "jealous God, visiting the iniquity of the fathers upon their children unto the third and fourth generation" (Ex. 20:5); and also as the "LORD God, merciful and gracious, longsuffering, and abundant in goodness and truth, keeping mercy for thousands, forgiving iniquity" (Ex. 34:6–7).

B. *The sublime conception of the Hebrew mind was perfected in Christ.* Every attribute of spiritual excellence was brought out into clearer distinction, and every element was enlarged and purified.

C. *Jesus did not say, "I bring light and truth," but "I am Light; I am Truth."* He is the Light of the World because in him is the glory of God. "The Father and I are one." In him dwelleth the "fulness of the Godhead bodily."

IV. Christ has made clear not only the idea of God but also of humans.

A. *Humans are different from other creatures in that they are moral beings.* They have relationships beyond nature and have wants and aspirations that connect them to the divine Ruler. Humans were the object of Christ's coming. Christ is the object of humankind's searching: "Is not life more than meat, and the body than raiment?" "Seek ye first the kingdom" (Matt. 6:25, 33).

B. *God has made humans in his own image and loves them no matter how they may have degraded that image and wandered away from divine good.* He claims people as his own—"Christ came to seek and to save that which was lost" (Luke 19:10).

C. Since Jesus has shown us what God is and what we ought to be, he has illuminated the profound abyss that separates people from God. He shows us how to span this abyss, "for God so loved the world" (John 3:16).

V. As the Light, Christ guides people.

A. "He that followeth me shall not walk in darkness" (John 8:12). As the pillar of cloud lighted the way for the Israelites, so Jesus lights our way. Whenever the people moved, the cloud moved; when they stopped, the cloud stopped.

B. Jesus promises us that if we walk with him we will not walk in the darkness. Many difficulties are cleared out of a person's road by the simple act of trying to follow Christ. Many are removed that we do not even know about.

C. Darkness is the scriptural term for the condition of the soul away from God. Our Lord declares that to accept him as the Light would mean that the darkness of sin would be driven out. Light drives the darkness back. There is darkness of ignorance, of impurity, and of sorrow. From this threefold gloom, thickening to a darkness of death, those who follow Christ find deliverance.

D. Not only is the promise made that we shall be led into the Light, but that we shall have that Light and become lights ourselves. Christ is our guiding Light even unto death.

Conclusion

Christ as the Light guides his followers to another and better life. Each of us can and must decide to trust and follow him. Come, repent of your sins, and by faith accept Jesus, the Light of the World, as your Light.

WEDNESDAY EVENING, APRIL 14

Title: The Call of Isaiah

Text: "Also I heard the voice of the Lord, saying, Whom shall I send, and who will go for us? Then said I, Here am I; send me" **(Isa. 6:8).**

Scripture Reading: Isaiah 6:1 – 13

Introduction

The prophets were men whom God raised up to meet a crisis in the life of Israel, and in that crisis God revealed much of his will to his messengers.

It was in a time of great crisis for Israel that God called Isaiah into the prophetic ministry. "In the year that king Uzziah died, I saw the Lord" is more than just a date in Hebrew history. It marks the spiritual birthday of one of Israel's greatest prophets.

I. Isaiah's background.

Little is known of Isaiah's early life. His name means "salvation of God." Isaiah was born around 760 BC, about the time that Amos appeared at Bethel. His father, Amoz, according to Jewish tradition, was a brother of Amaziah, king of Judah. If this tradition is true, Isaiah would have been Uzziah's cousin. Isaiah's familiarity with the successive monarchs of Judah has encouraged the belief that he was of royal descent. One can easily gather from the reading of his prophecies that he was of high social rank.

II. The time of Isaiah's call.

Isaiah's call to the prophetic ministry came in the year of King Uzziah's death. According to the best authorities, this was 740 BC. The condition of Judah was not unlike that of Israel in the north. While Jeroboam had been extending the power of the northern kingdom, Uzziah had been strengthening the kingdom of Judah.

It was a time of great postwar prosperity (2 Chron. 26:10, 15). Every type of social, moral, and spiritual degeneracy was evident in every bracket of public life. The noble were leaders in doing evil. Widows and orphans were oppressed. Land grabbing was the order of the day. The love of wealth and wine caused the people to degenerate. They became callous in worship and careless in life.

King Uzziah was not content with regal power. He snatched also at sacerdotal power. He wanted to be like the kings of other nations who served as priests in their pagan religions.

Second Chronicles 26:16 – 23 reveals how the priests protested Uzziah's act of impiety. They boldly withstood him. Their rebuke provoked his anger. While the red flush of anger was still burning on his brow, there appeared in it the white spot of a mortal leprosy. Thus he was smitten with leprosy by a holy God as a punishment for his lack of reverence and his flagrant act of compromise and disobedience. His fate was to live in isolation until his death. Jotham, his son, was to rule over his house.

136

How long it was before death ended the monarch's suffering the record nowhere states. Some have supposed that Isaiah, a young noble of Jerusalem, had been a hero worshiper during his youth. The object of his adoration was none other than the proud king of Judah. Perhaps he wondered why this terrible calamity had befallen the mighty king. As he mulled over this question, he came to a partial understanding of the seriousness of Uzziah's offense. He observed that the king had grown proud and self-sufficient. His success encouraged him to want to be like other kings. Isaiah probably observed that the king's "easy familiarity" with God was the besetting sin of the nation.

III. The temple vision.

Isaiah entered the temple with a sense of fear and uncertainty concerning the future. His mind was disturbed, and he was searching for certainty when he had an unusual experience in the temple.

A. *Isaiah had a vision of God.* In dramatic language, Isaiah relates how his inward eye was opened and he beheld God in all of his holiness and majesty (Isa. 6:1–4). The eye of his soul was opened and there dawned before him a splendid vision. With thoughts of a dead king and a vacant throne on his mind, there came to him a revelation of the divine King seated on the throne of the universe. Before his entranced eyes, the earthly priest saw angelic beings hovering about the Lord of the world to do his bidding. The fire of the earthly altar became that of the heavenly altar. There came to his ears the sound of the seraphim's song of adoration and praise of the thrice holy God.

B. *Isaiah's vision of himself and his people.* As this vision of the infinitely holy God presented itself to Isaiah's mind, he was made vividly conscious of his own sinfulness and of that of his people (Isa. 6:5). He was aware of his unfitness to stand in the presence of the thrice holy God. He feared the worst as a result of this personal encounter with God. Had Uzziah not died because of his intruding into the Holy Place?

C. *Isaiah's purification.* Instead of being driven from the presence of God because of his uncleanness, he experienced cleansing and forgiveness (Isa. 6:6–7).

D. *The call and surrender of Isaiah.* Only after Isaiah experienced the assurance of purification did he hear the voice of God calling. His lips having been cleansed, he was now prepared for personal conversation with God. He heard the question of the Lord, "Whom shall I send and who will go for us?" (Isa. 6:8). Mingled trembling and elation filled his soul as a response to this invitation came from his lips. "Here am I; send me" (Isa. 6:8).

Conclusion

There was no effort on the part of Isaiah to escape the call of God. There was no pleading of unsuitability. Isaiah volunteered in response to the divine invitation. The initiative was with God.

This experience was to Isaiah what the divine presence in the burning bush was to Moses. This experience was to him what the vision on the road to Damascus was to Saul of Tarsus. He volunteered to be God's spokesman to his generation.

Instead of waiting to be drafted for some place in the work of God and in service to others, we should be sensitive to hear the voice of God calling us. Some people have to be drafted. Others volunteer. Are you among the volunteers?

SUNDAY MORNING, APRIL 18

Title: How Christian Are You?

Text: "Now when they saw the boldness of Peter and John, and perceived that they were unlearned and ignorant men, they marvelled; and they took knowledge of them, that they had been with Jesus" **(Acts 4:13)**.

Scripture Reading: Acts 4:13–20

Hymns: "Open My Eyes, That I May See," Scott

"More About Jesus," Hewitt

"More Like Jesus Would I Be," Crosby

Offertory Prayer: Great God and Father of our Lord Jesus Christ, open our eyes and help us to see the wonders of your grace toward us. Help us to see the greatness of your all-inclusive love for all people everywhere. Help us to recognize where you are at work in the world, and help us to give ourselves to that work completely. This morning we bring our tithes and offerings as symbols of our desire to be living sacrifices in your service. Help us, as we give our substance, to give ourselves completely unto you in serving others. In Christ's name we pray. Amen.

Introduction

The word *Christianity* has in our day become a fallen term, having lost its original content and import. It now covers a multitude of religious ideas, error as well as truth, paganism as well as the revelation of God.

The term *Christian* covers rationalistic modernism on the one hand and frothy sentimentalism on the other. For some it includes gross worldliness and at the same time pharisaic self-righteousness. To others Christianity is something that is coldly ritualistic, while to others it involves heated emotionalism. Some present a cross without a Christ. Others present a Christ without a cross. The word *Christian* itself must be rescued and its original meaning restored. In the midst of the religious turmoil and confusion of our day, we need to search for and find a genuine Christianity. What is genuine Christianity? To find the answer, we must go back to the original sources. We need to reexamine the New Testament. We need to look again at the lives and activities of the apostles and other early Christians.

Genuine Christianity was not primarily a creed, and certainly it was not a competitive cult. Rather, it was a new way of life centered and built around the person and purpose of a crucified but risen and living Lord. God, in Christ, had revealed his divine concern for the redemption of people from sin. In Christ God had expressed his determination to deliver people from the penalty and power of sin.

The repentance of the disciples of our Lord and the faith that they placed in him produced a tremendous change in their attitudes and ambitions. In derision their enemies called them "Christians" (Acts 11:26). While they were accused of turning the world upside down, actually they were turning the world right side up. This brand of Christianity is the desperate need of the world today, for it alone can produce change in people's lives.

Our world needs desperately to rediscover an appreciation of the spiritual and become aware of the presence and power of God. As people seek to feed their souls upon bread alone, they discover a hunger that becomes more intense as time goes by.

As those who claim to know Christ as Lord and Savior, we need to reexamine the New Testament and evaluate our own faith and witness. What was the source of the spiritual effectiveness of the early disciples? How were they able to accomplish so much? Is it possible for us to experience the same inward transformation?

These early disciples lived Christ-centered lives. They did not turn the world right side up by living pleasure-centered lives. They did not change the course of history because of a passion for gold. They were not responsible for helping divide history into two great eras because of their love for comfort. Because Christ was at the center of their thoughts and activities and because they surrendered themselves to his mission of redeeming people, God could use them and bless them.

Is Christ at the center or on the circumference of your life? Is he a dear friend or a distant stranger? Are you on talking terms with him? Do you have full confidence in him? Are you willing to follow his counsel and take his advice? To what degree do you identify with the passion that brought him from heaven to earth and carried him to the cross?

I. The Christ-centered life is characterized by a glad surrender to the will of God.

A. *The supreme desire of Jesus was to do the will of God.* "My meat is to do the will of him that sent me, and to finish his work" (John 4:34). Jesus defined his mission in terms of the will of God: "I came down from heaven, not to do mine own will, but the will of him that sent me" (John 6:38). Again Jesus said, "I must work the works of him that sent me, while it is day: the night cometh, when no man shall work" (John 9:4). Even as he suffered the agony of Gethsemane, he was completely surrendered to the will of God, which was to involve the cross. He prayed, "Father, if thou be willing, remove this cup from me: nevertheless not my will, but thine, be done" (Luke 22:42).

B. *Many people have a false concept of the will of God.* Some consider it to be that which a cold, harsh fate imposes upon them. Others think of the will of

God only in terms of galling difficulties. Others think of the will of God as an unbearable burden over which they have no choice or control. Perhaps because of the surrender of Christ to God's will that led to the cross, we have come to think of it as something that is always unpleasant.

C. *God's will is always good in the long run.* God is both wise and gracious. His purposes for us and for others are in terms of his love.

Doing God's will may involve suffering and sacrifice. Jesus had faith to look beyond the cross to the joy of bringing the greatest possible glory to God and the greatest possible blessing to people. If you and I would find the highest possible happiness in life, we need to determine that God's will is to be our will always.

II. The Christ-centered life is a life of joyous sacrifice.

A. *There is a joy that can come through sacrifice.* If we would be followers of Jesus Christ, we must be willing to give ourselves to that for which our Savior gave his life. That which was of supreme value to him must become the object of supreme value to us. Mark says concerning him, "For even the Son of Man came not to be ministered unto, but to minister, and to give his life a ransom for many" (Mark 10:45). Christ defined his goal for living in terms of a complete sacrificial giving of himself to meet the deepest needs of others.

B. *The cross cannot be removed from Christianity (Luke 9:23).*

> *Must Jesus bear the cross alone*
> *And all the world go free?*
> *No, there's a cross for every one,*
> *And there's a cross for me.*

Most of us are guilty of searching for a costless religion. We would like very much to have a religion of comfort and convenience. We seem blind to the fact that all things of great significance are purchased through suffering and sacrifice.

If we want to save the world, we must find the cross that God wants us to bear. We must then put our life on the cross and give ourselves completely to bring redemption to those whom God is seeking to reach through us. It is a poor expression of Christianity to give God that portion of life that is left over after we have done that which we selfishly desire to do.

III. The Christ-centered life is a life of loving service.

A. *Christ defined true greatness in terms of service rendered (Mark 10:43–45).* It is said concerning the Christ that he went about doing good. He gave himself utterly and completely in ministries of mercy to those who were suffering. He did not restrict his love to those of his own village, or to his own group. He crossed racial barriers and religious barricades to minister to the outcast and to the unfortunate.

B. *The Holy Spirit would enable us to give of ourselves unselfishly in service to others.* He entered our hearts in the new birth experience. He would overflow our hearts with compassionate concern for the needy, for the troubled, for all of those whom God loves.

C. *God would have us to serve.* Paul wrote to the Ephesians (Eph. 2:10) that God has redeemed and created us anew for the purpose of good works. It is the will of God that each of us be his servants in the matter of redeeming a lost world.

Conclusion

Gratitude requires that each one who is redeemed give himself gladly in ministries to redeem others. The need of a world that is lost from God and from hope demands a radical commitment to obedience and to service on the part of those who know Jesus Christ as Savior. True fulfillment, the abundant life that Christ wishes to bestow, comes only to those who give themselves unreservedly to the cause that brought Christ from heaven to earth. He died that we might live. He calls us to live that others may not die eternally. May God help each of us to really see him and trust him, to the extent that we will forsake all that is unworthy and follow him in his quest to bring the world back to God.

SUNDAY EVENING, APRIL 18

Title: Jesus, the Resurrection and the Life

Text: "Jesus said unto her, I am the resurrection, and the life: he that believeth in me, though he were dead, yet shall he live" (**John 11:25**).

Introduction

The sixth key sign from John 11 speaks of life, death, and life hereafter. It contains a most heartening and courageous message for everyone who has a loved one gone and for all of us who may at any time suffer the bereavement of the loss of a loved one. Only Jesus can speak with authority on a subject like this. Philosophers of all ages have sought to unravel the mystery of death but have given up in despair. Anyone can speculate and offer theories, but Jesus speaks with authority and illustrates his teaching by his own power and experience. Apart from the teachings of Jesus, people would remain in utter darkness concerning proof of immortality, but we have the undisputable testimony of his own experience. He died, was entombed and arose, lives today, and is the author of these wonderful words: "Because I live, ye shall live also" (John 14:19).

I. Take a look at the scriptural account in John 11.

A. *The scene opens with a simple home scene in the little town of Bethany, about two miles from Jerusalem.* Distress had come to the two sisters of the home, Martha and Mary. Their brother, Lazarus, was seriously sick. They thought of

Jesus, which was natural, for they loved him, and the love was mutual. You think of Jesus when sickness comes, and you can understand their actions. Their distress was augumented by the fact that Jesus was away.

B. *Jesus was teaching, perhaps in Perea, some distance away.* The messenger arrived with the brief statement: "Lord, behold, he whom thou lovest is sick." They did not ask Jesus to come; they merely advised him of Lazarus's sickness. How perfectly natural and expectant it was!

C. *When Jesus received the message, he said to the disciples, "This sickness is not unto death, but for the glory of God, that the Son might be glorified thereby."* Here we find the first great statement. This sickness is not leading to the end of death but that God may be realized as the great "lifesaver." The Son is the declarer of the Father's glory.

D. *This was a home where Jesus felt a special closeness.* He loved the sisters but waited two days before making a start to see them. If we were in a desperate situation and called a doctor for an appointment and were told we had to wait two days, we would call another one. Jesus recognized the Father's purpose, and it could best be served by remaining two more days where he was. It is difficult to remain calm in an emergency, but complete trust in God will give us serenity.

E. *Finally, two days later, Jesus started for Bethany.* His disciples did not want to go. They knew Lazarus was sick, but they thought that he would get well. They were afraid the Jews would stone Jesus if they went back. They said, "If he is asleep, he is getting better." Jesus told them that he knew what he was doing. He was not walking in darkness, and things were not hidden from him. He told them plainly that Lazarus was dead and that he was glad for their sakes that they might come to believe.

F. *The home in Bethany was plunged into woe.* There were many mourners at this home, and when Jesus arrived he was told that Lazarus had been buried for four days.

II. Jesus comforts the sisters.

A. *Martha rushed out to meet Jesus while Mary stayed in the house.* "Lord," she cried, "if thou hadst been here, my brother had not died." Doubtless this was the cry of the sisters those four days. It seemed that Jesus had failed them in their hour of great need, yet they had not abandoned hope. She added quickly, "But I know, that even now, whatsoever thou wilt ask of God, God will give it thee." Here was real faith. This was Martha, not the supposedly more spiritual Mary.

B. *Jesus told her that Lazarus would rise, and immediately she replied that she knew he would at the last day.* She would have rejoiced had Jesus said, "Thy brother shall *live* again," but when he said, "He shall *rise* again," she thought of the resurrection at the last day. She did not disdain that glorious hope, but the resurrection seemed so far away, and her heart craved present reality. Jesus hastened to reassure her drooping spirit and vouchsafed to her a great assurance: "I am the resurrection, and the life: he that believeth in me, though he were dead, yet shall he live."

III. Jesus is the resurrection.

A. *"I am the resurrection, and the life."* The power of the resurrection is in Jesus now just as it will be at the last day, and he gives us that power that we might have a new and victorious life now. Here is the climax of John's gospel!

B. *In Jesus the resurrection is present because:*
1. There is a spiritual resurrection — believers live though they die.
2. Giving new life is the resurrection.
3. This is symbolized in baptism. It is pointing to another resurrection when that life will be clothed with a spiritual body.

C. *This means that all people will have either two births or two deaths.* If a person is twice born — once physically and the other spiritually, "from above" — then he or she will have only one death — physical. If he is born only once (the physical), he or she will have two deaths — physical and spiritual. Physical death is the separation of the soul from the body. Spiritual death, sometimes called the second death, is the separation of the soul from God. Jesus says, "The one believing in me shall never die this spiritual death."

"Do you believe this?" Jesus asked.

"Yes, Lord," Martha replied, "I believe that thou art the Christ, the Son of God, the one coming into the world."

IV. Jesus proves his power.

A. *The crowd followed Jesus and the sisters to the tomb.* Someone in the crowd sneered, "Could not this man, which opened the eyes of the blind, have caused that even [Lazarus] should not have died?" (John 11:37). The sneer reached Jesus' ears, but he ignored it and commanded that the stone be removed from the entrance to the grave. Mary protested that Lazarus had been in the tomb four days, and by this time decomposition had set in. Why expose the dead to the gaze of all? Jesus prayed that they could believe that he was the representative of God. If they had seen that, all the misunderstanding would have been avoided.

B. *Jesus called in a loud voice, "Lazarus, come forth!"* This was the shout of death's conqueror, and the dead man heard his voice. When he heard it, he came forth wrapped in his grave clothes. "Loose him," said Jesus, "and let him go."

V. Here we have the complete sign.

A. *Jesus is eternally the Resurrection and the Life.* We are going to experience that great eternal fact. If the story of Lazarus's resurrection had been a fable, we would have the words of Lazarus, but we do not. Although the body is dead Jesus can give life, for he is God. He declared, "The one that believes in me shall never die."

B. *Here we have the climax of the good news of God.* Paul states this great truth in Romans 14:7–9: "For none of us liveth to himself, and no man dieth to himself. For whether we live, we live unto the Lord; and whether we die, we die unto the Lord: whether we live therefore, or die, we are the Lord's. For to this end Christ both died, and rose, and revived, that he might be Lord both of the dead and living."

C. *Death had not separated Lazarus from Jesus; through resurrection it had brought him nearer in reverential love.* It had not divided him from his sisters; it had made the ties of affection stronger and holier than they had ever been before. It had not quenched one faculty of his being; for to Lazarus every power of sight, speech, and hearing would be more sacred and nobler than in his former life. In one word Christ showed this—there was in him a life that rendered death only the gateway through which life arose more perfect, holier, and freer.

Conclusion

The resurrection of Lazarus was an illustration of a fact that all believers in God will experience. Resurrection and eternal life are not simply *through* Christ but *in* Christ. Jesus said, "I am. . . ." God was in the Son; then the Son was essentially God in power. The one who believes shall never die. It is that simple. Christ not only demonstrated it by raising Lazarus but by his own resurrection. "Whosoever *liveth* and *believeth* in me shall *never* die" (John 11:26, italics mine).

When God so raises the souls of people to the level of his own holy and loving life, he will never allow death to destroy his handiwork. Would an artist, working long and hard to perfect a product, order its destruction after completion? Of course not, and those who believe in Christ shall have everlasting life. "Because I live, ye shall live also" (John 14:19).

WEDNESDAY EVENING, APRIL 21

Title: The Call of Jeremiah

Text: "The words of Jeremiah the son of Hilkiah, of the priests that were in Anathoth in the land of Benjamin: To whom the word of the LORD came in the days of Josiah the son of Amon king of Judah, in the thirteenth year of his reign" (**Jer. 1:1–2**).

Scripture Reading: Jeremiah 1:1–19

Introduction

The call of God to Jeremiah is disappointing to those who love the spectacular and the melodramatic. The account of how Jeremiah became a prophet of God, found in the first chapter of his prophecies, seems simple when compared to the calls of Isaiah and Ezekiel.

144

I. Jeremiah's spiritual heritage.

Anathoth, an hour's walk to the north of Jerusalem, was Jeremiah's birthplace and home until manhood. Since the days of Solomon, Anathoth had been the residence of a famous family of priests (1 Kings 2:26). Being "the son of Hilkiah, of the priests that were at Anathoth," Jeremiah could probably trace his lineage back to those who originally had custody of the ark. Nowhere would the best traditions of Israel and their God find a better repository than in a household whose forebears had guarded the most sacred symbol of Israel's invisible God.

There is every reason to believe that Jeremiah was reared in a godly Hebrew home. His name means "God hurls." Perhaps this was an expression of the hope of his parents that the Lord would use him in helping to solve the problems that had been created by the reign of the wicked Manasseh, who was ruling at Jeremiah's birth.

The religion of Israel had degenerated during the reign of Manasseh. Apostasy was rampant in the land, and worship of the Baalim was prominent. The nation was depending on alliances with neighboring nations for national security.

II. A dialogue with God.

The account of Jeremiah's confrontal by God in the deepest zone of his being is given in the form of a dialogue. Instead of the spectacular, Jeremiah describes the objects or events of common daily experience as the starting point for his perception of the divine truth and purpose for his life. We get the impression that the deep feeling that God was calling him into the goodly fellowship of the prophets came to him as a result of a growing religious experience.

If Jeremiah's experience of the divine call took the form of a vision, it was a "calm meditating vision" that was not accompanied by any spectacular phenomena. It was an experience with God on life's way. God chose him, met him, spoke to him, touched his lips, and commissioned him as a prophet.

A. *Predestination.* By some mysterious manner, God made it known to the young Jeremiah that he was a chosen instrument (Jer. 1:4–5). As Jeremiah meditated on the purpose of God for his life, the conviction was forced on his mind that a combination of things happened before his birth that were to be determining factors in his becoming a prophet. He came to realize that everything he had received or that had happened to him had worked together under the hand of God to prepare him for the work to which he was being called. The awareness that he had been a thought of God before his birth must have stirred this sensitive young man to the very depths of his being.

B. *Jeremiah's hesitancy.* His first reaction to this perception of God's purpose for his life was a feeling of utter insufficiency. We can sympathize with this when we recognize the immensity of the task that was before him. He was to be a prophet, not only to Judah, but "to the nations" as well.

Jeremiah's reply to the call of God was "I do not know how to speak; I am only a child" (Jer. 1:6 NIV). This was not a plea of unfitness of character

145

as in the case of Isaiah. Jeremiah was pleading his youth, his inexperience, and his lack of ability.

C. *The assurance of divine assistance.* God took steps to reassure the timid, hesitant, young prophet of divine help in the discharge of his prophetic duties. He was led to understand that he was to speak only that which God commanded him to speak. His own intellect was not to be the source for the oracles he was to utter; they were to come from God and would carry divine authority within themselves.

Jeremiah was then assured of divine deliverance from his enemies (Jer. 1:8). He was assured that God would put his divine words in his mouth.

Jeremiah hesitated to enter upon his ministry as is indicated by the visions of the almond rod and the boiling caldron (Jer. 1:11–15). These two visions gave him a sense of urgency and inner compulsion that told him that it was time for him to be at work (v. 17).

D. *The nature of Jeremiah's ministry.* Jeremiah was to be a prophet set "over the nations and over the kingdoms" (Jer. 1:10).

The effect of God's work in words spoken by Jeremiah would be two-fold—both destructive and constructive. The word would serve to "pluck up and to break down, to destroy and to overthrow" that which was displeasing to God. The constructive work of the word would be to "build and to plant" that which is good. Beyond a ministry and message of judgment, Jeremiah was encouraged to look forward to a better and more hopeful state of affairs.

Conclusion

Jeremiah describes the experience of how the call of God came to him in terms of a conversation with a friend. He must have spent much time thinking about the will and way of God as well as the needs of his nation. In connection with these, God came to him, laid his sovereign hand upon him, and called him to a ministry of usefulness and helpfulness.

If we want God to call us to something that is good and noble, we must provide time for meditation and contemplation. We must let God speak to the highest part of our intellect and to the deepest part of our emotions. God will speak to us as he spoke to Jeremiah if we will but listen.

SUNDAY MORNING, APRIL 25

Title: Our Great Salvation

Text: "How shall we escape, if we neglect so great salvation; which at the first began to be spoken by the Lord, and was confirmed unto us by them that heard him" (**Heb. 2:3**).

Scripture Reading: Hebrews 2:1–4

Hymns: "Blessed Redeemer," Christiansen

"What a Wonderful Saviour!" Hoffman

"All Hail the Power of Jesus' Name," Perronet

Offertory Prayer: Holy heavenly Father, you have given us the joy of being children in your family. You have blessed us with the assurance of forgiven sins. You have given us the opportunity to serve with you in redeeming the world from sin. We thank you for every opportunity to be a part of your redemptive work. Today we bring tithes and offerings and pray your blessings on them to the end that others might hear the good news of your love and grace. Accept them and bless them in Christ's name. Amen.

Introduction

The Bible is the book that reveals the way of salvation. It concerns itself with the salvation that God offers to people through faith in Jesus Christ. The salvation that God offers is of major concern not only to the churches but also to individuals, families, and even to nations.

The Bible speaks concerning how Christ came into the world to be our Savior. He died on the cross to save us from sin. He conquered death and the grave and lives eternally that he might be the Savior of all who come to God through him (Heb. 7:25).

Our text speaks of a great salvation. It is great because of the love that bought it. It is great because of the love that brought it. It is great because of the love that wrought it. It is a great salvation, yet the tragedy is that many see only one facet of the great salvation available to them through Jesus Christ. There are some who think of Jesus only as a funeral director for the soul. They believe that he is relevant and needed only in the time of death. There are others who think of the great salvation only in terms of a ticket to heaven. How tragic that anyone should hold such a limited concept of the great salvation that God offers so freely.

The word *salvation* is used in a number of different ways in the New Testament. It is used with reference to deliverance from physical harm, deliverance from failure, and deliverance from despair.

The great salvation that God offers to us through Jesus Christ is far greater than most of us realize. Some understanding of the length and breadth and height and depth of this great salvation will not only strengthen our faith and stimulate our energies, but it will also greatly increase our understanding of the teachings of the Scriptures.

I. Our great salvation includes deliverance from the penalty of sin.

Scripture tells us that all are sinners (Rom. 3:23). That the wages of sin is death (Rom. 6:23) is not only the verdict of Holy Scripture, it is a fact that we can observe. The death to which this passage refers is spiritual death, the separation of the soul from God.

Jesus affirmed that he came into the world not to condemn the world but that the world through him might be saved. He came that we might be saved from the penalty of sin, which is death (Isa. 53:5).

It is concerning salvation from the penalty of sin to which Paul refers in Ephesians 2:8–9: "For by grace are ye saved through faith; and that not of yourselves: it is the gift of God: Not of works, lest any man should boast." Paul here speaks of salvation as an accomplished fact. Those to whom he wrote were assured that through faith in Jesus Christ they were already saved. He refers to the deliverance from the penalty of sin, which is death. This takes place in the miracle of the new birth. Legally this is called justification (Rom. 5:1). Justification is the act of God by which he receives the believer on the basis of that believer's faith in Jesus Christ.

This is but the beginning of the great salvation that God offers through Jesus Christ. This is but the birth experience. It is in this experience that a relationship is established. The believer becomes the child of God, and God becomes the spiritual Father of the believer.

II. Our great salvation includes salvation from the power of sin.

God, the heavenly Father, was not interested in saving people in their sins. God was and continues to be interested in saving people from sin. Consequently, the New Testament speaks of salvation not only as a past accomplishment but also as a present process. The theological term for this experience is sanctification.

When God bestows on believers the divine nature, and when the Holy Spirit takes up residence in the hearts of new converts, God begins his good work of redeeming and delivering his children from the power and practice of sin (Phil. 1:6; 2:12–13).

Believers who would experience the great salvation that God has for them must cooperate with God if they want to experience deliverance from the power of sin or from the practice of sin in their daily lives. Even God cannot save people from the power of sin apart from their continuous cooperation with the work of the Holy Spirit.

Romans 7 presents to us a picture of the believer who would attempt to attain righteousness in the energy of the flesh by obeying a law. Such effort always ends in dismal failure. Romans 8 presents a picture of the victorious Christian who in the power of the Spirit of God cooperates with God to experience salvation from the power of sin in his or her daily life.

Salvation from the power or practice of sin in daily life is a part of God's great salvation for us. God has saved us for his glory. God has saved us for service. We have been created anew in Christ Jesus unto good works (Eph. 2:10).

III. Our great salvation includes salvation from the presence of sin.

Paul wrote to the Romans and declared, "Now is our salvation nearer than when we believed" (Rom. 13:11). The writer of the book of Hebrews speaks of a salvation that will be manifested when Jesus Christ returns to the earth again

(Heb. 9:28). In John's first epistle he speaks of a manifestation of sonship that will take place only when the Lord Jesus appears again (1 John 3:1–2).

There are a number of references in the New Testament to salvation in the future tense. Because of this, some have labored under the erroneous idea that assurance of salvation in the present is impossible and that we must wait until some future time before we can be certain that heaven is going to be our eternal home.

Conclusion

The New Testament speaks of salvation in the past tense, in the present tense, and in the future tense. Salvation in the present tense is sanctification. Salvation in the future tense is glorification. We must repent toward God and put faith in Christ Jesus for salvation from the penalty of sin. We must cooperate with the Holy Spirit day by day if we are to experience salvation from the power of sin. We must trust Jesus Christ and the precious promises of God for salvation from the presence of sin at some time in the future.

Ours is a great and wonderful salvation. Let us trust Christ sincerely. Let us cooperate with him continuously. Let us rejoice in him abundantly.

SUNDAY EVENING, APRIL 25

Title: Jesus, Immanuel — God with Us

Text: "They shall call his name Emmanuel, which being interpreted is, God with us" **(Matt. 1:23)**.

Scripture Reading: John 17:1–5

Introduction

This seventh key sign is the completion of all of the other signs God has revealed to Isaiah (7:14) that "a virgin shall conceive and bear a son, and shall call his name Immanuel." Immanuel means "God with us." John tells us in the prologue that Jesus is God and was with the Father in heaven before he was born of the Virgin Mary in Bethlehem. Heaven's doors swung outward to let Jesus out in order that they could swing inward to let us in. He came as a baby and pitched his tent among humans, living a perfect life among us in this world for thirty-three years, setting an example for all of us.

The other six signs have revealed his glory as to his power, salvation, and nature. This last sign helps us to see the extremes to which God was willing to go to save the world. We understand better that "God was in Christ, reconciling the world unto himself" (2 Cor. 5:19).

John 17 is the longest recorded prayer of Jesus. He offered it to his Father just before his arrest, trial, crucifixion, death, burial, and resurrection took place. The first five verses lay the basis for the sign. John 18–20 gives us the details, with the great miracle being the resurrection.

Jesus prays, "Father, the hour is come; glorify thy Son, that thy Son also may glorify thee" (John 17:1). The prayer continues with Jesus asking God's blessings upon the disciples (vv. 6–19), and then he prays for us (vv. 20–26). "Neither pray I for these alone, but for them also which shall believe on me through their word" (v. 20). Isn't it wonderful comfort to know that Jesus is praying for you?

When the prayer is finished, John tells us (18:1) that Jesus "went forth...." He was now ready to pay with his own life the penalty for the sin of the rebellious world. The greatest miracle of all was about to take place—the innocent dying for the guilty, the just for the unjust.

John introduces us to the different attitudes that were reflected by the people in the world that Jesus came to save. These attitudes are still prevalent today.

I. Open hostility—"Crucify him!"

A. *Jesus had come unto his own, but his own had received him not, and now their rejection broke into open, violent hostility.* They had been planning to kill him for some time and finally had found a way. A terrible weakness was discovered in one of his own men—Judas. The chief priests offered Judas money to tell them where Jesus could be found at a certain hour. Judas chose money over favor with God. He chose the jingle of coins over the "well done" of the best Friend he ever had, and he sold his Lord for thirty pieces of silver—the price of a slave.

B. *They found Jesus in the garden praying.* Among the "band of men and officers from the chief priests and Pharisees, coming thither with lanterns and torches and weapons" was Judas Iscariot. The very name seems like a curse word, yet many people today are selling Jesus for material gain. His Word is neglected, his church forgotten, justice perverted, and money mishandled all because of the "love of money" today. Judas found that he had made a terrible mistake, but it was too late to rectify it. He could not live with his sin, so he committed suicide. Many today who choose money over the Master will discover that they have played the fool.

C. *Among the group who came to arrest Jesus were "officers."* These policemen had arrested criminals before. They had been led to believe that they were out to capture the worst man who ever lived. They had seen criminals cringe with fear when apprehended, but they were not prepared for the action of Jesus. Jesus was not cringing but standing straight and tall when he asked them, "Whom seek ye?" They answered, "Jesus of Nazareth." He said, "I am he." His calmness and forthrightness so overwhelmed them that "they went backward, and fell to the ground." The question was repeated, and again Jesus told them who he was and asked for the release of his disciples (John 18:3–8).

D. *The world still cries out, "Crucify him!"* Try witnessing for Christ today and see if you don't meet hostile people.

150

II. **Weakness of supposedly strong ones.**

A. *How sad that Simon Peter denied ever knowing Jesus.* He had displayed a willingness to fight for Jesus and actually unsheathed his sword and cut off a man's ear. When Jesus told him to put up his sword, Peter knew nothing else to do but run. He would have died for Jesus fighting, but he went all to pieces without his sword in his hand.

B. *Our fears and emotions can do strange tricks to us.* Have you ever been in a place where you were ashamed to admit that you were a Christian? How many people deny Jesus daily by the lives they live? Some of his worst injuries have been afflicted by those who professed to love him. Zechariah 13:6 asked the question of the Messiah, "What are these wounds in thine hands?" The answer: "Those with which I was wounded in the house of my friends." It behooves each of us to be careful with our lives lest we hurt the one we love most.

III. **Indifference.**

A. *John points out the indifference of the soldiers during the time the greatest crime of all ages was being committed, the death of the very Creator of this universe, the King of Kings and Lord of Lords.* The soldiers gambled underneath his cross for his only worldly possession — his robe. Blind to the great tragedy around them, evidently not caring in the least about his suffering, they displayed more concern for his garment.

B. *One of the gravest sins of America today, if not the most serious, is just this — indifference.* Americans go merrily on their way of sex-crazed, pleasure-mad self-indulgences, ignoring or neglecting God's free gift of salvation. If we care whether people are saved or lost, now is the time to show it. If we are concerned about lost loved ones, now is the time to prove it. If we don't, indifference will be our undoing.

IV. **A tender love scene.**

A. *In the midst of this dark catastrophe, John singles out a scene so tender and touching that it shines like the noonday sun.* Jesus took time even while dying to think of his mother and make future provision for her. He committed her to the keeping of John and asked John to accept her as his mother. John was happy and honored to comply.

B. *Also, John introduces two men to us who displayed touching courage in the face of grave danger.* They are Joseph of Arimathea, a wealthy man, and Nicodemus, who had come to Jesus by night and was told that he must be born again. I think that this means that Nicodemus was now a Christian. It was a dangerous thing for anyone to identify himself with any part of Christ at this time, but these men came and asked for his body, and with tender loving hands they took it down from the cross and anointed it for burial. Joseph loaned his tomb to that sacred body and must have had a wonderful feeling inside in doing so.

V. God displays his might.

A. *What do you suppose God's thoughts were toward all this?* He had sent his only begotten Son into the world to save the world. The cruel, rebellious world had killed him. How could God refrain from unleashing a thunderbolt and wiping out the earth?

The story is told of young parents watching their four-year-old son playing in their front yard. A drunken driver careened his car off the road into their yard and killed their son. The horror-stricken father picked up the body of his dead son as the drunken man staggered up saying, "Forgive me." The distraught father screamed, "You dirty bum, I'll never forgive you!"

B. *Look back through the centuries to another Father, standing beneath the cross, holding in his arms the dead body of his only Son.* He looks the world that killed him in the eye and says, "You did this to my Son! I forgive you because he died for you."

Conclusion

John concludes by telling us that "these are written, that ye might believe that Jesus is the Christ, the Son of God; and that believing ye might have life through his name" (John 20:31).

WEDNESDAY EVENING, APRIL 28

Title: The Call of Ezekiel

Text: "The word of the LORD came expressly unto Ezekiel the priest, the son of Buzi, in the land of the Chaldeans by the river Chebar; and the hand of the LORD was there upon him" (**Ezek. 1:3**).

Scripture Reading: Ezekiel 2, 3

Introduction

A close study of Ezekiel's experience by the Chebar River will reveal that his inaugural vision did not come to him in a vacuum. An act of nature, the condition of the exiles, the prophet's search for meaning, his imaginative powers, and his literary ability, combined with the revelatory activity of God, cooperate to produce an experience and an account of that experience that has mystified even the most diligent scholars. The ancient rabbis decided that the first chapter of Ezekiel should be withheld from students below thirty years of age because it gave rise to theosophical speculations.

I. Ezekiel's background and training.

Eleven years before its final destruction in 586 BC, Jerusalem was captured by Nebuchadnezzar. The city was stripped of most of its best and noblest inhabitants. These were carried into exile, and among this group of exiles was a young priest, Ezekiel, the son of Buzi (Ezek. 1:3). It was a time of tragic grief and misery for those who had to leave their homeland. Especially was this true of one whose life was wrapped up in the services of the temple.

Ezekiel is said to have been a priest, and we have every reason to believe that he received the best religious training of his day. Most likely he heard the preaching of Jeremiah, for his earlier prophecies show some striking similarities to the prophecies of Jeremiah.

II. The exiles in Babylon.

The exiles got along rather well in Babylonia. They were permitted to possess their own houses (Ezek. 3:4), and there is no illusion to hardships imposed upon them by their heathen neighbors. Some of them prospered to the extent that later when they had an opportunity to return they chose to remain.

The majority of the exiles were gripped with a sense of despair. Many things had happened to shake their faith. They feared that God had either completely cast them off or that his power was inferior to that of the gods of the Babylonians. Either thought was enough to cast the exiles into the depths of despondency.

III. Ezekiel's inaugural vision.

The captives had been in Babylon five years without a true prophet when the Lord laid his hand on Ezekiel (Ezek. 1:2). It was with a disturbed mind concerning the condition of the exiles and God's plan for them that Ezekiel was by the banks of the Chebar on a stormy day. There he had a revolutionary experience, and he who had been trained to be a priest became a prophet. As a storm cloud began to sweep down across the plain toward him from the north, "the heavens were opened" and Ezekiel "saw visions of God" (v. 1).

In connection with this natural phenomenon, a frightening storm cloud, Ezekiel had a strange spiritual experience. This vision of God impressed vividly upon his mind both the transcendence and accessibility of God. The great God whom he and the other exiles had worshiped in Jerusalem had come into the land of exile. This transcendent God was calling him to a prophetic ministry. He was to be God's spokesman to the exiles.

IV. Ezekiel's commission.

Ezekiel recounts how God called and commissioned him as a prophet to the exiles. He was addressed as "son of man" and commanded to arise and stand upon his feet so as to hear the voice of God (Ezek. 2:1). "The spirit entered the prophet and caused him to stand upon his feet" (v. 2).

Ezekiel was then informed of the divine purpose for his life (Ezek. 2:3). He was made to realize that the exiles were rebellious, impudent, and stiff-hearted (vv. 3–4). He was given no guarantee of success in his ministry (v. 5). The actual commission of Ezekiel is different from that of any other prophet in the Old Testament. The message of God was given to him in the form of a scroll "written within and without: and there was written therein lamentations, and mournings, and woe" (v. 10). He was directed to eat the scroll. After digesting the scroll he would have a message for his people.

Once more Ezekiel was commanded to go to the people and speak the message that God had given him for them. Again he was given no assurance of success (Ezek. 3:4–11).

Conclusion

There are several important truths from the experience of Ezekiel that are relevant for the present. God will come to us in the most difficult and unfavorable of circumstances. He has a purpose for us and therefore will reveal himself to us. We, like Ezekiel, should "eat the book." By so doing we will give God a better opportunity to speak to us, and we will have a message for the people of our day. We are not called to be a success; we are called to be faithful.

MAY

■ **Sunday Mornings**

Topical sermons that deal with the needs of all and others that focus on individuals or specific groups are suggested for this month. Instead of having a central theme, these sermons are designed to help pastors respond to our Lord's command to Peter: "Feed my sheep."

■ **Sunday Evenings**

Life is made up of relationships. We become a part of all that we meet. This is true as we become intimately acquainted with the great characters of the Bible. "Becoming Acquainted with the Apostle Paul" is the theme for Sunday evenings. On the last Sunday evening of the month, a new unit begins, which is a sequel to the earlier sermons. The suggested theme is "Challenges from the Heart of the Apostle Paul."

■ **Wednesday Evenings**

Continue the series "The Call of God and Our Response."

SUNDAY MORNING, MAY 2

Title: The Authority of Jesus

Text: "And they were astonished at his doctrine: for he taught them as one that had authority, and not as the scribes" (**Mark 1:22**).

Scripture Reading: Mark 1:21–34

Hymns:　"All Hail the Power of Jesus' Name," Perronet

　　　　"Praise Him! Praise Him!" Crosby

　　　　"Great Redeemer, We Adore Thee," Harris

Offertory Prayer: Holy and loving Father, we thank you for the blessings of the past week and for the privilege of being with your people today in this house of prayer and worship. Particularly we thank you for the inward disposition of heart and mind that has brought us to this place of prayer and worship. Because you have given us so much, we come this morning to give ourselves afresh to you. Accept our tithes and offerings as symbols of our desire to be completely dedicated to your purpose in the world. In Jesus' name we pray. Amen.

Introduction

The enemies of Jesus were interested in discovering the source of his authority (Matt. 21:23–27). He violated their traditions and upset their customs, and they wondered concerning the source of his authority for his revolutionary attitudes and actions.

The friends of Jesus rejoiced in the fact that he spoke with authority. They heard him gladly (Matt. 7:28–29). There was something fresh, independent, original, positive, and relevant about everything he said and did. He knew the way to heaven, for he had been there. He knew the principles of the kingdom of God, for he was the God-man. He had the authority of an expert in the things of God.

On occasion Jesus demonstrated his authority, his power, his right to command, and his right to the obedience of his disciples. He demonstrated his authority over disease, over nature, and finally over death itself.

The need of our age is to recognize and respond to the authority of Jesus Christ. He has a right to speak to our generation and to be heard.

Those who recognized Jesus' authority and responded to it not only turned the world upside down; they turned it right side up.

I. Jesus' authority was the authority of his divine and unique person.

A. *Jesus was not merely the best man who ever lived.*

B. *Jesus was not merely a visionary who died a martyr's death.*

C. *Jesus Christ was the Son of God. He was God in human flesh.* In him God visited the earth. He is the Creator and Sustainer of the earth.

II. Jesus had the authority of one filled with the Spirit of God (Luke 4:1).

The Holy Spirit possessed Jesus' mind and heart. Jesus was instantly responsive and obedient to the guidance of the Holy Spirit. He labored in the energy of the divine Spirit. He was obedient to the Holy Spirit of God.

III. Jesus had the authority of absolute truth (John 14:6).

A. *There was no flaw in his teaching.*

B. *There were no errors in his precepts.*

C. *He spoke words of infallible truth concerning God, man, life, and eternity.*

IV. Jesus had the authority of indescribable love (2 Cor. 9:15).

He came as a symbol of God's love for us and to demonstrate the love of God for us. From the beginning to the end of his earthly ministry, his one great concern was to manifest and demonstrate the love of the heart of God for sinful humans.

V. Jesus had and still has the authority of a living and exalted Lord (Phil. 5:2–11).

In the Great Commission Jesus said, "All power is given unto me in heaven and in earth" (Matt. 28:18). The word translated "power" actually means authority.

Jesus is here declaring that all authority has been given to him in heaven and in earth. To him has been given the right to command the love and loyalty of his disciples.

The early disciples recognized and responded to Jesus' lordship. They became the channels through which the message of God's love was communicated to the hearts and lives of needy men and women.

Conclusion

Nature recognized the authority of Christ. The demons recognized his authority and obeyed him. Disease disappeared at his touch. Death itself surrendered its victims.

What about you? Have you recognized Jesus' authority and responded to it? You should, because of who he is. You should, because of what he has done. You should, because of what he can do in your heart and life and through your heart and life when fully surrendered to his love and mercy and grace.

SUNDAY EVENING, MAY 2

Title: Paul, a Chosen Apostle

Text: "But when it pleased God, who separated me from my mother's womb, and called me by his grace.... But what things were gain to me, those I counted loss for Christ" **(Gal. 1:15; Phil. 3:7).**

Scripture Reading: Galatians 1:15; Philippians 3:1–7

Introduction

It was the worst storm the sailors had experienced. The sails were ripped by the tempestuous winds. It left the ship without steerage. The cargo was cast overboard. The giant waves threatened to swamp the ship. Neither the sun nor the stars appeared for fourteen days. All hope of being saved was lost. Suddenly in the storm's darkness a shadowy figure cried out, "Sirs, be of good cheer, there shall no man's life be lost." Who is this man? Look! He is a felon; he is in bonds! What is his name? His name is Paul.

In these same waters some two thousand years later a man of high rank in government and commerce said to a missionary friend, "The apostle Paul is one of the few men of the ancient world who was absolutely modern. He changed the course of history." The historian Lecky says, "Civilization came to Europe in a ship with a man named Paul."

I. Paul's ancestry.

The Christian religion was cradled in Judaism. Behind it lay the amazing history of the Hebrew nation. Into it went the idealism, the faith, the divine revelation, and the providential guidance of the patriarchs and the fathers. Four thousand years of influence were compended here. Though Paul was born of the

Jewish faith, Christianity was to leave its ancestral home and be spread around the world. The seed sown in Judean soil was to become a tree whose leaves were for the healing of all the nations. Jesus, the divine founder, had given command: "Go ye into all the world, and preach the gospel to every creature" (Mark 16:15). But Christianity was in danger of becoming another Jewish sect like the Essenes, the Zealots, or the Pharisees. Then God chose a man, a man named Saul of Tarsus. Who was he? What was he like? I suppose we ought to let Paul tell his own story. He speaks of it in Philippians 3:3–7 and 1 Corinthians 15:8–10. He calls himself "Paul, an apostle."

The source of a stream is not where it arises in some green glen among the hills to make a tiny sparkling bit of water, but in the mighty sea that is drawn upward by evaporation to form the clouds. These then cast their droplets upon the mountains, and the drops come together to form the stream. So it is with a life. Paul felt that he had been foreknown and predestined by God. So he says to the Ephesians, "He chose us in him before the foundation of the world" (Eph. 1:4). In youth we suppose that our life plan is of our own choosing—that we are masters of our own destiny. In a sense this is true, for God will not violate the human will, yet in his infinite knowledge he knows what influences will move us. As we review our lives, we discover that we choose because we are chosen. We love because God loved us. We leave the sepulcher of our selfishness because God says, "Come forth." We are delivered from the sacraments of death because God already provided the living seed. How does a man's life come to be? The apostle Paul says, "By the grace of God I am what I am." This reminds us of the words of Whittier:

> *What to thee is shadow to Him is day*
> *And the end he knoweth*
> *And not on a blind and aimless way the spirit goeth,*
> *Like warp and woof all destinies are woven fast,*
> *Linked in symphony, like the melody of an organ vast.*

God said to Jeremiah the prophet, "Before I formed thee in the belly I knew thee, and before thou comest out of the womb I sanctified thee.... I ordained thee a prophet unto the nations" (Jer. 1:5). So Paul discovered the hand of God in his life. To the Galatians he said, "It was the good pleasure of God who separated me even from my birth and called me through his grace to reveal his son in me that I might preach him among the Gentiles." Paul would not have said this in his youth, but now he sees it.

God has a purpose for every life. Where we are yielded and acquiescent, that divine will is made known to us. One of the interesting studies of the human life is to see how circumstances and influences shape the determining will. Every thread is needed for the completion of the pattern. Where does the pattern begin to take shape? Early in life, yes, even before the life becomes such. Paul speaks of a prenatal grace of God. He reminds Timothy that the grace he has is a gift through "thy grandmother Lois and thy mother Eunice" (2 Tim. 1:5). What sacred obligations parents and grandparents have! To give your children all other gifts but the gift of grace is to beggar their soul. What shall a man profit if he gain the whole world and lose his own soul? There are hundreds of thousands of parents who by precept and profession are saying to their children, "It is important for you to get a good education, to have a good job, to choose a good companion for life, but God really doesn't count."

II. Paul's home.

We know little of Paul's home. In fact, his parents are not mentioned in the Bible. History says, through the pen of Jerome: "His father was a native of Gisehela in Northern Galilee. He was driven from his home by civil disturbance at the death of Herod. Then the family escaped to Tarsus." They were rather well-to-do, so Paul was afforded a good education. They were Roman citizens, and this in itself was no empty adornment. It saved Paul at one time from a scourging and at another from a crucifixion. As a Roman citizen, Paul had a right to appeal to the emperor. We are told in Acts 23 that Paul had a sister. The sister's son warned Paul of a plot to kill him.

In his defense at Jerusalem, Paul said that he was a Jew of Tarsus, a city of Cilicia, a citizen of no mean city. This was true, for Tarsus was the capital of the province, a city of at least a half million people. Tarsus was the crossroads of two continents. Here met the highways of the east and west. Behind the city of Tarsus the mountains stretched as an endless barrier to separate two worlds. Anything moving from Asia to Europe came through the Cilician Gate. Through Tarsus went the balsam of Jericho, the spices of Arabia, the sword of Damascus, and also the gospel. Here in Tarsus, in a Jewish home, in a Roman province, in a Greek land, Paul was born.

Paul's name means "ask for." I think his name speaks a bit of the piety of his home. Though this family was away from the land of promise, yet Paul's parents were faithful to the religion of their fathers. So as Paul says it in the Philippian letter, I was "circumcised the eighth day, of the stock of Israel, of the tribe of Benjamin, an Hebrew of the Hebrews" (Phil. 3:5). The last is a remarkable expression indeed. It really means that he was "sprung up" from the Hebrews. The phrase speaks of more than just nationality. It means to grow up among; it means all that a person is influenced by. It would be like one saying that he is typically American. He is born an American, reared in America, educated in America, influenced by America—all American.

That's Paul. He is proud of his Hebrew ancestry. In 2 Corinthians 11:22 he says: "Are they Hebrews? so am I. Are they Israelites? so am I. Are they the seed of Abraham? so am I." It never occurred to Paul to apologize for his race, not even among the cultured Greeks or the critical Romans. Paul's Jewish ancestry was always a cause of thanksgiving to him. He could say, "In Christ there is no east or west," yet he loved his Jewish ancestry. It is strange indeed that God would take this zealot, this Hebrew, this seed of Abraham, this Benjamite, and through him, lift Christianity from its Judean cradle and cause the love of God to embrace people of every race and nation.

We shall follow the course of the gospel's triumphant journey across the empire as we trace the footsteps of the empire's first missionary. We will find blood and agony in the pathway. Paul will be beaten, stoned, and shipwrecked; but at the sunset end of the journey he will say, "I have fought a good fight, I have finished my course, I have kept the faith: Henceforth there is laid up for me a crown of righteousness ... and not to me only but unto all them also that love his appearing" (2 Tim. 4:7–8).

WEDNESDAY EVENING, MAY 5

Title: God's Call Is Life's Greatest Opportunity

Text: "And he saith unto them, Follow me, and I will make you fishers of men" **(Matt. 4:19).**

Scripture Reading: Matthew 4:18–23 10

Introduction

God's call has always been a person's supreme opportunity. It was so with Abraham, Moses, and the prophets, and with all of the disciples and Paul.

If God had not called these men, and if they had not harkened to his call and found their place in his redemptive program, the world never would have heard of them. Their own generation would have ignored or forgotten them.

God's call is an invitation to faith, friendship, fellowship, and fruitfulness.

Those who have heard God's call and have responded have discovered in the laboratory of experience that people really begin to live when they heed God's call. The door of supreme opportunity begins to swing wide open before us when we hear and respond to the call of God to our hearts.

I. God's call is a person's opportunity to experience and understand the compassionate heart of God.

A. *God is love.* "In this was manifested the love of God toward us, because that God sent his only begotten Son into the world, that we might live through him" (1 John 4:9).

B. *God loves this sinful world.* We can discover and experience this love as we hear his call and respond to his good will.

II. God's call is a person's opportunity to lead others to the way of real life.

A. *To lead one to trust Christ is the greatest service one can render to God.*

B. *To lead one to trust Christ is the greatest possible service that can be rendered to our fellow humans.*

C. *This work must be done directly and instantly.* Consciously and unconsciously we should give our witness. Voluntarily and involuntarily we should share the good news of God's love. Deliberately and definitely we should press the claims of God's love on the hearts of those who need him.

III. God's call is a person's opportunity to see what God can do with one life.

Dwight L. Moody has often been quoted as saying that he wanted to demonstrate to the world what God could do with one man who was fully surrendered to his will. It is said that because of his ministry a million people were converted to Christ.

A. *The task of becoming a great Christian is not a human achievement alone.* It is the result of a person cooperating with the working of the Holy Spirit in his or her heart.

B. *Only God knows what your life could amount to under his miraculous touch.* Centuries ago Joshua said to the people, "Sanctify yourselves: for tomorrow the LORD will do wonders among you" (Josh. 3:5).

IV. God's call is a person's opportunity to discover the condition of his or her own heart.

A. *By means of X-rays and carefully worked out tests and examinations, a medical doctor seeks to discover the true physical condition of a patient.*

B. *People can discover their own spiritual condition by the response they make to the call of God.*

Conclusion

A deep awareness of a great need, combined with a conviction that God wants to meet part of that need with your time, talents, tongue, and treasure, constitutes God's call to you.

To each of us there comes the call of the highest, the pull of the lowest, and the appeal of the practical. How do you respond to God's call? Do you, like Jonah, say "I will not go"? Do you respond like Jeremiah did when he said, "I am too young and inexperienced"? It would be wonderful if you would respond like Isaiah did when he said, "Here am I, LORD, send me."

SUNDAY MORNING, MAY 9

Title: Mary: A Model for Modern Mothers

Text: "The angel went to her and said, 'Greetings, you who are highly favored! The Lord is with you'" **(Luke 1:28 NIV)**.

Scripture Reading: Luke 1:26–35, 46–56

Hymns: "Faith of Our Mothers," Patten

"He Leadeth Me," Gilmore

"O Love That Wilt Not Let Me Go," Matheson

Offertory Prayer: Holy and loving Father, for the beauty of this spring Lord's Day morning, we thank you. Gracious is your love and generous is your kindness. We rejoice today in all that you mean to us and all that you have done for us. We come today in worship, bringing not only our prayers, but also our tithes and offerings, asking that you receive these offerings and bless them to the advancement of your kingdom of mercy and love in the hearts of all people everywhere. Grant us this day a reverent, worshipful spirit with ears that can hear and a heart that will respond positively to your good will. In Jesus' name. Amen.

Introduction

In the Scriptures we should look for models to imitate. We will also find examples to follow and others to avoid.

Because Roman Catholic Christians have unduly exalted Mary, the mother of our Lord, to a position of worship, most non-Catholic Christians have neglected to benefit from the positive example of this great model of motherhood.

Today, on Mother's Day, let us look at Mary to discover something about her faith and her faithfulness. Let us look at the truth of her motherhood in order that we might discover some of the factors that contributed to her success as a mother.

I. Mary was chosen for a mission.

Mary became the mother of our Lord by means of a miraculous conception. The Savior was born of a virgin. He had an earthly mother without an earthly father.

The eternal God chose to clothe himself in human flesh and, in order to put on an "earth suit," he came by way of a miraculous virgin birth and became a man. It was not Mary's virginity alone that qualified her uniquely for becoming the mother of our Lord.

A. *Mary was a devout worshiper of the true God.*

B. *Mary was pure in heart and mind and body.*

C. *Mary was humble, recognizing her dependence upon the Lord.*

D. *Mary was obedient to the known will of God.*

E. *Mary was cooperative and willing to do what God wanted her to do.*

F. *Mary had an attitude of gratitude. She was thankful to the Lord for permitting her to assist him in his work.*

G. *Mary's life was one of consistency and self-control.*

These are the characteristics that are needed by the modern mother as well as by the woman who gave birth to Jesus.

II. Mary was chosen as a model, or example.

Mary was chosen not only for a mission, but also to serve as an example to other mothers.

A. *Mary responded positively to God's gracious plan for her life. Once she knew the will of God, she consented to participate as God desired.*

B. *Mary magnified the Lord in song for his goodness and graciousness. God puts a song in the hearts of those who trust him.*

C. *Mary worshiped the mighty God of Israel (Luke 1:49).* Mary's God was no wimp and no weakling. He was the great God, the creator God, the redeeming God. He was the God on the throne, and she responded to His authority.

D. *Mary worshiped the merciful God (Luke 1:50).* The love of God expresses itself in a persistent attitude of goodwill and helpfulness to His people. The psalmist described the God of Israel as "a very present help in trouble." Mary experienced this helping hand of God, and she became a helper to Him in His work of helping others.

III. Mary suffered the pains of motherhood.

There is pain associated with the birth experience. There are greater pains along the pathway of life for some mothers, and Mary became acquainted with these pains.

A. *When Christ was twelve years of age, Mary found it difficult to understand her son (Luke 2:49–50).* Mary could sympathize with modern mothers of teenagers.

B. *Later other members of the family in which Jesus grew up were unsympathetic toward him.* They did not accept him to be who and what he really was until after his resurrection.

C. *Mary no doubt experienced great pain when Christ was rejected by the people of His own home town, Nazareth (Luke 4:28–29).*

D. *Mary suffered the horrible humiliation of seeing her son arrested, falsely accused, convicted, condemned, and crucified, as if he were a common criminal.* "Now there stood by the cross of Jesus his mother" (John 19:25). In no way can we fully understand the agony in this mother's heart during these terrible hours when her Son was suffering as he did.

IV. Mary worshiped a risen and ruling Savior.

Following our Lord's resurrection from the dead, we find Mary present with those who were rejoicing at His victorious triumph over death. She was with them as they prayed in anticipation of the coming of the Holy Spirit (Acts 1:14).

Conclusion

Mary is a good model for the modern mother. Hers was a life of great faith, as evidenced by her song, which is called "the Magnificat" and is recorded by Luke (Luke 1:46–55).

Mary's heart was in tune with the Father God as she was continually open to communication from him. Prayer was a dialogue rather than a monologue.

Mary, the mother of our Lord, believed that God's will was good and that it was something to do rather than something merely to endure.

Mary, as a good model for rearing children, encourages purity and prayer and participating in the will of God.

SUNDAY EVENING, MAY 9

Title: Paul Is Debtor

Text: "I am debtor both to the Greeks, and to the Barbarians; both to the wise, and to the unwise" (**Rom. 1:14**).

Scripture Reading: Romans 1:1 – 16

Introduction

John Gibson Lockhart, in his famous biography of Sir Walter Scott, said, "He was making himself all the time, but he didn't know what he was until the years were past." And such it is with every life. We grow up never quite realizing the influences that shape us until we look back upon our lives from mature years. Paul wrote to the Romans, "I am debtor both to the Greeks, and to the Barbarians; both to the wise, and to the unwise." What are these influences that shaped the life of the apostle Paul?

I. History.

First of all, it was the influence of history. Paul said, "I am debtor to the Greeks, and to the Barbarians."

Paul was indeed debtor to the Greeks. Paul and the whole world owes much to those Hellenists! Under Philip the Macedon, the Greek states were united. After his assassination in 336 BC, his son Alexander, only twenty years of age, set out to rule the world. He conquered Persia in 334, then Babylon and Syria, Arabia and Egypt. With his armies came the Greek language, culture, art, and philosophy.

Rome and its Caesars took up where the Greek conquerors left off. Rome extended the empire from the Caspian Sea to the Atlantic, from Britain to the Nile, from Hadrian's Wall to the Euphrates. What would this mean to Paul and the spread of Christianity? It would mean peace and safety. There were Roman governors in every province. Paul's Roman citizenship saved his life often. From end to end of the empire ran the Roman roads. Travel was easy though travelers were often in danger of robbers. The whole world was joined under one law and authority. Before this time the world was not ready to receive the missionary message of the gospel. Now, by a common language and in the safety and protection of the Romans, Paul could take to all the world the message of redemption. What were the other influences that made Paul the man he was?

II. The influence of the Hebrew home.

The Jewish dispersion among the nations began with the forcible deportations under the Assyrian king Tiglath-Pileser about seven hundred years before Christ. By the time of Alexander there were colonies of Jews in every major city of the Greek world. While Jesus was still a boy, there was born in a Jewish home of Tarsus a boy who was destined to make the city's name famous for all time. Both of his parents were of pure Hebrew lineage and, though they were living outside

164

the land, the Jewish heritage was strong in their home. On the eighth day, at his circumcision, he was named Saul. Hebrew would be his native tongue, but he would be fluent also in Greek and Aramaic.

Paul was born into a home of means. By birthright, he was a Roman. He would be trained in the rabbinic schools. In paternal sternness, Paul was taught the law and manners of Israel. At the age of five, he began to memorize the Torah by oral repetition. The teacher would recite a sentence and the class would repeat it in unison. In this way Paul memorized the Jewish law. He would carry the lesson in his heart. He would need no copy book.

The education of the Jewish child was essentially religious. No one who had learned the elemental lessons of life could talk contemptuously of his first reader or teacher. At age ten, the Hebrew lad began learning the Mishna, the oral law. Many and sundry were the interpretations of rabbis concerning the law. There were more than 613 of them, all to be memorized and practiced. At thirteen the boy was initiated into manhood. No longer did he have to sit with his mother behind the screen or in the balcony at the synagogue, but now with the men on the main floor. He was more responsible, and he would practice the law.

In these years at home, Paul would saturate his mind and heart with the Old Testament Scriptures. He would know by memory the life and the writings of the patriarchs and the prophets. He could sing the Psalms. This boyhood knowledge would in later years serve him well. In the Philippian jail, Paul would remember the songs of his youth. In his arguments with the Judaizers at Antioch, he would be able to quote the Scriptures from memory. In his recitation before the philosophers at Mars Hill, he would remember the teachings of his youth. In his defense before King Agrippa, he would use well the lessons of his boyhood.

III. A third influence.

At age seventeen Paul left home for college. He would study at the time's most famous Jewish school, the school of Hillel at Jerusalem. The headmaster was the renowned Gamaliel. In Acts 22:3 Paul writes, "I am verily a man which am a Jew, born in Tarsus, a city in Cilicia, yet brought up in this city [Jerusalem] at the feet of Gamaliel, and taught according to the perfect manner of the law of our fathers." Paul was not only a "good Jew," but was also schooled at the headquarters. He studied religion and theology with the greatest teacher of his day. In fact, he was one of the most zealous pupils of Gamaliel, so in the Galatian letter he said, "I outstripped many of my classmates in my zeal for the tradition of our fathers."

Like many of his colleagues, Paul joined an extremist group on his campus called the Pharisees. They rebelled against any liberal cosmopolitanism. They jealously guarded a dogmatic traditionalism. They believed that Jewish tradition contained all the truth and that any other teaching was apostate and heretical. Paul believed that the only hope for the salvation of his nation was in obedience to the law and traditions of his father. So he developed an intense prejudice against all that was not Jewish. To persecute heretics was to do God a favor. A part of his daily prayers was to recite, "I thank Thee that I am not as other men." Paul

165

was proud of his "goody-goodness." He was contemptuous in his exclusiveness and meticulous in his ritual and worship.

Like all good Pharisees, Paul determined to win God's favor by good works. He was taught to carefully keep all the laws and traditions of his fathers. What is wrong with this kind of religion? First of all, it is a religion of redemption by human efforts. It is a religion of legalism, of righteousness through works. In this kind of religion, people are thrown back to their own resources. The law summons people to ceaseless toil at the hope of pleasing God. They must battle the world, the flesh, and the devil in their own strength. They must build their own highway to heaven. But what happens then? The building becomes a Tower of Babel. It reaches nowhere near to God. It ends in shame and confusion. People cannot save themselves by their own efforts.

This was Paul's great discovery after he knew the gospel of God's grace through Jesus Christ. In defense of this gospel, he later wrote, "By grace are ye saved through faith; and that not of yourselves: it is the gift of God: not of works, lest any man should boast" (Eph. 2:8–9). Paul discovered what Peter declared at the Jerusalem council recorded in Acts 15:10, the righteousness of the law is "a yoke upon the neck of the disciples, which neither our fathers nor we were able to bear." Paul was writing from personal experience when he said in his letter to the Galatians (2:16), "Knowing that a man is not justified by the works of the law, but by the faith of Jesus Christ, even we have believed in Jesus Christ, that we might be justified by the faith of Christ, and not by the works of the law: for by the works of the law shall no flesh be justified."

Many today, like Paul the Pharisee, are laboring for a righteousness which is in the law. They will never find it. Paul could not. For all his straight-laced righteousness, he cried out, "Oh, wretched man that I am! who shall deliver me from this bondage of death?" (Rom. 7:24). His outward life was exemplary, but his soul was torn by mortal strife. Like the young man who came to Jesus, Paul could say, "All these things have I kept from my youth up, what lack I yet?"

There was something else wrong with Paul's religion. It was a legalism of negatives. The religion of Paul kept saying, "Thou shalt not." The negative became the foundation stone of his creed. This indeed is burdensome. It is a religion that never sings or exalts. It is a dead weight that the soul must carry. It hounded and haunted the heart with its commands, "You must have proper meat, a proper drink, a proper bread." It talked about a certain length to the border of the robe and a certain number of tassels on it. There was always the legalism of straining the wine so that not even the hair on the third left leg of the fly would defile. It speaks about tithing the stalk and the leaf as well as the fruit. It commands a counting out of just so many steps for a Sabbath day's journey. One great rabbi spent all week writing down what he must not do in order to keep the Sabbath.

This yoke of legalism can never bring the peace of God to the heart of man. One of two things results—either there is a spirit of self-righteousness or of despair. For Paul it was the latter. The religion of his youth became a religion of utter despair. No Jew was so ardent, no Pharisee so punctilious, no rabbi so untiring in keeping the law as was the apostle Paul. He did not lie when he told the Philippians, "As touching the righteousness which is in the law, I am blameless." Yet for all of this there was something wrong. For all of this Paul's soul was restless. What was the matter? Paul tells us in Romans 7:18–25. Then again in 8:3 he says that what the law could not do, God sending his own Son could do.

There was only one thing left for Paul. That was to meet Jesus, God's gift of grace. Paul must change his religion of works for a religion of grace. So it is for many of you. You will never be happy and you will never have peace in your religion of works. It is a yoke of legalism. The law may point to the way of righteousness, but it can never give power to walk in it. Paul discovered that the only way to peace of heart and happy living was through surrender to Jesus, who said, "I am the way, the truth, and the life: no man cometh unto the Father but by me" (John 14:6). There was one thing left for Paul: He must have an encounter with Jesus Christ.

WEDNESDAY EVENING, MAY 12

Title: The Call to Abundant Living

Text: "Give, and it shall be given unto you; good measure, pressed down, and shaken together, and running over, shall men give unto your bosom. For with the same measure that ye mete withal it shall be measured to you again" **(Luke 6:38)**.

Scripture Reading: Luke 6:27–38

Introduction

Our Lord was issuing a call to his disciples to give and holding out before them the promise of abundant living. Because of the innate selfishness of the human heart, many have read this statement from the lips of the Savior without discovering the promise of abundance. They have seen only the initial call to a life of giving.

I. The Lord calls his disciples to concentrate on giving.

To study this text is to discover that the Lord did not specify what his disciples were to give. He said nothing about money or time.

    A. *The focus of attention and effort is to be on giving.* Instead of concentrating their thought and energy on obtaining, he suggests that they should define life in terms of an opportunity to give. This philosophy should be put into practice in the home, school, and workplace as well as in the church.

    B. *Our Lord encourages a life of continual giving.*

        1. He encourages us to give love—an unbreakable spirit of goodwill toward others.

        2. He encourages us to give mercy to those in need (Luke 6:36).

        3. He encourages us to give forgiveness to those who have mistreated us (Luke 6:37).

4. He encourages us to give praise where it is deserved.
5. He encourages us to give encouragement to everyone.
6. He encourages us to live in such a way that we inspire those who know us.
7. He encourages us to give gratitude toward all whose lives bless our lives or the lives of others.
8. He encourages us to give our time and our attention to others.

II. The Lord promises a rich reward from people.

Notice particularly the promise — or is it an observation? — in our text. Christ says, "It shall be given unto you." One man observed that it appears that our Lord is encouraging us to give with a selfish motive. He does appeal to the motive of self-interest. This may be surprising to some. The first word in the text is a command. The rest of the text is a promise. Christ describes how people will respond toward the individual who has lived his life by the philosophy that "it is more blessed to give than to receive." Jesus observed that people respond by returning:

A. *Good measure.*
B. *Pressed down.*
C. *Shaken together.*
D. *Running over.*

III. Do you live to get or to give?

This is a paradox isn't it? Many think the world owes them everything. But true living doesn't begin until we learn to give.

Christian Paradox

It is in loving — not in being loved,
The heart is blest;
It is in giving — not in seeking gifts,
We find our quest.
If thou art hungry, lacking heavenly food,
Give hope and cheer.
If thou art sad and wouldst be comforted,
Stay sorrow's tear.
Whatever be thy longing and thy need,
That do thou give;
So shall thy soul be fed, and thou indeed,
Shalt truly live.

—*Author Unknown*

Conclusion

May God help each of us to respond to the call of the generous giving of ourselves and of our substance to others. It is only as we live to give that we will live the abundant life.

SUNDAY MORNING, MAY 16

Title: The Kind of Church God Honors

Text: "And they, continuing daily with one accord in the temple, and breaking bread from house to house, did eat their meat with gladness and singleness of heart, praising God, and having favour with all the people. And the Lord added to the church daily such as should be saved" **(Acts 2:46–47)**.

Scripture Reading: Acts 2:1–4

Hymns: "The Church's One Foundation," Stone

"Onward Christian Soldiers," Baring-Gould

"Seal Us, O Holy Spirit," Meredith

Offertory Prayer: Grant to us, our Father, understanding by our own experience of the reality of the beatitude of our blessed Lord, who said, "It is more blessed to give than to receive." Forgive us that we are everlastingly consumed with the lust for getting, and help us to worship you by the inspiring stewardship of giving, even as you have given to us so bountifully through your love. In Jesus' name. Amen.

Introduction

Even a casual glance at the New Testament churches reveals to us that they were not perfect. The reason they were not perfect is that their membership was composed of sinners. They were sinners saved by grace, but they were sinners just the same. The church is not composed of stone and wood and steel and glass. The church is composed of people; and people, even redeemed by Christ, have feet of clay.

When someone says to me, "I won't join your church; you have hypocrites in it," I am tempted to reply, "All right, you look around until you find a perfect church. But when you do, they won't let you join, for you will spoil their record."

There is a sense in which we should be grateful that the church is not perfect. Because it is imperfect, we have been received into its fellowship. Because of its short-comings, we are challenged to work and grow within its ranks. No, the church is not perfect. But it should be more nearly perfect than it is. The imperfections and the shortcomings are a scandal and a drag on its journey of achievement for our Lord.

With all its faults, the churches of those New Testament years were marvel-ously blessed by God. Their numbers were small. They had no buildings. They had no organizations. They had no status. They had no printing press or elec-tronic communication facilities to spread the gospel. They had no money. Yet this small fellowship of nobodies, as the world viewed them, came closer to winning their generation to Christ than we have ever done since, with all our millions in money and members, and with all our methods and techniques of promotion, organization, and communication.

In the first two chapters of the book of Acts we find the secret of the blessings of God on the early church. Let us examine the things that qualified that church for God's prosperity.

169

I. The kind of church God honors is a praying church.

In Acts 1:14 we read, "These all continued with one accord in prayer and supplication, with the women, and Mary the mother of Jesus, and with his brethren."

A. *Everyone was present for the prayer meeting.* "These *all* continued." No one was absent. What would happen if every member of our church came to the prayer service next Wednesday evening? They couldn't all get in, for there would not be room. In all likelihood, someone else would have to be quickly drafted to lead the service, for the pastor would probably faint. In many churches the prayer service has died or has been abandoned. What could happen if all of God's people came together in the house of prayer!

B. *They were all in one accord.* "These all continued *with one accord* in prayer." Their hearts were knit in fellowship and love. They came with the same serious purpose and with a common sense of need. Here were 120 people, together in body and spirit, joined in prayer and supplication for the promised blessings of God.

A praying church is a spiritual church. God forgive us that often we have substituted the techniques of promotion and organization and advertising for the practice of prayer. There is no substitute for prayer—prayer in the secrecy of one's closet, prayer in the family circle, and corporate prayer in the sanctuary of God's house. God cannot give us his blessings unless we spiritually qualify for them, and we cannot spiritually qualify unless we pay the price in prayer.

II. The kind of church God honors is a witnessing church.

In Acts 2:4 we read, "And they were all filled with the Holy Spirit and began to speak...."

A. *They all began to speak.* In the New Testament church, all of the people witnessed. The Scripture does not say that the apostles began to speak or that the church leaders began to speak, but that even the most obscure and modest members spoke. What an exciting scene it must have been to see 120 excited, thrilling Christian witnesses telling the startled people on the streets of Jerusalem, "He is alive! He whom you killed arose from the grave! He is the Messiah, the fulfillment of prophecy! He is the Son of God and the Savior of the world! He has redeemed me from my sins, and he can and will forgive you if you trust him and ask him!"

Not only are the hinges to our prayer closets rusty from neglect, but our lips are silent and our tongues are still. We have left it for the professional to do our praying and our witnessing for us.

One of the greatest victories Satan ever won was when he convinced the average church member that the pastor and the evangelist and the song leader and the educational director and a deacon or two should do the witnessing.

Let me read you two significant verses from this dynamic book of Acts: "And at that time there was a great persecution against the church which was at Jerusalem; and they were all scattered abroad throughout the regions of Judea and Samaria, except the apostles" (Acts 8:1). What does that verse say? It tells us that a terrible persecution broke out in Jerusalem against the church and everyone fled, except the apostles — the pastors. They stayed behind, at the risk of their lives, to minister to the aged and infirm and others who could not flee.

Now let us read Acts 8:4. "Therefore, they that were scattered abroad went everywhere preaching the word." Who were scattered abroad? Not the preachers; the people were scattered — men, women, young people, and children. And those who were scattered abroad went everywhere witnessing, testifying, teaching, and preaching! And God richly blessed that church and the Christian growth of that generation.

What would happen today if every member of the church recognized that witnessing is every Christian's task and privilege? We would see another glorious Pentecost in our day.

B. *They were all filled with the Holy Spirit and began to speak.* Much of what little witnessing we do is mechanical and impotent because we are not filled with the Holy Spirit.

1. Being filled with the Holy Spirit gives us boldness. We may witness occasionally or by assignment if we are not filled with God's Spirit, but if we are filled with the Holy Spirit, we cannot help but speak. Even the stones would cry out if we remained silent when the Spirit possesses us. We do so little witnessing because the Holy Spirit possesses so little of us.

2. Being filled with the Holy Spirit gives us effectiveness. It is the Holy Spirit who convicts of sin. It is the Holy Spirit who works at both ends of the line — with us and with the person to whom we witness. It is the Holy Spirit who gives us guidance in our prayers of intercession for those without Christ. It is the Holy Spirit who gives us a radiance, a poise, a buoyancy that will make our faith contagious and will cause others to desire the joy and peace that are ours.

III. The kind of church God honors magnifies preaching.

The climax of the Pentecostal experience is recorded in the words, "But Peter, standing up with the eleven, lifted up his voice and said unto them. . . ." The Holy Spirit chose Peter to preach the sermon that great day. He preached Christ. He gloried in the cross. He preached with eloquence. He preached with conviction. He preached with boldness. He preached with power. He made definite demands. He presented the claims of the risen Christ. He called people to repent. He commanded believers to be baptized. He gave an evangelistic invitation, and thousands responded.

Someone has said that on the day of Pentecost one sermon was preached and three thousand responded but that today it takes three thousand sermons for one response. The church that God honors magnifies the sermon. God still honors preaching — Bible preaching, Christ-centered preaching, urgent preaching, Spirit-filled preaching.

It is my conviction that preaching today lacks the effectiveness God purposed for it because it is not preceded by the praying and witnessing of a Spirit-filled church. The sermon is not designed to do the job alone. It is intended by God to be the climax of the praying and witnessing of people and pastor. The sermon of Peter would have lacked its great effectiveness that day had it not been preceded by the praying and the witnessing of all of the church.

When a church today will dedicate its life to fervent, faithful, unceasing, agonizing prayer, God can bless that church. When the people are filled with the Holy Spirit and begin to speak, miraculous things will begin to happen all over again. Then, when the pastor opens God's Book to proclaim his gospel, there will be conviction, repentance, conversion, and commitment.

Conclusion

The crucified and risen Christ that Peter preached is still the persuasive Savior today. The love of God for you that prompted him to send his Son to die for your sins is just as deep and abiding today as in that day. If in your heart you feel that this is your hour to commit your life to Christ, this is his call, and we pray that you will respond.

If you already are a Christian and you are searching for a church, I challenge you to prayerfully consider membership and fellowship in this blessed church. We invite you to join us in building a church that God honors.

SUNDAY EVENING, MAY 16

Title: Paul Is Converted

Text: "And he trembling and astonished said, Lord, what wilt thou have me to do? And the Lord said unto him, Arise, and go into the city, and it shall be told thee what thou must do" **(Acts 9:6)**.

Scripture Reading: Acts 9:1–9

Introduction

Gamaliel's most famous student could never be accused of neutrality; the collegian Paul was a revolutionary. Even when his memories of youth were tempered by forty years, Paul confessed his part in the ardent persecution of the Christian church. In Galatians 1:13 he says, "Ye have heard of my conversation in time past in the Jews' religion, how that beyond measure I persecuted the church of God and wasted it." In Philippians 3:6 he says, "With great zeal I persecuted the church." And in his defense before King Agrippa recorded in Acts 26:11, he says, "I punished them oft in every synagogue, and compelled them to blaspheme; and being exceedingly mad against them, I persecuted them even unto strange cities."

All of this illuminates Luke's description: "And Saul, yet breathing out threat-enings and slaughter against the disciples of the Lord, went unto the high priest, and desired of him letters to Damascus to the synagogues, that if he found any of this way, whether they were men or women, he might bring them bound unto Jerusalem" (Acts 9:1–2).

In John 16:2 Jesus predicted that the time would come when the believers would be turned out of the synagogues and killed, and those who persecuted them would think they were doing God a service. This is exactly what Paul thought. He fervently believed that followers of Jesus were blasphemers, heretics, and deserters of the faith. It was his duty to stamp them out. Paul became the chief persecuter of the church. He heard that there was a group of believers at Damascus, so he took with him warrants from the high priest to arrest any who called themselves "disciples of Jesus."

I. Influences on Paul's conversion.

We all know of the dramatics on the Damascus Road—the light, the voice, the blindness, the complete change that came to Paul. When did it all start? What were the influences that brought Paul to his conversion? There is a moment of conversion, but there are many influences that work to bring about that change. This was true of the apostle Paul.

What were the influences that brought about his conversion? First, there was the disillusioned heart. Paul earnestly and zealously performed all the traditions of his fathers. He declared of himself, "... touching the righteousness which is in the law, blameless" (Phil. 3:6). Paul was like the young man who came to Jesus and asked, "What must I do?" And Jesus replied, "Keep the law." And the young man said, "All these I have kept from my youth up, what lack I yet?" (Matt. 19:20).

For all of Paul's goodness, for all of his churchgoing, he felt there was a lack in his life. He had faithfully performed all of the prescribed routine of ablution, of fasting, of praying, and of Sabbath observing, yet he had no peace. Instead, he had an empty heart. Paul's heart was troubled, he was disillusioned, but what could he do? He could work harder, he could redouble his efforts at righteous-ness. Isn't it strange that when works of righteousness bring us no peace we just try harder? We attend church more, we pray more, we pay more; but with all of this the peace of God escapes us. Whatever else Paul's religion had done for him, it had not brought him peace. The fury of his attacks against the Christians indi-cated that something was wrong in the heart of the apostle Paul.

A second influence that led to Paul's conversion was the lives of the Chris-tians. The early church was poor and persecuted, yet it had power. The apostles preached and witnessed with conviction. Even in the face of death the early Chris-tians had a calm confidence, a glad fearlessness, a rejoicing. Tertullian says, "All of this struck Paul with an inward misgiving." Had they found something that he had missed? It behooves us who are Christians to present to the world a positive profession. In everyday life, in spite of adversity, sorrow, or disappointment, we need to show forth the glories of our faith. One never knows when a Paul might

173

be watching. The strong influence in the heart of Paul was the martyrdom of Stephen. Stephen was not a Hebrew. Like Paul, he was a Hellenist, a proselyte to the Christian faith. He was not a preacher but rather a layman, a deacon. It was his job to witness to the gospel in the Greek synagogue, and this is what he did. It was in one of these visits to the synagogue that Stephen and Paul met (Acts 6:9–10).

One Sabbath something very disturbing happened. There was a sharp encounter with Stephen in the church and later in the halls of the council of the Sanhedrin. Paul and his rabbinic colleagues were outmatched. It must have been a humiliating experience. For all of their rabbinic degrees, their letters, and their dialectics, the members of the Sanhedrin were impotent. When they saw that they were about to lose their argument, they cried, "Blasphemy." It had worked a couple of years before at the trial of Jesus; it worked again at the trial of Stephen. So the deacon Stephen was dragged outside the city and stoned.

Stoning is peculiarly a Jewish form of execution. It is brutal and revolting. Everyone is expected to share in the sentence, for it is not a spectacle to be witnessed from a distance but something that is done at close hand. The first stones were cast by the witnesses against Stephen and then by the hands of everyone present. It was done in clumsy violence and bitter rage. Such a horrible execution would make an indelible impression upon Paul. He stood watching and even consenting to Stephen's death. Acts 7:58 says, "And they stoned him [Stephen]: and the witnesses laid down their clothes at a young man's feet, whose name was Saul." The Scripture adds, "And they saw Stephen's face as it had been the face of an angel" (Acts 6:15). I think in the days that followed, Paul kept seeing that face of Stephen. Paul never got away from these influences. His disillusionment with the old Pharisaic religion, the radiant lives of the Christians, and then Stephen's death, all influenced his conversion that followed.

Having purged Jerusalem of the heretics, Paul learned of a company in Damascus. Securing papers and letters of authority, he set out. It was a long journey of some 140 miles. During that week of journey Paul had time for reflection. He kept asking himself, "Could these Christians be right? Was Jesus really the long-awaited Messiah? Am I fighting against God?" It was high noon. The Syrian sun beamed down on the company of soldiers. In the distance could be seen the ancient city of Damascus. Soon Paul and his company would leave these stony wastes and begin to ride beside the pleasant Baradda River. What happened then is all a part of the sacred story. It is recorded in Acts 9:3–9.

II. Dramatics of Paul's conversion.

There are two things about the dramatics here—the voice and the vision. The voice said, "Saul, Saul, why persecutest thou me?" The words were spoken in Hebrew, Paul's mother tongue. There is a pleading iteration of his name. The question indeed is strange. It is not "Why do you persecute my disciples?" nor

"Why do you persecute my church?" but "Why do you persecute me?" From the beginning of his conversion, Paul was going to learn that the glorified Savior and his people are one—one body together. Jesus had said to his disciples, "Inasmuch as ye have done it unto one of the least of these my brethren, ye have done it unto me" (Matt. 25:40). If we persecute the church, we persecute Jesus Christ. If we serve the church, we serve Jesus Christ.

Conclusion

There was that voice and then the vision. Whatever else Paul saw that day on the Damascus Road, he saw the living Lord. He writes of it in 1 Corinthians 15:8: "And last of all he was seen of me also, as of one born out of due time." For Paul, this was the beginning of the new life. He calls it an "arrest, an apprehension." We call it conversion. It means a complete change. Paul was born again. He became the most conspicuous example in the New Testament of a complete and instantaneous conversion. Paul, in speaking of it, says, "I became a new creature in Christ Jesus: The things I once hated I now love, what before I loved, I now hate, so it is no longer I that liveth but Christ living in me."

That Damascus Road is not the only gateway into the kingdom. Your spiritual experience may lack the dramatics of Paul's conversion, but the conversion needs to be just as real—the salvation just as satisfying. There must come a time in your life when there is a personal confrontation with Jesus. Yours, too, must be a turning about. You also must be made new; you must experience conversion. There must come a time when you can say with the apostle Paul, "I have become a new creature in Christ Jesus—it is no longer I that liveth, but Christ living in me." Have you had your Damascus Road experience?

WEDNESDAY EVENING, MAY 19

Title: The Call to Personal Witnessing

Text: "But ye shall receive power, after that the Holy Ghost is come upon you: And ye shall be witnesses unto me both in Jerusalem and in all Judaea, and in Samaria, and unto the uttermost part of the earth" **(Acts 1:8)**.

Scripture Reading: Acts 1:1–14

Introduction

Some people believe that the greatest call God can extend is the call to the ministry. Others feel that the call of God to be a foreign missionary is the highest and holiest call that God extends. The truth is that neither of these calls constitutes the primary call of God.

The primary call of God to each of us is the call to be a witness. The call to be a witness takes precedence over the call to the ministry or to the mission field. We are called to be witnesses first and ministers or missionaries second.

I. Personal witnessing is our supreme task.

We are mistaken if we define our supreme task in terms of teaching, preaching, singing, or giving. Our supreme task is that of being a witness, and we may give this testimony through teaching, preaching, singing, or giving.

II. Personal witnessing is our most precious privilege.

To give a personal testimony is to share the good news of God's love, which can be used by the Holy Spirit to bestow the gift of faith that makes possible the new birth in the heart of another person.

III. Personal witnessing is our most pressing responsibility (Rom. 1:14–16).

Paul was aware of the great debt that he owed to God and that he owed to a lost world. He was ready with everything that was within him to meet his obligation to God and to the world. The only way he could meet this obligation was by the testimony concerning the wonderful grace and power of God through Jesus Christ.

IV. Personal witnessing is our most challenging opportunity.

Many opportunities confront us today—opportunities that would fill us with enthusiasm and command our total energy. However, if we would try to evaluate these various opportunities, not one would offer comparable dividends and satisfactions to that of personal witnessing.

V. Personal witnessing is the world's greatest need.

The world has many needs—the need for peace, food, education, better homes, better medical attention—but the world's greatest need is for our personal testimony concerning the goodness and mercy of God as it is revealed in the life of Jesus Christ.

VI. Personal witnessing to the saving power of Jesus Christ is the world's only hope.

Most of the unsaved people in the average community never attend the regular worship services of any church. If these people are to be converted, if they are to experience the grace of God, it will be because of the personal witnessing of those who go outside the walls of the church to share the good news of what God has done for them through Jesus Christ.

VII. Personal witnessing is the divinely ordained method of saving lost men and women.

Jesus Christ used the face-to-face method of telling others about the love of God. The one-on-one method would communicate the gospel to the whole world in ten years if each professing Christian were to win one other to faith in Christ during each of those years.

Conclusion

The unsaved world waits for our personal witness. The Holy Spirit waits to bless our personal witness. God has called each of us to be personal witnesses, and the need of the hour is for us to be faithful to our calling.

SUNDAY MORNING, MAY 23

Title: When Christ Comes

Text: "Go home to thy friends, and tell them how great things the Lord hath done for thee, and hath had compassion on thee" (**Mark 5:19**).

Scripture Reading: Mark 5:1–20

Hymns: "Come, Thou Fount," Robinson

          "Christ Receiveth Sinful Men," Neumaster

          "Since I Have Been Redeemed," Excell

Offertory Prayer: Blessed Father, today we thank you for both the great and the small blessings that you have bestowed on us through Jesus Christ. You are the source of all that is good and noble in our lives. We give you the honor and glory and praise. Today we come bringing tithes and offerings as an indication of our gratitude. Accept them as symbols of our desire to be completely dedicated to your redemptive purpose. Bless them to your glory and bless them to the spiritual welfare of a needy race of men. Through Jesus Christ our Lord we worship and pray. Amen.

Introduction

There was a sharp contrast in the reaction of various people when they received word concerning the birth of the Christ in Bethlehem. On one hand, there was great fear at the time when his birth was announced. The shepherds were frightened by the presence of the angels. Herod the king was frightened by the announcement that a baby had been born who was to be the King of the Jews. The angels rejoiced and urged all the earth to rejoice, for a Savior had been born.

Through the centuries the Christ who was born, who lived, who died, and who arose again has continued to confront both individuals and groups. Without exception, when Christ comes he still creates either a deadly fear or a great rejoicing. This is because he creates a crisis within the soul. To come face-to-face with the Christ produces a conviction of human frailty and sin. This conviction can lead either to conversion and life, or it can lead to despair if he is rejected.

That Christ creates a crisis within the soul can be dramatically demonstrated by the description of his visit to the country of the Gadarenes where he delivered a demoniac from the evil, unclean spirits who were in control of his personality. This encounter confronts us with three pictures of the Christ. First, Christ is

177

pictured as a disturber who would torment the evil that possesses us. He is also pictured as one who brings health and wholeness and happiness to those who permit him to heal them. Third, Christ is pictured as a worthy Master for those who would yield their hearts and lives to him in devoted service.

I. When Christ comes he creates disturbance (Mark 5:6–7).

Christ confronts the evil in our hearts, and this is always a disturbing experience.

A. *The man of Gadara was under the domination of evil.* The New Testament clearly teaches the existence of evil spirits that seek access to the hearts and souls of people. The purpose of these evil spirits is to bring harm to human lives. These evil spirits are the instrument of Satan.

The condition of the demonized man is revealed.

1. He was living in a condition of terrible isolation among the tombs in the region of death, as far as possible from his fellow human beings.
2. He was characterized by a terrible lawlessness that threw off all restraint.
3. His experience was one of inward, agonizing restlessness crying out night and day.
4. He suffered greatly from self-inflicted wounds as a result of cutting himself with stones.
5. He had become a menace to all people, making it dangerous for them to approach where he was.
6. He was at war with himself.
7. He was at war with others. He presents to us an exhibition of the ultimate effects of being possessed by an evil spirit.

B. *Christ confronted the demons who possessed the soul of this man, and he continues to confront the demons who possess the souls of people today.* He sets people free to live and love and labor as God intended they should.

C. *Christ always disturbs and torments when he comes.* "Think not that I am come to send peace on earth: I came not to send peace, but a sword" (Matt. 10:34). On one occasion when Peter was overwhelmed with the deity of the Christ, we hear him cry out, "Depart from me; for I am a sinful man, O Lord" (Luke 5:8).

When Isaiah experienced the vision of the holiness of God, he cried out of his unworthiness and said, "Woe is me! for I am undone; because I am a man of unclean lips, and I dwell in the midst of a people of unclean lips: for mine eyes have seen the King, the Lord of hosts" (Isa. 6:5). When Christ comes, he causes us to see ourselves as we really are. To come face-to-face with him is comparable to beholding our features in a perfect mirror.

D. *Christ disturbs us by showing us what we may become.* An unknown poet described this torment in a poem entitled "I Met the Master Face to Face."

> *I had walked life's way with an easy tread,*
> *Had followed where comforts and pleasures led,*

178

> *Until one day in a quiet place*
> *I met the Master face to face.*
> *I met him and knew him and blushed to see*
> *That his eyes full of sorrow were fixed on me,*
> *And I faltered and fell at his feet that day,*
> *While my castles melted and vanished away.*
> *Melted and vanished, and in their place*
> *Naught else did I see but the Master's face;*
> *And I cried aloud, "Oh, make me meet*
> *To follow the steps of thy wounded feet!"*
> *My thought is now for the souls of men;*
> *I have lost my life to find it again,*
> *E're since one day in a quiet place,*
> *I met the Master face to face.*

E. *Christ disturbs us by the call of human need.* He would sensitize our spiritual eardrums so that we could hear voices like that which spoke to Paul in the night, saying, "Come over into Macedonia, and help us" (Acts 16:9). Christ will disturb us in our comfort and complacency. He will disturb us in our devotion to the acquiring and accumulation of material possessions. He will encourage us to love to the extent that we will share with those who suffer need.

II. When Christ comes he comes to heal.

When Christ comes, he comes to offer abundant, joyous, eternal life.

A. *Christ commanded the unclean spirits to come out of the man of Gadara (Mark 5:8).*
   1. Christ was determined to deliver him from the evil spirit who dominated his life.
   2. Christ delivered him from his unnatural, evil, destructive life.
   3. Christ rescued him from living death.
   4. Christ cleansed him from the uncleanness of his life.
   5. Christ caused his homeless wanderings, miserable wretchedness, and disturbing restlessness to cease.
   6. With Christ there is forgiveness for sin, solace for sorrow, strength and courage for living in all situations.

B. *Christ gave the man a new purpose for living and made it possible for him to live with himself and for others.*

C. *Christ brought a unity into his personality that created peace and joy.* Christ gave him the strength to let his ideals have supremacy over his instincts. Christ always brings out the best in those who are willing to respond positively to his call. A woman past sixty came to her pastor on one occasion and said concerning herself and her husband, "This is our first anniversary as the children of God. We wouldn't swap this past year for all of the others put together." Christ brings a wonder and a joy into life that cannot be found anywhere else.

179

III. When Christ comes and we permit him to be our Master, life takes on new meaning, beauty, and purpose.

A. *The man who had experienced the redeeming power of Christ made a most natural request: "And when he was come into the ship, he that had been possessed with the devil prayed that he might be with him" (Mark 5:18).* Perhaps he was conscious of his personal weakness and wanted to stay close to Christ. It is possible that the fear of a recurrence of the inward hell that he had known in the past encouraged him to make this request. Or perhaps it was love and gratitude that bound him to his benefactor.

At first glance, the refusal of the Master to grant his request is a bit shocking. On other occasions, Jesus had invited his followers to come and follow him. In this case, the man who had been healed wanted to follow, yet Christ had other plans for him.

B. *The request of the man was denied because the Master had something better for him.* He was denied pebbles in order that he might have bread. He was denied serpents in order that he might have fish. Many times when God says no, he does so because he has something better for us.

C. *The Master's reply to the man's request was, "Go home to thy friends, and tell them how great things the Lord hath done for thee, and hath had compassion on thee" (Mark 5:19).*

D. *The Master requested that this man go home and be a living, walking, vivid, unanswerable demonstration of what Christ can do for every person.*

E. *The man of Gadara showed his gratitude to the Savior by his obedience.* In the very places where his former condition was best known and in the place where the marvelous change that had taken place could be best appreciated, he was to communicate the good news of salvation. By his very presence he would demonstrate the effects of the love and power of Christ in a person's life. Every person needs a master. Every person has a master. Every person has the choice concerning who or what will be the master of his life.

Conclusion

As Christ comes to disturb your conscience and your heart, his purpose is to bring health and happiness. For him to do so, you must let him become your Master and Lord and live a life of obedience to him who is infinite, indescribable love. Make him the Lord of your life now.

SUNDAY EVENING, MAY 23

Title: Paul Joins the Church

Text: "But rise, and stand upon thy feet: for I have appeared unto thee for this purpose, to make thee a minister and a witness both of these things which thou hast seen, and of those things in the which I will appear unto thee" **(Acts 26:16)**.

Scripture Reading: Acts 9:1–9; 26:12–20

Introduction

The following lines are an epitome of Paul's transformation:

The proudest heart that ever beat
Has been subdued in me,
The wildest will that ever rode
To scorn thy cause, or raid they foes,
Is quelled, My God, by Thee.
Thy will and not my will be done,
Henceforth I'd be forever Thine,
Confessing Thee, the living Word,
My Saviour Christ, My God, My Lord,
Thy Cross shall be my sign.

How different was Paul's entry into Damascus than he had anticipated! He thought he would be met there by the ranking ecclesiastical authorities. He had letters from none other than the high priest—the potentate of all Israel. Instead of entering the city in pomp and circumstance, they led Paul in by the hand. He was blind and shaking and trembling and helpless. The great conquistador for the inquisition was a stricken man. Acts 9:9 says, "For three days he lay helpless." During these days of darkness, his heart was blessed by the light of Christ, which he speaks of as a "heavenly vision." To his troubled soul God unveiled the secrets of his divine purpose.

Paul speaks of this in Acts 26:14–19. It is the story of his arrest by God—how he was struck down and stopped in his way. He speaks of it as his separation to a divine purpose, a calling to his vocation. In Acts 26:19 Paul says, "I was not disobedient unto the heavenly vision." Has this ever been your experience? Have you met the arrester of your soul? Has God made such a light in your heart? He can give you a heavenly vision if you will do as Paul says in verse 20: "Repent and turn to God."

A guide can still show you the street in Damascus called "Straight." Here, hidden away in some stall, Paul found refuge in his days of darkness. That short visit by Jesus had changed the direction of Paul's life. From persecutor he would become the purveyor of the gospel. From chief sinner he would become the chief servant. What would be next for Paul?

I. Paul is befriended (Acts 9:10–22).

It is strange that the great troubler of the Christians should have one of them to befriend him. In Paul's great hour of need, God sent a man named Ananias to be his friend. We know almost nothing about Ananias yet enough to know that he was a jewel. He is a man to whom the Lord could speak. He must have had an intimate prayer life. The Scriptures do not indicate that he held any important position in the early church. He was no apostle, no preacher, no deacon—just a holy man who lived a humble life. He was a simple saint, yet God chose him to be the friend of Paul at the crucial time of his conversion.

Ananias came to Paul with a Christian welcome. Notice his words, "Brother Saul." Those words must have brought a holy thrill to Paul. Pharisaism had never spoken to Paul like this. Theirs was a negative, legalistic ecclesiasticism that put barriers between people, pitting them against one another in a religion of works. Theirs was a religion of distrust, envy, and jealousy; but here was a Christian who said, "Brother," a name that reminds us of what we become when we join God's family.

II. Paul is baptized (Acts 9:7–18).

What a baptism Paul's must have been! There were tidal waves of emotion that Paul would long remember. He speaks of it in Romans 6:3: "We who were baptized were baptized into Christ Jesus; we were buried therefore, through baptism into his death, that we also might walk in newness of life."

Paul's baptism marked an irreversible break with his past. Now the die was cast. Paul could no longer go back to the old life. He would walk in newness of life with Christ and Christian fellowship. Paul began to witness to his new faith immediately: "And straightway he preached Christ in the synagogues, that he is the Son of God" (Acts 9:20). Paul did not wait for a pastor's class; he did not wait for a course on "How to Witness." He began telling the story of his own experience in Christ.

III. Paul is persecuted (Acts 9:23–35).

Now the chief persecutor is persecuted! The Pharisaic Judaizers had regarded Paul as their able ally, but now they discover that he has become quite the opposite. He is a renegade, a traitor. The same violence Paul had meted out to the Christians, he would now suffer. They said, "We will kill him."

Damascus was a walled city. It was easy enough to shut it up and to make a guard around it. Only a few gates allowed entrance and exit. These gates were posted and watched. One such gate remains until today. It is a part of the East Wall, a rocky structure that has three arches about forty feet high. What would Paul do? How would he escape Damascus? Under the cover of darkness he was smuggled to a house by the wall. There he was placed in a basket and lowered over the wall to the ground. Christian history hung precariously on that little rope that lowered Paul in a swinging basket. How different would the story have been had Paul not escaped! But God already had put his providential hand upon Paul, for the Scripture says, "He is a chosen vessel unto me, to bear my name before the Gentiles" (Acts 9:15).

IV. Paul becomes a member of the church (Acts 9:26–30).

It is not surprising that Paul's application for membership in the Jerusalem church would be questioned. Everyone in Jerusalem knew about Paul's past life. He was the persecutor, the destroyer of the church. Now he wanted to join it. The church at Jerusalem had probably heard about Paul in Damascus—how he claimed to be changed; how he preached the gospel of Jesus—but no man can change that much! Isn't it strange that we preach the power of God to change people's lives, and then when God does it, it is hard to believe and accept?

The language of verse 26 is strange indeed. It says, "He assayed to join the disciples." The word *assayed* means to attempt to bring about, to try several times in several ways. The same word is used in Acts 16:7: "We assayed to go into Bithynia but the Spirit suffered us not." The meaning of the word implies persistence. Why join the church at all? Paul was already saved and baptized. He had already received his special revelation from God and a commission to a life of service. He did not need man's ordination.

For Paul it might have been easier to have gone his own way. He could have become an independent evangelist, self-appointed, self-ordained, self-advertised, and self-supported. Or Paul could have started his own church, "The Independent Paulists." Why not? Here's why: Because Paul had already learned something about Christ and his church. Paul remembered the words of Jesus on the Damascus Road, "Why persecutest thou me?" The living Lord had identified himself with the church.

Paul understood that the church at Jerusalem, or Antioch, or Corinth, or Rome, is the incarnation of Christ for this age. So the Bible says, "Now ye are the body of Christ and members in particular" (1 Cor. 12:27). I am convinced that the "organized church," for all her faults and shortcomings, is the instrument through which Christ will work in this age. The New Testament says, "Christ loved the church and gave himself for it" (Eph. 5:25).

Conclusion

"But Barnabas took him." I thank God for such great-hearted Christians. The name Barnabas means "son of consolation." Barnabas was exactly that to the young convert Paul. The church in Jerusalem was big; one could get lost in its membership. One could drop out of its fellowship and scarcely be missed. But in that big church there was a man named Barnabas who took care of new members. Every church ought to have a Barnabas. Chrysostom described him as "sweetly reasonable, gentle, kindly accessible." When others would have cautiously kept Paul at arm's length, Barnabas drew this young man close to his heart and his fellowship.

This chapter of Paul's life closes with verse 29: "He spake boldly in the name of the Lord Jesus." Christians ought to do this. Christians who have recently been saved from their selfishness and sin ought to speak boldly in the name of Jesus. Christians who have known the grace of God, whose lives have been transformed by God's love ought to speak boldly in the name of Jesus. I am persuaded that some of you need to do what the apostle Paul did. He met Christ and pledged his life to him. He was baptized and joined the fellowship of the church. Immediately he began a life of Christian witness and service.

WEDNESDAY EVENING, MAY 26

Title: The Call to Faith

Text: "And Jesus answering said unto them, Have faith in God" (**Mark 11:22**).

Scripture Reading: Mark 11:15–26

Introduction

The call from God to have faith comes to the heart of every person. Our response to this call largely determines whether we will be capable of hearing other calls from God.

Jesus came that he might help people have faith in the great God. It was the lack of faith in the hearts of his disciples that limited what he could do in them and what they could do for others (cf. Matt. 17:14–21).

Let us give some consideration to some of the great truths concerning the call of faith.

I. Genuine faith is sometimes difficult.

A. *We are men of flesh who like to walk by sight.* This is a part of our human frailty. We want to follow the faith of common sense where no risk is involved.

B. *We have a natural tendency to live only for the moment.* We major in satisfying our stomachs and clothing our backs. We deny the uniqueness of our nature as creatures of eternity who are made in the image of God.

C. *There is much suffering in the world that causes some people to have serious questions concerning both the nature of God and the purposes of life.*

D. *Some people find it difficult to have faith because of the great variety of beliefs that offer themselves as the authoritative explanation of the gospel.*

II. Faith is not only reasonable but necessary (Ps. 14:1).

A. *It would be exceedingly difficult to be an atheist and to believe that there is no supreme power behind our wonderful and beautiful universe.* One cannot study astronomy or anatomy without being impressed with the mystery of things that the finite minds of humans cannot possibly explain. There must be a God. God is a logical necessity for a rational understanding of the world and of humans.

B. *The testimony of history reveals that the men and women who have put faith in God have been men and women who have lifted humanity.* The men and women who have had the faith to trust God and to cooperate with him as he has revealed himself have been the men and women who have found life meaningful.

C. *Many of us can bear testimony to the reasonableness of faith on the basis of our own personal experience.* With reverence we can say that, like Enoch, we have talked with God and that God has talked with us. Like Abraham we have walked with him. Like the disciples following the resurrection, we have experienced the presence of the living Lord as he has come near not only to comfort but also to counsel, to commission, and to change.

D. *Without faith life is empty and without ultimate purpose.* Without faith assurance is impossible and personal venture, which implies risk, will be at a minimum. Little faith or no faith will attempt nothing of real significance. Little faith was the undoing sin of ancient Israel. It also was the sin that greatly handicapped and limited the disciples of the Lord.

III. The way to faith.

A. *Faith is based on testimony.* We believe some things because of the testimony of our senses—we can see, taste, touch, and smell. But the faith based on our senses comes closer to common sense than it does to the faith that ventures.

B. *Faith is the gift of God (cf. Luke 17:5; Acts 14:27).* In a real sense, faith is the gift of God, yet it is a human response to God's revelation of himself.

C. *Our faith in God can grow.* God is faithful and can be depended on by those who trust him. The more we trust him, the greater our faith will become. A study of biblical and Christian history reveals that the spiritual giants were the men and women who out-believed their contemporaries.

Conclusion

By the testimony of the Scriptures, we are encouraged to a life of faith. By the testimony of the saints, we are encouraged not only to faith but also to faithfulness.

God calls us to put our confidence in Jesus Christ as Savior and Lord. Each of us needs to respond to this call.

SUNDAY MORNING, MAY 30

Title: How to Be Filled with the Spirit

Text: "And be not drunk with wine, wherein is excess; but be filled with the Spirit" (**Eph. 5:18**).

Scripture Reading: John 16:7–14

Hymns:　"Come, Thou Almighty King," Anonymous

　　　　 "Holy Spirit from on High," Bathurst

　　　　 "Holy Spirit, Faithful Guide," Wells

Offertory Prayer: We thank you, Father, for the gift of your Holy Spirit, who has worked the miracle of redemption within us and enabled us to walk among people as the children of God. Just as you have led us to your house, lead us in the bringing of our gifts to you. Accept the gift of our renewed lives behind the offering of our possessions, that these gifts of our stewardship may be acceptable to you. In Jesus' name. Amen.

Introduction

Most American people today believe that there is a God, but most would admit that they have never felt his presence. Their belief in God is an intellectual, impersonal acknowledgment that there must be a God somewhere out there.

The church today is filled with busy, hardworking people who view their vows as very practical and urgent. They sign pledges, give their tithes and offerings, read their Bibles, visit, witness, teach, and even preach without power and warmth. Are we not too often engaged in doing things *for* God rather than allowing God to do those things *through* us? Our fathers gloried in what they called their heartfelt religion. Today we sniff at emotion and disdain the sentimental. Our faith is intellectual and our works are mechanical. What we need is a spiritual relationship with God. This relationship comes through the work of the Holy Spirit in the heart and life of the believer.

The Holy Spirit is a person. He is not an "it." An inexperienced young preacher exclaimed to the new mother concerning her newborn child, "Isn't it pretty." "My baby isn't an it!" the mother indignantly replied. And the young pastor had learned a vital lesson. I can visualize the indignation and hurt of God when he, through his Spirit, is depersonalized. He is a person who reacts as other persons. He can be grieved, he can be quenched, he comforts, he convicts, he reveals, he regenerates, and he keeps us in God's grace.

The doctrine of the Trinity is a mystery that must be accepted by faith. I do not know all the answers, but I know that when a person or a church becomes "filled with the Spirit" things begin to happen.

The night before Jesus died, he told his disciples, "It is expedient for you that I go away: for if I go not away, the Comforter will not come unto you; but if I depart, I will send him unto you" (John 16:7). As long as Jesus was in the flesh on the earth, he was localized in his presence. He could not be in Galilee and Jerusalem at the same time. But since he went away and the Holy Spirit came in power into the church, the presence of Christ is everywhere all of the time. The world traveler feels Christ's presence in other parts of the world just as he does as he worships in his own church at home. God is a universal God, present and working in the lives of his children throughout the world.

The Holy Spirit comes into the heart of the believer in his experience of conversion. "Hereby know we that we dwell in him, and he in us, because he hath given us of his Spirit" (1 John 4:13). If you are a Christian, do not pray for the Holy Spirit to come into your heart. He is already there. He may dwell in a corner of your heart because you have crowded him out of the main rooms, but if you are a child of God, the Holy Spirit dwells in your heart.

Christians are commanded to be filled with the Holy Spirit. This is a step, an experience, beyond the presence of the Holy Spirit in our lives through salvation. Our usefulness, our joy, our peace of mind and heart, our boldness in witness, and our effectiveness depend on availing ourselves of the Spirit's infilling.

To be filled with the Holy Spirit is a gift. "If ye then, being evil, know how to give good gifts unto your children: how much more shall your heavenly Father give the Holy Spirit to them that ask him?" (Luke 11:13). To receive the gift of the Holy Spirit we must qualify. What must we do? Let me offer some suggestions.

I. We must earnestly long to be filled with God's Holy Spirit.

If we say, "I have as much of God as I desire," we cannot be filled. If we are satisfied to get along without God's power, we cannot receive the filling of the Holy Spirit. This wish must be all-consuming, the most important thing in our lives.

It must crowd out all else. We must be willing to pay any cost, and there is a cost. This gift does not come by a casual wish or a momentary whim. It is a big deal, the biggest deal in the Christian experience.

II. We must be willing to be emptied of all else.

This is logical. If a vessel is filled, it cannot be filled with something else unless the present contents are displaced. If our lives are filled with self, they cannot, at the same time, be filled with God. We must be emptied of self. If our lives are filled with sin, they cannot be filled with God's righteousness. To the extent our lives are filled with worldliness, to that extent they cannot be filled with eternal verities. We must be emptied of our pride, our self-righteousness, and our love for pleasure if we are to be filled with God's pleasure.

III. We must desire to be filled for Christ's glory and not for our own.

If we wish to be filled with God's Spirit in order to be successful in the Christian life or in the ministry or in church leadership, our motive is wrong, and we cannot qualify for his gift. If we wish to be filled so that we might have eloquence in our preaching and draw great crowds, have sensational revival meetings, and impressive statistics of baptisms, we are still filled with self, and the Holy Spirit is crowded out. Jesus said of the Holy Spirit's ministry, "He shall glorify me" (John 16:14). The Holy Spirit never glorifies the Christian. He does not even glorify himself. If one claims a gift of the Spirit that prompts him to glorify the Spirit rather than glorifying Christ, a question is raised as to the validity of the gift.

IV. We must yield wholly to God and his will.

This is unconditional surrender, absolute commitment, unquestioned consecration. This means that we sign the blank check and let God fill in the price and the details. We do not make a deal with God. We do not say, "Send me, Lord—but not to Africa," or "Use me, Lord—but not in the ministry." Some Christians are afraid to surrender fully because they fear that God will take advantage of them. God is not a tyrant who gleefully punishes us when we put ourselves in his power. He is a loving Father who always prescribes what is best and most useful and most satisfying to his child. Trust him! He wants only the best for you.

V. We must ask God to fill us with his Holy Spirit.

"How much more shall your heavenly Father give the Holy Spirit to them that *ask* him." We are simply to ask him to fill us with his Holy Spirit after we have done all we can to qualify for his gift. We must ask in great earnestness. Our desire must be all-consuming. And we must ask him to give us faith to believe that he has answered us. We must not bank on feeling. We must not expect an emotional upheaval. Some Christians have had such an experience, but most of us will react with quietness and growing assurance.

We must not expect a "once for all of a lifetime" experience. A few men like Charles Finney, Dwight L. Moody, and R. A. Torrey had an unusual experience for an unusual life assignment, but for most of us, to be filled with the Spirit is a recurring experience that comes when we feel a special need; when we have an overwhelming desire; when we feel the weight of an overwhelming assignment; and when we writhe under the burden of a selfish, empty, worldly, impotent Christian witness.

"Be not drunken with wine ... but be filled with the Spirit," is the command of Paul. Many Christians would die before they would be drunk with wine, but they ignore the positive side of this command.

Conclusion

Are you satisfied with the mediocre life you are living? Are you pleased with a dull and drab witness of the Christian life? Knowing that God has something better for you, do you want the best? Do you long to be filled with God's Holy Spirit? More than you could possibly want this blessed gift, he wishes to bestow it upon you. If you wish to be filled with the Holy Spirit, pray a prayer something like this:

O Lord, I long to be filled with your Spirit. Like a drowning man who wants air above all else, like the thirsty agonizing for water, like the hungry crying for food, I ask you for the filling of the Holy Spirit. Empty me of self. Purge me from my pride, my self-righteousness, my sin. I pray as did my Lord, "Not my will but Thine be done." I have asked. Now I pray for faith to believe that you have answered my prayer. Amen.

SUNDAY EVENING, MAY 30

Title: What Is a Living Sacrifice?

Text: "With eyes wide open to the mercies of God, I beg you, my brothers, as an act of intelligent worship, to give him your bodies, as a living sacrifice, consecrated to him and acceptable by him" (**Rom. 12:1** PHILLIPS).

Scripture Reading: Romans 12

Introduction

The word "sacrifice" in our text presents a problem to the minds of many devout Christians. They look upon a sacrifice as something that is painful, difficult, and unpleasant.

Perhaps the difficulty that many have when they think of sacrifice is a result of their false concept of the nature and purpose of our God. A proper understanding of the nature and character of God does not come accidentally or instantaneously. We can behold the greatness of God by studying the universe. We can discover the beauty of God by a study of the flowers. We can come to understand God's nature, character, and purpose only as we experience him as a loving Father through faith in Jesus Christ, his unique and divine Son.

Some look upon God as being tyrannical and unconcerned about the welfare of human beings. They unjustly blame him for all tragedies and catastrophes. This kind of attitude toward God causes them to react negatively when they are challenged to sacrifice themselves completely into the service of God.

Words have many different shades of meaning, and particularly is this true with the word *sacrifice.* In its verbal form, to sacrifice is to make sacred. As a noun, it can be used four different ways.

1. A sacrifice is an offering to a deity.
2. A sacrifice is anything consecrated and offered to God or to a divinity.
3. A sacrifice is a destruction or surrender of something desirable in favor of a higher object, or devotion of it to a claim deemed more pressing.
4. A sacrifice is a loss of profit or grievous loss incurred in selling under unfavorable conditions.

I am afraid that most Christians think in terms of the fourth definition. To hold this concept of sacrificing alone will wreak havoc with one's Christian consecration and service to God.

If we would realize that sacrifice does not always involve suffering, we might be able to make a more positive response to the challenge of full dedication of all that we are to the will of God. Paul is affirming on a spiritual level that which is a self-evident truth in other areas of life. He is emphasizing that success is built on sacrifice. For example, the young man who would be successful in playing football must make certain sacrifices in the area of discipline, and he must put the game before his own personal safety at times. He who makes no sacrifice at this point will never be an effective football player.

Successful home and family life is built on sacrifices that are made by each member of the family for the well-being of the group.

In obtaining an education, a student has to make certain sacrifices in order to secure that which is most desirable. He may have to decline some invitations to social or recreational events so that he might study and excel in his chosen field. Apart from sacrifice there is no success in any area of life.

Paul is declaring that if the child of God is to become a true servant of God, he must dedicate his total being to God and consider God's will as being the highest possible goal. He declares that the purpose of God for us should have top priority over all other claims. A number of things could be said concerning the nature of a living sacrifice.

I. The living sacrifice is a sacrifice that is alive.

In the Old Testament we read of the animals that were offered as burnt sacrifices. These sacrifices involved death, so that which was offered as a sacrifice was indeed a victim.

We think of Jesus as being one who sacrificed himself, and this involved death for him. We need to recognize that his sacrifice, even of his life, fell under the third definition of sacrifice. Jesus deliberately chose to die so that he might have the joy of glorifying God and saving people at the same time. This was the highest goal for him. It brought greater joy than escaping the cross ever could have brought (cf. Heb. 12:2).

Jesus was willing to become a dead sacrifice because he had experienced the joy of being completely dedicated as a living sacrifice.

Our text does not challenge us to die for our faith. It invites us to live for our God in complete dedication to his will.

II. The living sacrifice is to be a holy sacrifice.

Many of us are afraid of the word *holy*. We need not be. Positively, it means "to be dedicated to"; negatively, it means to be separated from and at the same time to be dedicated to. In modern terminology it means to be completely available to the good purpose of God. The Good Samaritan illustrates what it means to be a holy sacrifice unto God. He was available to render ministries of mercy to an unfortunate victim in a time of need. The priest and the Levite, supposedly men who were dedicated to the will of God, were not available for service in the time of need. Most of us are following in the footsteps of these two when the text would challenge us to follow the pattern of the Good Samaritan.

III. The living sacrifice is a complete sacrifice.

The challenge of the text is to a complete dedication of every facet of our being into the service of God. It does not call for a fractional type of consecration. It calls for something more than Sunday morning religion. It invites us to an acceptance of a full awareness of the stewardship nature of life. It challenges us to cooperate with God's good purpose for us in every area of life.

IV. The living sacrifice is a voluntary sacrifice.

There is no appeal to fear as a motive for surrender in this text. This is no demand for draftees. It is an invitation to volunteers who on the basis of gratitude respond "with eyes wide open to the mercies of God."

V. The living sacrifice is a joyful sacrifice.

Our Savior is the Good Shepherd who leads his sheep. He is not a driver who compels them to go where they do not wish to go.

Only those who have enough gratitude to motivate them to surrender will respond to this gracious invitation. Christian joy makes a living sacrifice possible.

VI. The living sacrifice is a satisfying sacrifice.

A. *The holy Father in heaven will be fully satisfied with you and your services if you fully dedicate yourself to his will.*

B. *You will experience an inward satisfaction and joy that will prove to be invaluable if you will make a full response and give yourself unreservedly and unconditionally into the service of your loving Lord as he reveals his way to you from day to day.*

The God who so loved you that he spared not his Son but delivered him up for you will not withhold anything from you if you dedicate yourself to him. You cannot outgive a God who delights to give. The more you give of yourself, the more you will be able to receive from him.

Conclusion

God has given his Son to save you from your sin. The only thing that you must give up to receive his salvation is that which is going to ruin you if you don't. God approaches you on the basis of his grace and mercy so that he might bestow upon you the richest gifts that one can experience. If you are willing to give to him the place that belongs to him, you can begin to know what it really means to live life on the highest plane and in its richest quality.

JUNE

■ **Sunday Mornings**

Topical sermons with an evangelistic and an ethical emphasis are suggested.

■ **Sunday Evenings**

Continue the series "Challenges from the Heart of the Apostle Paul."

■ **Wednesday Evenings**

Continue to use the theme "The Call of God and Our Response."

WEDNESDAY EVENING, JUNE 2

Title: The Call to Genuine Love

Text: "A new commandment I give unto you, That ye love one another; as I have loved you, that ye also love one another. By this shall all men know that ye are my disciples, if ye have love one to another" (**John 13:34–35**).

Scripture Reading: John 13:31–38

Introduction

Many officials are identified by means of the uniform that they wear, and this is especially true of the various branches of the military service. Jesus called his disciples to wear the uniform, or badge, of self-giving love as the credential that would identify them as his followers.

I. Jesus manifested his love by his perfect self-forgetfulness.

Jesus was so dedicated to the welfare of others that he often forgot his own bodily necessities. His primary concern was not that of feeding his mouth and clothing his back. His love for others caused him to forget his own sorrows and agonies. He was concerned to the extent that he gave himself unreservedly to meeting the needs of others.

An attitude of self-forgetfulness would make life more beautiful for all of us.

II. Jesus manifested his perfect love by his attitude of lowliness (Matt. 11:29).

Jesus did not possess a peacock complex. Never once did he strut or show off or express an attitude of superiority in a manner that would humiliate others. He was indeed a humble man.

192

III. Jesus manifested his perfect love by his persistent efforts to raise and serve the worst.

Jesus had the remarkable habit of always seeing the best in others. He could see something queenly in the face of the prostitute. He could see Matthew, the apostle and writer of the first gospel, in Levi, the hated tax collector. He did not specialize in searching for flaws and defects. He declared, "For God sent not his Son into the world to condemn the world; but that the world through him might be saved" (John 3:17).

IV. Jesus manifested his perfect love by his attitude of forgiveness toward those who mistreated him.

Jesus forgave his parents when they misunderstood his commitment to his Lord. He forgave his disciples when they responded so dully on many occasions. He even prayed for the soldiers who were crucifying him (Luke 23:34).

Conclusion

The kind of love the followers of Christ are called to demonstrate is made possible by his presence in their hearts and by the work of the Holy Spirit (cf. Rom. 5:5; 1 Cor. 13).

SUNDAY MORNING, JUNE 6

Title: Are You a Christian?

Text: "And the disciples were called Christians first in Antioch" (**Acts 11:26**).

Scripture Reading: Acts 11:19–26

Hymns: "We're Marching to Zion," Watts

"More Like Jesus Would I Be," Crosby

"Take the Name of Jesus with You," Baxter

Offertory Prayer: We come to you, Father, as Christians, aware that this is a privileged relationship that we enjoy because of your gracious and generous love. We love you because you first loved us. You have commended your love toward us in that while we were yet sinners Christ died for us. We bring our gifts to you in the light of your great gift of your Son. We give in his name even as we pray in his name. Amen.

Introduction

Years ago when *South Pacific* opened in New York, it was destined to become the greatest hit in Broadway history. It played to sellout crowds, and seats were hard to get unless you reserved them months in advance. One ticket seller wearily said, "More people want to get into *South Pacific* in one night than want to get into heaven in a year." Some were not just eager to see the show; they were even more eager to go home and tell their neighbors that they had seen it.

Some enterprising young men cashed in on the situation. They would pick up the discarded canceled ticket stubs for orchestra seats from the floor after each performance, add a used program, and sell them for fifty cents or so. Can't you see the phony tourist back at home displaying the evidence that he viewed the show from the front rows? Can't you hear him gush, "It was a great show. You should see it sometime," while thinking to himself, *That is, if you ever rise in the world to where you can rate such status.*

In the spiritual realm, some people show stubs and programs of the church service — the order of worship and the announcements. They know the pious words. They sing "Crown Him Lord of All" just like phony ticket holders hum "Some Enchanted Evening." They have never really seen the show; they have casually been exposed to the mechanics of a worship service. Their names are on the roll, but they are not involved in the life and witness and fellowship and work of the church.

Too long we have asked, "What church do you attend?" or "Where is your church membership?" Far more important than having one's name on the church roll is to have it inscribed in the Lamb's Book of Life. Christianity is not a body of doctrines or a system of ethics. Christianity is Christ. The relationship is a personal one with Jesus Christ.

Antioch, in the first century, was a city of a half million people. It was the third largest city in the world, exceeded only by Rome and Alexandria. It was a metropolis of great wealth, architectural magnificence, and fine pagan temples. It also was a hotbed of corruption and vice.

And to Antioch a group of believers traversed three hundred miles from Jerusalem to begin a church. This church blossomed and became the Gentile center of the Christian world. It was here that a new name appeared, but it was not invented by the church, for they were too busy to think up a new name. They called themselves brethren, saints, people of the Way, and believers. Jesus had called them disciples, followers, and friends. This name, "Christian," was given to them by their enemies and was used in derision and contempt.

The church accepted the name and clothed it with such honor and respectability that it has become our most precious designation. It shines like a star in the heavens. These jesters spoke better than they knew. The very fact that the world gave them a name shows us something of the impact they made on this wicked city.

I. The believers attracted attention.

Because the believers in Christ could be ignored no longer, they had to be given a name. Too often today we have so little influence on our community that they can ignore us. Sadly, the progress we attain can often be explained in worldly terms of promotion and organization. There is no miracle of power and transformation in the lives we touch. The citizens in Antioch knew something was going on, and they took note of it.

II. The believers were no longer associated with Judaism.

At least this was so in the eyes of the people. Until this time the followers of Jesus were classified as just another branch of the Jewish religion, but now society discerned that they were different.

Is your faith distinctive? Can people see that you are different from the world? Do you live a separated life that convinces unbelievers that you have something they do not have? And is your faith so radiant and contagious that they will desire it above everything else in life?

III. The people of Antioch named the believers for what they saw in them.

CHRIST-ian! They bore the name of Christ. They were "Christ's people." They belonged to Christ. When people saw them, they saw Christ. The business of Christ was their business. The human name of our Lord was Jesus, meaning "Jehovah is Salvation." If they had seen the human in them, they would have named them "Jesuits." Instead, they named them after his divine name, "Christ," meaning "the Messiah." The enemies of the church saw the divine in the followers of Christ.

The vagueness and all-inclusiveness of the name *Christian* today is distressing. People glibly refer to our nation as a "Christian" nation. We have many Christians in America, but we also have one of the highest rates of crime, alcoholism, and drug abuse.

A preacher tells the story that early in his ministry he helped block a liquor license and gambling project of a promoter in his town. The sheriff later told the preacher that this man was in his office one day inquiring about "that preacher who is fighting my club." Then he made this statement: "I'll have to go talk with that preacher. You see, I'm a Christian, too."

Conclusion

The story is told that a soldier was once brought before Alexander the Great on the charge of disobedience to military orders. "What is your name?" the great general asked. "My name is Alexander, sir," the soldier replied. "What did you say? What is your name?" the general asked intensely. "My name is Alexander, sir." Alexander the Great screamed out at him, "Then change your conduct or change your name!"

Our Lord asks, "What is your name?" We reply, "My name is Christian, Lord." He says, "Change your loyalties or change your name."

How does one become a Christian? Just like those early Christians in Antioch. We turn from our sins and yield ourselves to Christ. We ask him to forgive us of our sins and to give us the strength to live the Christian life. We open our hearts to his persuasion and let him possess us. We become Christ's people. His business becomes our business. His life becomes our life. Then the world will see that we are different and will take note of us. Are you a Christian? You can be right now.

SUNDAY EVENING, JUNE 6

Title: The Christian Use of the Body

Text: "I beseech you therefore, brethren, by the mercies of God, that ye present your bodies a living sacrifice, holy, acceptable unto God, which is your reasonable service" (**Rom. 12:1**).

Scripture Reading: Romans 12

Introduction

Phillips translates our text in the following way: "With our eyes wide open to the mercies of God, I beg you, my brothers, as an act of intelligent worship, to give him your bodies, as a living sacrifice, consecrated to him and acceptable by him." This verse contains a clear appeal for the dedication of our physical body to the will and purpose of God. Such an appeal may appear strange to some who consider the body to be basically evil rather than good.

Throughout the life history of Christianity there have been some who have held a very sub-Christian concept of the body. The belief that the body is evil is to be traced not to Hebrew thought but to the influence of Greek philosophies that considered all material as being basically evil. Because the body was made up of matter, it was considered essentially evil. This viewpoint was held by certain early church fathers and has had a profound influence in Christian thought through the centuries.

Dr. T. B. Maston declared that the idea of the body as being evil is not found in the Bible except as the latter is misinterpreted. In contrast to the Greek concept of the body, he declares: "The Hebrew perspective is revealed in the statement that 'God saw everything that he made, and, behold, it was very good' (Gen. 1:31). The body which is 'very good' from God's perspective can be used for good or evil purposes depending on the 'person' who lives in and controls the body."

I. Sub-Christian attitudes toward the body.

The attitude that one holds concerning the nature and function of his body is of great significance for daily Christian living.

A. *Some give too much honor to the body.* The woman who is blessed, or perhaps cursed, by having an unusually beautiful body may depend on physical attractiveness entirely too much and, consequently, neglect the proper development of her mind and spirit as well as character.

The young man who possesses a strong and handsome physique may concentrate on developing his muscular might to the detriment of the growth of his intellect and the development of the skills that will be necessary for effective living in a complex age.

B. *The body may be despised.* There are some who possess neither physical beauty or muscular strength, and because their physical bodies do not come up to their standards of acceptance, they react with an attitude of deep resentment and dissatisfaction toward their bodies.

196

C. *Many are discontented with their physical bodies.* Some who are overweight diet and exercise to lose weight, and some do so to extremes. Some who are tall wish that they were short, while some who are short are miserable because they are not tall. Jesus, in the Sermon on the Mount, said that there are some things concerning our physical stature that must be accepted if we are to live a full life. "Which of you by taking thought can add one cubit to his stature?" (Matt. 6:22). He points out how foolish it is to be anxious about physical features that cannot be altered. Along with evaluating ourselves and learning that we are worth more than sparrows, and dedicating ourselves, he suggests that we also accept ourselves. Since we have only one body and it is impossible to get a new one, the one we have must be accepted and utilized.

D. *Undue concern for the body is the result of little faith.* It was because of people's concern for food and drink and clothing for the body that Jesus addressed his comments in a major section of the Sermon on the Mount (Matt. 6:25–34). Jesus encourages us to concentrate our thoughts on living a great life for the honor of God and for the well-being of others rather than making the means of living the chief goal of our lives (Matt. 6:25–26).

Have you unintentionally accepted the sub-Christian understanding of the nature and function of the body you possess? Are you, like the rich fool, concerned primarily with feeding your stomach, while neglecting your mind, soul, and the very purpose of your earthly existence (Luke 12:16–21)?

II. A Christian understanding of the body.

Our text makes a plea for the dedication of the body to the will of God.

A. *Paul taught that the body is "for the Lord; and the Lord for the body" (1 Cor. 6:13).* Paul talks about Christians as constituting the body of Christ on earth. Our physical bodies become his body on earth through which he carries on his ministry of mercy and grace.

B. *We are to glorify God in our body (1 Cor. 6:20).* To glorify is to make known. By the way we live and by the manner in which we relate ourselves to others, we are to reveal in and through our bodies the nature and purpose of God in our world. To recognize that it is possible for our bodies to be so used is to bring a challenge to the spirit of every person.

C. *The body is the temple of the Holy Spirit (1 Cor. 3:16).* It is the shrine in which the blessed Holy Spirit has come to dwell. This truth can humble and excite the spirit of the believer at the same time.

These thrilling truths concerning the body would indicate that our attitude and use of our bodies are vital to our Christian stewardship.

III. The dedication of the body to the will of God is a fundamental requirement for living the Christian life.

As the mind must be filled with thoughts of God, even so must the body be dedicated to the uses for which God intended it.

The dedication of the body to the will of God is to be a definite and solemn action. It is to be dedicated deliberately, voluntarily, and completely.

Our text issues an appeal that every organ and appetite of the body recognize and respond to the loving lordship of Jesus Christ. This means at least the following:

A. *The brain or intellect will be dedicated to the will of God.* This calls for loving God with the totality of our intellect as well as with our emotions. It involves the bringing of our total intellectual life into harmony with the mind of Jesus Christ.

B. *The eyes will be taught to look for the good in others as well as in the world about us (Matt. 6:22–23).* They will see the needs of those who suffer and the opportunities to serve in the name of Christ.

C. *The ears will be made sensitive so as to hear the voice of God and at the same time hear the distress calls of those who are in need of the grace of God and of the ministries of his servants.*

D. *The tongue will be bridled so as not to bring harm to us personally or to others.* Instead of being used to curse, it will be dedicated to the blessing of others (James 3:3–12).

E. *Our hands will become the hands of the Savior to bless and to help others in need.* They will be holy hands lifted in prayer and at the same time merciful hands involved in continuing ministries in a needy world.

F. *Our feet will carry us into the paths of righteousness as well as service, and we will become the bearers of the good news of the gospel of peace (Rom. 10:15).* The childhood chorus says it this way:

> *Little feet be careful*
> *Where you take me to.*
> *Anywhere for Jesus*
> *Only let me go.*

Conclusion

Because of God's mercies, because of the need of a lost world, and because of the potential for personal satisfaction, it would be wise for each of us to deliberately, solemnly, voluntarily, and joyfully dedicate our physical body to the Lord for Christian uses.

WEDNESDAY EVENING, JUNE 9

Title: The Call to Praise God

Text: "Oh that men would praise the LORD for his goodness, and for his wonderful works to the children of men!" (**Ps. 107:8**).

Scripture Reading: Psalm 107:1–15

Introduction

In Psalm 107 the author issues a call to people everywhere to join in and give praise to the Lord for all of his goodness and mercy toward the "children of men." Our text is a refrain that occurs five times in this beautiful psalm.

Has it ever occurred to you that the call of God comes to each of us to praise him for his grace toward us and his power within us? Only as we give credit to whom it is due can we be a winsome witness to the saving power of Jesus Christ.

I. The offering of praise pleases God.

God does not need our praise because of a low ego. We do not need to praise him to build up his self-confidence. However, God is pleased when from sincere hearts we offer thanks and give voice to praise.

The offering of genuine praise to God will be one of our chief activities after we have entered the eternal home that Christ is preparing for those who love him (Rev. 5:11 – 14).

II. He who offers praise to God is blessed in doing so.

Not only is the heart of God pleased by our giving praise to him for his goodness, but our hearts are blessed also. We will find our hearts strangely warmed and encouraged if we will take the time necessary to enumerate the blessings of God. If we do more thinking about his grace and mercy, we will do more thanking him for his blessings upon us. The offering of praise encourages a positive outlook on life. It will aid us in practicing the presence of God.

III. Expressing praise for God will bring great blessings to others.

The Bible teaches us that unredeemed persons are dead in trespasses and sins. They are blind to spiritual reality. They are deaf to the voice of God's Holy Spirit. They are aware that something is missing, but until someone comes with the good news of God's love, mercy, and grace, they do not know what it is.

If each of us would use just a part of the opportunity that we have to offer praise to God, we would be surprised at the beneficial results in the lives of others.

Conclusion

The psalmist resolved that he would praise God continuously, "Every day will I bless thee; and I will praise thy name for ever and ever. Great is the LORD, and greatly to be praised; and his greatness is unsearchable. One generation shall praise thy works to another, and shall declare thy mighty acts" (Ps. 145:2 – 4). We must praise God for our own good. We must praise God for the benefit that it can bring to others. We must praise God if we would pass on to our children the benefits of our experiences with God.

SUNDAY MORNING, JUNE 13

Title: Have You Been Born Again?

Text: "Marvel not that I said unto thee, ye must be born again" **(John 3:7)**.

Scripture Reading: John 3:1–7

Hymns: "Praise Him, Praise Him," Crosby

"The Great Physician," Hunter

"Just as I Am," Elliott

Offertory Prayer: We are gratefully aware, Father, that you are the Giver of every good and perfect gift. We are further aware of our own unworthiness of your goodness and grace. Especially do we thank you, O God, for the gift of your salvation through Jesus Christ, your Son. We bring our gifts today, asking that you shall use our offerings in the effective extension of your gospel around the world. In Jesus' name. Amen.

Introduction

A couple stood one day in the spacious lobby of a hotel. The husband excused himself in order to step over to the information desk for a moment. When he turned to return to his wife, he noticed that she was talking to an elderly man who was neatly but modestly clothed. The husband courteously remained by the desk until the man walked away a few minutes later. As he approached his wife, he noted great agitation and distress in her face and her eyes.

"What did he say to you?" he bluntly asked.

"He asked me if I had been born again."

"Why didn't you tell him we are respectable and decent people?"

"He didn't ask me that. He asked me if I had been born again."

"Why didn't you tell him we are regular in our attendance at church?"

"He didn't ask me that."

"Why didn't you tell him it is none of his business?"

"If you could have seen the earnestness in his face and the concern in his eyes, you would have known that it *is* his business," she replied.

Seeing people born into the kingdom of God is Jesus' business. He confronted Nicodemus with this same issue. Most of those Jesus drew to himself were common people who heard him gladly. Here he dealt with an aristocrat, a big name in Jerusalem. He was a ruler of the Jews, a member of the Sanhedrin, the "Supreme Court" of the religious life of his people. We are privileged to look in on the conversation.

I. Nicodemus was sincere.

He was serious and earnest. Jesus dealt with him respectfully and patiently. He was impatient with insincerity and hypocrisy. Nicodemus was sincere, but Jesus said to him, "Ye must be born again." There is an old expression, "It doesn't make any difference what you believe, as long as you are sincere." But the truth is you can be sincere and still be sincerely wrong.

II. Nicodemus was morally clean.

As a religious leader, a Pharisee, Nicodemus's moral life was above reproach. He was overanxious in his legalism to observe even the minutest details of the moral law of Moses. Jesus did not say, "Clean up your life," for Nicodemus had a clean moral record. But Jesus said, "Morality and decency are not enough. You must be born again."

III. Nicodemus was religious.

He prayed, tithed, offered sacrifices, read his Bible, fasted, attended and even led public services in the synagogue, and frequented the temple. But being religious was not enough. Being zealous in religious exercises was not sufficient. Jesus said, "Marvel not that I said unto thee, Ye must be born again."

IV. Nicodemus was orthodox.

He was a Pharisee who knew the law and believed the law. He had exactly the right views about God. He cherished the blessed hope prophesied in the Old Testament that God would send the Messiah. He was a member of the Sanhedrin. Orthodoxy of doctrine is not enough. Satan is "orthodox" in that he "believes" and trembles. Commitment of heart and life to Christ, acting on our beliefs, is necessary. One can be orthodox and still be cold, hateful, and legalistic. One can hate heresy, but some go on to hate the heretic. No matter how orthodox your beliefs, "you must be born again."

V. Nicodemus was learned, cultured, refined, and wealthy, but Jesus said, "Ye must be born again."

Education does not make a person a Christian. Wealth does not qualify a person for heaven. Culture and refinement may get a person ahead in society but not in the kingdom of God.

Nicodemus had gone as far as Judaism alone could carry him. Yet he felt a lack in his life. There was no peace, no joy, no assurance, no abundant life. So he came to Jesus, seeking life in all its qualitative dimensions. And Jesus gave him the formula, "Ye must be born again."

Conclusion

Sin is a heart disease, and we all are afflicted with it: "All have sinned and come short of the glory of God" (Rom. 3:23). This disease is humanly incurable: "Salvation is found in no one else, for there is no other name under heaven given to men by which we must be saved" (Acts 4:12 NIV). Unless a disease is arrested or cured, it gets worse. Sin is never static. It cannot be arrested; it must be healed. Only the Great Physician can heal, and he heals by applying the remedy to the heart. Some people prescribe superficial cures: "Be decent." "Go to church." "Live a good, clean life." You cannot cure heart disease with a medicine applied to a skin rash. You cannot brighten the drab interior of a house by whitewashing the outer surface. And you cannot cure sin without the new birth, without the miraculous transformation of the inner man. "If any man be in Christ, he is a new creature: old things are passed away; behold, all things are become new" (2 Cor. 5:17).

The master novelist Victor Hugo has a story that describes the terror of sailors on a ship in a storm at sea. As the waves lash the frail vessel, the sailors feel a shudder and a thud. They look at each other and know: the cannon in the hold of the ship has broken loose from its moorings. Each lurch of the ship in the storm sends the cannon crashing into the wooden hull of the vessel.

The novelist describes the plight of the sailors who disappear into the dark hold, their faces drained of color. They crouch and dodge as the monster threatens to pin them to the wall and crush them. Finally, they desperately chain the cannon back in place, and the ship is saved.

This is a parable of our own lives. Something is wrong down inside of us. This monster threatens to wreck us. But a Deliverer available. There is salvation from the raging storm. Put your soul, your life, your destiny, and your sins in the hands of Jesus, and you will be born again. And in that new birth there is safety and assurance and a safe arrival at his harbor.

SUNDAY EVENING, JUNE 13

Title: The Peril of Conformity

Text: "And be not conformed to this world: but be ye transformed by the renewing of your mind, that ye may prove what is that good, and acceptable, and perfect, will of God" **(Rom. 12:2)**.

Scripture Reading: Genesis 13:10–13

Introduction

Phillips translates our text: "Don't let the world around you squeeze you into its own mould, but let God re-mould your minds from within, so that you may prove in practice that the plan of God for you is good, meets all his demands and moves toward the goal of true maturity." The text is a negative admonition issuing a challenge to nonconformity. Paul urges his readers to stop being fashioned by the world.

Terrific pressure is brought upon each follower of Jesus Christ to fit the moral society in which he lives. "This world" stands for the sphere of life that is contrary to God. The moral standards of the world are false and sinful. The thought patterns of the world are ungodly and give no consideration to the spiritual nature of life.

Romans 12 begins with a plea for a complete, deliberate, joyful, and voluntary commitment of the body to the will and work of God. This challenge is followed by the imperative prohibition of the text. If we would respond positively to the challenge of complete dedication, we must also respond positively to the negative admonition of the text.

Several great truths are self-evident if serious consideration is given to the challenge of the text. First, evil is contagious and aggressive. Like a fatal disease, it will invade every cell of our being if we consent to let it have its course. Second, spiritual progress is to be made in spite of handicaps. The world about us will not congratulate us because of our utter devotion to God. Third, the Christian life is not to be thought of as "business as usual." There must be some great negatives if we truly are to be God's people in our world. In our attitudes, ambitions, and actions there must be something that distinguishes us from the materialist who lives as if the primary reason for being is to provide food, shelter, and clothing.

I. The pressures that promote conformity.

The world about us is active and aggressive. It insists on conformity. It resents and opposes nonconformity. Jesus was referring to this danger in the parable of the soils as he described the fate of the seed that fell among the thorns. "And that which fell among thorns are they, which, when they have heard, go forth, and are choked with cares and riches and pleasures of this life, and bring no fruit to perfection" (Luke 8:14).

We can describe the pressures to conform as "the world, the flesh, and the devil."

A. *We have a built-in tendency to conform.*

    1. We are imitators by nature. A child imitates his parents or older children. A student imitates his teacher. In youth one imitates his heroes. We learn both good and evil from those whom we accept as our patterns for thought and conduct.

    2. By nature we like to belong to a group. We are gregarious creatures, and we have a fear of being distinctly different. This is true with adults as well as with teenagers. We associate with groups or join organizations and put forth some effort to conform to the principles and practices of the group.

    3. We have a deep inward desire for security, and conformity to a group makes a contribution toward this desire for safety and security. This desire for security has a tendency to whip us into line at times when our conscience disturbs us and we have doubts concerning the propriety of certain ideas or actions that are proposed.

B. *The power structures in our society wield a powerful influence at the point of promoting conformity.* People are not free to be individualistic and nonconformist as they would like to be. They feel that they must conform or be ostracized or eliminated from consideration for possible business or professional advancement.

C. *Specific pressure groups promote conformity on the part of all so that they might achieve their desired objectives.*

D. *The entertainment media are very effective in promoting attitudes, habits, customs, and dress that result in large groups conforming to a certain way of life.* High-pressured advertisements that appeal to subconscious emotional needs of viewers and listeners influence our choice of foods, clothing, and automobiles. Cigarette advertisements try to convince us that the way to relaxation

203

is by using a particular brand. Beer advertisers try to convince us that the only way to really enjoy life is by regularly consuming their product.

Are you a conformist? Have you let the world squeeze you into its own mold? Do you think like the average unsaved person thinks? Do you act like your neighbor who has no love for God and no awareness of the spiritual dimension of life? Have you accepted a materialistic scale of values as your standard for success? Each of us needs to heed the words of our text: "Don't let the world around you squeeze you into its own mold."

II. Areas of conformity.

A. *Some people have let the world squeeze them into a nonspiritual conformity in that they either ignore or forget God as they make their decisions and choices.* Lot, the nephew of Abraham, gave no consideration to the will of God when he lifted up his eyes and looked toward Sodom. He was concerned only about prosperity and the good life from a materialistic standpoint. Do you fit into this mold?

B. *Economic conformity.* The devil tempted our Lord with the bread theory of life (Matt. 4:3). He made the subtle suggestion that since man has to live, Christ should turn the stones into bread. Jesus replied by saying that it is more important that a man live by the Word of God than that he feed his stomach. Some people make all decisions on the basis of the economics involved.

Are you Christian in your business practices? What are the primary goals of your life? What is your attitude toward money? Could it be that you are like the rich fool who treated himself as if he were nothing more than a pig by thinking that he could feed his soul on the things that he could store in a barn (Luke 12:15–21)? Do you fit into this mold?

C. *Conformity in speech.* Our speech in many respects reveals our character. It is a window through which one can look into our mind. If we are genuine followers of Jesus Christ, profanity, smutty jokes, untruthfulness, and unkindness should be eliminated.

D. *Conformity in personal habits.* In his epistle to the Ephesians, Paul challenged his readers to walk worthy of the Lord and therefore not as the Gentiles walked (Eph. 4:17). He insisted that there needs to be a distinctive difference in the conduct of those who have come to know Jesus Christ in an experience of forgiveness and new life. Have you eliminated those personal habits that are destructive of the highest and best in your life and detrimental to the lives of others, or have you permitted the ways of sin to cling to you? Have you let the world about you provide a pattern for your personal habits or have you let the Spirit of God help you rise above the ways of a world that does not know God?

E. *Conformity in recreation.* We live in a time when people are obsessed with the idea of having fun. There are many forms of recreation whose primary appeal is to the lower appetites of human nature. Things such as adult films and alcoholic beverages lead downward rather than upward.

F. *Conformity of attitudes toward other persons.* Do you let the customary attitudes of your community and your culture determine your attitude toward minority groups such as those of a different race or creed? One of the most painful problems facing America today is the unchristian attitude that many of us hold toward persons who belong to groups other than our own. We need to see every individual as one for whom our Lord died. We need to see everyone as a potential child and servant of God.

As these various areas of conformity are recognized, it is easier for us to see the urgency behind Paul's challenge "Don't let the world around you squeeze you into its own mould, but let God re-mould your minds from within, so that you may prove in practice that the plan of God for you is good, meets all his demands and moves toward the goal of true maturity."

III. The harmful effects of conformity.

A. *To conform to the world is to decline our spiritual heritage.* The challenge of the text is to the effect that the Christian as an individual and Christians as a group are to serve as thermostats rather than thermometers in their community. A thermometer merely registers the temperature and does nothing to affect the temperature one way or another. A thermostat helps determine the temperature. A thermostat makes it possible for us to have a cool temperature in the hot summer and a warm temperature in the cool days of winter. Christians are to serve as salt that preserves society from decay and as a light that provides warmth, reveals the way, and makes abundant life possible.

B. *To conform to the world is to bring disrepute to the gospel of Christ.* Christ expects us to be different because of the transforming presence of the Holy Spirit in our hearts. The new nature, received in the new birth, makes conformity to the world inconsistent. The unsaved world expects the Christian to be different. Not to be different is to deny the saving power of a risen Lord.

C. *If we conform to the world, we destroy our potential testimony for Christ.* Our unsaved friends will refuse to give heed to the words of our lips unless they see something in our conduct that confirms the truth of our testimony. An unbelieving world needs the testimony of transformed lives as well as the testimony of our lips before they will seek the Savior as the Lord of their lives.

D. *To conform to the world is to experience disrespect on the part of those who could be blessed by our lives.* If an unbelieving neighbor cannot see a new quality in your life, she is not very likely to give a great deal of attention to your efforts to persuade her to join your Bible class, to attend your church, or to trust your Savior. If there are flagrant contradictions in your conduct, she will not only be indifferent, but she will be disrespectful if you should attempt to encourage her to give consideration to becoming a Christian.

E. *To conform to the world will cause you to experience the displeasure of God.* Lot saw the accumulation of his efforts go up in smoke and down in ashes. God not only acted in judgment against Sodom, but he acted in judgment against the works of Lot, for Lot had lost his influence even with his family.

God sent a great storm into the life of Jonah because Jonah was conforming to the attitude of his society toward the inclusion of non-Jewish people in the redemptive concern of God. Jonah's disobedience is but an illustration of the disobedience of the nation to the holy will of God. Both Jonah and the nation experienced the displeasure of God.

Conclusion

If we would serve God significantly, we must refuse to let the world around us squeeze us into its own mold. This is no weak plea for purity. It is not an appeal for an attitude of toleration. It is an affirmation that there is a negative side to the life of complete dedication to the will of God. There must be some great refusals if you are to become what God would have you to be.

Our text challenges the unconverted to come to Christ and to make a full commitment to him and to cease to conform to the way of life that they have known in the past. Each one can experience victory over the sinful world and can know spiritual transformation by the renewal of the mind and by a positive response to the indwelling Spirit of God when he or she takes Christ seriously and trusts him as Lord.

WEDNESDAY EVENING, JUNE 16

Title: The Call to Worship

Text: "O come, let us worship and bow down: let us kneel before the LORD our maker" (**Ps. 95:6**).

Scripture Reading: Psalm 95

Introduction

The Bible from its beginning to its close is an invitation to humankind to worship the true and living God. Repeatedly throughout the Psalms we find an invitation to join the worship of the true God. Our Lord Jesus Christ came that people might know the nature of God and give their hearts and lives in his worship and service.

I. A call to worship the true God.

The psalmist invites us to recognize and respond to the true and living God by worshiping him with our minds and hearts.

Because people are made in the image and likeness of God, they are worshipers. We worship because we must. We are made with a God-shaped vacuum within our hearts that only the true God can satisfy.

When people do not worship the true God, they worship a false god and become idolaters. The object of our worship is that which we consider to be of supreme worth.

II. The necessity of worship.

A. *We must put forth an effort to worship God in spirit and in truth if we are to bring our will into harmony with his.*

B. *We must bow down before God in confession of sin if we are to experience the joy of forgiveness and cleansing and release from the deadly effect of guilt.*

C. *We must bow before God if we are to receive the divine guidance that we need for living the abundant life.*

D. *We must bow down before God if we are to overcome fears that are associated with being human.*

E. *We must bow down before God to receive new commissions for the living of a responsible life.* God wants to guide us from day to day.

III. The nature of worship.

William Temple sought to define worship in the following manner: "To worship is to quicken the conscience by the holiness of God, to feed the mind by the truth of God, to purge the imagination by the beauty of God, to open the heart to the love of God, and to devote the will to the purpose of God."

Worship contains at least three essential elements: adoration of God, communion with God, and dedication to God.

To worship we must concentrate our minds and our hearts on God as we understand him to be. We can come to the best possible understanding of God as we look at and respond to the life and teachings of Jesus Christ. In him we can find the truth about God. In him we find the way to worship and serve God. In him we find the life that God is so eager to give to those who worship.

To genuinely worship we must be honest enough to confess our sins. One of the results of genuine worship is that of experiencing an awareness of the imperfections and shortcomings of one's life.

A genuine experience of worship will always bring with it a recognition of the needs of others. In the experience of God, we will hear his call or commission to give of ourselves in helping to meet those needs.

Conclusion

With mind, heart, energy, and time, let us bow down in recognition of God's good purpose for our lives. In both public worship and private worship, let us offer ourselves to him for the doing of his will. "O come, let us worship and bow down: let us kneel before the LORD our maker" (Ps. 95:6).

SUNDAY MORNING, JUNE 20

Title: The Forgotten Father

Text: "Then Joseph being raised from sleep did as the angel of the Lord had bidden him" (**Matt. 1:24**).

Scripture Reading: Matthew 1:19–25

Hymns: "God, Our Father, We Adore Thee," Frazer

"Faith of Our Fathers," Faber

"All the Way My Savior Leads Me," Crosby

Offertory Prayer: Our Father who art in heaven, we thank you that we may be called your children; heirs of God and joint heirs of Jesus Christ. We thank you for our fathers who have given good gifts to us. We thank you that even more our heavenly Father gives the Holy Spirit to his children. Grant that your Holy Spirit may guide us as we worship you through our gifts. And grant, Father, that your Spirit may fully bless and guide our lives. In the name of our blessed Lord we pray. Amen.

Introduction

When Christmas rolls around, the spotlight settles on the infant Jesus, the virgin mother, the shepherds, the angels, and the wise men. Have you ever heard a sermon on Joseph, the husband of Mary, who fulfilled the role of human father in the early life of our Lord? In my entire library I have found only one printed sermon on him.

The Roman Catholic Church has canonized Jesus' earthly father, and he is called St. Joseph. But Protestantism has virtually ignored him. He deserves better. He must have been a remarkable man for God to have chosen him of all the men on earth to play the role of earthly father to his Son. Let us use the occasion of Father's Day to do him honor.

Matthew supplies most of what we know about Joseph. Royal blood coursed through his veins. He was of the lineage of David. He had a dignity and gentleness about him that reflected his family heritage. He was present when Jesus was born; he witnessed the adoration of the shepherds; he took Mary and the baby to Egypt to escape the slaughter of infants. He took Jesus to the temple at least twice. He presented him in his infancy and offered a humble sacrifice. When Jesus was twelve years of age, he took him to Jerusalem and the temple. Jesus called him father and was subject to him. Joseph was a hardworking, God-fearing man who supported his family in a rustic town disdained for its obscurity and provincialism.

Joseph drops out of the historical accounts of the Gospels. It is likely that he died while Jesus was a young man; and our Lord, as the elder born, assumed the responsibility of the carpenter shop and the support of his family. He did not relinquish the role of village carpenter until the younger brothers were old enough to take over. Then he entered his public ministry.

Although little is written about Joseph, we see enough to know something of his greatness.

I. He was a just man.

"Then Joseph her husband, being a just man ..." (Matt. 1:19). It is with delicacy and frankness that the Bible tells us of the conception of Jesus by the Holy Spirit.

    A. *Joseph was sensitive to society's moral standards.* He could not ignore what people would think and say. All his life he had been abiding by this high standard. Apparently Joseph had no dynamic, overwhelming personality. He was a good man, a just man, a man of ordinary abilities, but he put those abilities in God's hands and God used him. In the same way God wants to use you.

    B. *Joseph was sensitive to his own reputation.* When someone says, "I don't care what people think as long as I consider I am right," he is only trying to fool himself. Being right is most important, but what people think of you is also important. You may be truly right, but if people think you are wrong, you have lost your opportunity to help them. The reputation of a religious man is very important.

    C. *Joseph was sensitive to Mary's plight.* "While he thought on these things ..." (Matt. 1:20). He delayed any harsh judgments. He did not want to believe the worst. He was compassionate in his consideration of her plight. He was willing "to put her away privily," if that would protect her from the cruel gaze of hostile neighbors. We marvel at his emotional balance in this great crisis.

II. Joseph was sensitive to a heavenly vision.

Like Paul, Joseph was not disobedient to the heavenly vision. It took supernatural proof to prove a supernatural birth. After the dream, he had no further doubts. He accepted Mary unreservedly as his wife. They had perfect faith in each other.

III. Joseph was a faithful father.

He provided Jesus with a human example for his sublime teachings about God as our heavenly Father. John Stuart Mill could not pray the Lord's Prayer because of the cruel, unreasonable discipline of a tyrannical father. To think of God as a Father like his father was not complimentary to God.

Jesus seemed to reflect warmly on his own remembrance of Joseph's gracious generosity to his children: "If ye then being evil, know how to give good gifts unto your children, how much more shall your Father which is in heaven give good gifts to them that ask him?" (Matt. 7:11).

Conclusion

Most revealing of all is the teaching of our Savior as he gives us the parable of the prodigal son. This moving story might more appropriately be called the parable of the loving father. The most thrilling part of the story is the return of the boy from the far country. The father never ceased to watch for him. ("While he was yet a far way off the father saw him.") "He ran," denoting his own anxiety for reconciliation. "He fell on his neck and kissed him," thus welcoming him home. Then followed the ring and the shoes and the robe and the fatted calf and the joyous festivities. The father said, "This my son was lost and is found."

Jesus tells us God is like that. Though you might have strayed far from him, he is a loving Father who longingly looks for your return and who will give you forgiveness and restoration and reconciliation and the place of a son in his house if you will turn your back to the old life and your face toward the Father and home.

SUNDAY EVENING, JUNE 20

Title: The Blessing of a Burdened Heart

Text: "Brethren, my heart's desire and prayer to God for Israel is, that they might be saved" (**Rom. 10:1**).

Scripture Reading: Romans 9:1–3

Introduction

Some of God's greatest blessings come to us in the form of burdens to be carried. This may seem strange to those who have accepted the idea that happiness is to be found through either avoiding or escaping burdens. The study of history and a critical examination of the present will reveal that those who achieve significance are those who accept a burden and then bear it courageously and triumphantly.

In our text the apostle Paul reveals the burden of compassionate concern that filled his heart for those of the Jewish faith. This burden came to him because of his desire to share what he had discovered in Jesus Christ. Paul was convinced that Jesus was the Messiah for whom his nation was waiting. This burden came to him by the command of Christ. The Holy Spirit placed this burden of concern upon and within the apostle's heart. It is possible that had it not been for this burden that Paul talks about that he would never have achieved either the significance or the success that are now recognized.

One of the greatest blessings that God bestowed upon Paul was this burden for God's people. Paul accepted the responsibility voluntarily and carried it out triumphantly. In fact, it lifted him from mediocrity to a place of immortality.

Have you rejected the blessing of a burden? Do you avoid anything that appears to be difficult? Have you laid aside a burden when you discovered that it was heavy? In all kindness I pray for you the blessing of a burdened heart similar to the burden that Paul describes, and there are a number of reasons why I pray this for you.

I. A burdened heart will cause us to forsake unworthy goals.

The great majority of people make the mistake of giving a first-rate loyalty to third-rate causes. To obtain the right kind of burden that is permitted to become the magnificent obsession of life will cause one to eliminate things of minor significance in order to major upon that which is of supreme importance.

A. *Some live only for pleasure.*

B. *Others strive for a position of power and prestige in their chosen area of interest.*

C. *The majority define the purpose for being in terms of acquiring an excess of material goods so as to enjoy a life of leisure.*

II. A burdened heart will call forth the best that we have in us.

No one can possibly evaluate himself or another properly unless consideration is given to the depth and degree of that which motivates his actions. Psychiatrists are sometimes amazed at the major transformation that takes place when some people suddenly take on new drive. Why is it that some people with average or below average motivation suddenly begin to produce in an extraordinary manner? The explanation, in some instances, can be found in the fact that the individual involved received some kind of intense desire or challenging burden that called forth energies and abilities that had been lying dormant.

In a pamphlet entitled "Uncle Gideon's Advice to Young Preachers," the author suggests that it will be impossible for a pastor to secure three men to travel even a short distance with him to kill a mouse, while he affirms that he can get fifty men to walk a mile with him to help him kill a bear.

Only as we accept the burden of something beyond our limited abilities will we dedicate our highest and best toward the achievement of the desired goal.

As Paul faced his burden of responsibility which was at the same time his greatest opportunity, he describes his concentration and determination in the following way. "Brethren, I count not myself to have apprehended: but this one thing I do, forgetting those things which are behind, and reaching forth unto those things which are before, I press toward the mark for the prize of the high calling of God in Christ Jesus" (Phil. 3:13–14).

III. A burdened heart will cause us to voluntarily follow a rigid program of spiritual discipline.

Most of us have a built-in tendency to concentrate on the faults of others. We can see the splinter in the other person's eye, yet we fail to recognize that we have a plank in our own eye (Matt. 7:3–5).

We would make much greater progress in our spiritual growth as well as in our ministry to others if we sat in rigid judgment upon ourselves. We need to bring our methods and our motives under the mind of Jesus Christ. Paul describes the rigid discipline of the athlete who would excel and then makes an application to the disciple of Jesus Christ (1 Cor. 9:24–27).

If it were necessary for the apostle to rigidly discipline himself and to give the knockout blow to evil inclinations, it might be wise for each of us to recognize that we could profit by the same.

If Satan could gain control of the mind and the tongue of one like Peter, it is altogether possible that he can do the same with you (Matt. 16:23).

IV. A burdened heart will draw us closer to our Lord.

We live in a world of great need. This need takes many forms: material, physical, mental, emotional, social, and educational. Jesus Christ is our contemporary, and he wants to walk among us in the midst of all our needs. Through each of his followers he would seek to meet the deep spiritual needs of the multitudes that make up our world.

To face world needs is to be overwhelmed with our human inadequacy. As the branch cannot bear fruit apart from a vital living union with the vine, even so, we cannot bear fruit and meet the spiritual needs of those about us (John 15:4).

   A. *To be burdened for those about us should cause us to search the Scriptures deliberately that we might be wise with the wisdom of God.*
   B. *The need of our own heart as well as the need of others should cause us to come again and again to the throne of Christ in prayer for mercy and help in every time of need (Heb. 4:16).*
   C. *The Holy Spirit dwells within the heart of each believer to give guidance and assistance.* As we seek to meet the needs of others, we must recognize and respond to his divine guidance.

V. A burdened heart makes possible earth's greatest joy.

Apart from the blessing of a burdened heart there will be very little Christian witnessing or Christian ministering. When the heart is filled with compassion, there will be both witnessing and ministering.

   A. *Witnessing and serving bring joy to the heart of the witness and servant as one experiences the blessings of God upon his or her effort.*
   B. *Christian witnessing and Christian ministering make the love of God real to the hearts of those who need Jesus Christ as Savior.* They will experience the joy of becoming the children of God. Those who permitted God to bestow upon them the blessing of a burdened heart will now have hearts filled with joy.

Conclusion

If your life is mediocre, you should be concerned. If there is no fruit that indicates a degree of achievement in the vineyard of God, you should be personally disturbed. Perhaps the blessing that you need most is the blessing of a burdened heart. A genuine concern for others is the command of God, and it is a gift from God. Receive it now and respond to it through the balance of your life.

WEDNESDAY EVENING, JUNE 23

Title: The Call to Prayer

Text: "Ask, and it shall be given you; seek, and ye shall find; knock, and it shall be opened unto you: For every one that asketh receiveth; and he that seeketh findeth; and to him that knocketh it shall be opened" **(Matt. 7:7–8).**

Scripture Reading: Matthew 7:1–12

Introduction

Our Lord lived in an attitude and atmosphere of prayer. He was in continuous communion with the loving Father. This is not to imply that he always had his head bowed or that he was always on his knees. He was always in immediate contact with God. He was open to God and responsive to God.

On many different occasions our Lord went apart into a private place for prayer (Mark 1:35; Luke 5:16; 9:18, 28).

Because of the rich benefits of prayer, one of Jesus' disciples requested that he teach them to pray (Luke 11:1).

I. Why do we neglect to respond to the call to prayer?

A. *Is it because we feel self-sufficient because of our own human resources?* Is it that we feel no need for the wisdom, power, and grace of God?

B. *Is it because we do not have our heart in the work of our Lord?* Do we have a burden of compassionate concern in our hearts that causes us to recognize the lostness of people about us?

C. *Do we neglect to pray because we are too busy with the common tasks of life in which we are seeking to feed our stomachs and clothe our backs?*

D. *Do we neglect to pray because we do not like to face our sins?* This can be a painful and humiliating experience. The heavenly Father reveals our sins to us only that he might grant us forgiveness, cleansing, and victory.

E. *Do we neglect to pray because of our blindness to our own spiritual poverty and to the needs of those about us?*

II. The rewards of prayer.

Repeatedly Jesus encouraged his disciples to believe that the heavenly Father is a prayer-hearing and a prayer-answering God. He compares the heavenly Father to a wise and generous earthly father. He declares without hesitation that it is the good pleasure of the Father to give good things to those who ask him.

A. *It is the will of God to give salvation to all of those who call upon him in repentance and faith (Rom. 10:13).*

B. *The model prayer, often called the Lord's Prayer, was intended by our Lord as a call to prayer.* He describes the manner for effective praying. He infers the beneficial results that will come to the disciple who enters into the closet of prayer. This model prayer is designed to assure the disciple of the loving fatherhood of God. It is intended to bring the one who prays into harmony with the will of God.

C. *We can experience forgiveness of our sins when we respond to the call to prayer and confess those sins.*

D. *We can be blessed with the guidance of God as we come to him in our times of uncertainty.*

E. *We can receive the power of the Holy Spirit for victory over evil in our own lives or for a ministry to others (Luke 11:13).*

Conclusion

Charles Haddon Spurgeon said that the Christian who departs for the day's work without first talking to God is like a soldier who departs for battle without his weapons. By prayer we check in with the heavenly headquarters. It is in the experience of prayer that the heavenly Father communicates his wishes to us. It is when we pray that he gives us commissions and responsibilities.

SUNDAY MORNING, JUNE 27

Title: Some Tests for Right and Wrong

Text: "Wherefore, if meat make my brother to offend, I will eat no flesh while the world standeth, lest I make my brother to offend" (**1 Cor. 8:13**).

Scripture Reading: Romans 14:13–15

Hymns: "I Would Be True," Walter

    "Let Others See Jesus in You," McKinney

    "Take Time to Be Holy," Longstaff

Offertory Prayer: Holy Father, we lift our hearts to you in worship and praise. Today we bring a portion of the fruits of our labors and place them on the altar as an indication of our desire to be completely dedicated to your redemptive purpose in the world. As you have given yourself in mercy to us, help us to give ourselves to being the channel through which your blessings can reach the hearts and lives of others. Help us to recognize the role that we are to play in your continuing work of rescuing people from the waste and ruin of sin. Bless these tithes and offerings to the advancement of your kingdom and to the redeeming of men and women and boys and girls from the consequences of sin. In Christ's name we pray. Amen.

Introduction

In the text Paul gives voice to a principle that is relevant for much that concerns us in the modern day even though few of us will be bothered concerning the eating of meat that has been offered on a pagan altar. Paul was referring to a local problem of great significance to new disciples in Corinth. They were recent converts from paganism, and it had been their custom to offer meat sacrifices on the altar of their pagan gods. They looked upon this eating of meat as being an expression of worship. The more mature Christians recognized that these pagan idols were actually "nothings." They did not believe that the eating of this meat was harmful or sinful as far as they personally were concerned.

Paul urged upon them that love and concern for the weaker brother should be the guiding principle that controlled their behavior. He declared that he would abstain from eating meat rather than be the cause of a weaker brother falling into sin because of his doing so. He gave voice to a principle rather than to a rigid law.

The principle is applicable as we face the continuing necessity of making moral decisions concerning proper conduct in our day. Those who look for a special prohibition against every form of evildoing will find themselves in great difficulty. We must seek to discover principles and then with the help of the Holy Spirit apply them to the complexities of the modern world. There are eight tests that we can use to help us make decisions concerning right and wrong. It would be beneficial for parents to observe these tests, and it would be most helpful to young people if they were to memorize and observe them.

I. The spiritual test.

Is this action or attitude expressly forbidden in the Word of God? Am I aware of what the Bible teaches concerning this issue? Am I willing to let the teaching of the Bible be authoritative and determine my conduct?

II. The prayer test.

Is this something concerning that which I can ask for both the approval and the blessings of God? Can I count on God to smile upon it and to bless it?

III. The personal test.

Will doing this particular thing make of me a better Christian? Will it aid my spiritual growth? Will it cause me to become more Christlike?

IV. The social test.

Will my doing this particular thing influence others to be better Christians, or will it provide a stumbling block before their feet?

V. The practical test.

What will the results be if I do this particular thing? Will they be desirable or undesirable? Will they produce happiness or unhappiness for me or for others?

VI. The stewardship test.

Will I be fulfilling God's purpose for my life, or will I be wasting that which God has entrusted into my care?

VII. The universal test.

What would happen if everyone did this? Would the community be better or worse?

VIII. The publicity test.

Is this something that I would be willing for everyone to know about? Will it stand the gaze of the public without causing me to blush?

IX. The missionary test.

Will it help or hinder the progress of the kingdom of God around the world?

X. The evangelistic test.

Will this cause others to want to know my Savior? Or will it cause them to lose confidence in him whom I claim as my Savior?

Conclusion

As Christians face the question "Is it right or wrong?" they will find that the Holy Spirit can guide them in moments when decisions need to be made if they will apply these tests to the issues under consideration.

SUNDAY EVENING, JUNE 27

Title: The Security of the Children of God

Text: "For I am persuaded, that neither death, nor life, nor angels, nor principalities, nor powers, nor things present, nor things to come, nor height, nor depth, nor any other creature, shall be able to separate us from the love of God, which is in Christ Jesus our Lord" **(Rom. 8:38–39).**

Scripture Reading: Romans 8:31–39

Introduction

Paul sought to encourage the Roman Christians who were exposed to the possibility of terrible suffering by leading them to concentrate on their perfect security in the grace and plan of God. He assured them that God works in all things for good for those who love him (Rom. 8:28). He assured them that the great God whose purpose of redemption is eternal would not be prevented from accomplishing his good purpose in them (vv. 29–30).

I. The certainty of the believer's security (Rom. 8:31–34).

Paul writes to a group whose physical security may be greatly in doubt. He affirms that they need have no anxiety concerning their eternal security. He seeks to illustrate this by asking a number of questions. The answer to these questions is either given or implied. The purpose of each is to affirm that there will be no accusation brought against them on that great day when they stand before God.

A. *"What shall we say to these things?"* Paul is left speechless as he contemplates the wonders of our great salvation.

B. *"If God be for us who can be against us?"* The answer is given in Romans 8:32. God is for us to the extent that he gave his Son for us.

C. *"Who shall lay anything to the charge of God's elect?"* In the latter part of verse 33, Paul affirms that it is God who justifies us. That is, God, on the basis of his grace and our faith in Jesus, accepts us as if we had never sinned. Consequently, he will not be bringing any accusation against us.

216

D. *"Who is he that condemneth?"* Certainly Christ will not condemn us. We can be sure of this on the basis of at least four facts: Christ died for us, Christ is risen again for our justification, Christ is at the right hand of God exalted and triumphant, and Christ makes intercession for those who trust him (Heb. 7:25). Our Lord's crucifixion, resurrection, ascension, and present ministry should give us an overwhelming sense of security in the grace of God.

II. The eternity of our security in Christ (Rom. 8:35–39).

The previous questions that Paul raised deal with the believer's security as far as the past and the present are concerned. What about the future? Paul mentions a frightful possibility: "Who shall separate us from the love of Christ?" In view of this possibility Paul mentions seven possible threats to the bond of love as people normally understand it.

A. *Shall tribulation and the cruel oppression associated therewith separate us from the love of God?*

B. *Shall distress with the anguish and the acute pain that people often experience separate us from the love of Christ?*

C. *Shall persecution and malignant pursuit by those who are the enemies of God separate us from the love of Christ?*

D. *Shall famine or starvation be interpreted as the withdrawal of the love of Christ?*

E. *Shall the defenselessness of nakedness and poverty be interpreted as an absence of God's love for us?*

F. *Shall the peril of exposure to harm and suffering and death separate us from the love of Christ?*

G. *Shall the possibility of death by sword or some other horrible manner imply that the love of Christ has been withdrawn from us?*

Conclusion

How shall we respond to the security that is ours in the love of God through Jesus Christ? It should be easy for us to love God warmly with all of our being. We can well afford to trust him implicitly with our past, our present, and our future. We should obey him gladly in his every wish. And without hesitation we should make ourselves available to be the channels through which his love can flow and work in the lives of others.

WEDNESDAY EVENING, JUNE 30

Title: The Call to Faithfulness

Text: "Therefore, my beloved brethren, be ye steadfast, unmoveable, always abounding in the work of the Lord, forasmuch as ye know that your labour is not in vain in the Lord" (**1 Cor. 15:58**).

Scripture Reading: 1 Corinthians 15:51–58

Introduction

Paul brings his great message on the resurrection of Christ and the resurrection of the saints to a climactic conclusion by an appeal to steadfast faithfulness in the Lord's work.

God needs faithful servants. God uses and blesses faithful servants. The world needs men and women who are faithful to God.

I. Faithfulness is reasonable.

Faithfulness of children to their parents and of parents to their children is logical and reasonable.

Faithfulness to God is not only admirable but absolutely necessary. We must be faithful to him in our home life, business life, and church life. Faithfulness is most influential; it gives power to preaching.

II. Faithfulness is difficult.

A. *There are reasons within ourselves that make faithfulness sometimes difficult.* If we suffer from a lack of physical rest or if we have neglected to secure adequate spiritual nourishment, we may find it difficult to be faithful to that which God would have us to do.

B. *There are reasons outside ourselves that make faithfulness difficult.* The demands of a highly competitive economic system combined with a person's natural acquisitive instinct sometimes would encourage him or her to be less faithful to the will and work of God.

C. *Each of us, whether we recognize it or not, has an enemy in the devil who walks about seeking whom he may devour.* In a multiplicity of ways, he tempts us and would lure us away from our faithfulness to the will of God.

III. The necessity of faithfulness.

A. *We must be faithful to the opportunity to grow if we are to become what God would have us to be.* Faithfulness in worship, prayer, study, and witnessing is essential for continued spiritual growth.

B. *Faithfulness is absolutely essential if we are to overcome the arguments of unbelievers and demonstrate that Jesus Christ really makes a difference in the lives of those who trust him.*

C. *Faithfulness is absolutely essential if we are to enjoy our religion.* Jesus spoke of his desire that we have fullness of joy (John 15:11).

D. *We must be faithful to show our gratitude to our Lord, who was faithful to his mission on our behalf to the point of dying on the cross for us.*

IV. The rewards of faithfulness.

A. *Faithfulness is perhaps the best defense that one can build against the evil that is within him and the evil that is about him.*

B. *The joy of a clean conscience is one of the great rewards that comes to the man or woman who is faithful (2 Tim. 4:7–8).*

C. *Another satisfaction that comes to the faithful is the assurance of a permanent achievement.* Our text assures us, on the basis of the resurrection, that our labor for the Lord will not be wasted or in vain.

D. *Each one who has experienced the joy of receiving forgiveness and the gift of eternal life desires to do something to express his gratitude to the Lord.*

Conclusion

He who would be faithful must do so day by day. Life is divided up into moments as well as decades. Because of our Lord's love for us, because of our love for him, and because of the world's desperate need for Christ, we can and should be faithful.

JULY

■ Sunday Mornings

Following the first Sunday morning with its patriotic theme are sermons in a series called "Facing Life's Problems Triumphantly."

■ Sunday Evenings

"Inspiration and Encouragement from the Apostle Paul" is the theme for the Sunday evening messages. Everyone needs encouragement, for one of the devil's chief weapons is discouragement. We must continually study and apply the Word of God to our lives that it might lift our spirit.

■ Wednesday Evenings

"Romans for Today's Living" is the suggested theme for an expository study of the book of Romans. This study can both enrich and inform the spiritual life of your people.

SUNDAY MORNING, JULY 4

Title: Let Freedom Ring

Text: "Proclaim liberty throughout all the land unto all the inhabitants thereof" (**Lev. 25:10**).

Scripture Reading: Psalm 33:1–12

Hymns: "O God, Beneath Thy Guiding Hand," Bacon

"My Country, 'Tis of Thee," Smith

"God of Our Fathers, Whose Almighty Hand," Roberts

Offertory Prayer: Almighty God, Ruler of heaven and earth and before whom all individuals and nations are judged, we bow this day before you in earnest prayer to thank you for the good gifts we have from your bounty. We are grateful for the personal uplift that comes to us as our own spirits contemplate the joys of leaning each day on you for strength, wisdom, and guidance. We thank you for all the blessings you have given to our land; for our national heritage; for the faith of our fathers; and for the spirit of dedication that caused those who have gone before to build for us a republic dedicated to the proposition that all men are created equal before you and have been endowed by you with certain inalienable rights, including life, liberty, and the pursuit of happiness. As we present our gifts of gratitude this morning, may we realize how much we owe you. Help us to realize that along with our gifts of money we are to give ourselves

220

to you—completely and willingly. Bless us as we give, our Father, and may we be a blessing in return to others. In Jesus' name we pray. Amen.

Introduction

In recent years bells have rung throughout the United States at high noon on July 4. This annual Independence Day celebration in towns and cities throughout our land serves to remind us of the sacrifices, character, ideas, ideals, and faith that have gone into the making of our national history. The sound of these bells calls us back to that meaningful day, July 4, 1776, when our nation was born. Those of us in the Judeo-Christian tradition look back further to such events in biblical history as that indicated in our text when the Lord spoke through Moses and said, "Proclaim liberty throughout all the land unto the inhabitants thereof."

I. A time to remember.

A. *The price of what we enjoy.*

> *Freedom isn't free . . .*
> *You've got to pay the price,*
> *You've got to sacrifice,*
> *For your liberty.*

Days of hardship and grave uncertainty accompanied the efforts of those colonial leaders who led us to attain our freedom as a sovereign nation.

B. *The principal Person who provided our liberty.* In Leviticus 25:2 reference is made to keeping "a sabbath unto the LORD." The word "sabbath" means rest. Perhaps the word is used here as a remembrance that God the Creator rested (Gen. 2:2) at the completion of his creation. The emphasis, however, does not belong on the idea of "rest"; the context indicates that the emphasis belongs to the idea of who it was who did the creating—*Elohim*—the mighty God, the Sovereign of the universe. It was this same God who delivered Israel from Egyptian bondage, led the tribes through the wilderness, and helped them conquer Canaan, the land of promise. The sabbatical year mentioned in Leviticus 25 was commanded in the law of Moses as a reminder to them of how they came to receive their liberty from bondage.

Our founding fathers, too, carved a nation out of a wilderness—a national wilderness, a political wilderness, and a spiritual wilderness. From such wildernesses they fled to our shores to find freedom, and under God, to build here a country dedicated to freedom and justice for all. Our God did all of this for us just as he did for his people long ago.

II. A time to return.

A. *To first principles: work, sacrifice, discipline, patriotic devotion, love of justice and freedom, honesty, high purpose, and respect for the rights of others.* These were first and basic principles in the foundations of our nation.

B. *To free enterprise.* Individual initiative, private industry, the freedom to choose and work for a way of life — these are fundamentals of life in a free society. All are primary factors in a government of free people, and they are diminishing factors in the way of life we know in our age.

III. A time to recognize.

A. *Evils of our materialistic, power-crazed, technological age.* Millions never know what it means to go to bed at night without feeling hunger, yet our nation spends money on things of little importance, so much so that we have the highest national debt in our history. If Edison thought we needed to take time out scientifically to catch up with ourselves spiritually, what would he think if he were living today?

B. *Ills of our status-minded society.* We spend money we do not have to buy status symbols we do not need, to keep up with people we do not know and probably would not like if we did know them.

C. *Dangerous trends of our times.* For years the trend has been to withdraw religion from our public schools and government institutions. In the past, American tradition has kept government closely allied with religion. Our presidents have used the Bible in taking the oath of office; Congress opens its sessions with prayer; our pledge to the flag includes the phrase "One nation, under God"; our coins are inscripted with "In God We Trust"; and the first sentence of the Declaration of Independence uses the word "God," recognizing him as our Creator, and the last sentence uses the phrase "With a firm reliance on divine providence."

The Bill of Rights (Articles I–X) of the Constitution begins with the First Amendment, in which we read, "Congress shall make no law respecting an establishment of religion, or prohibiting free exercise thereof." Serious students of history know this had to do with one specific contextual matter, a "state church." The framers of the Constitution never dreamed that this nation would ever forget God!

One may ask what special insight has come to people today to enable them to interpret as unconstitutional these time-honored traditions. One may respond that there had never been a court case on this. Again, one may ask, Why? Thomas Paine wrote *The Age of Reason* (published 1794–96), an attack on religion that embodied the spirit of German rationalism and French atheism. Paine was an ardent leader in the Revolution.

By the end of the Revolution and the adoption of the Constitution in 1788, religion had reached a low ebb in the new nation — fewer than 10 percent of the people had any church relationship. So why was the subject of "religion" left in obscurity until 1963 when someone had to tell us what was meant by "establishment of religion"? The answer: Because those close to the day of its origin knew what it meant. Their sole purpose was to preserve and protect the people's freedom so that they might be sure they would not be harassed by a state church that could interfere with their consciences. The exercise of religion itself was a fundamental principle in government and private life, but it too was to be a free, voluntary act. It should forever be so!

IV. A time to renew.

A. *Our allegiance to God and country.* It is significant that in many churches the American and Christian flags are displayed together; they are not in opposition one to the other, but they complement each other.

B. *Our faith in God, the cause of freedom and the meaning of our text for today, "Proclaim liberty throughout the land."*

Conclusion

Let all the bells in the land ring; all the choirs sing; and all the preachers, teachers, editors, statesmen, and others proclaim liberty in our land. Let freedom ring so that the matchless words of Abraham Lincoln may come true, "that this nation, under God, shall have a new birth of freedom, and that government of the people, by the people, and for the people, shall not perish from the earth."

SUNDAY EVENING, JULY 4

Title: Rich in Everything

Text: "That in everything ye are enriched by him" (**1 Cor. 1:5**).

Scripture Reading: 1 Corinthians 1:1–9

Introduction

One of the dominating motives of the business world is the desire for riches. Some people dedicate their total being to achieving financial riches. Only a few in each community or city or county achieve outstanding financial success. Others spend their lives in despair because of their inability to become rich.

The words of our text sound like a letter of congratulations to a group of people who had come into a great fortune, and according to Paul they had done exactly that. Their treasure ship had arrived. The apostle was referring to spiritual riches that are of permanent value rather than financial riches that are of temporary value.

In the verses of our Scripture reading, we notice the manner in which Paul dwells lovingly on the name of the Savior. Nine times in these nine verses he makes use of this name. He also does so in the next verse. Christ is the central figure and the primary subject of these nine verses. Paul lovingly lingers over the precious name of Christ, for he glories in the Christ (Gal. 6:14).

The apostle speaks of the grace of God that his readers had experienced through Jesus Christ as a treasure of incredible riches. He sought to help them realize the extent and to appreciate the nature of their newfound riches in Jesus Christ.

An early missionary was visiting an African village. He noticed the children playing with some odd looking stones, and a close examination revealed that they were diamonds in the rough. Similarly, those of us who have trusted Jesus Christ as Lord and Savior are rich beyond our fondest dreams, but many of us fail to recognize the nature of our riches.

Paul wrote to the Romans concerning their riches in Christ Jesus (Rom. 2:4; 9:23; 11:33). He was vividly aware of the spiritual riches that had come from God to the Ephesians (Eph. 2:4, 7; 3:8). In his second epistle to the Corinthians, Paul speaks of how those who receive Jesus Christ as Lord and Savior are rich in the things of God (8:9).

These riches are ours through Christ Jesus. As believers, we need to recognize the wonders of our spiritual estate. This will cause us to more properly love and appreciate our Savior. Those who have not yet trusted Jesus Christ need to recognize what they are missing as a result of their neglect and refusal to let Christ Jesus become the Lord and Savior of their lives.

There are at least three ways in which we are enriched by and through Jesus Christ.

I. We are enriched by a new relationship to God.

A. *Through faith in Christ, we become the children of God (John 1:12; Gal. 3:26).* The daughter-in-law of a multimillionaire gave birth to a son. By virtue of the home in which this child was born, the newspapers spoke of him as a millionaire on the day of his birth. Perhaps there are times when you have wished that you might have been born with a silver spoon in your mouth. While this may be the case, we should recognize and rejoice that the blessings associated with being children of God are far greater than any legacy that can be passed on from earthly parents. Harriet E. Buell put it this way:

> *My Father is rich in houses and lands,*
> *He holdeth the wealth of the world in His hands!*
> *Of rubies and diamonds, of silver and gold,*
> *His coffers are full—He has riches untold.*
> *I'm a child of the King,*
> *A child of the King!*
> *With Jesus my Savior,*
> *I'm a child of the King!*

B. *Through faith in Christ we become partakers of the divine nature (2 Peter 1:4; 1 John 3:9).* In the birth from above, God bestows on us the gift of eternal life (1 John 5:11–12). This new life from God is qualitative as well as quantitative. It causes us to love the things that God loves. It causes us to want to do the things that God would want us to do.

C. *Through faith in Christ we receive the assurance of victory over death and the promise of an eternal home above (John 14:1–3; 1 Cor. 15:51–57).* Great is the security of those who have placed their faith in a Savior who conquered death and the grave and who has promised to give that same victory to those who trust and follow him. He who served as a carpenter in Nazareth has gone into the heavenly carpenter shop to prepare a home for those who love him.

II. We are enriched by inexhaustible resources for living a victorious life.

A. *The inerrant teachings of the Bible and the unblemished example of Jesus Christ, our living Lord (John 8:12).* To follow Jesus Christ in his attitudes, ambitions, and actions is to discover the reality of the abundant life in the here and now. He provides light for the pathway in the present, and he will continue to do so in the future.

Jesus has promised that those who not only hear but also heed his teachings will find a stability and security in life that will provide them with the inward resources that are essential when the storms of life beat down on them (Matt. 7:24–25).

B. *The presence and power of the Holy Spirit who comes to dwell in the heart of the believer (1 Cor. 3:16).* The Spirit of God takes up his residency within the heart of each believer at the time of conversion. The Holy Spirit dwells within the heart both to create the desire and to make possible the ability for the believer to do the will of God (Phil. 2:13).

C. *The fellowship of the church that our Lord loved and which he commissioned to evangelize the world.* Everyone needs a cause to live for, a cause to give to, and a cause to die for. There is no greater cause on the earth than that for which the church came into being. The believer can find within the church great spiritual resources for the living of a triumphant life.

III. We are enriched by the rewards of a loving heavenly Father.

A. *Rewards in the present.* Right conduct is its own reward. God has so designed the universe that he who lives for God and for others will discover an inward joy that comes about as a result of doing that which is right.

The assurance of worthy achievement in a worthwhile enterprise makes a tremendous contribution toward happiness. As we give ourselves into the service of our Lord in a ministry of mercy to a needy world, we will be able to see the fruits of our labors. We will discover that happiness is a by-product of giving ourselves to something that is bigger and better than ourselves.

God will bless us with victory over difficulty and handicaps. When we live for him and work with him, we receive his wisdom, energy, and guidance.

The happiest people on earth today are not the wealthiest or the most highly educated or the most powerful. The happiest people are those who have a right relationship with God and who are seeking to do his will in every area of their lives.

B. *Rewards in the future.* Our Lord taught his disciples to invest their energies and resources in treasures of eternal significance (Matt. 6:19–21). In these statements he was giving to his disciples what we would call sound financial advice. He was pointing out the permanent value of some things in contrast to the temporary value of other things. He would encourage each of us to live our lives with the issues and values of eternity in mind (Rev. 22:12).

Each of us can have the privilege of hearing the Master say, "Well done, thou good and faithful servant" (Matt. 25:21).

Conclusion

Are you enjoying the rich rewards of God in the present? Are you investing your life and energy in such a manner as to have a promise of rich rewards in the future? This was one of the hopes that sustained and comforted the apostle Paul as he faced death (2 Tim. 4:7–8).

If you have never trusted Jesus Christ, then you are indeed poor. You are poor in your relationships, resources, and rewards. Make him the Lord of your life so that he might work his work within you and through you. He will enrich others through you if you will but let him.

WEDNESDAY EVENING, JULY 7

Title: Paul and His Purpose

Text: "For I am not ashamed of the gospel of Christ: for it is the power of God unto salvation to every one that believeth; to the Jew first, and also to the Greek" **(Rom. 1:16)**.

Scripture Reading: Romans 1:1–17

Introduction

Historically God has used the book of Romans to awaken the church. The Great Reformation of the sixteenth century can be traced to Martin Luther's study of the book of Romans. "Justification by faith" was rediscovered, and Christianity was reborn.

Two hundred years later when the church was again spiritually dead, the book of Romans lit the fires of revival through the conversion of John Wesley. From this experience the flame of evangelism began to blaze.

Again, in this generation, the theological world has taken on a renewed study and appreciation of the Word of God, and the message of Romans is heard anew.

It is possible that God could use this same book to awaken us in this day. Let us look at Romans 1:1–17.

I. The man who wrote (1:1).

A. Paul, who wrote this epistle, met Jesus Christ on the road to Damascus as recorded in Acts. His own life had been transformed by this gospel he preached.

B. *Paul called himself "a servant of Jesus Christ."* The word "servant" here means "slave" and carries the implication of the lordship of Christ. We cannot serve in the same way, but we can serve in the same spirit.

C. *Paul described himself as "called an apostle."* He was not acting in his own right; God had called him to the task. Happy is the man who knows his mission and purpose in life as did Paul.

D. *Paul said that he was "separated unto the gospel of God."* In Galatians 1–5 Paul discussed this. His Jewish background, his training as a Pharisee, and his Roman citizenship all were part of this preparation.

II. The Master Paul served (1:3–6).

A. *Paul discussed the person of Christ.* The fact that Jesus was "born of the seed of David" stresses his humanity.

B. The fact of Jesus' resurrection stresses his divinity.

C. As Truett said, "He was man as if he had never been God and God as if he had never been man."

III. The people Paul addressed (1:7–8).

A. *Paul addressed his letter to "all that be in Rome."* Rome was the center of the world of that day. Here all commerce, culture, and religion met. It was also a center of sin as seen in verses 18 and following.

B. *Paul called them "saints."* They were set apart by God by virtue of God's call. If one could be a "saint" in Rome, one could be a saint anywhere.

C. Paul gave thanks for them because their faith was "spoken of throughout the whole world."

IV. The mission Paul proposed (1:9–14).

Paul had intended many times to come to Rome but was always hindered. They, perhaps, had questioned Paul's failure to come to Rome. Was it fear? Unconcern? Paul gave three reasons for wanting to come:

A. *"That I may impart some spiritual gift"* (v. 11). Paul was always concerned about edifying the church.

B. *"That I might have some fruit among you"* (v. 13), or that he might win some to Christ. Winning people to the Savior was always uppermost in Paul's mind.

C. *"That I may be comforted together with you"* (v. 12). Any pastor knows that in seeking to help others, he or she is blessed as well.

V. The message Paul proclaimed (1:15–17).

A. *Paul was coming to proclaim the gospel of Christ.* He said that he was ready to preach in Rome because he was "not ashamed of the gospel" (v. 16). He well might have been. The gospel had no official standing; it was a minority religion — despised and rejected by people as was its Christ. Paul was confident and bold in his readiness, however. What a contrast to Christians of our day who are silent and ashamed. He was not ashamed because it is:

1. "The gospel of Christ." The gospel is the good news that Christ came to earth, died, and was raised—the good news concerning sin and humankind and God—the good news concerning life and death and eternity.
2. "The power of God." Paul knew the power of Rome, but he also knew a greater power. He knew that the gospel was equal to all the sin and vulgarity, all the wisdom and learning, all the power and might of Rome.

B. The gospel offers salvation to all who believe.

Conclusion

The same gospel that Paul proclaimed is ours. The same power that Paul experienced is available to us. Therefore, let us with the same determination serve our Christ.

SUNDAY MORNING, JULY 11

Title: Life Hanging in Doubt

Text: "If you are not careful to do all the words of this law which are written in this book, that you may fear this glorious and awful name, the LORD your God. . . . your life shall hang in doubt before you; night and day you shall be in dread, and have no assurance of your life" (**Deut. 28:58, 66 RSV**).

Scripture Reading: Deuteronomy 28:1–10, 58–68; 30:19

Hymns: "When Morning Gilds the Skies," Caswall

"O God, Our Help in Ages Past," Watts

"I Am Coming to the Cross," McDonald

Offertory Prayer: Grant to us, O God, a greater awareness of our daily dependence on you. In such awareness, we joyfully acknowledge our trusteeship of manifold blessings from you. Receive this separated portion, and bless its use at each station along the way to the end that your kingdom might come in the lives of many. Through Jesus Christ our Lord. Amen.

Introduction

The prophetic writer in Deuteronomy pictures the Hebrew people standing before the tribunal of God. In the great trial scene, the judgment hangs upon one tremendous "if." God is represented as saying, "*If* you are not careful to observe all the provisions of this code . . . by standing in awe of this glorious and awful name, the LORD your God, [then] your life shall hang in doubt before you; night and day you shall be in dread, and have no assurance of your life."

In preparation for Israel's entering their land of promise, Moses had given detailed instructions from the Lord. Deuteronomy 28 is sometimes referred to as the declaration of blessings and curses or rewards and punishment. But this chapter is not merely a shallow religion of moralism, as though in vending machine fashion Israel could put in a dollar's worth of obedience and get back a dollar's

228

worth of divine favor. These longtime slaves of the Egyptians desired their own country where they could enjoy freedom and a truer identity.

Israel as a nation — as a social, political, and economic organism — existed in covenant with the Lord. To break this covenant or to rebel against it or deny it was to violate that which had created, sustained, and composed nationality. To disobey God was to betray life itself as Israel understood it. Consequently, the choice was indeed between life and death, for the blessing, the reward, was life, and the curse, the punishment, was death. That word "if" hung over the nation like a suspended sword. Israel felt the cutting edge of that sword many times.

The life of each generation of the human race hangs in doubt, and the reality represented in that word "if" has to be reckoned with. "The twentieth century has put the human race on trial for its life," according to Quincy Howe in his book *World History in Our Times.*

Let us make the matter personal. What was true of Israel as a nation is true of you and me as individuals. So often our chief problem is ourselves. We go down to defeat, not because outward circumstances overwhelm us, but because things are not right within. For us, too, life hangs in doubt, and the verdict of the great Judge is determined by our response to his instructions.

I. With life hanging in doubt, we need to feel the responsibility that rightly belongs to us.

The choice is always yours. This has been said forcefully by many people. Herodotus wrote, "The destiny of man is in his own soul." Cassius, in one of Shakespeare's plays, says, "The fault, dear Brutus, is not in our stars, but in ourselves."

Christianity's first interest is the condition of a person's inner life. It does not fumble with outside situations but goes straight to the inner life and deals with the problem. When persons have faced themselves and are remade by God's grace, they are ready to confront the wrongs in their society.

II. The life of Christian usefulness hangs in doubt for the person who uses the circumstantial alibi.

The assumption behind the excuses we make for ourselves is that if we can discover alibis outside ourselves, we can escape responsibility for being what we are. "It is not our fault," we can soothe ourselves by saying. Abraham Lincoln reportedly explained the character of a village scoundrel by saying, "He's got the can't-help-its." The man habitually explained his behavior in terms of people and things over which he had no control. He couldn't help being like he was, he "alibied," because other people made him that way. Shifting the blame is an old excuse.

When a life of Christian usefulness hangs in doubt, alibis are a luxury one cannot afford. Honest self-examination is the beginning of maturity, even as it was with the disciples with Jesus in the upper room when each began to ask, "Master, is it I?"

Conclusion

I would now speak a word to those of you who are not professing Christians. Your life in the Spirit is in doubt. There is a great question about the life that has eternal quality in it as far as you are concerned. Put your eyes upon Jesus and keep them there. Hear his words of instruction, study his life, ponder his claims and call. Give yourself in full commitment and trust to him. Your life need not hang in doubt.

SUNDAY EVENING, JULY 11

Title: Continued Effort Encouraged

Text: "And let us not be weary in well doing: for in due season we shall reap, if we faint not" **(Gal. 6:9).**

Scripture Reading: Galatians 6

Introduction

There were times when even our Lord became weary and exhausted. It is possible that even he experienced the depression that comes as a result of disappointment. There were probably many times when the apostle Paul was weary in mind as well as in body.

Are you plagued with chronic fatigue? Are you weary in body and mind? Are you ready to give up the struggle and quit? Even the most faithful will admit that they have been tempted to throw in the towel.

Physical, emotional, and even spiritual fatigue can cause the servants of the Lord Jesus Christ to be tempted to give up the struggle to achieve the will of God in their lives or to see the will of God experienced in the lives of others.

As a veteran soldier of the cross, Paul wrote to the Galatian Christians to encourage them to continue in well-doing. He promised them that there would be a sure reward at the end of the way if they did not give out, give in, or give up.

I. Constant well-doing is the will of God for his children (Eph. 2:10).

   A. *By its very nature, the spiritual birth, which makes us children of God, creates within us a desire to do the will of God.* The desire for evil is replaced by a desire to do good (2 Cor. 5:17).

   B. *By the good works of a life dedicated to the glory of God and to the service of our fellow humans we reveal the difference that Jesus Christ makes (Titus 3:8).*

II. Discouragement is the foe of spiritual achievement.

Someone has said that the devil uses the tool of discouragement more than any other tool to defeat the servants of God. There have been times when each of us has been greatly discouraged. We had legitimate reasons for being discouraged.

   A. *There are things within ourselves that can produce discouragement.* The lack of physical rest and nourishment can produce exhaustion. A body that is not rested and refreshed is much more subject to discouragement than one that is enjoying the vitality of regular and consistent rest.

The lack of spiritual nurture that comes as a result of genuine worship can cause one to be defeated by discouragement. As the physical body must be refreshed by food, even so the soul must be refreshed by the devotional study of God's Word. The soul must be strengthened by communication with God in prayer. God is the source of the spiritual vitality of the inward person. Many of us are experiencing discouragement, and we are tempted to give up the struggle because of spiritual malnutrition.

The struggle of our old fleshly nature against our new spiritual nature can be so intense as to bring about discouragement. We find it much easier to hate than we do to love. We find it much easier to grow weeds in the garden of our lives than we do flowers. Our own personal failure to be what God would have us to be can contribute to discouragement.

B. *There are many things in the world about us that have a tendency to discourage us.* The world with all of its evils, with its unchristian attitudes and ambitions and customs, makes it difficult for us to always be what God would have us to be. Satan and all of the demons of hell oppose us as we seek to make progress in our own spiritual growth. Every effort to witness for Christ is an offensive effort against the host of evil.

Some believers find that there are some in their own family circle who would hinder them and discourage them and cause them to forsake the will of God for their lives.

C. *There are many things in the Lord's work itself, which at times contribute toward our being discouraged.* There is nothing easy about being genuinely Christian. It is a rather simple matter to trust Jesus Christ and to become a child of God through faith, but to be genuinely Christian in every area of life requires a constant struggle. We never achieve the ideal of being completely Christian in every area of life.

Often we are discouraged by the great variety of opinions that we find among those with whom we worship and fellowship and attempt to cooperate with in the Lord's work.

Sooner or later all of us have the breath knocked out of us by someone who has tragically failed to be the Christian he or she professed to be.

The Lord's work is hard work, requiring struggle and sacrifice to achieve success. We must swim upstream and against the tide if we would do God's will.

III. Continued effort is necessary.

A. *Our Lord always encouraged his disciples to count the cost before they undertook a task.* At no time did he deceive them into believing that it would be comfortable and convenient to be one of his followers. The cross itself was the symbol that he lifted up before them.

B. *Paul sought to encourage the Christians of Galatia by the sure and certain promise of a harvest in due season.* He encouraged them to be faithful at the task and to leave the results to God. The harvest may not come when we expect it or when we desire it. It may not even come during our lifetime. The great God of heaven is not limited by time as we think of time. There are instances in which it takes a decade for the seed that we grow in human hearts to germinate and sprout and come to life.

C. *We must not quit.* The devil will not quit attempting to defeat us and discourage us. He will not turn away from his malicious purpose of destroying the work of God.

The Holy Spirit is not going to quit. The living God is not going to quit loving a lost world. We must not quit. We must keep at the good work to which God has called us.

Conclusion

The New International Version translates our text, "Let us not become weary in doing good, for at the proper time we will reap a harvest if we do not give up." We must continue to be faithful to our Lord and his church. We must continue to give our Christian testimony to those who are unsaved. We must continually try to be genuinely Christian in every area of our lives. God will bless our faithfulness with success.

WEDNESDAY EVENING, JULY 14

Title: There Is No Difference

Text: "For all have sinned, and come short of the glory of God" (**Rom. 3:23**).

Scripture Reading: Romans 1:18–3:24

Introduction

The philosopher Seneca once said, "We must say of ourselves that we *are* evil, *have been* evil, and unhappily, I must add, *shall be* evil in the future. Nobody can deliver himself; someone must stretch out a hand to lift him up." This is what Paul is saying in this section of Romans.

I. All have sinned (Rom. 1:18; 2:17–3:23).

A. *The Gentiles are condemned (Rom. 1:18–32).* Paul paints a dark and painful picture of the pagan world, but it is even more distressing when we realize that classical authors depicted it in even more revolting detail.

1. They had a knowledge of God but had rejected him (1:18–23).

a. They were inexcusable (v. 19).

(1) God was known in creation (v. 20). The psalmist said, "The heavens declare the glory of God; and the firmament sheweth his handiwork" (Ps. 19:1).

(2) God was known in conscience, but they refused to listen. When communication was first established with Helen Keller, she was told about God. She replied, "I always knew about Him but did not know His name."

    b. Their action was deliberate (vv. 21, 28). They chose not to glorify him nor even retain him in their knowledge. It was not a sin of ignorance.

  2. The results of the rejection of God are seen (vv. 24–32).

    a. "God gave them up." This is the solemn repetition of verses 24–28. Dr. Herschel H. Hobbs says that this is like a man trying to tame a rebellious horse. After so long a time, God took off the bridle and permitted sinful humans to run loose to their own destruction.

    b. Their condition is progressive—they become debased (vv. 26–27).

    c. "The wrath of God is revealed ... against all" (v. 18).

    d. The climax is reached when it is seen in verse 32 that they not only do these things themselves but also encourage others to do them.

  3. One has only to read this list of sins to see how low humans can fall. Every metropolitan newspaper carries accounts of the same sins in today's ungodly society. This is what happens when a people turn their backs on the living God.

B. *The Jews are condemned (2:17–3:8).*

  1. They occupied a position of prestige (2:17–20). They were a chosen race and a covenant people.

  2. They had failed to keep the law (2:21–24). God pronounces them guilty in regard to honesty, purity, and idolatry.

  3. Outward conduct is insufficient (2:25ff.).

C. *The whole world therefore is condemned (3:9–23).* Paul brings a fourteen-point indictment against the human race. Each charge that he makes is a quotation from the Old Testament, mostly from Psalms and Isaiah. In analyzing this section, Dr. H. H. Hobbs has pointed out that:

  1. Paul speaks as a philosopher (vv. 11–12).

  2. Paul speaks as a physician (vv. 13–14).

  3. Paul speaks as a historian (vv. 15–23). Paul's conclusion is reached in verse 23: "All have sinned, and come short of the glory of God." All are condemned.

II. All shall be judged (Rom. 2:16).

Jew and Gentile alike shall be judged by Jesus Christ (v. 16). This judgment shall be:

A. *According to the truth (vv. 1–5).*

B. *According to one's deeds (vv. 6–10).*

C. *According to the gospel (v. 16).*

III. All can be saved (Rom. 3:24).

A. *By God's grace (v. 24)*. All have sinned and have been pronounced guilty, but God's grace can save. In fact, people can be saved only by grace (Eph. 2:8–10).

B. *Through redemption in Christ Jesus (v. 24)*. In Romans 5:8 Paul says, "But God commendeth his love toward us, in that, while we were yet sinners, Christ died for us."

Conclusion

This is not a pretty view of humankind's condition. We are helpless, and judgment is waiting. Yet Scripture promises, "God's kindness leads you toward repentance" (Rom. 2:4 NIV). He stands ready to save any who come in repentance.

SUNDAY MORNING, JULY 18

Title: When Bereavement Comes

Text: "Praise be to the God and Father of our Lord Jesus Christ, the Father of compassion and the God of all comfort" (**2 Cor. 1:3 NIV**).

Scripture Reading: Isaiah 41:10; John 14:1–3; 1 Cor. 13:12; 1 John 3:2

Hymns: "Great Redeemer, We Adore Thee," Harris

"Like a River Glorious," Havergal

"In Heavenly Love Abiding," Waring

Offertory Prayer: Our gracious and loving Father, in our sorrows we have found that your consolation never fails us. Yet we are made to sorrow when we realize how often we fail you. May the giving of yourself on our behalf inspire us to give ourselves and our substance for your work in the world. We ask for enablement from you, through Christ our Savior and example. Amen.

Introduction

"And the king was much moved, and went up to the chamber over the gate, and wept: and as he went, thus he said, O my son Absalom, my son, my son Absalom! would God I had died for thee, O Absalom, my son, my son!" (2 Sam. 18:33). Such is the cry wrung from the heart of a man hit by the sledgehammer blow of bereavement some three thousand years ago.

When a loved one dies, there is nothing anyone can say in a sermon, prayer, poem, personal conversation, or act that will take away the reality of the loss. Society has devised some ways of trying to hide it, and well-meaning friends may try to disguise it with distracting words or sentimental theology. The best first reaction in bereavement is usually to face the stark reality—the joy of mutual day-to-day involvement with the loved one has ceased, and it is time for weeping tears unashamed.

It is important that we know how to come through bereavement, however. It can become a snare and render us unfit for useful living. Protracted grief can shut us off from our primary source of help.

I. When bereavement comes, recognize certain barriers to consolation if they exist.

A. *Guilt may be one barrier.* It is easy to take people for granted, especially those nearest to us. We hurt others or deny them the fullness of our love, often unawares. Or we rationalize our miserliness in understanding and affection, blaming it on circumstances or job pressures, etc. In love, as in life generally, *now* is the time of salvation, but we say *later.* Then when death takes the loved one, it is too late for that earthly relationship to be built that could have brought real joy.

B. *A second possible barrier to consolation may be resentment.* "Why did this have to happen to me?" expresses it. Sometimes this is a good question, and the questioner is capable of giving the answer. Often there is no human answer to the question, and too often the wrong answers are given. We cannot lay everything at God's door with a pious or resentful reference to God's will. When the bereaved blame God *for* the tragedy they cut off the main source of strength *beyond* the tragedy.

C. *A third possible barrier to consolation is the dread of the future.* It may be fear of loneliness or financial burdens.

We can never prepare ourselves fully for the hour of bereavement, even if we could know the moment of its arrival. But in this regard, the old proverb applies, "An ounce of prevention is worth a pound of cure." Concerning guilt, follow the scriptural injunction, "Never let the sun go down on your wrath." As for resentment, learn of God and of his loving ways and revealed will. He is our Friend, not our enemy. Concerning the dread of the future, get into a sound life insurance program in keeping with your financial ability and survivor needs.

II. When bereavement comes, know the comfort of God.

We are prone to make the word "comfort" a synonym for "pity," "soothe," or "make comfortable." Paul wrote to the Corinthians, "Praise be to God ... the God of all comfort." The word breaks into two parts. *Com* means "with" and *fortis* means "strong." To be comforted is "to be strengthened by being with." The Holy Spirit is referred to as our Comforter or Paraclete, the one who stands by one's side to encourage, to strengthen, to give confidence. The comfort of God is the strength that comes from being with God.

III. When bereavement comes, keep in mind the happy estate of your departed loved one if he or she "died in the Lord"—to use a New Testament term.

A long list of Scripture references support this statement. In the presence of

235

these biblical promises, we should avoid both an attitude of evasiveness and an attitude of a know-it-all.

Dr. Arthur J. Gossip, following his wife's untimely death, preached a sermon titled "But When Life Tumbles in, What Then?" He said:

> We Christian people in the mass are entirely unchristian in our thoughts of death. We have our eyes wrongly focused. We are selfish, and self-centered and self-absorbed. We keep thinking aggrievedly of what it means to us. And that is wrong, all wrong. In the New Testament we hear very little of the families with that aching gap, huddled together in their desolate home ...; but a great deal about the saints in glory, and the sunshine, and the singing, and the splendor yonder.... Would you pluck the diadem from their brows again? Would you snatch the palms of victory out of their hands? Dare you compare the clumsy nothings our poor blundering love can give them here with what they must have yonder where Christ himself has met them?" (*The Protestant Pulpit*, comp. Andrew W. Blackwood [Abingdon-Cokesbury, 1947], 202)

Conclusion

When bereavement comes, in addition to the above-mentioned, give yourself to be an instrument for God's use. Submit your life to God's will and way, and thus the life of your beloved will be memorialized and your life will be radiant in our Father's world.

> *How shall we honor them, our deathless dead?*
> *With strew of laurel and the stately tread?*
> *With blaze of banners brightening overhead?*
> *Nay, not alone these cheaper praises bring:*
> *They will not have this easy honoring.*
> *How shall we honor them, our deathless dead?*
> *How keep their mighty memories alive?*
> *In him who feels their passion, they survive!*
> *Flatter their souls with deeds and all is said!*

SUNDAY EVENING, JULY 18

Title: The Strength of the Christian

Text: "I can do everything through him who gives me strength" (**Phil. 4:13 NIV**).

Scripture Reading: Philippians 4

Introduction

To be aware of our weakness, on the one hand, and on the other to recognize the source of sufficient strength to do the will of God, is a blessing of the first magnitude.

There are some who think they can do all necessary things in their strength alone. There are others who think that they can do nothing, even with the help of God's grace.

The text teaches us two great truths. There are many things for us to do. We can do all things that are necessary through Jesus Christ.

I. We have many things to do.

A. *Life was not given to be wasted. It is a trust from God. It is an opportunity for achievement and service.*

B. *We face the task of making a living by honest toil.*

C. *We are confronted with the opportunity for service in the realm of the spirit.*

D. *We daily face the need for the cultivation of a Christlike spirit.*

1. We must continually seek to walk in paths of true piety.

2. We must with endurance fight the good fight of faith.

3. It is the will of God for us to do good to all people, especially those who are of the household of faith.

E. *We may have much to do with suffering.* Some of us may suffer great affliction and even persecution. Death will take our loved ones and leave us with extra burdens to bear.

II. We can do all things through Christ.

Paul was thinking in terms of the things that need to be done. He was expressing the confidence of his heart that through faith in Jesus Christ he could be adequate. You and I need that confidence today.

A. *Our natural strength, whether small or great, comes from God.*

B. *Spiritual strength has its source in the grace of God (John 15:5; 2 Cor. 3:5; Eph. 6:10).*

C. *The Spirit of God communicates the strength of God to believers (Eph. 3:14–19).*

D. *Strength comes through genuine prayer (Isa. 40:30–31).*

E. *Power comes when the work is to be done.* Some of us would like to have the power before it is needed. God has promised that it will be available when it is needed.

Conclusion

The thrilling truths of this great text leave the poor trifler without excuse. At the same time, these precious truths should give courage and hope to the heart of each follower of Jesus Christ. The truths of the text honor the Redeemer and declare that the creative power of God is available to his followers as they seek to do his will and to carry on his ministry in the world.

Each of us, if we will give ourselves, can say with the apostle Paul, "I can do everything through him who gives me strength."

WEDNESDAY EVENING, JULY 21

Title: Can a Person Be Justified?

Text: "Being justified freely by his grace through the redemption that is in Christ Jesus **(Rom. 3:24)**.

Scripture Reading: Romans 3:21–4:25

Introduction

Job asked the question millennia ago, "Can a man be justified before God?" and human hearts have been asking that question ever since.

Paul gives the answer in Romans 3 and 4.

I. The meaning of justification.

A. Justification *is the key word of Romans and occurs about fifty times.*

B. *Justification means* "to pronounce *righteous," not to* make *righteous*. It means that the believer is viewed in Christ as righteous and is treated as such by God. It is the opposite of "condemnation," which Paul discusses in the previous portion of the epistle.

C. *Paul introduces the subject by saying,* "But now" *(v. 21).* This is both "logical," contrasting condemnation and justification, and "temporal," contrasting the past with the present.

II. Motive of justification (3:21–26).

Paul says that we are "justified freely by his grace, through the redemption that is in Christ Jesus" (3:24). Luther said, "This is the chief point and central place of the epistle and of the whole Bible."

A. *This righteousness or justification that God provides is:*
1. "Manifest" (v. 21). It was revealed by God. People could not discover it for themselves.
2. "Witnessed by the law and the prophets" (v. 21).
3. Necessary because of people's sin (v. 23).

B. *Justification is provided by God (3:24–25).* Paul uses three figures from contemporary life to illustrate what Christ has done for us.
1. The illustration from the courtroom is seen in the word *justification.* Here the judge acquits the prisoner who is condemned.
2. The illustration from slavery is seen in the word *redemption.* Here one pays the price, and the slave is freed.
3. The illustration from religion is seen in the word *propitiation.* Here the priest offers the sacrifice that is acceptable to God.

C. *God is in this manner "just, and the justifier of him which believeth" (3:26).*

III. The means of justification (Rom. 3:27–4:25).

A. *This justification is by faith (3:27–28). Faith* is another of the key words of Romans (used sixty-four times).

B. *Paul uses Abraham to illustrate this principle (4:1–25).*
1. Abraham was justified by faith and not by works (4:1–8). If anyone could have been justified by works, it would have been Abraham, for he was "the friend of God."
2. Abraham was justified before his circumcision (4:9–12). Religious ceremonies and ordinances cannot justify.
3. Abraham's justification was not by means of the law (4:13–23). Keeping the law and obeying its precepts will not justify.
C. *In the same manner, we can be justified by faith in the death and resurrection of Christ (3:24–25).*
1. Faith is *only* the *means* of our justification. It is Christ's work on the cross that justifies. Faith is the channel.
2. Faith is the *only means* of our justification (Rom. 3:28; 4). This excludes works, morality, law, etc. William Temple, in his *Nature, Man and God*, says that "the only thing of my very own which I can contribute to my redemption is the sin from which I need to be redeemed."

Conclusion

Justification is not something done *by* us or *in* us. It is what God has done *for* us in Christ Jesus.

SUNDAY MORNING, JULY 25

Title: Human Suffering and Divine Love

Text: "For our light and momentary troubles are achieving for us an eternal glory that far outweighs them all. So we fix our eyes not on what is seen, but on what is unseen. For what is seen is temporary, but what is unseen is eternal" **(2 Cor. 4:17–18 NIV).**

Scripture Reading: 2 Corinthians 4:16–5:5

Hymns: "Blessed Assurance," Fanny Crosby

"Love Is the Theme," Fisher

"O Master, Let Me Walk with Thee," Gladden

Offertory Prayer: O God, Creator and Sustainer of our lives, we remember the words of the great apostle that "as many as are led of the Spirit of God are the sons of God," and we are made to examine our ways. As you know the intent of our hearts in all our giving and doing, so may we be enabled to know them. If our motives or objectives are wrong, forgive. Receive these offerings that your kingdom may go forward. With this giving may we come to give ourselves to you more fully in service and in that service find our deepest joy. Through Jesus Christ, our Lord. Amen.

Introduction

Dr. John Redhead, in his book *Learning to Have Faith*, relates the story of a great sultan who instructed an aide to compile a history of the human race. Upon the completion of the task, the sultan was confronted with five hundred volumes of historic lore. This irritated him, and he commanded that the material be reduced to readable proportions. "Sire," said the aide, "all these volumes may be reduced into a single sentence: 'They were born; they suffered; they died.'"

We see all around us widespread suffering both of individuals and of entire nations. Some people are crushed by the hard march of events; they have suffered great losses or have endured illness that is almost more than can be borne.

The battle against disease is one from which there are no exemptions. Sooner or later everyone knows what sickness means. It is usually accompanied by pain and discomfort. Some people seem to be drafted for lifelong struggles against chronic ailments or disabilities.

I. God is not the source of suffering.

God allows many evil things to happen and uses them, but he does not intend them to happen. Likewise, a mother allows her toddler to fall on the floor in the kitchen or in his playpen and uses the fall to teach the child to walk. But she does not intend the child to fall, or she would push him over.

When Jesus met suffering, he dealt with it. When he healed the sick, he was not acting against God's will. He saw a woman who was bowed down by physical infirmity and referred to her as "this woman . . . whom Satan hath bound, lo, these eighteen years" (Luke 13:16).

God gets blamed for many things for which he should not be blamed. Sometimes our suffering is a direct, immediate result of our sin. It may be from sins of ignorance or sins of sensuality and folly. It may be from the guilt that follows. Sometimes our suffering is a result of an exaggerated sense of duty or importance—inducing hypertension. Sometimes it is the result of someone else's error. Often suffering cannot be traced to known sources in the sense of the "why" of it. Surely we will not believe that God hands out cancer to this man for being a bad man or diabetes to that woman because she has not said her prayers. But even so God can use the suffering that he permits as a means to worthwhile goals. Purification and strengthening can come through it.

II. God in his love permits human suffering as a means of leading us to worthwhile goals.

C. S. Lewis, in his book *The Problem of Pain*, says that God pays us the intolerable compliment of loving us in the deepest, most tragic, most inexorable sense. Suffering is a means by which some people may come into higher communion with God.

When trouble assails us, we may cry out to God, saying, "I wish he would leave me alone. All I want is to be happy." Though the trouble may be intolerable to us at the time, it is a supreme compliment that God will not leave us alone. This would indicate less care and love, not more. God will use any means, including the suffering he does not will, to shape us so that at last we may enter into communion with him in a way deeper than we have ever fathomed.

III. God relates himself to us in ways that are consistent with his love.

Divine love in human suffering may be seen better if a distinction is made between love and kindness. Parents are sometimes torn between these two. An underage son wants to drive the car. All his friends do, he says, and he is upset because he can't. Parents, motivated principally by kindness and desiring to see him "happy," give in. Love has a sterner note. It considers the end result—the help or hurt given to character development.

Kindness is often a love substitute that we offer to people whom we may not love or cannot be bothered to love. God relates himself to us on the basis of love, not kindness. He loves us and wants to bring us into communion with himself, and herein lies our deepest and most complete happiness.

God's love is a costly love, and the cross is proof of that. Hebrews 2:10 tells of Christ being made perfect through suffering. This can happen to us. We can make the best of our suffering or let it make the best of us. Christ's suffering on the cross tells us something about the use of pain. It can be turned into good use not only for the sufferer but for others as well. When the Jewish leaders nailed up the Christ, they thought they had finished with him. But it wasn't so.

Conclusion

God makes possible for us the glory of being his children and living in fellowship with him. We are honored by his love and brought into communion by his endless patience and the suffering that both he and we endure. This relationship can strengthen us in the day of our anguish and sustain us in the hour of our distress. We have only to look into our own heart to be certain that if God were content with us as we are, it could only mean that he had stopped caring.

SUNDAY EVENING, JULY 25

Title: The Attitude of Gratitude

Text: "Thanks be unto God for his unspeakable gift" (**2 Cor. 9:15**).

Scripture Reading: 2 Corinthians 9

Introduction

An attitude of gratitude can be detected in all of the writings of the apostle Paul. He was grateful beyond words to God for his mercy and grace through Christ Jesus. The apostle lived and labored that his life might express the gratitude of his heart. When Paul attempted to express his gratitude in words, he found that his vocabulary was inadequate, and so we have the words of our text.

To recognize the greatness of God's generosity toward us through Christ Jesus can stimulate an attitude of gratitude within our hearts. Gratitude is one of the strongest motives for service beyond the call of duty. We need to recognize and appreciate God's generosity that our own faith might be encouraged.

God's unspeakable gift saves us from an unspeakable fate. God's unspeakable gift saves us for a high and holy and noble purpose. God's unspeakable gift saves us to a glorious destiny in eternity.

I. The nature of God's unspeakable gift.

A. *It is unspeakable in its greatness.*
B. *It is unspeakable in its freeness.*
C. *Unspeakable is our need for it.*
D. *Unspeakable, indescribable is this gift in its availability to man once he recognizes his need for the forgiveness of sin and the gift of new life.*
E. *Unspeakable and indescribable is this gift in its effects on the lives of those who respond to it.*

II. A gift requires a response.

A. *One may ignore God's unspeakable gift in Christ Jesus.* It is possible for a person to treat a gift as if it had never been offered. To do so is to insult the one who seeks to bestow the gift.
B. *One may deliberately decline God's unspeakable gift.* To do so is to snub the Giver.
C. *One may formally accept God's unspeakable gift without any thought of using it.*
   1. Have you received God's unspeakable gift as you would receive a book without any intention of reading it?
   2. Have you received God's unspeakable gift as if it were no more than a trinket that you would never care to wear?
D. *One may accept God's unspeakable gift gladly, gratefully, and wholeheartedly.* He is the Water of Life for the thirsty man. He is the Bread of Life for those who are aware of their spiritual hunger. He is like health to those who recognize the moral sickness of the soul. He is like a rescue party to the person who is lost in a meaningless existence. He is an infallible Teacher who would guide us into a knowledge of truth about life. He is the Friend who loved us to the extent that he died for us on the cross.

III. What is your response to God's gift?

A. *Have you ignored the Christ?*
B. *Have you neglected the Christ?*
C. *Have you rejected the Christ?*
D. *Have you made him the Lord of your life so that he can be your Redeemer, Savior, and Friend?*

Conclusion

The wisest response that you could possibly make would be that of wholehearted acceptance and full committal of your life to him who gave his life for you.

God's unspeakable gift produced in Paul an attitude of thanksgiving. He responded in reverent humility and with genuine love and obedience to the goodness of God. He found the love of God to be so great and so good that words were not adequate to express the deepest sentiments of his soul. So may it be with each of us.

WEDNESDAY EVENING, JULY 28

Title: The Blessings of Justification

Text: "Therefore being justified by faith, we have peace with God through our Lord Jesus Christ" **(Rom. 5:1)**.

Scripture Reading: Romans 5:1–21

Introduction

A firm in New York investigates obsolete securities and informs their owners whether or not they have value. This company estimates that there are hundreds of millions of dollars from trust funds and inactive companies that go unclaimed. If this is true in the material realm, it is much more so in the spiritual. There are multitudes of Christians, ones "justified by faith," who are "heirs of God and joint heirs with Christ," who fail to claim the riches in Christ Jesus that are theirs.

In Romans 5 Paul enumerates the "blessings of justification"—the riches that belong to every believer who will claim them.

I. These riches belong to the "justified by faith" (5:1).

A. *"Therefore" points to the past: It is based on all Paul has said in chapters 1–4.* People have sinned (3:23), and the wages of their sin is death (6:23).

B. *"Therefore being justified" points to the present.* It is aorist, which means that our justification is now a present reality—it is already accomplished by faith in Christ. This means that our sins *are* forgiven. We *are* reconciled to God. But there is more! Years ago when Spain was at the zenith of its power, it inscribed upon its coinage a representation of the Pillars of Hercules. These pillars were erected on either side of the Straits of Gibraltar and were the extreme limit of Spain's extensive empire. Over this inscription were engraved the words *Ne Plus Ultra*, which mean "Nothing More Beyond." But when Columbus discovered America and other lands, Spain struck out the negative, *"Ne,"* and left the inscription *Plus Ultra* ("More Beyond").

Paul is saying that there is more beyond for the one "justified by faith." He then begins to catalog the blessings that are ours.

II. These blessings are now ours (5:1–21).

A. *We have peace with God (v. 1).*

1. Sometimes we do not appropriate the peace that is ours. This can be illustrated by the Battle of New Orleans, which was fought after the

243

treaty of peace was signed because General Jackson and Sir Edward Packenham did not know a peace treaty had been agreed upon.

2. Peace is what modern people want. People eagerly read books on the topic. They strive for peace while God gives it freely through faith.

3. Christ, the Prince of Peace, wants us to have peace: "My peace give I unto you." Leonard Griffith has said, "The Romans *read* about 'peace with God' in Paul's letter to them, but they *saw* 'peace with God' when the great apostle later came to Rome in chains."

B. *We have access to God (v. 2).* The picture is that of an Oriental court. One can enter the presence of the king only when he is entitled to or when he is properly introduced. The believer can enter the presence of the King of Kings through his blood.

The writer of Hebrews says, "Let us come boldly unto the throne of grace, that we may obtain mercy, and find grace to help in time of need" (4:16). This privilege is possible because we are justified.

C. *We have hope in God (vv. 2, 5).* Hope is not wishful thinking. It is certainty—assurance.

1. Hope is necessary for abundant living. There was a time when *hope* was a word used largely by preachers. Now psychologists and psychiatrists, as well as pastoral counselors, are saying with the apostle Paul, "In this hope we were saved" (Rom. 8:24).

Most medical doctors have seen many patients get well who have a strong hope, while the hopeless will most surely die. Teachers tell of pupils who give up and do much more poorly than their equally talented classmates because their hope fails.

2. People frequently have hope in the wrong things. Paul says, "Hope does not disappoint us" (v. 5). This is true when our hope is in Christ.

> *My hope is built on nothing less*
> *Than Jesus' blood and righteousness;*
> *I dare not trust the sweetest frame,*
> *But wholly lean on Jesus' name.*
> *On Christ, the solid Rock, I stand,*
> *All other ground is sinking sand.*

D. *We have assurance in tribulation (5:3–10).*

1. We make a mistake if we think a relationship with Christ excludes us from the tribulations of life. There are still sorrows and heartaches, trials and temptations, persecution and abuse to be endured.

2. Jesus warned his disciples of this: "In the world ye have tribulations."

3. Paul had experienced them (cf. 2 Cor. 4:10).

4. Even though we are not exempt from tribulations, we have assurance in the midst of them because:

a. We know we are loved by God (vv. 5, 8). If God loved us when we were enemies (v. 10) and sinners (v. 8), how much more does he love us now that we are in Christ Jesus?

    b. We have the Holy Spirit to help (v. 5). He is the "Comforter."

    c. We know that God is at work in our trials for a purpose (Rom. 8:28).

> *When thru fiery trials thy pathway shall lie,*
> *My grace, all sufficient, shall be thy supply;*
> *The flame shall not hurt thee — I only design*
> *Thy dross to consume and thy gold to refine.*

E. *We have security in Christ (vv. 9–10).*

    1. We belong to him, and he will keep us secure. The wrath to come holds no fear. "We shall be saved by his life" (v. 10). A better translation is "We are *kept safe* by his life." This does not refer to Christ's earthly life but to his present life at the right hand of God in heaven. Jesus made this promise in John 10:28–29, and Hebrews 7:24–25 lends further support.

    2. A life without this assurance of security is not only unnecessary; it is unsatisfactory. If a person is not certain he is on the right road, he cannot enjoy the journey. If one is not certain, he is liable to be led astray by any new doctrine. Without a sense of security, he feels that something is missing, and he will grab at any promising teaching (cf. Eph. 4:14).

Conclusion

The blessings of justification belong to anyone who will "receive the atonement" (v. 11). Sin may abound, but let grace much more abound (v. 20). Accept Jesus Christ as Savior by faith!

AUGUST

■ Sunday Mornings

The theme for Sunday mornings is "The Precious Promises of God."

■ Sunday Evenings

The primary objective of the Sunday evening sermons is evangelistic. No specific theme is suggested. At times it is most helpful for a pastor to concentrate on messages designed specifically to call people to repentance and faith that they might become the children of God.

■ Wednesday Evenings

Continue the series "Romans for Today's Living."

SUNDAY MORNING, AUGUST 1

Title: The Promise of God's Provision

Text: "My God shall supply all your need according to his riches in glory by Christ Jesus" (**Phil. 4:19**).

Scripture Reading: Philippians 4:14–23

Hymns: "A Child of the King," Buell

"Great Is Thy Faithfulness," Chisholm

"God Will Take Care of You," Martin

Offertory Prayer: Our Father, we thank you for all of the wonderful blessings that you have bestowed on us. As we lay before you our gifts, all of which were earned through your blessing on our labors, we do so with the prayer and expectation that you will bless the givers and use the gifts in proclaiming the gospel to those who do not know our Savior. Help us to discover the blessedness of generous and cheerful giving through Christ, in whose name we pray. Amen.

Introduction

Paul was confined in a dark, damp, and dismal dungeon in the Mamertine prison in Rome. Separated from friends who knew him most intimately and loved him most dearly, deprived of the opportunity of earning an income with which to obtain the necessities of life, and awaiting an impending death, Paul was in real need.

In his deep poverty and great need, Paul was remembered kindly and generously by his devoted Christian friends in the little church at Philippi. Out of their poverty they gave cheerfully and generously to send a love gift to Paul, as they had done previously (Phil. 4:16). Their gift was sufficient to meet Paul's needs, and it awakened in him a joyous gratitude. Their thoughtfulness revived him, their love encouraged him, and their sympathy comforted him.

In his letter to the Philippians, Paul acknowledged their love and generosity, expressed his deep gratitude to them, and assured them of his contentment even within prison walls. Any life that is filled with the consciousness of God's presence can take the shattered bow of disappointment and the broken strings of adversity and fill the soul with the sweetest melody.

I. The need.

Thinking about the problems that these donors would encounter as they journeyed through life, Paul committed them to God in the assurance that he would meet their needs through Christ Jesus.

Obviously, from birth to death each of us is a bundle of needs. All of us have many needs in common but certain needs that are peculiar to each of us. As Paul was in need of one thing and the Philippian Christians were in need of others, each of us is in need of something. Regardless of what we may have today and of how well satisfied we may be when we lie down tonight, we shall awaken in the morning with a new need. Our physical, intellectual, social, moral, and spiritual needs are many, varied, great, and constant.

II. The supply.

Deeply grateful to the Philippians for having supplied his needs repeatedly, Paul positively and unequivocally declared, "My God shall supply all your need." What an encouragement to them!

A. *The source of the supply.* The God of the Bible is the source of the supply of our needs. Having known him personally and intimately, Paul rejoiced to refer to him as "My God." He had found him to be both able and willing to supply every need of his.

God's infinite storehouse is open to his children. His righteousness is imputed to them and is theirs. His treasury of love and grace is at their disposal. His unlimited and inexhaustible resources are available to all believers in Christ who need and desire them.

B. *The sureness of the supply.* This sureness of supply is guaranteed in the statement, "My God shall supply all your need." This plain and positive declaration does not convey any thought of uncertainty. God has solemnly promised to meet the needs of his children, regardless of what those needs may be; and he is able, willing, and ready to fulfill that commitment. The assurance that God will supply all our needs should remove every doubt and fear from our minds, for his resources are adequate and inexhaustible.

> *Though troubles assail, and dangers affright;*
> *Though friends should all fail, and foes all unite;*
> *Yet one thing secures us, whatever betide, —*

> *The Scripture assures us "The Lord will provide."*
> *In some way or other the Lord will provide;*
> *It may not be my way;*
> *It may not be thy way;*
> *And yet in His own way, the Lord will provide.*

C. *The sufficiency of the supply.* God does not grant all of our whims or wishes or wants, but he does promise to supply every need of his children, whether it be material, physical, intellectual, social, moral, or spiritual. Sometimes we need to learn to do without what we think we need. Frequently we need trials to bring us closer to the Lord and into a more complete dependence on him. Often we need his guidance, encouragement, and strength. When we are in the midst of trying circumstances, he gives us poise. When we have so many things to do, he gives us power. When we have a multiplicity of needs, he gives us plenty. Due to the amplitude of God's grace, no real need will go unsupplied.

A Christian woman was traveling to the United States and became so desperately seasick that the ship's physician ordered that she not have anything to eat except oranges, lest she die. In a few days the steward came to her with the sad news that the supply of oranges was exhausted.

Undisturbed, the woman replied, "My Father knows my need and will undertake for me."

Surprised, the steward answered, "Madam, you forget we are in the midst of the ocean."

She replied, "My Father is able to open a window in heaven if that were necessary."

Hours later the steward returned to her cabin, his arms laden with oranges. "Your God has undertaken; just see here," he exclaimed.

"How did it happen?" inquired the sick woman.

"Did you not hear a siren?" the steward asked. "Well, that was a vessel in distress. The storm had driven it off its course and all of its fresh water was used up. We were able to supply their need of water. That ship had a cargo of oranges, and out of their gratitude the crew gave us a plentiful supply."

God is on the sea and the land. Oranges do not grow on the ocean, but God has "a way on the sea." He can drive a vessel from its course and trade fresh water for oranges for his sick and needy child. If oranges are really needed, God will supply them according to his promise. All of the resources of earth and heaven are at his disposal for the purpose of supplying the needs of his children.

D. *The standard of the supply.* The standard by which God measures his gifts to his children is not the number or the enormity of their requests but "according to his riches in glory." Like himself, God's riches are infinite. He is gloriously rich. His riches are inexhaustible and undiminishable. We cannot imagine how rich he is. It is not just "out of," but "according to his riches in glory" that God supplies our needs. He supplies our needs on a scale that is commensurate with his resources.

Christians can no more exhaust the riches of God's goodness, grace, and glory than a person could empty an ocean with a thimble. The standard by which he supplies our needs is such that at times his blessings seem too great for us to receive, but he assures us that they are not too much for him to give. There is no reason why we should draw lightly upon God.

> *For His grace and power are such*
> *That none can ever ask too much.*

E. *The stream of the supply.* From God's bounty, his riches in glory flow into the souls of his children through Christ Jesus, the one Mediator between God and humans. All of the riches of his grace and all of his infinite blessings upon his people are channeled through his Son and our Savior. If you are a Christian, you may rest assured that God will supply every need of yours through Christ.

Conclusion

Christian, now and henceforth claim this precious promise of God's provision: "My God shall supply all your need according to his riches in glory by Christ Jesus."

SUNDAY EVENING, AUGUST 1

Title: The Gospel of Saving Grace

Text: "By grace are ye saved through faith; and that not of yourselves: it is the gift of God: Not of works, lest any man should boast" **(Eph. 2:8–9)**.

Scripture Reading: Ephesians 2

Introduction

It is almost impossible to give an adequate definition of God's grace. J. H. Jowett said, "Grace is holy love in spontaneous movement, going out in eager quest toward the unholy and the unlovely." W. H. Griffith Thomas said that grace is "God's mercy pitying, it is God's wisdom planning, it is God's power preparing, and it is God's love providing." C. Roy Angel has said that God's grace is "something needed but not deserved." God's grace has been described as the unmerited favor of God toward sinners. God's grace is mercy, love, kindness, and compassion in spontaneous motion toward the undeserving sinner.

Our text suggests five thoughts that each of us should deposit in our heart: The grace of God seeks the sinner, the grace of God saves the sinner, the grace of God sustains the sinner, the grace of God satisfies the saved, and the grace of God is sufficient for all.

I. The grace of God seeks the sinner.

A. *God is not an impassive bystander who waits for the sinner to come to him.* The Bible pictures God as the compassionate father who in one way or another seeks the sinner. God seeks the sinner through his Son (Luke 19:10; John 3:17; 2 Cor. 5:21).

B. *God always takes the initiative (Rev. 3:20).* One of the most beautiful pictures of the compassionate heart of God is found in this great verse that pictures the living Christ standing at the heart's door knocking for entrance. He comes to us with purposes of love. He pleads for entrance into our heart that he might bring the grace, mercy, and peace of God.

II. The grace of God saves the sinner.

A. *Salvation is by the grace of God (Eph. 2:8–9).*

B. *Salvation is not by the works of the law (Gal. 2:16).*

C. *Salvation comes to us through the channel of faith.* The faith that saves is the faith that accepts Christ to be all that he claims to be and trusts him to do all that he has promised to do.

III. The grace of God sustains the sinner.

When God saves a person, he does more than rescue him from drowning: he teaches him how to swim. The apostle Paul gave all of the praise and credit to God for his salvation. He paid tribute to the grace of God.

A. *"But by the grace of God I am what I am" (1 Cor. 15:10).*

B. *"My grace is sufficient for thee: for my strength is made perfect in weakness" (2 Cor. 12:9).* Paul was afflicted with a thorn in the flesh. He prayed for the removal of this handicap on three different occasions. God replied negatively and informed Paul that his grace would be sufficient.

C. *God continues to deal graciously with us.* Paul was convinced that the God of grace who had begun a good work in the conversion experience would persist in his purpose to completely redeem and deliver his children from sin (Phil. 1:6).

IV. The grace of God satisfies the saved.

Throughout the epistles of Paul grace and peace are combined, although grace always preceded the gift of peace. Where there is not grace there can be no peace. The child of God can have peace, joy, and happiness because of God's grace.

A. *By God's grace, we can rejoice in the glad consciousness of forgiven sin.*

B. *Because of God's grace, we can rejoice in the blessed assurance of divine sonship.*

C. *Because of God's grace, we have access to an inexhaustible source of spiritual power for the service that God wants us to render.*

D. *By the grace of God, we can have the strength that is necessary to achieve victory over evil.*

E. *By God's grace, we need have no fear of death.* Our salvation does not depend on our good works. It is based solidly on and within the grace of a loving God.

V. The grace of God is sufficient for all.

The supply of God's grace is inexhaustible. We need have no fear that the bank of heaven will ever go broke.

A. *If your heart is thirsty, then come to him who is the Fountain of Living Water.*

B. *If you are hungry, then come to him who is the Bread of Life.*

C. *If you are weary and tired and depressed, then come to him who alone can give you the rest for which every heart hungers.*

D. *If you are staggering under the burdens and responsibilities of life, then cast your burden on him who cares for you.*

E. *If you are a guilty, unsaved sinner laboring under the burden of guilt, then come to him who alone can forgive (Isa. 1:18).*

F. *If you are helpless under the grip and power of evil, then come to him who alone can set you free (John 8:36).*

G. *If you are old and helpless and afraid of death, then come to him who said, "In my Father's house are many mansions."*

Conclusion

Each of us should look to him who said, "Look unto me, and be ye saved, all the ends of the earth: for I am God, and there is none else" (Isa. 45:22).

WEDNESDAY EVENING, AUGUST 4

Title: The Spirit of Victory

Text: "Nay, in all these things we are more than conquerors through him that loved us" **(Rom. 8:37)**.

Scripture Reading: Romans 8:1–39

Introduction

To step from the seventh chapter of Romans into the eighth is like stepping from a dark, dismal dungeon into the brilliant warmth of the sun. It is stepping from failure into victory, from despair into hope, from doubt into certainty. It is going from the power of Satan into the presence of the Holy Spirit of God.

Paul introduces this transition by saying, "There is therefore now no condemnation." It points to the past and to all that Paul has said in the first seven chapters. It points to the present and to the new life as a result of the indwelling of the Holy Spirit. It points to the future and to the glory that belongs to every believer. All of this is the work of the Holy Spirit. Paul develops these ideas in the verses that follow.

I. The Spirit gives life (8:1–13).

A. *Jesus said, "I am come that ye might have life and have it more abundantly" (John 10:10).* This abundant life comes as a result of being "born of the Spirit" and

251

his living within us (v. 2). Paul describes this as being "in Christ" (v. 1), one of his favorite expressions. (He uses it thirty-three times in his letters.)

B. *All of the barriers to life—the abundant life—are removed.* One can look back to the past with joy and serenity because all has been forgiven. He looks about himself today with peace and happiness, for there is no "sword of Damocles" hanging over him in judgment. He can look forward with anticipation because death and judgment are removed. Paul does not say that there will be no trials or temptations, no failures or falls, but he does say, "There is . . . now no condemnation" (v. 1).

C. *The evidence of this "life" is seen in that the justified ones "walk not after the flesh but after the Spirit" (v. 4, and see vv. 5–13).* There is a contrast here between life in the flesh, or unregenerate man, and life in the Spirit, or redeemed man. One lives to fulfill the lusts of the flesh, the way of the world. The other lives under the direction of the Holy Spirit and by his power. He then bears the "fruit of the Spirit." This is the only life that is satisfying to self and to God, for to live after the flesh "cannot please God" (v. 8).

II. The Spirit gives sonship (8:14–17).

A. *Paul uses the figure of "adoption" to show that we "have received the Spirit of adoption" (v. 15) and have become the "children of God" (v. 16).* Adoption refers to the position and privilege of the believer. Regeneration and the new birth refer to a believer's new nature and union with Christ. There is no conflict in the two.

B. *Several truths come under this figure.*
1. The adopted one is under the complete control and authority of the new father.
2. The adopted one will become heir of the father.
3. In Roman law there were witnesses to authenticate the claim of new sonship. The Holy Spirit bears witness that we are God's children (v. 16).
4. The adopted one has become a part of a family, as have the adopted children of God.

III. The Spirit gives help in suffering (8:18–30).

Suffering is a part of the Christian life. There are trials and tribulations, sorrows and heartaches, abuse and persecution that must be endured, but we are not alone in them. The Holy Spirit helps us.

A. *The Holy Spirit helps us to see that there is no comparison with the glory that shall be ours (vv. 17–25).* Suffering is temporary. Glory is eternal. He gives patience and hope in these experiences.

B. *The Holy Spirit helps us to pray aright in these experiences (vv. 26–27).* He intercedes for us, taking our requests and interpreting them before the throne of God. The poet has said:

> *We ask for strength that we might achieve;*
> *we are made weak that we might obey.*

We ask for strength that we might do greater things;
  we are given infirmity that we might do better things.
We ask for power that we might have praise of men;
  we are given weakness that we might feel our need of God.
We ask for things that we might enjoy life;
  we are given life that we might enjoy all things.

C. *The Holy Spirit helps us to understand that God is at work in all things for good (vv. 28–30).*

1. The Holy Spirit does not say that "all things are good" but rather that God works in all things. In the eighteenth century William Cowper believed it when he wrote:

   God moves in a mysterious way
   His wonders to perform;
   He plants His footsteps in the sea,
   And rides upon the storm.
   Ye fearful saints, fresh courage take;
   The clouds ye so much dread
   Are big with mercy, and shall break
   In blessings on your head.
   Judge not the Lord by feeble sense,
   But trust Him for His grace;
   Behind a frowning providence He hides a smiling face.

2. This promise is not for all people but to those who "love God … and are called according to his purpose" (v. 28).
3. The highest good that can come from these experiences is "to be conformed to the image of his Son" (v. 29).

IV. The Spirit Gives Security (8:31–39).

God is for us! This is certain since he gave us his Son; therefore we can trust him for all else.

A. *There is no condemnation because of the death of Christ (vv. 31–32) and because of the resurrection of Christ (vv. 33–34).*
B. *There can be no separation from God.* The things of this world — the circumstances of life — cannot separate (vv. 35–36). The things of the world to come cannot separate (vv. 37–39). Paul lists ten things that are unable to separate and then adds, "nor anything else." We are secure in the love of God in Christ Jesus our Lord.

Conclusion

Many believers go through life with doubts and fears, with problems and perplexities when God never intended it to be so. He freely gives the Holy Spirit to all who will surrender completely and claim his presence.

SUNDAY MORNING, AUGUST 8

Title: The Promise of God's Peace

Text: "Peace I leave with you, my peace I give unto you: not as the world giveth, give I unto you. Let not your heart be troubled, neither let it be afraid" (**John 14:27**).

Scripture Reading: John 14:15–31

Hymns: "Sweet Peace, the Gift of God's Love," Bilhorn

"It Is Well with My Soul," Spafford

"Is Your All on the Altar?" Hoffman

Offertory Prayer: Heavenly Father, our hearts of gratitude and love prompt us to present to you a portion of that which you have enabled us to earn. We pray that your blessing will multiply the usefulness of our gifts in advancing the cause of Christ. We also beseech you, O God, to pour your holy light into our souls that we may ever be yielded to you by whose power we were created, by whose mercy we were redeemed, and by whose providence we are governed. In Christ's name. Amen.

Introduction

Near the close of Jesus' earthly ministry, when the forces opposed to him were wild with fury and the conflict was approaching its darkest and most desolate hour, he gathered the apostles about him in an upper room in Jerusalem for a period of instruction. He was about to experience the betrayal of trusted friends, the desertion of those who had sworn allegiance unto death, the savage insults of a fickle rabble, the lying calumnies of false accusers, the bitter mockery of brutal men, the agony of sin, and the terrible pain of a horrible death on the cross. Facing the ordeal of the cross, the awful loneliness of the hour when even the Father would forsake him, Christ was concerned deeply and primarily about his bewildered and discouraged followers, whom he sought to calm and reassure by bequeathing a legacy to them.

For three years the apostles had been associated with Christ. Even though his life had been full of strenuous work, they had seen clearly that his heart was ruled by the peace of God. He had never been victimized or rendered impatient, anxious, or rebellious by outward circumstances. On every occasion he had been the Master of the circumstances. Often the apostles had marveled at his calmness and self-control. Now that he was about to say good-bye to those whom he had loved so tenderly and who loved him with a love unlike that which they had felt for any other person, Christ measured the extent of their grief and sought to comfort them by bequeathing his peace unto them.

What is peace? Thayer wrote, "Peace is the tranquil state of a soul assured of its salvation through Christ and so fearing nothing from God, and content with its earthly lot whatever sort it be." Peace is that rest of soul that comes from the establishment of a right relationship with God and living in harmony with his will.

254

What was Christ's peace? It was the peace of spirit that came from his oneness with God, his complete harmony with the will of the Father. Sorrows deeper than we can imagine broke over him; a cup bitterer than we can conceive was given him to drink; yet he was at peace. Harmony with God was the secret of his peace. He declared that the doing of the will of God was his meat and drink. Christ's legacy to his friends was not the peace of exemption or escape but that of serenity and victory.

I. The pursuit of peace.

Whether life is viewed today from the standpoint of the individual, the family, or the community, from its national aspects, or from the larger international relationships, obviously there is a tremendous lack of peace. Sin has separated and alienated people from God. People cannot be in rebellion against God and have peace at the same time. "There is no peace, saith the LORD, unto the wicked" (Isa. 48:22). Of the unsaved Isaiah says, "The way of peace they know not" (59:8).

Solomon tried to find peace in the things of the world. He pursued knowledge and wisdom on the human level in quest of peace and enduring satisfaction. Disappointed in that quest, he threw aside all restraints and plunged into a life of dissipation. Eventually he discovered that he had been pursuing peace and satisfaction in the wrong courses. The result of his pursuit is recorded in Ecclesiastes 2:10–11.

Confusion, frustration, unrest, tension, violence, and distress are widespread in our world. Great unrest prevails in every heart that is not in harmony with the will of God. Longing for peace, people search for it in many places where it cannot be found. Many think that if they only had plenty of money they would have peace, but the possession of money does not guarantee peace. Some of the unhappiest people have enough money to buy almost anything they desire, anything money can procure.

People will crown you one day and then curse you the next. One day the crowd spread their garments before Christ and cried, "Crown him!" A few days later they placed a crown of thorns on his head, scourged him until his back was a mass of bloody flesh, and then nailed him to a cross. Pursuers of peace should be taught that God is the only source of real, satisfying, and abiding peace.

II. The provision of peace.

Not only is peace to be desired, but it is available. Christ procured peace with God for those who would believe on him when he suffered and died on the cross. "But he was wounded for our transgressions, he was bruised for our iniquities: the chastisement of our peace was upon him; and with his stripes we are healed" (Isa. 53:5). The basic fact of the gospel is that Christ Jesus "made peace through the blood of his cross" (Col. 1:20). We must never overlook the fact that sin had to be atoned for because it had broken the fellowship between God and humans. Christ's death on the cross dealt fully with that, satisfying the justice of God and paying the penalty for the breaking of the law. "For he is our peace, who hath made both one, and hath broken down the middle wall of partition between us" (Eph. 2:14).

When Christ was bidding his apostles farewell as they stood around him in speechless sorrow, he did not promise them an easy way, a release from all burdens, or freedom from discouragement or temptation. Rather, he frankly told them that they could expect hardship, persecution, and even death for loyalty to him. The one gift that he offered to bestow on them as a parting legacy was peace. He said, "Peace I leave with you, my peace I give unto you: not as the world giveth, give I unto you." Included in this legacy that he provided was a quiet strength to bear the burdens of life, a new spirit in which to meet and master discouragement, adequate reinforcement to withstand temptation, and available strength to surmount all obstacles.

Uninstructed people sometimes tell an unsaved person to "make your peace with God." Once a dying man was asked if he had made his peace with God, and he replied, "No!" He was then asked, "Then, don't you think that you had better do so at once?" Again he replied, "No!" adding, "My peace was made more than two thousand years ago by Jesus Christ on the cross." Having believed what the Bible said and having accepted the peace that his Savior had provided, he knew that he was ready to meet God.

III. The possession of peace.

Coming into possession of peace is conditioned upon "repentance toward God and faith toward our Lord Jesus Christ." Through a personal trust in and reliance on Christ, who made an atonement for sin, the believer comes into possession of the wonderful peace that Deity has provided. "Being justified by faith, we have peace with God through our Lord Jesus Christ" (Rom. 5:1).

Christ imparts this peace to all who receive him as their personal Savior, and they become its happy possessors. The world can neither give to you nor take from you Christ's peace. No combination of distressing circumstances can ever remove it from you. "And the peace of God, which passeth all understanding, shall keep your hearts and minds through Christ Jesus" (Phil. 4:7).

Conclusion

Many already possess this wonderful peace because they accepted it as a gift from the Lord Jesus. Do you possess and prize this peace? If not, wouldn't you like to have Christ's perfect peace in your heart? If so, you can come into possession of his wonderful peace here and now if you will by simple faith receive Christ as your personal Savior. Salvation and peace are yours for the taking.

SUNDAY EVENING, AUGUST 8

Title: The Devil's Blindfolds

Text: "But if our gospel be hid, it is hid to them that are lost: In whom the god of this world hath blinded the minds of them which believe not, lest the light of the glorious gospel of Christ, who is the image of God, should shine unto them" (**2 Cor. 4:3–4**).

256

Scripture Reading: 2 Corinthians 4

Introduction

The annals of ancient history reveal that often the conquerors put out the eyes of their enemies when they were captured in war. This was the fate of Samson when he fell into the hands of the Philistines (Judg. 16:21). This cruelty was also inflicted on King Zedekiah when he fell into the hands of Nebuchadnezzar (2 Kings 25:7).

The most diabolical work of the demonic forces of Satan is that in which the minds of lost people are blinded lest the light of the glorious gospel of Christ shine into them so that they can be saved. This explains why many go through life without ever responding to the good news of God's love for them.

I. The devil blinds the minds of people to the terrible consequences of sin and to their need of salvation.

From the beginning of human history Satan has sought to create the impression that sin is not serious. In the Garden of Eden the serpent said to the first couple, "You will not surely die" (Gen. 3:4 NIV). Satan continues to use the big lie concerning sin, and people fall for it hook, line, and sinker. It is commonly believed that one can sin and escape suffering. Some people believe that one can sow wild oats in youth and never reap a harvest. Some believe that they can play with sin and still win the game of life. Many believe that they can be social drinkers and escape alcoholism. Some believe they can step from morality into immorality without experiencing hurt.

With all of the cunning of hell, Satan encourages people to treat sin lightly.

II. The devil blinds the minds of people to the joys of being a child of God.

Some people believe that if they become a Christian they can no longer have any fun or happiness. For some reason many associate being a Christian with a drab, monotonous, boring way of life. They think that Christianity is for sissies and that real men do not need God.

A. *The unsaved are blind to the joys of sonship.* They do not recognize how wonderful it is to be a child of God.

B. *The unsaved are blind to the security of the perfect peace that comes to those who have trusted Jesus Christ.* Consequently, they seek security in their own personal achievement or in the pursuit of financial security. They fail to recognize that the only real security and peace that one can have is that which is to be found in the grace of God.

C. *The unsaved are blind to the joys of the Christian.* Their lives often are incomplete and unhappy, and they do not recognize that the only way to find completeness and happiness is to let God occupy the place that belongs to him in the human heart.

D. *The unsaved are blind to the joys of Christian service.* They cannot understand why the children of God regularly go to the house of God for prayer, worship, study, and fellowship. They do not have an appetite for or appreciation of the things of God.

III. The devil blinds the minds of people to the power of the gospel.

The gospel is the power of God unto everyone who believes. This includes those who have felt the grip of a degrading habit for many years and those who feel helpless and are filled with despair as they face the evil within their own lives. Satan keeps them blind to the fact that God wants to come in and deliver them from the power of evil and from the grip of their degrading habits.

IV. The devil blinds the minds of people to the wonder of God's love.

Many people identify God with their guilty conscience; they think of him as a policeman searching for a fugitive. They labor under the impression that God is against them and that his only purpose toward them is to punish them for the evil in their lives. It seems too good to be true that God would love them in such a gracious and lavish manner as sending his Son to die for their sins. However, this is the gospel, the purpose behind the ministry of Jesus Christ. He came to reveal that God does love the sinner and that God's purposes toward the sinner are purposes of love.

V. The devil has blinded the minds of people to the simplicity of the way of salvation.

People have accepted a materialistic and commercialized view of life. They believe that they must purchase or merit every good thing. They refuse to believe that salvation is the gift of God (John 3:16). They can understand how that the wages of sin is death, but somehow they find it difficult to believe that the gift of God is eternal life through Jesus Christ our Lord (Rom. 6:23).

Conclusion

The devil will use many things to blindfold you from seeing your need for the grace of God. It is time for you to cast off these blindfolds and come face-to-face with your need for the forgiveness of sin and the gift of spiritual life through faith in Christ Jesus.

Do you need help in putting off the blindfold that Satan has placed on your mind? If so, then try to evaluate your life in comparison, not with those who have failed to be genuinely Christian, but with the finest Christian that you have ever known. Look at the cross and see how Jesus suffered and died so that he might be your Savior. Contemplate the issues and the values of eternity. Recognize the emptiness and incompleteness of your life without God. Face up to the fact that without God the influence of your life will be such as to lead others away from God. Become aware of the brevity of life and the certainty of death. Recognize the eternal significance of the present. As these thoughts penetrate, they can help you to throw off the blindfolds so that the light of the glorious gospel of Christ can shine in that you also might be saved.

WEDNESDAY EVENING, AUGUST 11

Title: My Heart's Desire

Text: "Brethren, my heart's desire and prayer to God for Israel is, that they might be saved" **(Rom. 10:1)**.

Scripture Reading: Romans 9–11

Introduction

Poet William Ewer has said in "Chosen People":

> *How odd*
> *of God,*
> *to choose*
> *the Jews.*

Paul is saying in Romans 9–11 that it is not odd at all that God chose the Jews, for he had a purpose in their selection. Note how Paul develops his theme:

I. Paul's Concern for Israel (9:1–3; 10:1).

Paul is in the train of Moses, who was willing to be blotted out of God's book for Israel (Ex. 32:32); and of Jeremiah, who wished his "eyes a fountain of tears, that I might weep, day and night" (Jer. 9:1); and of Jesus who wept, "O Jerusalem, Jerusalem, how oft would I have gathered you unto myself," and then went to the cross for them and us. This must be our concern for Israel and for all people everywhere. Anything less is not worthy of the name Christian.

II. God's dealings with Israel (9:4–11:32).

A. *Israel had been chosen and blessed by God (9:4–5).*
  1. They had been blessed with the privileges of adoption. God had adopted the nation as his son (Ex. 4:22).
    a. They had "the glory"—God's *shekinah* (presence) to lead.
    b. "The covenants" to Abraham, Moses, and David were theirs.
    c. "The law" had been given them.
    d. "The services" of the tabernacle, sacrifices, ritual, etc., were all theirs.
    e. "The fathers," such as Abraham, Isaac, and Jacob, had been given.
    f. "The promises" of the Old Testament were all theirs.
    g. Finally, Christ himself had come (9:5), and they had rejected him (John 1:11).
  2. They were to have been a priestly nation and as such were to represent God before all peoples (Ex. 19:5–6). This was the purpose of their election.
B. *Israel had rejected God (9:30–10:21).* Much of this section must be autobiographical as Paul senses his own rejection before his conversion. The reasons for rejection were:
  1. They sought him not by faith but by works (9:30–33).

259

2. They failed to see Christ as the end of the law (10:1–7).
3. They forgot that salvation was for all people (10:13).

C. *God had rejected Israel (9:6–29).*
1. God had rejected them because they had rejected him.
2. Promises were to spiritual, not physical, Israel (9:6–8).
3. God is sovereign—illustrated by Jacob and Esau (9:9–13). God has a right to exercise his sovereignty in mercy (9:15–16). He can also exercise it in wrath and judgment (9:17–18).
4. Paul is not speaking of salvation but of service. Election is for service.

D. *Israel is promised salvation (11:1–32).*
1. Israel's rejection is not complete (11:1–10). There is a remnant of believers, even as in Elijah's day.
2. Israel's rejection has meant that the gospel has been preached to the Gentiles.
3. Israel's rejection is not final. There shall be a great turning to God. When? We do not know. How? Again we do not know. Our responsibility is to preach the gospel and leave the outcome to God.

III. God's invitation to all (10:8–21)

A. *The gospel includes all people (10:13).* "Whosoever shall call" includes Jews and Gentiles alike. It includes all races, all economic classes, all cultural and educational levels.

B. *The gospel must be believed (10:9–10).* This is one of the earliest Christian statements of faith and plans of salvation.
1. One must believe that Jesus Christ is Lord. This includes a belief in his sacrifice but also an acknowledgment of his lordship—his sovereignty over life.
2. One must believe that Christ is raised from the dead—that he is alive.
3. One must confess Christ for salvation.

C. *The gospel must be preached (10:14–21).* The world cannot hear the "good news" unless there are those to preach and those to send. God's concern is that this be done. This was the purpose of our calling—that people might hear and be saved.

Conclusion

Should not all people everywhere be told the Good News? William Carey thought so and left his cobbler's shop in England to tell those in India's darkness. Adoniram Judson thought so and left his comfortable life in America to rot in a Burmese prison that those lost in sin might know the way of salvation. David Brainerd thought so and gave himself without reserve that the Native Americans of our land might know the gospel. John Knox thought so and cried, "Give me Scotland or I die." Many others thought so and died at the hands of the enemies of God that people might be saved. And so must we dedicate our lives to sharing the Good News no matter the cost!

SUNDAY MORNING, AUGUST 15

Title: The Promise of God's Presence

Text: "And he said, My presence shall go with thee, and I will give thee rest" (**Ex. 33:14**).

Scripture Reading: Exodus 33:12–23

Hymns: "Guide Me, O Thou Great Jehovah," Williams

           "Trust and Obey," Sammis

           "Never Alone," Anonymous

Offertory Prayer: Almighty God, the fountain of wisdom and the inspirer of men, we bring our tithes and offerings to you and humbly beseech you to receive and use them for the furtherance of the gospel of Christ. Grant that these gifts may be the pledge of our purpose to let you guide us in the performance of all our duties unto your glory. So inspire and challenge us that the thoughts of our minds, the words of our mouths, and the deeds of our lives may be acceptable and glorifying unto you. We pray in the matchless name of the Lord Jesus Christ. Amen.

Introduction

To the great longing of God's people for the assurance of his presence with them, God has responded graciously and generously with some precious promises in his Word, such as this one that he spoke to Moses at the time of a great crisis.

I. The circumstances of this promise.

Under the direction of Moses, whom God had called to lead his people out of bondage, the Israelites had left Egypt, which to them was a place of toil, oppression, and misery. They were journeying through the wilderness on their way to Canaan, which they believed was a place of freedom, rest, abundance, and happiness. As they journeyed, God manifested his presence with them by preserving, protecting, and providing for them in miraculous ways.

While Moses was on Mount Sinai communing with God and receiving his commandments and instructions, the people quickly turned to idolatry. When Moses descended the mountain and found them worshiping a golden calf, he was disappointed, disillusioned, and disheartened. Knowing that God had declared a breach between himself and his people due to their willful and terrible sins, Moses could not see anything ahead except defeat, disintegration, and disaster. He resolved that this disaster must be averted at all costs.

It is not surprising then that, in response to Moses' longing and praying for the assurance of God's presence with him and his people, God spoke the comforting promise: "My presence shall go with thee, and I will give thee rest."

II. The content of this promise.

That priceless "My" pledges to God's children the side-by-side, step-by-step, and heart-to-heart fellowship of God himself.

A literal translation of the first clause in the text is "My face shall go with thee." How richly expressive! It bespeaks intimacy of fellowship. How wonderful it is to be able to converse with one who is strong enough to supply all of the guidance and strength that a child of God needs! What an inspiration this promise brings to us!

This precious promise is not ambiguous, involved, or hard to understand. Rather, it is unequivocal, positive, and clear.

A. *Companionship.* Darkness cannot prevail in the life in which regular communion with God keeps the soul bathed in the glorious light of the divine smile. Repeatedly God assures his obedient children of his companionship. To Joshua God said, "As I was with Moses, so I will be with thee" (Josh. 1:5). To Jeremiah he said, "Be not afraid of the king of Babylon ... for I am with you to save you, and deliver you from his hand" (Jer. 42:11). To Paul the Lord said: "Do not be afraid ... for I am with you, and no one is going to attack and harm you" (Acts 18:9–10 NIV). Later Paul testified: "The Lord stood with me, and strengthened me" (2 Tim. 4:17).

Years ago a Christian missionary, Felix of Nola, was being pursued by a hostile tribe. His strength was almost gone, and seeing a narrow cave, he crawled into it, prayed for safety, and committed himself to the care of God. Scarcely had he entered when a spider began to weave a web across the entrance to the cave. Before long his pursuers came and were about to search the cavern when one of them noticed the spider's web and said: "It is useless to enter there, for had he gone in he would surely have broken that web." They hastened on in search of him, and the servant of God escaped. God's resources are infinite, and he sustains and protects his children.

Every child of God has the glorious privilege of having and enjoying the companionship of the Lord. Not knowing what burdens we shall be called upon to bear, what troubles we shall meet, or what difficulties we shall encounter, it is stimulating and helpful to receive the promise of God's companionship. To his own God has said: "I will never leave thee, nor forsake thee" (Heb. 13:5). Our paths will change, but the Partner and the presence will never change.

B. *Rest.* "I will give thee rest." How comforting is this promise of rest in toil, meaning an internal and deep repose and liberty of spirit! God's presence gives rest from doubts, fears, anxieties, dangers, and afflictions.

III. The consequences of this promise.

To know that God is with you, as the pressures of life become harder each day, gives you an assurance of at least three things that are invaluable.

A. *Safety.* God's presence with us guarantees our protection and safety. What a cheering word for us as we face the unknown future!

B. *Strength.* God's presence may not always keep us from temptations and trials, but it does guarantee our deliverance and victory over them. It enables us to say with Paul, "I can do all things through Christ which strengtheneth me" (Phil. 4:13).

C. *Satisfaction.* God's presence accompanies those who travel the highway of Christian obedience. It enriches all earthly blessings and makes them worth having. All of us need the presence of God every hour of every day.

Conclusion

Let us practice the presence of God, and then our pathways will be illumined with a divine light that will burn more brightly until we go to heaven. When God is with us we shall have, enjoy, and appreciate safety, strength, and satisfaction.

SUNDAY EVENING, AUGUST 15

Title: God Cares for You

Text: "Likewise, I say unto you, there is joy in the presence of the angels of God over one sinner that repenteth" **(Luke 15:10)**.

Scripture Reading: Luke 15:1 – 24

Introduction

One of the basic fears of people outside of God's kingdom is that God does not care for them. But Jesus' parables teach us that God does care for lost sinners. The parables of lost things symbolize and communicate the compassion and the heart of God for sinners. Jesus' parables of the shepherd who lost a sheep, the woman who lost a coin, and the father who was waiting for a wayward son describe the sorrow of God because of sin. They describe God's search for the sinner and his joy and delight over the recovery of that which was lost.

I. The sorrow of God because of sin.

A. *God's attitude toward sinful humans is like that of a compassionate, loving shepherd who grieves over a lost sheep.*

B. *The sorrow of God is like that of a woman who is greatly concerned because of a lost coin.*

C. *The sorrow of God is like that of a suffering father who is greatly disturbed because of a wayward son who is away from home.*

II. The activity of God with reference to sinful humans.

God is not one who dwells in the distant somewhere. He is not impassive and unmoved by people's distresses.

A. *God is like the shepherd who goes out into the darkness of the night searching for lost sheep.*

B. *God is like the distressed woman who diligently sweeps the floor until she finds her lost coin.*

C. *God is like the waiting father who watches eagerly and who daily feeds the fatted calf in anticipation of the day when the wayward son will return and they can feast.*

III. The joy of man is nothing compared with the joy of God when someone responds to Jesus Christ and makes him the Lord and Savior of life.

Jesus, in these parables of lost things, pictures for us the joy of the Redeemer when a person returns to the home that was forsaken because of sin.

A. *God rejoices like a shepherd who returns home with a lost sheep that has been found.* There is rejoicing even in the presence of angels over one sinner who repents.

B. *God rejoices like the woman rejoices with her friends when she recovers the lost coin.* Again Jesus says, "There is rejoicing in the presence of the angels of God over one sinner who repents" (Luke 15:10 NIV).

C. *The joy of God is like that of a father who receives a wayward son.* God is far more eager to forgive than he is to punish. God has no pleasure in the death of the wicked. His desire is that the wicked turn from evil, destructive ways and return to the home where love and forgiveness are offered and where eternal life is the gift of God (Ezek. 33:11; 2 Peter 3:9).

Conclusion

God does care for you. He demonstrated this care in the gift of his Son Jesus Christ who died on the cross for you. By means of this grace, mercy, and demonstration of love, God would woo you and persuade you to forsake the empty life, the wayward life, the wasteful life, the life that will not satisfy.

WEDNESDAY EVENING, AUGUST 18

Title: The Service Is Beginning!

Text: "I beseech you therefore, brethren, by the mercies of God, that ye present your bodies a living sacrifice, holy acceptable unto God, which is your reasonable service" (**Rom. 12:1**).

Scripture Reading: Romans 12:1–13:14

Introduction

A man who came in late to a worship service asked an usher, "Is the service over?" The usher replied, "The preaching is over. Now the *service* begins."

This is what Paul is saying in our text. In the first eleven chapters, Paul has given a theological foundation. Now he gives a practical application. He is saying, "The service begins now." Notice how Paul develops this idea for the Christian.

I. The plea for consecration (Rom. 12:1–2).

Paul begins by making an appeal for his readers to be consecrated to Christ Jesus: "I plead with you brethren" (v. 1). By faith the believer is "in Christ." His voluntary act of baptism symbolizes this. "Now," says Paul, "let your life show it in consecration." He gives us the:

A. *Motive of consecration: "by the mercies of God."* What are "the mercies of God"? Paul refers to what he has said in Romans 5:8: "But God commendeth his love toward us, in that, while we were yet sinners, Christ died for us."

B. *Manner of consecration: "present your bodies a living sacrifice."*
  1. It is characterized by humility. Man is "not to think more highly of himself than he ought" (v. 3). He must not have an exaggerated sense of his own importance.
  2. It is characterized by usefulness (vv. 4–8). Whatever a person's gift, he will use it in the proper manner. He will assume his place in the church, as a part of the body, doing what God has given him to do.
  3. In the attitude we display to other Christians (12:9–13). One is not to be hypocritical. His love toward others is to be "without dissimulation" (vv. 9–11). He is to be enthusiastic (v. 11); hopeful, patient, and prayerful (v. 12); and generous (v. 13).
  4. In the spirit we show to others outside the church (12:14–21). The Christian will not retaliate (v. 14) and will not show partiality (v. 16). He will live peacefully with all people (vv. 17–21). This is the spirit Christ himself showed.
  5. In the responsibility we assume as citizens (13:1–7). The Christian is a citizen of the state and is responsible to his government as well as to God. Paul, proud of his Roman citizenship, says, "I am a citizen of no mean city." People once condemned Dwight L. Moody for taking such an active part in the affairs of government, to which he replied, "I am a citizen of heaven, but right now I vote in Cook County, Illinois." The idea of sacrifice was familiar to his readers, but Paul asks for a different kind of sacrifice.
    a. They were to offer "themselves," not an animal. It is not enough to offer time, talent, or possessions.
    b. It was to be "living" not dead.
    c. It was to be "holy," without impurities.
    d. Such a sacrifice will be "acceptable," or "well-pleasing," to God.

C. *Manifestation of consecration: "be not conformed."* Paul offers a negative and a positive exhortation.
  1. "Be not conformed." "Don't let the world around you squeeze you into its own mold," as Phillips translates it. Don't let the world set your standards. Don't be like a chameleon, which changes its color to fit in with its environment.
  2. "Be ye transformed." These are the same words used of the transfiguration of Christ. Dr. H. H. Hobbs says that it means to change your outward appearance from what it is to correspond to your inward nature. Only God can do this through the indwelling of the Holy Spirit. "Be transformed" is in the passive voice and indicates someone's doing something to you.

II. The pattern of life (Rom. 12:3–13:7).

Paul reveals that transformed lives will show themselves in the service we render as members of the "body of Christ" (12:3–8).

III. The path of love (Rom. 13:8–10).

Five times in these three verses Paul uses the word "love." It is the word used of God's love for us in John 3:16. We are to manifest this same type of love toward others. This is our debt to all people.

Such love is a fulfillment of the law. Paul cites the commandments dealing with adultery, killing, stealing, and coveting, but all are summed up by saying, "Thou shalt love thy neighbor as thyself."

IV. The promise of his coming (Rom. 13:11–14).

"The day is at hand," says Paul, referring to the second coming of Christ. We, therefore, must:

A. *Be alert: "awake out of sleep" (v. 11).*

B. *Walk decently: this is the meaning of "honestly" (v. 12).* He then gives three opposites of this:

1. No reveling and drunkenness.
2. No chambering and wantonness (impurity covers both).
3. No strife and jealousy.

C. *Make preparation: "put on the Lord Jesus Christ and make no provision for the flesh" (v. 14).* We must burn all bridges behind us and be ready for his coming.

Conclusion

Peter says, referring to the Second Coming: "Seeing that all these things shall be dissolved, what manner of persons ought ye to be in all holy living and godliness, looking for and hasting unto the coming of the day of God" (2 Peter 3:11–12). This must be our attitude as "living sacrifices."

SUNDAY MORNING, AUGUST 22

Title: The Promise of God's Protection

Text: "Fear thou not; for I am with thee: be not dismayed; for I am thy God: I will strengthen thee; yea, I will help thee; yea, I will uphold thee with the right hand of my righteousness" **(Isa. 41:10).**

Scripture Reading: Isaiah 41:10–20

Hymns: "The Haven of Rest," Gilmour

"O God, Our Help in Ages Past," Watts

"Jesus, Lover of My Soul," Wesley

Offertory Prayer: Holy Father, who has revealed yourself to us, redeemed us from our sins, and reconciled us unto yourself, we rejoice in your loving-kindness and pray that you will increase our faith in you, our love for you, and our devotion to you. We thank you that through the presentation of our gifts and your blessing upon them, we can participate in proclaiming the gospel of Christ, in bringing others into your family, and in rendering ministries of mercy to those who are in need. Bless these our gifts in Jesus' name. Amen.

Introduction

It is doubtful that there has ever been a generation as frightened as ours about the unfathomable present and the unknown future. Many of our fears, which prevent our happiness and lower our efficiency, can be traced to self-interest. There has never been a time when God's children needed the encouragement, support, and comfort of the words "Fear thou not," more than we need them today. If we will only appropriate these challenging words, we will be sheltered beneath God's wings, protected by his omnipotence, and provided for by his immeasurable and unfailing love.

Note the fivefold promise of God's protection in the text:

I. "I am with thee."

These encouraging words derive their value from the one who spoke them. He has never made a promise that has not been or will not be fulfilled.

God's presence cheers and inspires us with fearlessness. Our circumstances and surroundings may seem dark and discouraging, but we shall be safe when God is with us. He is fully able to cope with any situation, regardless of how serious it may be. He is equal to every emergency. Most of life's perplexing problems will vanish when God is with us. The assurance of his presence with us applies to our struggles, afflictions, and trials.

It is good to know that God is with his children in the midst of their great enterprises, unusual responsibilities, and strenuous labors, imparting to them a joy and a peace that surpass all understanding. It is impossible to explain fully the exhilaration that the children of God have in the consciousness of the nearness of him who is sufficient for all emergencies. His presence does not mean that we shall never have any trials, but it dispels our fears. It increases our faith to hear him say, "I am with thee." This assurance of God's presence is not only a comfort, but it is a challenge also. It not only begets confidence, but it calls us also to obedience to him.

II. "I am thy God."

"Be not dismayed; for I am thy God." "Be not dismayed" may be translated "Look not around you," meaning, "Do not focus your eyes upon your environment." If you look around you today, you will see trouble on every hand and be made to wonder what will happen to you tomorrow.

"I am thy God." This fact implies the infinitude of his love and the unspeakableness of his mercy. On our part, "I am thy God," implies reverence, submission, and obedience. On God's part it implies guardianship and blessing. God takes special care of his own. They are always safe when he is with them. In him are all the resources that they shall ever need. He will never fail those who trust, worship, and serve him.

III. "I will strengthen thee."

All who have truly believed on Christ certainly have a right to claim this glorious promise. It is encouraging to know that we shall never be in a position where God, who is adequate for all circumstances and emergencies, cannot strengthen us. He will always be with his own in sustaining power. He will infuse strength into our fearful hearts and invigorate our spirits. When we are confronted with some gigantic task or with some duty that seems to appall us, it is strengthening to know that there is not anything that is too difficult for God. No matter how seemingly impossible the task, nor how heavy the load, his resources will be sufficient. In our weakness we need the strength that he promises and he alone can impart.

IV. "I will help thee."

God's promise "I will help thee" suggests that we have something to do and that God will help us to do it. It speaks of cooperation in a glorious task. This promise means "I will render you personal assistance." It implies that as we go down life's pathway we will have burdens to bear that will be too heavy for us. We will need help from God when we are taxed beyond our ability—physically, mentally, and spiritually. God is both willing and able to give us all of the help that we need when and as the needs arise. He may not help us just at the time and in the manner that we desire, because our way may not be best. His way of helping us will be best.

V. "I will uphold thee with the right hand of my righteousness."

The grasp of the hand signifies present and close friendship. The right hand is an emblem of power, and in this verse it signifies omnipotent power. With God there is not any sinister or left-hand work; it is all right-hand work. His faithful and victorious right hand can be relied upon to support those who have placed their trust in him. God will never fail to uphold his own, and his strength will be sufficient for all of their needs. The assurance of his presence and power is the source of a courage that danger cannot dispel, suffering cannot exhaust, and death cannot destroy.

Conclusion

One wonders if there is any encouragement to surpass that which is contained in these five glorious promises of God to his children who appropriate and apply them.

SUNDAY EVENING, AUGUST 22

Title: What Must I Do to Be Saved?

Text: "Sirs, what must I do to be saved? And they said, Believe on the Lord Jesus Christ, and thou shalt be saved, and thy house" (**Acts 16:30–31**).

Scripture Reading: Acts 16:25–34

Introduction

The question the jailer put to Paul and Silas is the greatest question in all of the world. The Bible was written to answer this question. God gave his Son Jesus Christ that there might be an answer to this question. Christ Jesus, the sinless, spotless Son of God came and died on the cross and conquered death and the grave that there might be an answer to this question. The church is in the world today to publish the answer to this question.

I. The question implies that there is a need for salvation.

A. *People need to be saved from the penalty of sin, which is death.* It is the testimony of Scripture that "all have sinned and come short of the glory of God" (Rom. 3:23).

B. *People need to be saved from the pollution of sin.*

C. *People need to be saved from the power of sin.*

D. *People need to be saved from the presence of sin.*

This deliverance from the presence of sin will take place when the Lord returns to effect the resurrection (1 Cor. 15:51–57). Our mortality will put on immortality. We will lay aside the corruptible to receive that which is incorruptible. We shall be like him, for we shall see him as he is (1 John 3:2). Our loving Lord who has conquered death will give us new bodies fashioned like unto his glorious body. We shall be delivered from the very presence of sin (Phil. 3:20–21).

II. This question implies that there is an answer, a way, a plan, a means whereby one can be saved.

There are many different suggested answers to the question, "What must I do to be saved?" Some people say, "Just be sincere." Others say, "Just do the best that you can." Still others say, "Everything will turn out for the good in the end." But the Bible tells us that the only way that we can be saved is by believing on the Lord Jesus Christ.

Notice the nature of the Lord in whom we are to trust. He is Jesus Christ. By the name Jesus, Paul was emphasizing his redemptive office. He came that he might be our Savior from sin (cf. Isa. 53:5–6; Mark 10:45; 1 Cor. 15:4).

By speaking of him as Lord, Paul was emphasizing his kingly office. He was Lord in every area of life. He was Lord over the angels, the demons, disease, nature, and death. He has been exalted to a position of lordship over the universe. In trusting him as Savior we are to make him the Lord of our own life.

III. Let us consider the nature of the salvation that comes to those who trust Christ.

What does it mean to be saved? There are a number of different answers to that question because it means many different things.

A. *Salvation involves the forgiveness of the sin that separates a man from God (Acts 10:43).* When we receive Christ as Lord and Savior, our sins are forgiven, and we are cleansed by the blood of the Lamb of God (1 John 1:7).

B. *Salvation through Jesus Christ brings us into a parent-child relationship with God (cf. John 1:12; Gal. 3:26; 1 John 3:1).*

C. *Salvation through Jesus Christ bestows the gift of eternal life upon the believer (cf. John 3:16, 36; 5:24).*

D. *Salvation through Jesus Christ makes possible the indwelling of the Holy Spirit in the heart of the believer (Titus 3:5).* The Holy Spirit dwells in the heart to produce within the believer the character of Jesus Christ (Gal. 5:22–25).

Conclusion

Every person stands in need of the great salvation that can come only through Jesus Christ. People can learn of the power of God and of the existence of God by studying nature, but the only way by which people can come to know him personally is through Jesus Christ, our Redeemer and Savior.

WEDNESDAY EVENING, AUGUST 25

Title: You're on *Candid Camera*

Text: "Let us not therefore judge one another any more: but judge this rather, that no man put a stumbling block or an occasion to fall in his brother's way" (**Rom. 14:13**).

Scripture Reading: Romans 14:1–15:13

Introduction

There used to be a television program called *Candid Camera.* People were always being filmed when they least expected it. The program ended by saying, "Smile. You're on *Candid Camera.*" Actually, we are always "on camera," for people observe our example every minute of every day. Paul, in our text, says our influence and example can save or destroy others. Notice how he develops this concept.

I. The Christian is an example (Rom. 14:1–23).

There was a division in the church at Rome over the observance of special days and the eating of meats and herbs. Paul made no attempt to settle their specific problems by declaring which side was right or wrong. He was more concerned that the fellowship be maintained in a spirit of brotherly love. To do this each one had to watch his or her actions, for they were being watched.

A. *Don't reject your brother (14:1).* He is your brother and must be treated as such. In 15:7 Paul says, "Receive ye one another, even as Christ also received us." The opposite of this is seen in the Pharisee's attitude toward the publican in the temple (Luke 18:9–14) and in the elder brother's rejection of the prodigal son (Luke 15:28–30).

B. *Don't judge your brother (14:1–9).* There were some who condemned those whose practice was not like their own. This you cannot do, says Paul, because no man can criticize another man's slave (v. 4). The owner alone has this right. Paul had opened his letter by calling himself a slave. Now he reminds them that they are also slaves.

Jesus said that we ought not to judge in a manner in which we would not want to be judged (Matt. 7:1–2). Also no man is perfect enough, himself, to judge another (Matt. 7:3–5).

C. *Don't offend your brother (14:13–23).* The Christian must consider how his action or attitude will affect his brother. Men are not accountable to one another but are responsible for one another (v. 12).

A blind man was seen walking down the street at night carrying a lantern. "Why do you carry the lantern if you cannot see?" asked a friend. The answer was classic: "Because I don't want anyone to stumble over me."

In one situation, Jesus said, "It were better for him that a millstone were hanged about his neck, and he cast into the sea, than that he should offend one of these little ones" (Luke 17:2).

II. The Christian is to follow the example of Christ (Rom. 15:1–13).

Paul says that when we consider our relationship to others as brothers, we must follow Christ's example. Peter speaks of Christ's "leaving us an example, that ye should follow his steps" (1 Peter 2:21). He has given us an:

A. *Example of love: "bear the infirmities of the weak" (v. 1).* To bear the burdens of others is to love them. Christ has done this for us. Isaiah 53:4 says, "He hath borne our griefs and carried our sorrows." Peter says that he "bare our sins in his own body on the tree" (1 Peter 2:24). When Paul speaks of bearing the weakness of others, he uses the same word used of Christ's bearing his cross (literally in John 19:17 and figuratively in Luke 14:27). Since Christ has loved and served others rather than self, we must follow his example.

B. *Example of unselfishness: "not to please ourselves" (v. 1).* "For Christ pleased not himself" (v. 3). Phillips translates this: "not to go our own sweet way." Jesus said, "I came ... not to do my own will but the will of him that sent me" (John 6:38). Had Christ sought to please self, the suffering and agony of the cross would not have been his; he could have avoided it. The wilderness temptations were an offer to do so, but he thought only of others.

C. *Example of patience:* "*The God of patience and consolation grant you to be likeminded one toward another according to Jesus Christ*" *(v. 5).* How patient Christ was when reviled and persecuted. How patient he was with weak and willful Simon Peter. How patient we must be with our brothers and sisters.

III. The Christian's own example shall be judged (Rom. 14:10–12).

A. *This judgment is certain.* "As I live saith the Lord." God assures its certainty. Hebrews 9:27 and Acts 17:31 also emphasize this.

B. *This judgment is universal.* "Every knee shall bow to me, and every tongue shall confess to God."

C. *This judgment is personal.* "Everyone shall give an account of himself." We shall not account for our brother whom we judged but for ourselves—our example and influence.

Conclusion

A stone marker for a young girl buried in a cemetery bears this inscription: "A child of whom her playmates said, 'It was easier to be good when she was with us.'" We must be this type of Christian by example.

SUNDAY MORNING, AUGUST 29

Title: The Promise of God's Power

Text: "Thy shoes shall be iron and brass; and as thy days, so shall thy strength be" **(Deut. 33:25).**

Scripture Reading: Deuteronomy 33:24–29

Hymns: "Grace Greater Than Our Sin," Johnston

"A Mighty Fortress Is Our God," Luther

"How Firm a Foundation," Unknown

Offertory Prayer: Ever adored God, our Father, we express to you our grateful and joyous praise for your multitudinous blessings. Accept our offerings as one expression of our obedience to the commandment of Christ and as evidence of our longing for others to know him as their Savior. Grant that through our worship here we may receive inspiration to holy living, heroic endeavor, and high achievement. In Christ's name. Amen.

Introduction

Life's problems and burdens should cause God's children to search out, appropriate, and plead the precious promises from God's Word, such as the one in this text. God's promises are applicable to the conditions and circumstances in our lives.

I. A pilgrimage.

After a long and useful life, Moses was approaching the end of his earthly pilgrimage. From experience he had learned what God's children may expect from selfish people around them and from the God of grace above them. Before surrendering his leadership of God's people to his successor, Moses assembled the people and commended them to God and to the work of his grace.

To Asher and his tribe, whose inheritance was a strip of rugged hill country extending from Carmel to Sidon and over which traveling was very difficult, was given this special promise: "Thy shoes shall be iron and brass; and as thy days, so shall thy strength be." One making a pilgrimage through the region that Asher received had to tread on sharp-edged stones. Unless his footwear was of an appropriate quality, his feet were left torn, bleeding, and sore. Consequently, God, through Moses, promised Asher shoes of iron and brass to wear while walking on the sharp-edged stones. God also assured Asher that, while his life would be beset by many difficulties and hardships, he would be supported and sustained by an unseen power.

This precious promise is timeless in its application to the children of God. When we are called upon to travel over rough places on the journey of life, as we frequently will be, we may rest assured that we will receive from him what is appropriate and adequate for our needs in our particular circumstances.

On life's pilgrimage all of us will encounter rough places, for all of life has its difficult stretches. Instead of having flowers strewn in our pathways or being led through sunny meadows, those who make this pilgrimage will have to face the rugged roads of struggle, the steep hills of hardship, and the lonely paths of toil and sacrifice. We should not be surprised or shocked when disappointments loom before us and cut across our dearest hopes. We have not been promised an escape from the roughness and steepness of life's road.

In case you wonder why the stones have not been gathered up, why the obstacles have not been removed, and why the roads of life have not been paved for you, it is because God has left the conditions as they are for the development of your Christian character and for the increase of your usefulness.

There is much hill climbing to do in the Christian life. Some people have hills to climb because they have descended them. Those who have spent considerable time going downhill need not be surprised when they have to take a turn at climbing. When we persist in running down a hill, we should expect to be called upon to climb it again. Many of the difficulties that we encounter are of our own making. When we find ourselves in a storm, as Jonah found himself, it is frequently because we have tried to run away from the performance of some duty.

II. A pledge.

When we are called upon to travel rough roads on life's pilgrimage, as is often the case, it is encouraging to know that God will provide for us shoes of "iron and brass" and make us superior to our circumstances. Here is his pledge: "Thy shoes shall be iron and brass; and as thy days, so shall thy strength be." God also said,

273

"When thou passest through the waters, I will be with thee; and through the rivers, they shall not overflow thee" (Isa. 43:2).

Many things that take place today cause us to be disquieted, dismayed, and discouraged, but God's Word reminds us that he is still on his throne and will fashion footwear suitable to the needs of our times. God will not continue to give us life without giving us the strength we need to live it aright.

The famous nineteenth-century British preacher Henry Moorehouse had a daughter who had a physical disability. One day he came home with a package, and when he was about to carry it upstairs, she said: "Let me carry the parcel, Daddy." He said, "But how can you, my little daughter who cannot even walk, carry the parcel?" "Daddy, I will carry the parcel, and you will carry me." God does something like that for us when we need help. We carry the load but find ourselves being carried.

A strange physical condition caused Paul great misery. He asked God to remove this disability so that he might serve him better. God did not grant Paul's request, but he said to him, "My grace is sufficient for thee: for my strength is made perfect in weakness" (2 Cor. 12:9). God does not always remove our burdens and disabilities, but if not, he gives us grace and strength to carry them. In our text is his pledge to give us shoes that will be appropriate for the roads that we will travel. Do not hesitate or be afraid to wear the shoes he offers you. Wearing them will enable you to turn a minus into a plus.

What the future holds in store for you, what your days are to be, you cannot know. But there is one thing about the future that you can know: "As thy days, so shall thy strength be." We are promised strength for the day when it comes and for what it brings, but we are not promised strength for the day before it comes or for a day that may never come.

Riding the circuit in Illinois once, when heavy rains had flooded the rivers, some of the lawyers who accompanied Lincoln were in great anxiety about how they could ford the Fox River. In reply to their appeal, Lincoln said, "I have often forded the Fox River at all times of the year and in all kinds of weather, but I never ford the Fox River until I come to it." Do not try to ford your rivers until you reach them, but have faith to believe that when you reach them God will help you to cross them. "As thy days, so shall thy strength be."

God's pledge covers all of the days that he gives to us. His Spirit dwelling in us will make us equal to every demand that the days make on us. Regardless of how many days we may have, God has promised us sufficient strength for them. He did not say "as thy life is" or "as thy years are" or "as thy weeks," but "as thy days, so shall thy strength be."

Conclusion

Let us learn the art of living a day at a time, depending on God for the strength we shall need. Let us heed the timely advice of Augustine: "Trust the past to the mercy of God, the present to His love, and the future to His providence." God does not give us enough grace and strength at any point in life to carry us all

274

the way through, because we would not have the capacity for them. But God has promised, "As thy days, so shall thy strength be." The prayer of an unknown saint is appropriate for each of us.

> *Lord, for tomorrow and its needs, I do not pray;*
> *Keep me, my God, from stain of sin, just for today.*
> *Let me both diligently work, and duly pray;*
> *Let me be kind in word and deed, just for today.*
> *Let me be slow to do my will, prompt to obey;*
> *Oh, keep me in Thy loving care, just for today.*
> *Let me no wrong or idle word, unthinking say;*
> *Set Thou a seal upon my lips, just for today.*
> *Let me in season, Lord, be grave, in season, gay;*
> *Let me be faithful to Thy grace, just for today.*
> *So, for tomorrow and its needs I do not pray;*
> *But keep me, guide me, love me, Lord, just for today.*

SUNDAY EVENING, AUGUST 29

Title: The Tragedy of Neglect

Text: "How shall we escape, if we neglect so great salvation?" (**Heb. 2:3**).

Scripture Reading: Hebrews 2:1–9

Introduction

Have you ever known a person who deliberately intended to come down to the hour of death without having made preparation for his or her trip into eternity? Most people believe in the existence of God, and most also believe that a human being does not cease to be when death comes. Almost without exception people believe that some preparation must be made for meeting God. However, for some reason people neglect to make that preparation. Why is this?

Perhaps an understanding of some of the reasons that contribute toward this policy of postponement can help the individual Christian bear a more winsome testimony and at the same time help the individual who has not yet made a decision to trust Christ to recognize the urgency for doing so.

I. Some neglect the great salvation because they are not acutely aware of their lost condition.

They are aware that they have not made a public profession of faith in Jesus Christ. They are aware that they have never followed him in baptism and become a member of his church. However, the absence of these is not enough to convince some people of their need for salvation.

Many people are unaware that to have the life of God in their heart and to be a member of the family of God they must experience the birth of spiritual life that

Jesus talked about in his conversation with Nicodemus, "Jesus answered and said unto him, Verily, verily, I say unto thee, Except a man be born again, he cannot see the kingdom of God" (John 3:3).

II. Some neglect the great salvation because they are unaware of how great God's love is for them.

From the beginning of time, Satan has been seeking to misrepresent the nature and the character of God. He did so in the Garden of Eden. The serpent misrepresented the nature of the Creator and implied that he was seeking to restrict and to hinder and deprive the first couple of that which they were entitled to have. When they questioned the goodness of God, they fell into sin. The same continues to be true in the present when people misunderstand the nature and motives of God.

III. Some neglect the great salvation because of the grip of sin upon their life and their fear of failure to measure up as a Christian.

All of us have known those who were slave to an evil habit. No one was more aware of the need for a change in their lives than they. Some of these have sought by every means at their command to break the enslaving grip of evil upon their lives, yet they have experienced failure after failure. They are inclined to give up in despair and to believe that there is no hope for them. To these people we need to communicate the good news that Jesus Christ is more than a soul Savior. He will do more than just throw a life preserver to a drowning man. He will teach him how to swim.

When Jesus Christ is permitted to come into a person's heart, the power of God becomes available to enable that person to overcome the degrading effects of sin. With the help of God, a person can conquer the sin that has enslaved him or her.

IV. Some neglect the great salvation because of the failures of some who profess to be Christian.

There have always been those in the church who fail to live up to the high ethical teachings and the ideals set before us by Jesus. But the person who has never trusted Christ needs to face up to the fact that the spiritual birth does not produce a full-grown Christian; it produces only an infant Christian. Only time, growth, and struggles can help that new child of God become all that he should be as a child of God. There are many times when even the sincerest person will stumble in the struggle to become what God would have him or her to be.

Instead of looking at the failures of others, each individual needs to face up to his or her own responsibility to make preparation for life, for death, and for eternity. What another person has done or has failed to do will never provide us with a legitimate excuse for doing the wrong thing.

V. Some neglect the great salvation because of erroneous ideas about the nature of sin.

Many believe that once a person becomes a Christian there is no more joy to be found in living, that one must give up that which has brought joy, happiness, and excitement to life.

Sin is that which is destructive to human personality and the highest values of life. Sin is that which brings harm into the lives of others. The only thing that a person must give up to become a follower of Jesus Christ is that which is going to ruin him or someone else if he does not give it up.

Conclusion

There are undoubtedly other excuses that people use for neglecting the great salvation.

God's salvation is great because of the love that thought it, because of the love that brought it, and because of the love that wrought it upon the cross. It is great because of what it can save you from and because of what it can save you to.

SEPTEMBER

■ **Sunday Mornings**

The suggested theme is "The Ministry and Message of the Church in the Modern World."

■ **Sunday Evenings**

"The Bible Speaks to Our Condition" should be a theme that is close to the pastor's heart and mind at all times. This series could continue indefinitely.

■ **Wednesday Evenings**

"God Speaks through the Prophets" is the suggested theme for Wednesday evenings this month.

WEDNESDAY EVENING, SEPTEMBER 1

Title: Amos, the Prophet of Righteousness

Text: "The words of Amos, who was among the herdmen of Tekoa, which he saw concerning Israel in the days of Uzziah king of Judah, and in the days of Jeroboam the son of Joash king of Israel, two years before the earthquake" (**Amos 1:1**).

Introduction

A study of the prophet Amos can be both a disturbing and profitable experience. While there is a vast difference between the world of his day and our world, some things remain the same. God has not changed. The laws of God have not been altered. The law of gravity has not changed, nor has the law of righteousness. The laws of cause and effect are still linked together. The penalties of sin and the rewards of righteousness go on and on from generation to generation. While God remains the same, so also does human nature. The human heart is now what it has always been. No new instinct has been added to our human nature. No new basic appetite has been generated. No new passion has been introduced. The modern psychologist deals with the same instincts, emotions, appetites, and anxieties with which Amos dealt. Human needs remain the same as they were then.

I. Amos's home was in Tekoa.

Tekoa was a rather barren place twelve miles south of Jerusalem. Because of his proximity to Jerusalem, it was possible for Amos to be aware of what was going on in his nation.

278

II. Amos was a shepherd and a dresser of sycamore trees, a simple and common occupation of his day (Amos 7:14).

III. Amos's times.

Most scholars believe that Amos's ministry falls within the decade of 760 to 750 BC. This was during the reign of Jeroboam II in Israel. His regime is described briefly in 2 Kings 23–29. He was the greatest king that northern Israel had, yet he was profane and idolatrous. No king of northern Israel received the approval of the Scriptures.

IV. Social conditions.

A. *There was no middle class in the land.*

B. *There was a class of the very rich.*

C. *There was a class of the very poor.*

V. Religious conditions.

A. *There was much worship of the Baals and of the nature gods of the Canaanites.* Israel had gone into idolatry.

B. *The worship of Jehovah God was corrupted and compromised.* The false prophets of Baal were serving as the professional prophets of the king.

VI. Amos's character.

A. *He was simple in his wants and wishes.*

B. *He was fearless before those in positions of authority.*

C. *He was a man of great spiritual discernment.*

D. *He had a strong sense of divine mission.*

E. *He was a great literary artist even though he was a shepherd.*

VII. Amos's call.

Amos's ministry was in northern Israel. We cannot know how long it lasted. Some people think that it was only a brief preaching mission and that it stirred up so much opposition that he was martyred.

Amos describes his call to the prophetic ministry in Amos 7:14–15. He emphatically declared, "I was no prophet, neither was I a prophet's son." By this he was repudiating any relationship to the professional prophets of northern Israel who were in reality false prophets. He declared that he was God's spokesman because of a divine constraint that he had found to be irresistible.

VIII. A summary of his message.

A. *Fundamentally, Amos's message was a redefinition of the nature and character of God.*

B. *Amos was a crusader and a reformer.*

C. *Amos's message was one of judgment and doom.*

D. *Amos's message contained only a faint ray of hope.*

Conclusion

This man of God who lived in the past has a message for the present if we will but take time to listen to what God says to us.

SUNDAY MORNING, SEPTEMBER 5

Title: The Church Jesus Made

Text: "Then they that gladly received his word were baptized: and the same day there were added unto them about three thousand souls" **(Acts 2:41)**.

Scripture Reading: Acts 2:37–47

Hymns: "O Worship the King," Grant

"Lead on O King Eternal," Shurtleff

"I Love Thy Kingdom, Lord," Dwight

Offertory Prayer: Our Father, who has given to us the responsibility for bearing divine treasures in these frail vessels of earth, we thank you for the providence that has brought us to this time in your holy purposes. Out of our personal experiences and from your inspired Word we hear again the call to be bearers of your truth to the uttermost parts of the earth. We ask your blessing on the resources and endowments you have provided for this task. May your richest blessings be on those who serve you across our hungry world. Give our missionaries the realization of your care and your presence. Lord, help us to understand that material blessings can never be disassociated from the dedication of our lives to your will. Receive now these tithes and offerings we present to you. By these we wish to honor your name and bless the lives of others around the world. In Jesus' name. Amen.

Introduction

Jesus established his church on the earth and said, "The gates of hell shall not prevail against it" (Matt. 16:18). The questions for our time are these: "What kind of church did Jesus establish?" "What are the ingredients?" "What are the characteristics?"

The pattern for the church made by Jesus is clearly cut for us in the book of Acts. When J. B. Phillips translated the book of Acts, he called it "The Young Church in Action." This is not all that the early church was, but it was that. Here were a people who were blessed by God and in the power of his Spirit marched into the world and made a real difference.

I. The book of Acts assumes redeemed people.

These people of the upper room were not just any people; they were peculiar people. They had no name as yet. Buildings were not a consideration. Methods and techniques were not a major item in their program. They were the "people of

280

God." They had heard Jesus say, "Flesh and blood hath not revealed it unto thee" (Matt. 16:17). These were people touched by the grace of a living God. They were not just another gathering of people interested in changing their world. They were people of a common experience: Christ had come into their hearts!

II. These were a Spirit-filled people.

Peter set the bystanders straight as to what it was that was motivating the believers to be persistent in their purposes. He said, "These are not drunk ..." (Acts 2:15). They were filled with the Spirit. The great movements of the early church were initiated, motivated, implemented, and consummated by the leadership of the Holy Spirit of the Lord. The genius of the Spirit took the dedication, the enthusiasm, the resources, and the small number of souls and led them through seemingly impossible tasks.

III. They were a praying people.

The young church found itself face-to-face with an impossible task. Their world was too big and their human resources too small, but they found a "plus" that no church can afford to take lightly: power in prayer.

God's church faces many seeming impossibilities in our day. Our world is filled with lives adrift. Insecurity is a characteristic of our time. The world has become a destructive force that human resources have serious difficulties managing. But God's church can find power anew in claiming the "plus" of prayer.

IV. They were a witnessing people.

Witnessing is a natural expression of redemption. These young Christians had something to say to their world, and they said it by their lips and by their lives. The young church had "good news" for their world, and they couldn't contain it. This account of the church Jesus made helps us to understand the basic witness of God's church in the world. They preached, but they did it in simplicity. They taught, but they taught with practical and meaningful methods.

The witness of the church was done in their homes, in the marketplace, in the synagogue, and on the busy highways. No single day of the week was reserved for this vital expression of their lives. The church of today must witness as well.

V. They were people involved in breaking barriers.

The young church faced numerous barriers. There were barriers between male and female. Women had no real position as individuals then. There were political barriers. The Roman government had power over the lives of people. There was an economic barrier. The wealthy kept the poor in poverty. And there was a racial barrier. The Jews and Gentiles were on opposite sides of a very difficult fence.

Philip moved across barriers in his witness to the man from Ethiopia. The Spirit of the Lord led Peter to Cornelius at Caesarea. The young church moved on to other cultures and strange shores. Paul underscores this ingredient of the young church in his letter to the Ephesians (Eph. 3:18–19). They did not do this simply or without human tension. But the church that Jesus made is one that must see every life as one loved by our Lord and Savior Jesus, and we must learn how to love that other life as he has loved us.

VI. They were a worshiping people.

This ingredient in the church made by Jesus is the adhesive force. We, as people of God, need first to have "face-to-face" experiences with our Lord before we make any attempt to witness face-to-face with the world.

The first-century Christians were people who learned how important it was to look up to God before they went out to the world. The young church learned the art of personal and private worship. They knew, too, the necessity of corporate worship. They worshiped in their homes, on riverbanks, in the hold of a prison ship, in prison cells, in synagogues, and in busy marketplaces. Worship may be helped by the environment of a life, but it is not dependent on certain kinds of surroundings for its effectiveness. Method and means are not the primary concern. The church that is meaningful to the world must first be meaningful in personal experiences with her Lord.

Conclusion

The ingredients that make up Jesus' church are personal ones; each of us must respond to his call to minister to others. He expects us to be alert to and to meet the needs of those around us who are bound by sin. We are to be filled with his Spirit of power and are to testify boldly of his love, break barriers that keep people from his love, and pray effectively. Begin this review of personal effectiveness with the upward look to your Lord. Your seriousness in worship will help to make this necessary evaluation.

SUNDAY EVENING, SEPTEMBER 5

Title: The Bible Speaks about Itself

Text: "All scripture is given by inspiration of God, and is profitable for doctrine, for reproof, for correction, for instruction in righteousness: That the man of God may be perfect, thoroughly furnished unto all good works" (**2 Tim. 3:16–17**).

Introduction

Innumerable volumes of books have been written about the Bible. The great majority of these have sought to explain its nature and its purpose. An entire volume could be filled with growing testimony concerning the value of the Word of God both to the individual and to the nation.

A number of books have been written that are critical of the Bible. Their intention is to destroy the Bible by undermining its authenticity and denying its authority.

Some claim too little for the Bible, while others may claim too much. It can be most profitable for us to listen to what the Bible has to say concerning itself.

I. The Bible speaks concerning the source of the Scriptures (2 Tim. 3:16).

A. *The apostle Paul speaks of the Scriptures as being "God-breathed."* He declares that Holy Scripture owes its existence to the direct creative activity of God himself. Although man wrote it, it is God who brought it into being. Its content and character have been divinely determined. There is an Old Testament background that throws light on the graphic metaphor that Paul used in declaring God to be the source of the Scriptures. The phrase "inspired of God" literally means "God-breathed." The psalmist spoke of the heavens as coming into existence because of this creative activity of God. "By the word of the LORD were the heavens made; and all the host of them by the breath of his mouth" (Ps. 33:6). The writer of the book of Genesis declares that man became a living being by virtue of this breath of God. "And the LORD God formed man of the dust of the ground, and breathed into his nostrils the breath of life; and man became a living soul" (Gen. 2:7). Again, in Job 33:4 we read, "The spirit of God hath made me, and the breath of the Almighty hath given me life." "The breath of God" is the term used to describe God as the first and moving cause who created the heavens. In the same way in which God is the Creator of our world and Creator of life, Paul declares him to be the source of the Holy Scriptures.

B. *The Holy Scriptures are the product of the activity of the Holy Spirit of God himself (2 Peter 1:20–21).*

II. The Bible speaks concerning the unique nature of the Scriptures.

The Bible is different from all other books in that it has a divine origin and a divine purpose. It contains the life and energy of God.

In a day when words are considered lightly and of very little significance, it might be helpful for us to know that the ancient Hebrews looked upon words as having special significance. Words were thought of as having an independent existence once they were uttered. They were considered almost as living things either for good or bad. This is illustrated in the book of Isaiah. God speaks through the prophet, "So shall my word be that goeth forth out of my mouth: it shall not return unto me void, but it shall accomplish that which I please, and it shall prosper in the thing whereto I sent it" (Isa. 55:11).

The writer of the book of Hebrews speaks of the unique nature of Holy Scripture. "For the word of God is living and active. Sharper than any double-edged sword, it penetrates even to dividing soul and spirit, joints and marrow; it judges the thoughts and attitudes of the heart" (4:12 NIV). There are several truths contained in this passage of great significance for each of us.

A. *The Word of God is alive and active.* It is not dead or asleep.

B. *The Word of God is effective.* When God's Word is taught or proclaimed publicly, privately, or both, it produces an effect in the minds and hearts of the hearers. The Word of God does not need a defense as much as it needs a proclamation. The creative and dynamic power of God accompanies it when it is permitted to find a destination in the minds and hearts of people.

    C. *The Word of God penetrates, detects, judges, and exposes the secret thoughts, motives, and meditations of the mind and heart.* As the surgeon uses a scalpel to penetrate the human body to remove a diseased organ or to repair some malfunction, even so God uses his Word to perform needed miracles in the thoughts and motives of people.

A recognition of the unique and dynamic nature of Holy Scripture can do much to encourage both a pastor or a layperson to be optimistic in proclaiming the message of the Word of God to a needy world. Apart from the proclamation of his divine Word, there is no hope for miracles in the heart or for improvement in society as a whole.

III. The Bible speaks concerning the function of the Scriptures (2 Tim. 3:15–17).

The Bible has been used in a thousand different ways for a thousand different reasons—some legitimate and some illegitimate. Let us now consider three functions as revealed in these verses.

    A. *Scripture reveals the nature of God and the way of salvation (2 Tim. 3:15–16).* Much can be discovered concerning the mystery, majesty, and power of God by a serious contemplation of the natural world. If we would come to know God personally and to experience his salvation, we must give consideration to the written record of his activity of revealing himself and his purpose for humans in the Bible. Only in the Bible can we discover the Savior and the way of salvation. The Bible reveals to us that through faith in Jesus Christ as the Son of God, we can come to know the Creator as a loving and merciful Father. Were it not for the Bible, people would still be in utter darkness and dismay concerning our origin, nature, and purpose for being. We would have no divinely suggested way of escaping from the tyranny and consequences of sin.

    B. *Scripture provides authoritative guidance for conduct that is pleasing to God (2 Tim. 3:16).*

      1. It is profitable for teaching. It contains the great ideas that can lift life to the heavenly level. It can teach us a proper concept of God, man, life, death, and eternity.

      2. It is profitable for reproof. The writer of Proverbs said, "Faithful are the wounds of a friend; but the kisses of an enemy are deceitful" (Prov. 27:6). Even the best of us occasionally need rebuke or reproof. The Bible is uniquely equipped and qualified to rebuke us when we need to be reprimanded. We need to be reminded again and again that "there is a way which seemeth right unto a man, but the end thereof are the ways of death" (Prov. 14:12).

A reverent and responsible reading of the Word of God will occasionally provide us with a severe rebuke—internally and invisibly as far as anyone else is concerned. When we recognize how subject we are to self-deception the value of the reprimanding function of the Scriptures will be appreciated more and more.

3. It is profitable for correction. It is not enough to know what is wrong. We also need to know what is right. The study of God's Word will not only reveal the attitudes and ideas that need to be eliminated, but it will reveal the attitudes and ideas that should have complete command of our being. When we permit God to correct us by means of his Word we have begun not only the improvement of our own life, but we have also begun to make progress toward greater usefulness in helping others.

4. It is profitable for instruction in righteousness. The nature of the Christian experience itself causes the new convert to hunger and thirst after righteousness. The new birth creates a desire for righteousness. We will discover instruction in the ways of righteousness in the Word of God and supremely in the life and teachings of Jesus Christ.

C. *Scripture equips the receptive and responsive believer for fruitful service (2 Tim. 3:17).* God is eager that each of us be well trained, experienced, and competent as his servants. If we neglect to study his Word and to follow his teachings, there is no way by which we can be effective.

Inefficient and shoddy work on the part of those who should be spiritually mature is inexcusable. God has given his inspired Word, which contains divine instructions and guidance not only for the living of our personal lives but also for the manner in which we are to minister to others.

IV. The Bible speaks concerning our personal response to the Holy Scriptures.

A. *Jesus emphasized the supreme importance of not only hearing but also heeding the words of divine truth (Matt. 7:24–29).* He concluded the Sermon on the Mount by describing two possible responses. He encourages us to follow the example of both hearing and heeding and putting into practice these teachings that we might be like the wise man who built the house of his life on solid rock. This house was able to withstand the pressure and tensions when the storms of life swept down upon it. He warns us that to merely hear and not heed is to follow in the footsteps of the man who unwisely built his house on sand. When the times of testing came, it collapsed.

1. We should study the Bible historically. If we would interpret and apply it, we need to put forth an effort to get back into the historical situation so that we might apply it properly to our lives today.

2. We should study the Bible grammatically. We need to understand the meaning of the words the Bible uses, because the meaning of words

285

change as time goes by. The use of modern translations can be very helpful. Every field of knowledge and experience has its own unique vocabulary, and such is true with the Bible. We need to put forth an effort to learn the meaning of strange and unfamiliar words and phrases.

3. We should study the Bible logically. The Bible is a unity and does not contradict itself when understood properly. Each phrase should be studied in the context of the sentence, and the sentence in the paragraph. The paragraph should be studied as a part of the chapter, the chapter as part of the book, and the book as part of the whole Bible. The so-called discrepancies are in the mind of the reader rather than in the Word of God.

4. We should study the Bible spiritually. Because it is inspired by the Holy Spirit, it follows that only the Holy Spirit can help us to interpret it properly. The Bible cannot be understood with appreciation by the natural man (1 Cor. 2:14). The Bible can have real meaning for us only when we permit God to open up our understanding as we open up the Scriptures in an earnest search for the truth (Luke 24:45).

B. *We should trust the Word of God implicitly.* The word *success* occurs only once in the King James Version of the Bible. The idea of success appears in many places, but the word appears only once. Success is promised to Joshua providing he put a proper faith in the "book of the LORD" that came to him from Moses, the former leader of the nation of Israel. He was to meditate upon it day and night, and he was to observe its teachings in everything he did. On condition that he follow these teachings he was promised, "Then thou shalt make thy way prosperous, and then thou shalt have good success" (Josh. 1:8).

While some might want to question the inspiration of the Scriptures and argue about this, the world would be a different place if those who believe in its inspiration would respond to its authority. The Scriptures were not recorded merely that we might have a historical record of the past. These records provide us with a prophecy of what can happen in the future providing we respond to our opportunities with faith and faithfulness.

C. *We should teach the Word of God to others (2 Tim. 2:2).* By serving as teachers of the Word of God, we not only please God, but we also become the means whereby the blessings of God come into the lives of others.

If we have been taught, we should in turn teach others. Each follower of Christ is a teacher. Our only choice is at the point of the quality of our teaching. We teach in the home. We teach during our times of leisure. We teach while we work. We must not limit teaching to a classroom situation. Some of the most significant lessons that we have learned did not come to us in a classroom, but in a conversation with someone who had entered into a deeper experience of the grace of God.

Conclusion

The Bible speaks for itself if we will listen. The Bible will speak through us to the hearts of others if we are willing to let it. The Bible speaks to the deepest needs of us all. May God help each of us not only to hear it but also to heed it, study it, apply it, and proclaim its teachings to others.

WEDNESDAY EVENING, SEPTEMBER 8

Title: Judgment against the Nations

Text: "And he said, The LORD will roar from Zion, and utter his voice from Jerusalem; and the habitations of the shepherds shall mourn, and the top of Carmel shall wither" (**Amos 1:2**).

Scripture Reading: Amos 1 – 2

Introduction

Amos gave the times and circumstances under which he conducted his ministry for God to northern Israel.

I. Sins against the human conscience (Amos 1:3 – 2:3).

Amos expressed his faith in the sovereignty of God. He revealed that he believed that God is concerned about the affairs of people and is active in the processes of history. He also affirmed that people are responsible for their actions.

Amos used a psychological approach to bring the message of God to bear upon the hearts of the people in Israel. He used the "yes, yes," approach on his hearers. He began by condemning the sins of the surrounding nations. The things that he said concerning these nations are things his listeners would agree with.

A. *Judgment upon Syria to the northeast (1:3 – 5).* Syria was guilty of extreme cruelty.

B. *Judgment upon Philistia to the southwest (1:6 – 8).* Philistia had shown contempt for human personality.

C. *Judgment upon Tyre to the northeast (1:9 – 10).* Tyre was guilty of infidelity or covenant breaking.

D. *Judgment upon Edom to the southeast (1:11 – 12).*

E. *Judgment upon Ammon to the east (1:13 – 15).* Ammon had shown no compassion for the helpless.

F. *Judgment upon Moab to the southeast (2:1 – 3).* Moab had shown no concern for human feelings and no reverence for that which was appropriate.

The judgment of God was going to come upon all of these nations. The prophet spoke of that which was yet in the future as if it were already completed action, for he was certain that God was going to do it.

287

II. Sins against the revealed law of God (Amos 2:4–5).

Amos then turned his attention to Judah, Israel's neighbor to the south. He declared that because Judah had rejected the law of Jehovah and had refused to walk in his ways, wrath would come upon the nation. Judah could not plead that they were ignorant of the law of God, for they knew it and failed to keep it. They were guilty of following falsehood. Judgment was bound to come upon Judah.

III. The sin of Israel was a sin against the love of God (Amos 2:6–16).

A. *Evidences of God's love.*

1. God had delivered Israel from their enemies (2:9).
2. God had given Israel their national origin (2:10).
3. God had provided for their spiritual need through the prophets (2:11).

B. *Israel's response. Instead of responding with obedience to the will of God, Israel had rebelled against it.*

1. They were guilty of persecuting the helpless (2:6).
2. They were given over to covetousness (2:7).
3. They were guilty of perversion (2:7).
4. They were guilty of immorality (2:8).
5. Drunkenness was the order of the day (2:12).
6. True religion was inhibited and prohibited (2:12).

Conclusion

Divine retribution was on its way (Amos 2:13–16). Israel was loaded down with their own sins (2:13), and their strength would decline (v. 14). Their military skill would be lost (v. 15), and catastrophe would befall the nation (v. 16). Amos was a prophet of judgment and doom upon a nation. Because Israel refused to repent, they fell to a foreign invader some twenty-five years after these words were spoken. Does God have a message through Amos for the day in which we live?

SUNDAY MORNING, SEPTEMBER 12

Title: Assignment Number One!

Text: "And he said unto them, It is not for you to know the times or the seasons, which the Father hath put in his own power. But ye shall receive power, after that the Holy Ghost is come upon you: and ye shall be witnesses unto me both in Jerusalem, and in all Judaea, and in Samaria, and unto the uttermost part of the earth" (**Acts 1:7–8**).

Scripture Reading: Acts 1:1–11

Hymns: "All Hail the Power of Jesus' Name," Perronet

"He Leadeth Me," Gilmore

"Make Me a Blessing," Wilson

Offertory Prayer: Our Father and our Lord, we thank you for the assurance of your presence in the tasks you have given us. We thank you for the endowments of time, talents, and material blessings provided by your divine hand. Let us know that these are yours and that you have committed to us a stewardship of their use. Bless these gifts we now offer to you. May they be used as directed by your Spirit to bless the lives of others and extend your kingdom to the uttermost parts of the earth. We ask these petitions in the name of Jesus. Amen.

Introduction

Some experiences in the life of every Christian are unforgettable. We would like to sweep some of those lasting experiences under the rug. Others we remember vividly and do not ever want to forget.

There was such an unforgettable scene as this on Mount Olivet near Jerusalem. Jesus, in his resurrection body, gave his followers instructions to wait in Jerusalem until they were baptized with the Holy Spirit. This was "Assignment Number One." When Jesus had finished giving them their assignment, "he was taken up and a cloud received him out of their sight." Obediently they gathered together in an upper room to wait for further instructions. These people lived by Jesus' last words. They rang loudly in their ears and lay heavy on their hearts. This assignment was never altered for them or their successors. It remains the basic assignment for his church through the ages.

I. The assignment carries a well-defined task.

A. *It was an answer to their question: "Will you at this time give the kingdom back to Israel?"* The people did not have the right perspective for their task. They insisted that God was only for Israel and that their former behavior would prevail. The answer lifted them to higher motives and methods, for Jesus had said, "Ye shall be my witnesses."

B. *The assignment was a responsibility, not a privilege.* It is never arbitrary but is always by divine command.

C. *This assignment calls on the believers' experience with Christ.* They understood that they were to testify about what they saw and heard from their own personal experience. The young church became contagious in their world, not for their knowledge of methodology or their skill in organization, but because of their vital witness.

D. *The command to witness is a timeless one.* It is not reserved for one day per week or a given hour in a designated day. It is for any moment on any occasion during any given day of your life.

E. *The command to witness is a universal one.* The Lord did not single out a few of his followers and declare them to be witnesses; he calls each of us.

II. The field of operations: "In Jerusalem and Judaea, Samaria, and the uttermost parts of the earth."

A. *The nature of the gospel of Christ is universal.* Israel had this all mixed up. They felt God was only for Israel. Genesis 12:3 indicated clearly to Abram that God expected his people to be a blessing to all others. This commission was forwarded to Isaac and Jacob and verified to the prophets of the Lord. The guilt of Israel was that of "hoarding their beliefs and their witness."

B. *The assignment given by Jesus' to his followers indicated that the world with all the people in it was their field!* Acts 1:8 outlines the book of Acts. The young church went to the world: they went to Jerusalem and Judea and Samaria, and by the conclusion of the book, they were scattered to remote points of the known world!

C. *The assignment is not purely geographical but practical.* It is more than an outline of the geographical progress of the gospel. No church can justify a limited perspective that confines its task to its immediate members and to the people who live a few blocks from their church building. Joseph Parker, the late pastor of City Temple in London, insisted that when he stood in his pulpit, the back of his auditorium extended to the Rocky Mountains.

D. *The young church accepted this assignment and had both God and the world on their hearts at the same time.* The late Dr. W. O. Carver, professor of missions at Southern Baptist Theological Seminary, used to say that "a Christian is a redeemed personality living under the lordship of Jesus Christ." Carver told of a Japanese evangelist who once responded, "The missionaries did not bring Christ to us; Christ brought the missionaries" (*Christian Missions and Today's World* [Broadman Press, 1942], 112).

III. There is a divine promise in this assignment: "Ye shall receive power."

A. *Jesus' followers did receive power.* The Spirit of the Lord was poured out on them. It was the completion of the promise of the Paraclete (John 16:7–15). This power continues to be available for the seeking, for the asking, and for the knocking. To pray for the power of the Spirit and not be ready to do his bidding is a mockery of both our faith and our prayer. These Christians were ready when the power came!

B. *The power for the assignment is* dunamis *power, enabling power.* It is a power from above, a power of inward strength and a power of divine presence. Jesus really meant it when he said, "I am with you alway, even to the end of the earth." The people of the Old Testament called this power of Spirit, *ruach* (the wind). Jesus told Nicodemus that you cannot tell from which direction it is coming nor where it is going, but you can always know its presence!

Conclusion

We have heard again the last words of our Master. He has summarized our position, our responsibilities, and our place in his purpose. And he has assured us of his presence with his people in this work of witnessing in the world. There are three voices today that speak to our hearts: the voice from above, "Go ye to the uttermost parts of the earth and be witnesses of me"; the voice from the outside, "Come over and help us"; and the voice that speaks from the inside of every God-fearing Christian, the voice of our own hearts bearing personal responsibility, "I am debtor ... I can, I will, I must!"

SUNDAY EVENING, SEPTEMBER 12

Title: The Bible Speaks about the Home

Text: "Submitting yourselves one to another in the fear of God" (**Eph. 5:21**).

Scripture Reading: Ephesians 5:21 – 6:3

Introduction

Of the four basic institutions that make up our society—the home, the school, the state, and the church—the home is the most basic. The home is God's first institution for the welfare of society.

We live in a day in which sociologists, psychologists, law enforcement officers, journalists, and a variety of other authorities are seeking to communicate their wisdom and suggestions to the home. Numerous magazines carry articles every month that deal with the problems and privileges and perils that confront the home. It would be most profitable for us to examine what the Bible has to say concerning the home.

I. The Bible reveals the divine origin of the home (Gen. 1:27 – 28, 31; cf. Matt. 19:4 – 6).

The inspired writers looked upon marriage and the family as being a part of the divine plan and provision for humans. Marriage and the home should be considered as something other than just a legal contract or human arrangement. Marriage and the family are a part of the divine plan for the stability of society and for the well-being of humankind.

A. *By the creative act of a good God, we were made male and female.*

B. *Humankind was commissioned to "be fruitful, and multiply."* The relationship of man and woman in God's continuing work of creating life is thus designated as being a part of the divine plan of the Creator for his creatures.

C. *"And God saw everything that he had made, and behold, it was very good" (Gen. 1:31).* From the dawn of human history it has been part of God's plan for a man to have his wife, and for a woman to have her husband, and for them to live together in mutual love, faith, and faithfulness.

II. The Bible contains divine laws to safeguard the home.

The home is God's first institution for the welfare of the race. It was born in the heart of God and for the benefit of humankind. By divine decree God has given laws by which the sacredness of the home is to be perpetuated.

A. *The relationship of children to their parents (Ex. 20:12).* Humankind's primary duty as far as fellow humans is concerned is toward those within the circle of the family. The first responsibility of children is a proper respect for and a right relationship to their parents.

B. *The sacredness of sex and the preservation of purity (Ex. 20:14).* From the very beginning God has sought to instill within the heart of people a concept of the sacredness of sex. God sought and continues to seek to preserve the moral purity of his people. By this law he seeks to safeguard the welfare of the innocent and to preserve security for children.

Those who are guilty of disregarding the commandment that preserves sexual and moral purity break the holy law of God and degrade themselves. They misuse and abuse others. They strike a destructive blow at the foundation stones of a stable society.

III. The Bible speaks of the witness of the family (Deut. 6:4–9).

The Old Testament teaches that devout parents should assume the sacred responsibility for the teaching and training of their children in the law of God. Parents are instructed to diligently teach the truths of God to their children, both in the home and in the daily walk of life. They are to deposit the great spiritual and moral truths of God in the hearts and minds of their children.

The modern family seems to have abdicated its responsibility at this point. Many assume that because they take their children to Sunday school and Sunday morning worship that they have provided adequate moral and spiritual training. Most families are rearing a generation of spiritual illiterates, and the tragedy is that they fail to recognize it.

The church must do all that it can to provide guidance for Bible study and for instruction in the great principles of the Christian life. The church needs to help prepare parents to teach their children. Parents must recognize their responsibility and assume their responsibility for the moral and spiritual nurture of those whom God has placed in their home.

IV. The Bible contains guidelines for wholesome and creative family relationships (Eph. 5:21–6:3).

A. *Counsel for parents.*
1. Parents are responsible to God for their conduct toward each other and for the manner in which they teach and train the children that God blesses them with.
2. Parents are responsible for bringing up their children in the nurture and admonition of the Lord (Eph. 6:4).

B. *Counsel for wives.*
1. Wives are to act in submission to their husbands (Eph. 5:22–24). The Christian wife will want to properly adapt herself to her husband as being the head of her household. This does not mean that he is to

assume a lordly attitude and boss her around in an unkind manner. It does imply that every organization must have a head and that God holds the husband responsible for being that head.

2. Wives are to reverence their husbands (Eph. 5:33). It is possible for a Christian wife to so relate herself to her husband as to cause him to be more worthy of her reverence. At the same time it is possible for a wife to so influence her husband as to be less worthy of her reverence.

C. *Counsel for the husband.* The apostle Paul states that the husband is to relate himself to his wife in terms of Christian love.

1. Husbands are to love their wives as Christ loved the church (Eph. 5:25). Christ loved the church to the extent that he gave himself for it completely. He died for his church. The devoted husband will be so devoted to his wife.

2. Husbands are to love their wives as they love their own bodies (Eph. 5:28–30). Christian marriage involves the vital, indissolvable union of a man and woman in a union of their two lives together. The devoted husband will consider the well-being of his wife as part of his own well-being. He will treat her with the same regard with which his right hand treats his left hand.

D. *Counsel for children.* The Bible commands children to honor, respect, and obey their parents. They are to recognize that God has given their parents authority over them and that they are to respond positively to this authority. To reject this authority and to mistreat their parents is to break the holy law of God.

Conclusion

The home comes before the state, the school, and the church. It is the most basic institution in our society. The Bible speaks clearly concerning its nature, purpose, and preservation.

A Christian home is a home where Christ is loved, trusted, and obeyed sincerely and steadfastly.

Are you making progress toward the ideal of a Christian home? Are you making your individual and distinctive contribution toward making your home Christian, as a husband, wife, mother, father, son, or daughter? Each one has a contribution to make. You can be certain that God will work with you to help you achieve his ideal for your home.

WEDNESDAY EVENING, SEPTEMBER 15

Title: The Responsibility of the Privileged

Text: "You only have I known of all the families of the earth: therefore I will punish you for all your iniquities" (**Amos 3:2**).

Scripture Reading: Amos 3

Introduction

Israel occupied a unique place of privilege in the plan of God for the redemption of humankind. This was first revealed to Abraham (Gen. 12:1–5) then repeated to the patriarchs and also to the nation by Moses (Ex. 19:3–8). Amos had a message for Israel on the basis of Israel's unique relationship with God.

I. Israel's place of privilege demands a corresponding responsibility (Amos 3:1–2).

Amos flattered the national vanity of his listeners when he spoke for God, saying, "You only have I known of all the families of the earth." The people thought that because of their unique relationship with God that they had a monopoly on him. They believed that they belonged to him and that he belonged to them. They believed that God was unconcerned about other people.

Amos declared that because of their unique position of opportunity, they also had a corresponding responsibility to respond to their opportunity.

II. Amos presents his letters of ordination (Amos 3:3–8; 7:10–17).

Amos presents the basis upon which he has had the courage to speak the words that he is speaking. He uses several illustrations to explain how that his message is both logical and reasonable. He announces that God always warns before he brings judgment upon a people (3:7–8).

III. God's universal law in the sphere of privilege and responsibility (Amos 3:9–15).

A. *Rejected responsibility leads to insensitivity to the voice of God and conscience (3:9–10)*. Spiritual blindness is a result of one's refusing to do the known will of God. To lose spiritual perception is an irreparable loss.

B. *Rejected responsibility brings the judgment of God (3:11–15)*. The position of privilege will be withdrawn, and judgment will fall upon both the rich and upon those who consider themselves to be religious.

Conclusion

To occupy the position of privilege is to occupy a position of great responsibility. Some consider the position of privilege a gift to be enjoyed to the limit. Instead of being humbled by the position of privilege, they react with an attitude of superiority and arrogance. Israel had been guilty of both responses. The judgment of God was coming upon Israel, and the judgment of God continues to come upon those who reject the responsibilities that always accompany the position of privilege.

SUNDAY MORNING, SEPTEMBER 19

Title: Life's Mysterious Plus

Texts: "And, behold, I send the promise of my Father upon you: but tarry ye in the city of Jerusalem, until ye be endued with power from on high" (**Luke 24:49**).

"These all continued with one accord in prayer and supplication, with the women, and Mary the mother of Jesus, and with his brethren" (**Acts 1:14**).

Scripture Reading: Acts 1:6–14

Hymns: "There Shall Be Showers of Blessing," Whittle

"I Need Thee Every Hour," Hawks

"Open My Eyes," Scott

Offertory Prayer: O Lord, we understand that in your great purposes you intend to bring all things unto yourself, through Jesus Christ, your Son and our Savior and Lord. You have taught us, too, O Lord, that you intend to use your people, frail vessels of earth, to bear witness of the treasures of heaven. If we understand your divine purpose, we are humbled in your presence because of human limitations. You have taught us, Lord, that all things are possible by belief and through prayer. As we offer these material gifts to you, we pray that as you use them to extend your kingdom, you will continue to provide guidance for us as we dedicate ourselves to you. We ask your continued presence here as we wait on you. In Jesus' name we pray. Amen.

Introduction

It has been said that man's extremity is God's best opportunity. When the church lays its mission alongside of its human resources, there is a great gulf. God asked his church to do what they could not do when they depended completely on human resources. There is no more persuasive picture of the church than that pictured in Acts 1–3. It is the picture of an insurgent spirit against incredible odds.

I. The church had experienced defeat.

A. *Many had gone away (John 6:66).* They were spiritual dropouts. When people in the church live only for material things, they will receive only what material things can give.

B. *There was a moment shortly before the Holy Spirit came into the Upper Room when Simon Peter was about to abdicate.* He said, "I am going fishing." He really meant to return to his former way.

C. *The treasurer of the group had already gone out and hanged himself.* The disciples were afraid. Their leader was gone. It would seem that the whole movement was about to fall apart.

295

II. What is the Christian attitude in the hour of crisis?

A. *The positive story is told.* The disciples did not fall apart, nor did they turn to intensify human efforts. Study committees and promotional programs have limitations.

B. *A great conviction came upon them.* The scene in the upper room is one of eagerness bathed with realization of divine presence. They realized that somewhere out of what would humanly seem to be defeat would come a victory!

C. *There were tremendous odds against the believers—approximately 120 people in the upper room and millions in the world about them.* But they had the words of Christ ringing in their ears and on their hearts, "Go ye therefore and teach all nations."

III. What was the object of the believers' prayer?

A. *These people had received their pattern of prayer from Jesus.* They remembered that prayer was a real part of the curriculum in the school of Christ. They learned from Jesus that prayer must be done early in the morning, late at night, when the body is tired, or in the midst of an oppressing throng. They understood that prayer is not to be limited by moods, impatience, or busyness.

B. *They prayed for the way of God to be known to them in terms of vocation, strength for the works God would have them to do, a vital realization of divine presence, and power to resist temptation.* In some instances, even as far as the example of Jesus, some died praying (Stephen).

C. *They prayed enough to be equal to their task.* We should not ask the Lord to give us tasks equal to our strength and abilities, for these would suffer tremendous human limitations. The "young church in action" lifted their hearts to the Lord, requesting that he give them power to enable them to do the divinely given task.

Conclusion

As a result of the early believers' discovery of "Life's Mysterious Plus," we have the story of Pentecost. It is the story of how God is able to make the impossible possible. And is not this the story of our Bible? And is this not the story of God's grace for every life? "Men ought always to pray and not faint." We cannot afford to faint and cease prayer.

SUNDAY EVENING, SEPTEMBER 19

Title: The Bible Speaks about Christian Growth

Text: "But grow in grace, and in the knowledge of our Lord and Savior Jesus Christ. To him be glory both now and for ever" (**2 Peter 3:18**).

Introduction

One of the most grievous heresies is the idea that the child of God is born full grown. This erroneous idea is often held by a majority of the members of a church and is evidenced by the fact that they expect the new convert to demonstrate mature Christian character and conduct. They are not only disappointed but resort to severe criticism when the new convert stumbles in his efforts to achieve spiritual maturity. Instead of criticizing, the more mature members of the Christian family should be compassionate and understanding and should put forth a special effort to assist the new, immature convert in his struggle for release from the old ways of life.

Frequently a new convert will labor under the mistaken idea that because he has trusted Jesus Christ and united with the church that he should immediately find release from the chains of habit that have been formed possibly over a period of decades.

To discover the presence of unchristian attitudes and even appetites can be a very disturbing and discouraging experience. The majority of unsaved men and women in our society labor under the mistaken idea that a conversion experience should completely solve the sin problem and immediately produce a person not only with a changed heart but also with a completely different philosophy of life and manner of conduct. Because of their own failure to think proper thoughts, their inability to break enslaving habits, and their lack of self-confidence in their own power to enable them to live a transformed Christian life, they hobble along in unbelief.

It would be extremely helpful to all concerned to face up to the fact that the new birth produces not a mature Christian but a spiritual infant who is capable of growth in the moral and spiritual likeness of Jesus Christ. Only growth, time, and experience will solve some problems. Continued immaturity on the part of some Christians has plagued the church throughout its history. Examples of some of the problems created by the neglect of growth emphasize the need for spiritual growth.

I. The need for Christian growth.

A. *Continued immaturity creates discord within the church fellowship (1 Cor. 3:1–3).* Paul was greatly disturbed because of the immaturity of the Corinthian Christians. He discovered that they were engaging in a controversy over pastors similar to the manner in which children fuss and fight over toys. He declared that they were acting like babies instead of like mature men. To achieve maturity in any area is never easy. This is especially true in the spiritual realm. Most church fusses are due to the immaturity of some individual or a group within the membership.

B. *Continued immaturity creates an instability of character that reflects upon the cause of Christ (Eph. 4:14).* Growth makes possible a stability and steadfastness of character that reveals the worthwhileness of being a follower of Jesus Christ. To grow is to gain some convictions concerning what is right and what is wrong. To grow is to develop an inward consciousness of what is right and what is wrong and makes responsible action possible. There is a wisdom and an understanding that comes with growth that cannot be obtained or utilized as long as one remains in infancy.

297

C. *Continued immaturity makes an effective Christian witness impossible (Heb. 5:12–13).* In every area of life it is assumed that growth and progress will follow birth. There is always sadness and disappointment when some accident or disease hampers the natural process of growth.

An infant can understand only the things of an infant. An infant cannot do the work of a man. Even so the infant child of God cannot possibly be the effective servant of God that he is capable of being after years of steady growth.

D. *Continued immaturity deprives the new convert of the moral and spiritual insight that is needed (Heb. 5:14).* No one expects the kindergarten graduate to have the same ability or insight or understanding of the world situation as the college graduate. God does not expect of his little babes that they demonstrate either the understanding or the efficiency of those who are mature. But our Lord does expect each one to be on the way toward maturity.

E. *Continued immaturity implies that the new convert retains the attitudes and actions of the unconverted (1 Peter 2:1–2).* The new birth alone does not eliminate the unwholesome attitudes and habits of the non-Christian life. These are eliminated as spiritual growth takes place. The leaves of the oak tree do not fall when the killing frost comes. They cling to the tree and fall off only when the sap rises and the new growth begins the following spring. Even so the new convert will be able to cast off "all malice, and all guile, and hypocrisies, and envies, and all evil speakings" (1 Peter 2:1). Only when the new growth from the inside causes these attitudes and actions to slough off will the new convert be able to manifest the fruits of his faith.

II. Areas for Christian growth.

As the new child grows physically, mentally, and emotionally, even so there are a number of different areas in which the child of God is to grow.

A. *The child of God needs to grow in grace (2 Peter 3:18).* God's grace is the divine side of the salvation experience. God's grace is God's activity of moving to meet the sinner's need on the basis of divine love and mercy rather than on the basis of human merit. It is grace on God's side that makes it possible for people to be saved by the human response of faith (Eph. 2:8–9). Through faith and obedience the new convert can enter more and more into a deeper experience of God's grace (cf. 1 Cor. 15:10).

B. *The child of God needs to grow in the knowledge of our Lord and Savior Jesus Christ (2 Peter 3:18).* This growth should be both intellectual and experiential. By the study of the New Testament, we can discover both the mind and the manner of Jesus' dealing with different types of people. It is reasonable to believe that Jesus will relate himself to us in the same manner in which he related himself to these persons whom we read about. Intellectual knowledge alone is insufficient. We need to know him personally. We can experience the presence and power of Christ as we respond to his living presence and as we relate to the world about us in a redemptive manner. As the years go by, we should not only know more about him, but we should know him better.

C. *The child of God needs to grow in spiritual competency (2 Tim. 2:15).* Paul used a term familiar to tent makers as he described the efficiency with which the servants of God should work. Concerning "rightly dividing the word of truth," he wrote in terms of cutting it straight or cutting it correctly according to the pattern so that all of the pieces fit together. He is challenging them to become vocationally efficient in interpreting and applying the Word of God in such a manner that when they put all of the pieces of the doctrine together, they will fit together like the pieces of a tent.

We live in a day in which great emphasis is placed on vocational efficiency. Rigid standards must be met for an individual to serve as an electrician, brick mason, engineer, teacher, or physician. These people must be able to perform efficiently. Paul is challenging each of us to study so that we might grow in efficiency so as to hear words of divine approval from God.

D. *The child of God needs to grow in doctrine and convictions (Eph. 4:14).* The follower of Jesus Christ should be ashamed if after years of professing faith in Jesus Christ he or she does not understand and is unable to relate, at least in elementary terms, basic Christian ideas and convictions. It is sad but true that the great majority of those who claim to be followers of Jesus Christ do not know what they believe.

E. *The child of God needs to grow in obedience (Eph. 5:1).* The new birth does not produce instantaneous loving obedience in the heart of a new convert. While there may be a desire to be obedient in all things, it usually takes a degree of spiritual maturity to produce an attitude of loving obedience to the will of God. We should be more obedient today than we were a year ago.

F. *The child of God needs to grow in Christian love (1 Cor. 12:31).* Paul declared love, the God kind of love, to be the supreme gift of the Spirit. He declared that love is more important than all other attitudes or achievements. This kind of love does not come cheap and easy. It does not come instantaneously. It comes as a new convert permits the Holy Spirit to work within his or her heart (Rom. 5:8). This kind of love has been described as the badge of Christian discipleship by which we identify ourselves as the followers of Jesus Christ (John 13:34–35).

III. The resources for Christian growth.

A. *The nature of the Christian experience itself (1 Peter 2:2).* The Christian experience is not the establishment of a legal relationship but rather the forming of a living relationship. This experience imparts life with its appetite for spiritual things. As a new baby needs nourishment, the child of God will have an appetite for the things of God (Matt. 5:6).

299

B. *The milk and meat of the Word of God (1 Peter 2:2; Heb. 5:12–14).* The heavenly Father has provided ample nourishment and a well-balanced diet for the nurture and growth of the spiritual nature.

C. *The church as a spiritual family (Eph. 4:11–16).* While there are many functions which the church is to fulfill in the world, one of its primary roles is that of serving as a family for the new convert. The church has a responsibility for the growth of the little ones whom our Lord commits into our custody (Matt. 18:5–6).

D. *The inward work of the Holy Spirit (Phil. 1:6; 2:13).* In the new birth God comes into the heart of the believer to work from within to reproduce the mind, character, and conduct of Jesus Christ. If we are to grow, we must recognize and respond to the inward impulses that come to us from the Holy Spirit.

Conclusion

The desperate need of a lost world for our complete Christian testimony makes continued growth imperative. Each of us must respond to our responsibilities for spiritual growth.

WEDNESDAY EVENING, SEPTEMBER 22

Title: Unheeded Warnings

Text: "Hear this word, you cows of Bashan on Mount Samaria, you women who oppress the poor and crush the needy . . ." **(Amos 4:1 NIV)**.

Scripture Reading: Amos 4

Introduction

Amos communicates God's message to the people in terms of a spiritual analysis and interpretation of the significance of events that have befallen the nation. He declares that God has been speaking to the nation but that the people have turned a deaf ear to the loud voice of God as he spoke to them in historical events.

I. Words of warning to the leaders of society (Amos 4:1–3).

Amos directs these words to the first women of northern Israel. He speaks words of irony and satire to these women who are going to suffer most because of the spiritual deafness of both the religious and political leaders of the northern kingdom.

II. Words of warning to corrupt religious leaders (Amos 4:4–5).

Again Amos uses words of irony and challenges the people of northern Israel to go to their places of worship and to be guilty of sin. This is a caustic condemnation of heartless ritualism. There was no response of the people to the moral demands of Israel's God.

III. Words of warning that were unrecognized (Amos 4:6–11).

God spoke words of warning through various catastrophes and disasters, but the people did not have eyes to see and ears to hear. They saw these only as acts of nature. They did not look for a divine significance. Amos, as a divinely inspired news analyst, gives them the significance of these events.

A. *Famine (4:6).*
B. *Drought (4:7–8).*
C. *Calamity (4:9).*
D. *Plague (4:10).*
E. *War (4:10).*
F. *Earthquake (4:11).*

Conclusion

The judgment of God is going to be poured out on the people of a wicked nation that refuses to heed warnings and that refuses to respond to the chastisement of a God who wants to give them every possible hope.

Amos could not bear to tell the people what was going to come upon them (4:12). He simply declared that they must get ready because God was going to come in judgment (4:12).

The chapter closes with Amos's concept of God, who is both adequate and powerful to accomplish his purpose. He is the Creator. He is omniscient, omnipotent, and omnipresent. He is the God who places ethical demands on his people. The chapter closes without a ray of hope.

SUNDAY MORNING, SEPTEMBER 26

Title: There Is Good News Today!

Text: "And daily in the temple, and in every house, they ceased not to teach and preach Jesus Christ" (**Acts 5:42**).

Scripture Reading: Acts 5:29–42

Hymns: "Tell Me the Old, Old Story," Hankey

"He Lifted Me," Gabriel

"Crown Him with Many Crowns," Bridges

Offertory Prayer: Our Father, who has given to us the revelation of yourself through your Son Jesus, we thank you that in your great and eternal purpose you have made us your servants in these days. We thank you for bread for our table, clothes for our bodies, and shelter. We thank you for the resources that you have given to us in the very earth on which we walk. Lord, we pray your blessings on these gifts we now present to you and ask that you would help us to realize that these material blessings issue from divine sovereignty and result in our stewardship. Receive these gifts, O God, in the name of your Son, Jesus, who has given to us the blessings of eternal life. In Jesus' name. Amen.

Introduction

The "young church in action" was a fellowship of redeemed people involved in preaching the good news of God in Christ as the hope for a troubled and apathetic world. The words of Jesus rang in their ears and in their hearts, "As ye go, preach!" (Matt. 10:7); "Go ye into all the world, and preach the gospel to every creature" (Mark 16:15). The first frontal attack of the gospel of Christ in the world was the preaching of the Word of the Lord by his church.

If God expects preaching of the Word of the Lord to be a vital force in his church today, we should examine his command and its implications and our personal involvement in it. We do well to ask: What is it? Who is to do it? Where is it to be done? How can we get on with it?

I. What is this preaching expected of Christ's church?

A. *It is proclamation!* It is the good news that God is reconciling the world to himself through Jesus Christ.

B. *There is an excellent guideline for the preaching ministry of the church in Acts 2:14: "Peter stood with the eleven."* An examination of the proclamation of the early church gives us these conclusions:

1. It began with the good news about God.
2. The Good News came from God.
3. It came to this world in the person of the only begotten of the Father, Jesus.
4. It became a vital experience in the lives of persons so that they felt in their heart and proclaimed in their lives, "This Jesus is both Lord and Christ" (Acts 2:36).

C. *The early church's proclamation was not intended to change cultures or to adjust society but to "tell all men what God has done for them and how he has compassion on every life."* Conviction and redemption are powers that belong to God, and only he can bring salvation to pass.

II. Who shall do this work of preaching?

A. *It is usually our understanding that preaching is reserved for the clergy.* We think of preaching for the most part as what goes on in the pulpit, not in the pew or on the streets. But it was not just a few who received this command to preach and proclaim the "good news"; it was the responsibility of the entire church, the corporate fellowship.

B. *The early church involved every member in preaching.* Philip preached while on a trip to Samaria. Stephen, a deacon in the church, preached, and his preaching cost him his life. Paul preached. John Mark, one of the young men of the church, preached. Lydia preached in Macedonia. Apollos was the dramatic preacher from the schools of North Africa, but Priscilla and Aquila preached, and they were but simple tent makers.

C. *There have been several levels of understanding in recent years concerning preaching.*

1. The concept that one man of the local fellowship is the "preacher." We labeled him; we assigned this task to him only. We thought of him as our professional.
2. We said that "the laypeople were to help the preacher." They were to "hold up the preacher's hands" in preaching the Word of the Lord. The preacher was to take care of the pulpit and the laypeople the business matters of the church.
3. We have reached a higher level in our day. We have moved from the pages of the book of Acts right into the needs of our time. The minister is not to be helped by the laypeople in the task of preaching. Instead, the minister is to help laypeople evangelize the world. The modern minister must see every member as an evangelist!

III. Where is this preaching to be done?

The New Testament says that it is to be done everywhere. Look at the scenes of the book of Acts. The people of God were on the streets, on the open highways, in their homes, in prisons, in synagogues, and in places of business. The local church was the basis for their fellowship, the center of their worship, and the source of their teaching, instruction, and prayer. But when the worship was concluded, they were released to the world everywhere.

IV. How may preaching be done by the church today?

A. *In the backdrop of sin.* We are not salespeople but witnesses. We must understand that people have sinned and "come short of the glory of God" (Rom. 3:23). We must see again what Ezekiel saw when he looked on the valley of dry bones. There is no life, only death, in the person whose goals are in opposition to those of a sovereign Lord.
B. *By faith in its Author.* We must understand that the power to change life belongs to the Lord. The preaching church is one that exercises great faith in the Author of redemption. Only God can produce that!
C. *With much dependence on worship, prayer, and witness.* Worship is the prelude to witness and preaching in the world. The young church in action found great strength when they assembled together before the Lord for ethical instruction and inspirational motivation. The preaching of the church is before the world. It must be preceded by people whose hearts come openly and prayerfully before their God!
D. *In vital and compassionate love.* There is no real preaching where there is no real love!

Conclusion

God has in no way adjusted the design and the purposes of gospel preaching. He continues to use the "foolishness of the thing preached" to save that which is lost. Many years before the advent of Christ, and in those days when there was the development of a moral overtone in society, God called Ezekiel and asked him, "Can these dead be made to live?" Ezekiel wisely answered, "O LORD, Thou knowest." God commanded him to preach to that which was dead. Bones came to bone, joint to joint, and that which was dead stood upon their feet, an exceedingly great army! God continues to use the genius of good news from God brought to this world by Jesus and experienced in personal confrontation through faith as a vital force in the life of his church!

SUNDAY EVENING, SEPTEMBER 26

Title: The Bible Speaks about Witnessing

Text: "But ye shall receive power, after that the Holy Ghost is come upon you: and ye shall be witnesses unto me both in Jerusalem, and in all Judea, and in Samaria, and unto the uttermost part of the earth" (**Acts 1:8**).

Scripture Reading: Luke 24:45–48

Introduction

The mission of the church, as well as the mission of the individual follower of Christ, is defined in terms of witnessing.

I. The meaning of Christian witnessing illustrated.

A. *The word "witness" is used to define the ministry of John the Baptist (John 1:8, 15, 19, 32, 34–37).* John the Baptist gave a verbal testimony concerning his personal knowledge of Jesus Christ. His testimony is in the form of an authentic record of what he knew to be true concerning Jesus Christ.

B. *Jesus used the word "witness" to help define his mission and ministry (John 3:11; 18:37).* That which he spoke was absolute truth, as if it had been given under oath by a witness in a trial before a jury.

C. *In the book of Acts the words "witness" and "testify" are used in thirty-five different instances to describe both the mission and the task of the church (cf. 2:32; 4:20, 29, 33; 5:19–20, 33, 38).* While the witness of a life that is utterly devoted to ministries of mercy in the name of Christ is of inestimable value, we need to recognize the need for a verbal witness also. The witness of a noble example lived daily is not sufficient within itself to enable the world to know Jesus Christ as Savior. The witness of one's lips is as necessary as the witness of one's life.

II. The motives for witnessing to the unsaved.

The need of the modern church is not for better organization but for a deeper and more compelling motivation. Particularly is this true with reference to our opportunity and responsibility of witnessing for Christ to an unsaved world.

A. *The early disciples witnessed continually because of the irrepressible joy of sharing life's greatest discovery (Acts 8:4, 8).* They had discovered in a refreshing and life-changing manner that the eternal God is a God of love. This had been made known to them through the life, teachings, death, resurrection, and constant presence of Jesus Christ. They simply could not contain the good news.

B. *The early disciples felt that telling the good news was a proper response to lordship of Jesus Christ (Matt. 28:18–20).* They believed that he had a right to command their person, their time, and their energies. They understood their primary function to be that of proclaiming the wonderful love of God (Acts 2:11).

C. *The early disciples were vividly aware of the leadership of the Holy Spirit (Acts 4:31).* The Holy Spirit came to them and caused them to lose their timidity and fear. Without hesitation they gave testimony concerning their assurance that God had raised Jesus Christ from the dead and that he was a living Savior. They encouraged others to receive him as Lord of life (Acts 4:33).

D. *The early disciples were motivated by a personal conviction of the world's deep need for salvation through Jesus Christ.* They were gripped by the conviction that man was away from God, lost and without hope and without a knowledge of the way home to God.

III. Resources for witnessing in our world today.

The early disciples had some resources for witnessing that we do not have. Some of them were eyewitnesses of the crucifixion. Some of them were eyewitnesses of the empty tomb. Some were eyewitnesses to the ministries of the living Christ following his resurrection. One hundred and twenty of them were actually present in the upper room when the Holy Spirit came to authenticate them as the people of God and to enable them to become his spokespersons.

As is the case with a witness in a law court, God's spokesperson can give verbal testimony concerning only that which is a part of his personal experience with Jesus Christ.

A. *We can relate our personal experience of receiving Jesus Christ as Lord and Savior.* We can relate the factors that led to our decision. We can and should describe the changes that receiving Christ produced in our life. We can bear testimony concerning what Jesus Christ means to us in the present.

B. *We can and should give testimony concerning our personal experience of the truth and dependability of the Holy Scriptures.* This testimony will be determined by the degree to which we have studied the Scriptures and responded to its promises and to its instructions. To the degree that it has been a blessing to our lives, we have a testimony to give. The Holy Spirit can use this to bring conviction to others.

C. *From personal experience we should give testimony concerning our access to God through the unclosed gate of prayer (Acts 4:31).* If we have tarried in the throne room in dialogue with our heavenly Father, we have a story that others need to know about. As you would describe the privilege of becoming acquainted with some famous person, even so relate your experience of communication with the heavenly Father.

D. *We should not hesitate to describe our personal recognition of and response to the leadership of the indwelling Holy Spirit (1 Cor. 3:16).* To give this testimony can provide great encouragement, particularly for an adult, to receive Jesus Christ as Savior. To relate how the Holy Spirit works within the heart can encourage the one who is hesitant to make a break with sin and to receive Jesus Christ as Lord. Many believe that they must live the Christian life in the power of their own will. They fail to recognize that the Holy Spirit will come to dwell within to enable them to do God's holy will.

E. *Our personal awareness of the world's unsatisfied spiritual hunger and its desperate need for Christ as Savior should compel us to be busy at the task of telling them of this wonderful Savior.* Christ is the only one who can provide bread for the soul and can meet the deepest need of the human heart.

F. *Our personal conviction of the power of the gospel to save one and all (Rom. 10:1) should motivate us to cast aside our timidity and fear of failure.* We should relate the good news of God's love and desire to save, and then trust the gospel and the Holy Spirit to do the rest.

Conclusion

What kind of a witness for Christ are you? Have you been content to just try to live a good life and let that be your only witness?

How long has it been since you let God lay the blessing of a deep personal concern for some unsaved friend upon your heart? Are you seeking week after week to give testimony concerning Jesus that will be convincing so that someone near to you and dear to you will have the courage to trust him as Savior?

The Holy Spirit will lead you as you are available. Your personal experience with Christ and the Scriptures you already know can be adequate when the Holy Spirit is leading. An unsaved person waits for you to bring the good news. Do not disappoint this unsaved person by remaining silent. Do not disappoint your Lord by refusing to tell what you know about his love. It is the teaching of the Bible that God expects each of us to be a personal witness.

WEDNESDAY EVENING, SEPTEMBER 29

Title: Unheeded Chastisement

Text: "And I also have given you cleanness of teeth in all your cities, and want of bread in all your places: yet have ye not returned unto me, saith the LORD" (**Amos 4:6**).

Introduction

Amos the prophet lived in a time of great postwar material prosperity. The people thought that God had indicated his pleasure in them by giving them victory. They thought that everything was exactly as it should be.

There were primarily only two classes of people in the land—the very rich and the very poor. The rich enjoyed great luxury and indulged in all the pleasures that money could provide. The poor were continually oppressed, and injustice was practiced in the courts.

True religion had been compromised to the extent that it was a mere form of religion. The religion of the people produced no moral effects in their lives.

The nation depended on financial and military might for existence among the nations of the earth. It seemed that all was right with the world. The prophet of God, however, was able to see signs of decay, evidences of poison in the bloodstream, and inevitable calamities ahead for these people who were unable to read the signs of the times.

I. Divine chastisement was unrecognized and unheeded.

A. *God sent famine upon them.* "And I also have given you cleanness of teeth in all your cities, and want of bread in all your places: yet have ye not returned unto me, saith the LORD" (Amos 4:6).

B. *God withheld the rain.* "And also I have withholden the rain from you, when there were yet three months to the harvest; ... yet have ye not returned unto me, saith the LORD" (Amos 4:7–8).

 The people simply thought that they had had a drought. When rain was needed, it did not come. Many people incorrectly assume that the laws of nature take care of such things as Amos is speaking about.

C. *God sent agricultural failure.* "I have smitten you with blasting and mildew: when your gardens and your vineyards and your fig trees and your olive trees increased, the palmerworm devoured them: yet have ye not returned unto me, saith the LORD" (Amos 4:9).

 The people thought that the season had produced an unusually large number of insects. Many times God is like a dentist; he has to inflict pain that better things may result.

D. *God chastised his nation with war.* The people were so dull that they did not recognize that God was trying to tell them something. "I have sent among you the pestilence after the manner of Egypt: your young men have I slain with the sword, and have taken away your horses; and I have made the stink of the camps to come up unto your nostrils: yet have ye not returned unto me, saith the LORD. I have overthrown some of you, as God overthrew Sodom and Gomorrah, and ye were as a firebrand plucked out of the burning: yet have ye not returned unto me, saith the LORD" (Amos 4:10–11).

II. God continues to chastise.

A. *God chastises nations.* One cannot study the Bible without recognizing that the biblical writers believed that God had the power to sway the destiny of nations. The God of grace and justice rewards the nations that fear him and serve him and punishes the nations that ignore him and oppress the helpless.

The study of history reveals that those who usurp the place of God and ignore the laws of justice and mercy are eventually destroyed. History has been described as "His story." The Bible declares and history verifies the truth that "The wicked shall be turned into hell, and all the nations that forget God" (Ps. 9:17). There are nations today strutting across the stage of human history that must either change or experience the radical justice of a holy God.

B. *God chastises individuals.* A church member was injured quite seriously while driving under the influence of alcohol. His chest was crushed and his limbs were broken, and his life hung by a narrow thread. Someone could have said that the accident was due only to the loss of his mental faculties while intoxicated. His explanation was different. After months of lying on his back looking up, looking backward, looking inward, and looking forward with the language of faith, he declared that the loving heavenly Father had caused him to have the accident to bring him to his senses. He rededicated his life and renewed his vows and resumed the discipline of discipleship. As the years went by he became a trusted and respected servant of Jesus Christ as well as a blessing to his family, his church, and his community.

An unbelieving husband and wife were blessed with the birth of a precious baby. The years went by, and they refused to worship and bring the child to church. While still an innocent child the girl became ill and died. Shortly thereafter both the father and mother were converted and became faithful in both worship and work for God. They had to experience loss in order to experience the highest possible gain.

III. The purpose of chastisement needs to be understood.

A. *Chastisement is the proof of the fatherhood of God.* "If ye endure chastening, God dealeth with you as with sons; for what son is he whom the father chasteneth not?" (Heb. 12:7).
1. Where discipline is lacking, true fatherhood is wanting.
2. Because we are his sons, God chastises and educates us.

B. *In the distresses and trouble of life God deals with us in terms of his love.* "For whom the Lord loveth he chasteneth, and scourgeth every son whom he receiveth" (Heb. 12:6).

C. *God disciplines and chastises his children according to the dictates of perfect wisdom that we might be changed into the image of his holiness.* "Furthermore we have had fathers of our flesh which corrected us, and we gave them reverence: shall we not much rather be in subjection unto the Father of spirits, and live? For they verily for a few days chastened us after their own pleasure; but he for our profit" (Heb. 12:9–10).

D. *Chastisement properly understood and accepted produces peace and righteousness.* "Now no chastening for the present seemeth to be joyous, but grievous:

308

nevertheless afterward it yieldeth the peaceable fruit of righteousness unto them which are exercised thereby" (Heb. 12:11).

Conclusion

The psalmist said, "It is good for me that I have been afflicted: that I might learn thy statutes" (Ps. 119:71). God seeks people by means of his grace and goodness.

The apostle Paul asked, "Despiseth thou the riches of his goodness and forbearance and longsuffering; not knowing that the goodness of God leadeth thee to repentance?" (Rom. 2:4).

By the goodness of his love and by his mercy revealed in the gift of his Son, Jesus Christ, God seeks us. If we turn a deaf ear and heart toward God's goodness, he may seek us through affliction and trouble. He uses this method only as a last resort, to bring the greatest possible good to us after his entreaties of mercy have been spurned. Isaiah challenges each of us: "Seek ye the LORD while he may be found, call ye upon him while he is near" (Isa. 55:6).

OCTOBER

■ Sunday Mornings

Continue with the theme "The Mission and Message of the Church in the Modern World."

■ Sunday Evenings

"Have You Met the Master?" is the theme for Sunday evenings. The sermons are based on personal encounters with Jesus Christ. The compassionate Christ wishes to confront each of us in order to bring to us the truth and love of God.

■ Wednesday Evenings

Continue with the theme "God Speaks through the Prophets."

SUNDAY MORNING, OCTOBER 3

Title: The Saint, the Sinner, the Sword, and the Spirit

Text: "Then Philip opened his mouth, and began at the same scripture, and preached unto him Jesus" **(Acts 8:35)**.

Scripture Reading: Acts 8:25–40

Hymns: "Come, Thou Almighty King," Anonymous

"The King's Business," Cassel

"Crown Him with Many Crowns," Matthew Bridges and Godfrey Thring

Offertory Prayer: O Lord, our God, we thank you for the blessings of the week just past; and we thank you for the privileges and the opportunities you give us this day. As we make this offering of material blessings, we pray that you will help us to be aware that these are gifts of your love and a part of the expression of our concern that your gospel might be carried to the uttermost parts of the earth. Bless us as we continue to wait upon you. We ask these things in Jesus' name and for his sake. Amen.

Introduction

Our Lord gave us an assignment that involves our witness of the good news of Christ in our hearts, beginning where we are and on to the uttermost parts of the earth. And he gave his church the power to accomplish this task. According to the leadership of the Lord, the church developed its method.

The young church in action learned about mass evangelism (Acts 2–3) and about missionary evangelism (Acts 7–8). "The disciples were scattered abroad and went everywhere preaching the gospel." The young church learned the significance of lay evangelism. Stephen and Philip are classic examples. The church practiced pastoral evangelism through the witness of Peter and James and the other apostles. The young church in time learned about cooperative mission evangelism. The Spirit of the Lord put it on the heart of the church to set apart Paul and Barnabas and assured them of their cooperative efforts to make it possible for them to be witnesses of the Lord on foreign fields. Family evangelism was practiced by the young church. Cornelius and the Philippian jailer's families were involved in the gospel.

There is no method in evangelism that will supersede personal witness. Acts 8:25–40 tells us of four factors involved:

I. The saint: The deacon, Philip.

A. *A great awakening was creeping throughout Judea and was spreading into Samaria.* In our Scripture lesson we find a layman, busy in his weekday world, who turned a corner of his life and found another personal opportunity to bear his witness of God.

B. *Philip was a layman, one of the first deacons.* It is said that "he was filled with the Holy Spirit, with wisdom, and with faith."

C. *The layman applied his Christian faith in personal experiences day by day.* He did not reserve his Christianity for one hour or one day in the week. He was near to God, where the Spirit could use him and was available on call.

II. The sinner.

This man was not of the culture of the Jews. He was a stranger to their ways and a visitor in their territory. He was a sinner.

A. *Why a sinner?* Because all people are in sin and "come short of the glory of God."

B. *His traits were admirable.* He was a man of reputation, inclined to worship and eager to understand the Scripture.

C. *He was characteristic of a spirit of conviction.* His will and desire were one — seeking fellowship with God.

D. *He had a faulty understanding of relationships.* He asked, "Here is water; what doth hinder me to be baptized?" Such an attitude reflects an institutional understanding of relationships. It was the task of the Christian to lead this man from this level to a level of personal relationship with his Lord. How did he do it?

III. The sword: the Word of the Lord.

A. *The eunuch was reading a passage from Isaiah.*

B. *The Bible has a unique way of speaking to the hearts of serious people concerning an eternal God.*

311

C. *The Christian began at this point and told him the meaning of Christ for his life.* Here is the place where personal witness begins.

D. *The love of God for an individual can best be understood in terms of a cross.* The meaning of the cross comes alive by a person's personal faith: "If thou believest, thou mayest."

But there is a fourth factor in the scene of personal witness:

IV. The Spirit.

A. *The Spirit said to Philip, "Go 'glue' yourself to the chariot."* The Spirit was provoking both the saint and the sinner to speak from the truth of God's Word.

B. *Philip learned what Ezekiel learned years before.* God can bring the dead back to life, and the instrument is the power of his Spirit. "Without the Spirit of Christ, you are not his."

Conclusion

The experience of the Christian with the Ethiopian leaves us with speculation. We wonder if this man was not a vital force among his people upon his return. Whether he was or not, his salvation was the result of personal witness in the early church. The Lord had said to his people before he ascended unto the Father, "And ye shall be my witnesses." Whatever else occupies the attention of God's church, personal, vital, daily witness must be its mission!

SUNDAY EVENING, OCTOBER 3

Title: A Divorcée Meets the Master

Text: "Come, see a man, which told me all things that ever I did: is not this the Christ?" (**John 4:29**).

Scripture Reading: John 4:1–42

Introduction

The story of the Savior and the Samaritan woman at Jacob's well is one of the most instructive and inspirational stories in the entire Bible. The story takes place in Samaria, a country surrounded on the south by Judea, on the west by the Mediterranean (Great) Sea, on the east by Perea and Decapolis, and on the north by Phoenicia and Galilee. The country got its name from its capital city, Samaria. Jacob's well today is located near the modern town of Nablus.

The story teaches us many wonderful lessons: (1) Jesus has great insight, (2) Jesus has living water for parched souls, (3) converts must become evangelists, (4) a person with an unholy past can do good works for Jesus Christ as he or she repents and accepts him as Lord, and (5) the greatest of all gifts is eternal life, the living water.

The story is inspirational. Let us look at the divorcée who met the Master at Jacob's well. She had:

I. A religion that had been long ignored.

In her conversation with Jesus she showed that she had a religious problem. "Our fathers worshipped in this mountain; and ye say, that in Jerusalem is the place where men ought to worship" (John 4:20). She had ignored her religion, yet she had a religious hope. "I know the Messiah cometh" (John 4:25).

II. A life in which the fires of passion had burned out.

The woman at the well had yielded herself to passion. She had spent herself in a life of sin.

III. A thirst that had never been quenched.

You cannot satisfy life with the thrills of passion and the possession of material things. The soul longs for something better. This divorcée was a woman of sadness, weariness, and disillusionment. She had not found in life what she really needed.

When Jesus talked to the woman about living water and spiritual worship, hope sprang into her parched soul. She had a thirst that only God could satisfy. Her experience is our experience. God can satisfy the deepest thirst of the soul.

IV. A moment with destiny, and she grasped it.

Notice how Jesus dealt with this divorcée. He appealed to her kindness (John 4:7), then her curiosity (v. 10), then her thirst (v. 14), then her sin (v. 16), and finally to her sense of God (vv. 19–24). He revealed himself as the Messiah (vv. 24–25). She came face-to-face with the truth about the Savior and salvation, and she grasped it.

V. A gospel, which she shared.

She said, "Come, see a man, which told me all things that ever I did: is not this the Christ?" (John 4:29).

A. *Come see a Man who knows you through and through.*

B. *Come see a Man whom you can trust.*

C. *Come see a Man who has life's resources — living water.*

Conclusion

I don't know what the woman at the well sang after she was saved, but it could have been something like this:

> *He was better to me than all my hopes,*
> *Better than all my fears;*
> *For he made a bridge of my broken signs,*
> *And a rainbow of my tears.*

WEDNESDAY EVENING, OCTOBER 6

Title: The Nature of True Religion

Text: "Seek good, and not evil, that ye may live.... Hate the evil, and love the good, and establish judgment in the gate" (**Amos 5:14–15**).

Scripture Reading: Amos 5

Introduction

The prophets have a message for our day and for every day. This is true because they were experts in the knowledge of God rather than being mere predictors of events that were to take place in the future. They brought the truth of God to bear upon the social and political upheavals of their day. They were the communicators of timeless truths concerning God and life. They applied this truth of God to the situation that then existed.

While the circumstances of our day are different, God remains unchanged in both his provisions and in his demands. Man was a sinner in need of God's grace then, and he continues to be a sinner in need of God's grace today. The God of the prophets was a moral God who expected a moral and social response on the part of his people. The God of the prophets and the God and Father of our Lord Jesus Christ continues to expect us not only to look to him in worship but also to relate ourselves to others in terms of justice and mercy.

The prophets lived in a day and time when true religion was neglected. Micah defined true religion in terms of acting justly, loving mercy, and walking humbly before God (Mic. 6:8).

Amos lived in a day, like ours, in which formalism and ritualism were accepted as substitutes for genuine worship. The people were indifferent toward God. They were guilty of compromise; they were given over to idolatry, and they depended on materialism and military might for their security. True religion had almost completely disappeared. In the fifth chapter of his book, Amos emphasizes both the nature of and the need for true religion.

I. The chapter begins with a dirge (vv. 1–3).

A. *Amos sings a song of sadness over his nation.* His spirit wears a shroud as he sings. Because Israel had not heeded the chastisements of God, judgment is going to come (4:6–11).

B. *Calamity is upon them.* The nation will be ravished by an invader.

II. The root cause for the collapse of Israel was a false concept of true religion.

Israel had a false concept of the nature, character, and purpose of God. Consequently, their concept of worship was false and inadequate.

A. *Israel thought that God was limited to certain places and that he could be pleased with the observance of ritual ceremonies (5:4–5, 21–23, 25–26).*

B. *Israel failed to realize that they could not mistreat other human beings without experiencing divine retribution (5:10–13, 27).*

C. *Israel held the erroneous idea that religion and morality were two separate things (5:14–17).* Like many moderns, the people of ancient Israel failed to recognize that the only way by which we can express love for God is by loving people.

D. *Israel failed to recognize that the judgment of God is on an inward basis rather than on an external basis (5:18–20).* They had the erroneous idea that because they were the people of God, he would bless them on this basis. They failed to recognize that God looked on the heart and that God held his people responsible for a proper response to his grace.

III. Superficial reform will fail to meet the need of the human heart (5:21–27).

Amos brings a message of warning concerning a doom that is inevitable if the people make only a superficial response to the moral demands of a holy God. It will take something infinitely more than better attendance at their places of worship and more generous offerings. Something other than an external expression of religion is demanded. There must be an inward change of the heart in reference to the will of God if the individual is to please God and if the nation is to be spared.

Conclusion

Amos expresses the need for a radical turning to God in repentance and faith (5:6–9, 14–15). The situation is so serious that Amos hesitates to make a definite promise that catastrophe can be avoided. Note his uncertainty at this point in verse 15. He declares that if this repentance takes place, "it may be that the LORD God of hosts will be gracious unto the remnant of Joseph." There is a faint hope that the nation can be spared the catastrophe that seemingly is inevitable. Only true religion can save them. Does God speak through Amos to our day?

SUNDAY MORNING, OCTOBER 10

Title: Great Crowds Followed Him

Text: "When he came down from the mountain, great crowds followed him" **(Matt. 8:1 RSV).**

Scripture Reading: Matthew 5:1–2; 7:28–8:1

Hymns: "Come, Thou Almighty King," Anonymous

       "Christ Receiveth Sinful Men," Neumeister

       "My Savior's Love," Gabriel

Offertory Prayer: Holy Father, you have been so gracious and generous to us. Today we thank you for the glad consciousness of forgiven sin. We thank you for the precious privilege of being members of your family. We rejoice in the privilege of serving you and working with you to help others come to know the great salvation that is available through Jesus Christ. Accept our tithes and offerings. In Jesus' name. Amen.

Introduction

The passage of Scripture that falls between Matthew 5:1 and 8:1 is known around the world as the "Sermon on the Mount." Perhaps it would be correct to call it the "Lecture on the Plain," because our Lord was teaching rather than preaching.

It is significant that this message was delivered to the crowds that had begun to follow him. It is significant that once he had completed this message, the crowds followed him down from the mountain.

The really significant thing is that the crowds continue to follow Jesus Christ after nearly twenty long centuries have rolled by. By the grace of God, it has been given to us to be among the crowds that follow him and that listen to him.

What is the secret of this magnetism of the Teacher who spoke these remarkable words? What is it that causes crowds to follow him after twenty centuries? Why is it that you and I continue to follow him?

I. We follow him because of who he is.

Certain celebrities attract a crowd wherever they go. To enjoy any privacy at all, they must conceal their identity and their presence.

Jesus was and is the God-man. He was the eternal God clothed in a human body. He was the Messiah promised by the prophets. He was the one for whom Israel had been waiting.

Peter verbalized the conviction of his heart when he declared, "You are the Christ, the Son of the living God" (Matt. 16:16 NIV).

Jesus was more than just a good man. Jesus was more than just a great teacher. Jesus was more than just the best man who ever lived. He was God in human flesh. Because of who he is, we continue to follow him.

II. We follow him because of what he did.

Across the length and breadth of the United States, whenever Arnold Palmer was on the golf course at the height of his career, there was always a group of followers called "Arnie's army." They followed him because of who he was but also because of what he did on the golf course.

Around the world Muhammad Ali was a famous character who enjoyed great popularity in spite of his reputation as being "a big mouth"–or perhaps partly because of it. He enjoyed this tremendous popularity because of what he achieved as a boxer. He enjoyed the distinction of being a champion's champ in the boxing ring. Because of what he did there, he has always had a following.

We follow Jesus Christ because of what he did during his lifetime. He ministered to the sick. He comforted the grieving. He gave hope to the discouraged.

316

He fed the hungry. But his greatest achievements were on a cross and in a tomb. On the cross he took our place, demonstrating the height and depth and breadth of the divine love for unworthy sinners. On the cross he paid our debt, dying as a substitute for each one of us.

In the tomb our Lord conquered death and the grave. From the tomb he demonstrated the fact that death will not have final victory over those who trust him. By conquering death and the grave, he became a living Savior, able to save unto the uttermost those who would come unto God by him.

Because of what he did, we continue to follow him after nearly two thousand years.

III. We follow him because of what he can do.

We follow him because he is able to forgive our sins and make us clean and acceptable to the Father God.

We follow him because he can give the gift of eternal life and cause us to love the things that are lovable in the eyes of God. He gives us a new quality of life, a new kind of life.

We follow him because he is able to give us victory over the evil within us and the evil that threatens us from without.

We follow him because he is able to live a life of poise in the midst of turmoil. He is able to help us be productive and victorious in living the abundant life. We follow him because it is through him that we can achieve our highest possible personhood.

IV. We follow him because we need him.

Children need their parents. A husband needs his wife. A wife needs her husband. We need our friends. We need certain professionals who can provide us with services in times of need. All of us are in need of others.

More than anyone else in all existence, Jesus Christ is the one we need.

We follow him because we need him. With selfish motives and with the best of interests, we follow him because "it pays to serve Jesus. It pays every day. It pays every step of the way."

V. We follow him because he needs us.

We would not be presumptuous in making statements like this concerning Jesus Christ. It is in the divine plan that God uses men and women to share the good news of his love with others. God could have chosen to use the angels to tell the message of his love, but he didn't.

God could have chosen to use the sky as a great television screen on which to reveal the message of his love, but he didn't.

We follow him because he needs us. If we do not follow him, the work he began and wishes to continue will come to an end. George Buttrick wrote, "Unless Christianity begins with the individual, it does not begin; but if Christianity ends with the individual, it ends." We follow him because he needs us.

VI. We follow him because others need him.

People have many needs. They need education, justice, jobs, medical care, insurance. They need at least some of the gadgets that are available in today's world. They need food, clothing, and shelter.

Humankind's greatest need is for a right relationship with God. This comes through repentance toward God and faith in the Lord Jesus Christ.

You meet others' greatest need when you help them to receive the forgiveness of sin and the gift of new life that comes only through Jesus Christ.

Conclusion

Crowds followed Jesus eagerly during his earthly ministry. Crowds have followed him zealously through the centuries. You and I can rejoice over the privilege of being among the crowds that followed him.

If you have not yet begun to follow him, right now would be a good time to forsake the way of life that ends in disappointment and come to him who alone can give hope and peace and joy. Become a true follower of Jesus Christ because of who he is, because of what he has done, and because of what he can do in your life.

SUNDAY EVENING, OCTOBER 10

Title: A Politician Meets the Master

Text: "And he made haste, and came down, and received him joyfully" (**Luke 19:6**).

Scripture Reading: Luke 19:1–10

Introduction

"I guess you are wondering what I am doing here at six o'clock in the morning watering this sycamore tree. You surely must be a stranger in town or you would not be looking at me with such amazement. Let me finish pouring this bucket of water on the tree, and then I want to tell you about the tree."

I stood back for a moment and watched with amazement as this small man poured water around the roots of the tree. He gently touched and caressed the trunk of the tree with his hands. He stood there in silence and with bowed head as if in prayer and deep contemplation. I was a stranger in town, and I was witnessing a strange sight. Had this small man lost his senses over this short sycamore tree with its thick, forked branches?

He finally finished his ritual and picked up his bucket and walked over to me. "You are a stranger in Jericho," he said, "Welcome to our city. My name is Zacchaeus." I greeted him with an apology for intruding on what obviously had been an act of love.

I. "Let me tell you about my city."

"Jericho is a city of priests and Levites. Much Hebrew history has been recorded here. Jericho was first captured by Joshua as the children of Israel

318

opened their campaign to take Canaan [Josh. 6]. Five miles east of Jericho you will find the Jordan River. John the Baptist baptized there, and Jesus was baptized there. It is indeed a famous spot. The Dead Sea is found seven miles south of Jericho. The water is salty, and no fish live in its waters. See those rocky, barren mountains over there? That is where Jesus was tempted. The people used to call that mountain Quarantina; now thy refer to it as the Mount of Temptation. Say, did you know that Jericho was Rahab's city?"

Zacchaeus stopped talking long enough to catch his breath. I thought that Jericho was indeed a beautiful historic city, an oasis city, in the midst of a barren desert. Zacchaeus started talking again.

II. "Let me tell you about myself."

A. *"I am a Jew. I believe I told you my name is Zacchaeus. My name means 'pure.'*
B. *"I am a chief publican.* Do you know what it means to be a publican? A publican is a tax collector. I really wish I had another job, because people hate tax collectors. Tax collectors do not find many friends among the people. There are two reasons why people hate me:
   1. "I represent the Roman government, the establishment.
   2. "I also used to collect more than just the per capita tax. Some people felt that I was a robber, an extortioner.
C. *"I am rich.* Even though I do not like my job, I will have to admit that it is a good-paying job. I have become rich by collecting taxes.
D. *"I am little of stature.* If you are to understand about that sycamore tree, you have to understand about my height. I am extremely short. I don't know why. One thing I do know; God made me this way."

 I started to leave and thanked Zacchaeus for telling me about Jericho and himself. As I was leaving, he caught me by my coat sleeve and said, "There is one other thing I must tell you."

III. "I want to tell you about my Savior."

"The reason I love the sycamore tree so much is because it was here that I first came in contact with Jesus, the Savior. He is the most unusual man I have ever known. In fact, he is more than a man; he is the Savior of men. He is God's Son. "Let me tell you some of the things I know and like about Jesus.

A. *"He seeks us out.* When he came to Jericho a short time before he was crucified, he was the most popular and, at the same time, the most hated man in Palestine. The crowds were so great that a little fellow like me didn't stand a chance of seeing him. Out of my curiosity and determination, I climbed up into that sycamore tree to see Jesus. When he came by, he said to me, 'Zacchaeus, make haste, and come down for today I must abide at thy house' [Luke 19:5].

 "I have often wondered how he knew my name. I have a feeling he knows all about us.

B. *"Another thing I like about Jesus is that he commands in terms of necessity.* He said to me, 'I must abide at thy house today.' What he says, he means. He commands in terms of necessity.

C. *"He is kind.* His way is the way of kindness. He was so tender with me.

D. *"Another thing I like about Jesus is that he changes people; he saves people.* I had always grasped for money, but after he changed me, I was giving it away. What happened to me is best expressed by his own words: 'This day is salvation come to this house' [Luke 19:9]. I am saved; I am a changed man.

E. *"Another thing I like about Jesus is that he gives joy to the sinner.* Jesus did not come to make us solemn and sad.

F. *"I know you have to go, but there is one other thing I like about Jesus, and that is that his mission is our mission.* I heard him say, 'For the Son of man is come to seek and to save that which was lost' [Luke 19:10]. By the way, mister, are you a follower of Jesus Christ? Has he saved you?"

Tears were now streaming down my face. "Yes, Zacchaeus, I am a Christian! He called me to preach, and I am so happy in him!"

WEDNESDAY EVENING, OCTOBER 13

Title: At Ease in Zion

Text: "Woe to them that are at ease in Zion, and trust in the mountain of Samaria, which are named chief of the nations, to whom the house of Israel came!" **(Amos 6:1)**.

Scripture Reading: Amos 6

Introduction

Amos brings an indictment against his nation. He declares that they will reap the harvest of their love of selfish luxury. He indicts the people with being guilty of apathy and indifference toward God and toward the state of the nation.

I. Conditions of complacency described (6:1–6).

A. *Their customs, dress, and perfumes were the richest (v. 4).*

B. *They enjoyed the richest foods and rarest delicacies available (v. 4).*

C. *The pursuit of pleasure was their chief objective (v. 5).*

D. *They were given over to drunkenness (v. 6).*

II. The causes of this complacency.

The people were living in a postwar period when their nation enjoyed unrivaled national power and unparalleled prosperity. Religious activities were popular.

A. *They placed great trust in military resources for security (6:1).*

B. *They had a tendency to dismiss all serious thought concerning the possibility of peril for their nation (6:3).*

C. *The pursuit of profit and prosperity was of supreme importance (6:4).*

D. *Their hard-heartedness was indicated by the lack of grief and compassion for the sickness of their nation (6:6).*

III. Calamity and captivity were to befall the nation.

Amos was probably considered as a radical, pessimistic, religious fanatic who did not know what he was talking about. He warned his nation concerning the judgment of God and the advance of the enemy (6:1, 7, 9–11, 14).

Conclusion

Some people look upon the prophets as prophets of doom who offered no hope to their nation. The fact that God was using them as his spokesmen would indicate that there was at least a little hope.

SUNDAY MORNING, OCTOBER 17

Title: The Falling of the Wall

Text: "Then Peter opened his mouth, and said, Of a truth I perceive that God is no respecter of persons: But in every nation, he that feareth him, and worketh righteousness, is accepted with him" **(Acts 10:34–35).**

Scripture Reading: Acts 10:25–48

Hymns: "The Church's One Foundation," Stone

"Must I Go, and Empty-Handed?" Luther

"Send the Light," Gabriel

Offertory Prayer: O Lord, our God, we thank you for the demonstration of your love and concern for us. We pray that as you have taught us by your Son, Jesus, how great your love for us is, that we can learn completely that this love is for every life. When we come now, O God, to this opportunity to give unto you of our material blessings, let us understand that your purpose includes all people to the uttermost parts of the earth. We here dedicate these gifts of our hand to extend your kingdom by your direction and by your Spirit unto the uttermost parts of the earth. As we give these material blessings to you, let us give of our own persons to the needs of lives whom we touch. In Jesus' name we pray. Amen.

Introduction

The message of the "good news" is a universal one. God intended this message to include all people everywhere. Written at the highest point in the gospel is "Whosoever will may come." The young church was faced with what seemed like an impossibility at this point, for there were barriers on the horizon of their mission that needed to be broken through: the sex barrier—male and female were not equal; economic barriers; political barriers—conflicts between Romans, Greeks, and Jews; and cultural barriers, such as the militarism of Rome, the intellectualism of Greece, and the religious orientation of Israel. The inclination of such decisive barriers is one of exclusiveness. Israel tended to shut out others.

If the church is to be effective in bearing the Good News to this earth, similar barriers must be broken through.

The event recorded in Acts 10 is the story of the work of God moving to new frontiers. It is a story of adventure, faith, courage, and personal relationships.

I. The human situation: Pointed up in two men.

These men resided only thirty miles apart, but by reason of barriers they were at opposite poles in their ability to communicate.

A. *Cornelius was a Roman citizen, Italian-born, subject to Roman government, and oriented in the backdrop of Grecian culture.* He lived in the city of Caesarea, a Roman capital. He was a leader of men, a man of wealth, and a man of great influence.

B. *Simon Peter was a Jew, a common fisherman, one who carried serious loyalty to a covenant given to Israel by Jehovah, and one who was dedicated and loyal to the moral laws of his religious forebears.*

There is great diversity here. We see two men close together and yet far apart. Is not this a parable of our current situation? Our world has come close together. Mass media and modern communication give us the opportunity of being seen and heard by multitudes, yet because of barriers, the people of the church stand with great diversity over against the people of the world. There are national barriers, a culture gap, sex barriers, economic barriers, and political and moral barriers. The question for our time is, How does the Lord's person relate the good news of God to people with whom he or she finds it difficult to communicate?

II. The divine communication.

A. *To Cornelius.* God intervenes on the scene of the human situation. Cornelius was at prayer. He was expressing a spiritual need; there was a vacuum in his soul. He was looking in the right direction for spiritual assistance — up to God — and God came down to him! God gave him two things: a recognition (Acts 10:4) and instruction. He told him to send to the seaport town of Joppa and seek out the man Simon Peter, who was residing at the home of Simon the tanner.

B. *To Simon Peter.* Here is the man of the church. God came to him in a vision. Three times he caused the sheet filled with a variety of animals to be lowered and commanded Simon, "Kill and eat!" Peter insisted that he would be loyal to his tradition and refused. God instructed him, "Call thou not common what I have made clean." Peter was beginning to learn that God looks upon all people, regardless of culture, nationality, religious creed, or moral circumstance in a different way than humans do. He instructed Peter to go with the visitors from Caesarea.

C. *The intervention of the Spirit of God is the third factor in the picture of impossibilities.* Here is one man with a spiritual need and another man whose responsibility it is to communicate the Good News. It was the Spirit of God who put these two men face-to-face.

III. The consequent fellowship: These two men became brothers.

A. *The confrontation.* Your imagination can give you a vivid picture of the scene that happened in the home of Cornelius. We have two men facing each other over insurmountable barriers! How would they react?

B. *Simon Peter communicated: He told Cornelius what news there is from God concerning man's spiritual need.* He communicated to this man that God is love—that God loves all people regardless of their background. But Simon Peter went further that day than he had ever gone before with the gospel of God. He added a third factor: God wants us to love each other as he has loved us!

C. *What does this story say of God's church?* There is one bond in common, and that is that each is loved by God and bound together in a mutual fellowship and given a commission to bear the good news of God to others.

Conclusion

The church in which God is involved these days would have to be that community of redeemed people who follow divine guidance by his Spirit and face insurmountable barriers, expecting again the falling of the wall!

SUNDAY EVENING, OCTOBER 17

Title: A Man with Means Meets the Master

Text: "And when he had gone forth into the way, there came one running, and kneeled to him, and asked him, Good Master, what shall I do that I may inherit eternal life?" (**Mark 10:17**).

Scripture Reading: Mark 10:17–31

Introduction

The rich young ruler was a fascinating young man. He possessed all the characteristics of charm. He was clean, discerning, humble, courageous, and prominent (Mark 10:17–20). He was a "ruler"—a leader, a presider over the synagogue, a member of the Sanhedrin. He possessed character, worldly position, courteousness, reverence, aspiration, and wealth. Let us look at him as he meets the Master.

I. A man with means meets the Master and realizes that the Master loves him.

Great opportunities are created by wealth (Luke 16:9), and great perils are created by wealth (Luke 12:15). It is difficult for a rich man to be saved (Mark 10:23–27).

Often rich men feel unloved. The rich young ruler will not ever be able to say he was unloved by Jesus. The Scriptures bear record to the love Jesus had for this man: "Then Jesus beholding him loved him" (Mark 10:21).

Jesus loves the good and the bad. He may rebuke, but he loves. Jesus' love is firm and can be severe; it never softens the requirements of discipleship.

II. A man with means meets the Master and knows something is lacking in his life.

The rich young ruler possessed many fine characteristics, but something was lacking in his life. He said to Jesus: "What lack I yet?" (Matt. 19:20). Jesus told him he lacked one thing: "Yet lackest thou one thing" (Luke 18:22). Scholars divide themselves when they discuss what he lacked. Some say he lacked poverty. However, the Scriptures indicate that he lacked following Jesus (Mark 10:21). He lacked a Savior and eternal life. He lacked putting his life under the Lord's control. He lacked submitting to his authority, crowning him King. Yes, he lacked following Jesus.

You can have all else, but unless you follow Jesus, you have nothing!

III. A man with means meets the Master and comprehends that being good does not make one a child of God.

The rich young ruler believed in God, believed in the law of God, and had been obedient to that part of the law that had affected his relationship with others. He had not committed murder or adultery, nor stole, nor borne false witness. He had honored father and mother and loved his neighbor as himself.

Having done all these things, he still was not a child of God.

IV. A man with means meets the Master and discerns that a good man can be wrong.

As wonderful and as good as the rich young ruler was, he was wrong about several things:

A. *He was wrong about salvation (Mark 10:17).*
B. *He was wrong about goodness (Mark 10:20).* He was satisfied with external respectability. He needed internal cleansing. He needed a new heart to be good.
C. *He was wrong about Jesus (Mark 10:17).* Jesus is more than good; he is God!
D. *He was wrong about money (Mark 10:22).*

V. A man with means meets the Master and is made aware that life needs control from one other than self.

Human life is too great for human management. If we are to find pardon, peace, power, and poise, we must seek the Lord's help. To attain the full realization of life's capacities and possibilities, we need the Lord's help and guidance. We need an authority greater than ourselves, whose ability is transcending, whose love is certain.

VI. A man with means meets the Master and sees that he must surrender what hinders him from following Jesus (Mark 10:22, 27–31).

A. *We may have to surrender money to follow Jesus.*

B. *We may have to surrender loved ones to follow Jesus.*

C. *We may have to surrender our homes (lands) to follow Jesus.*

D. *We may have to surrender acceptability (be persecuted) to follow Jesus.*

E. *We may have to surrender our lives to follow Jesus.*

The rich young ruler's money stood between him and eternal life. If something else had been there, he would have had to give it up. We must surrender whatever keeps us from following Jesus.

VII. A man with means meets the Master and understands that to reject Jesus means sorrow.

"And when he heard this, he was very sorrowful: for he was very rich" (Luke 18:23). The light faded from his face and the hope went out of his heart when Jesus told him to sell what he had, give it to the poor, and come take up the cross and follow him. His bubble burst, his earnestness evaporated; he kept his possessions, and he lost Christ. How tragic! He went away sorrowful. When a person turns away from Jesus, it always spells sorrow.

Conclusion

To gain Jesus is to gain everything. To lose Jesus is to lose everything. Hear what Paul said about his loss and his gain: "I count all things but loss for the excellency of the knowledge of Christ Jesus my Lord: for whom I have suffered the loss of all things, and do count them but dung, that I may win Christ, And be found in him, not having mine own righteousness, which is of the law, but that which is through the faith of Christ, the righteousness which is of God by faith" (Phil. 3:8–9).

Claim Jesus as your Savior. "The gift of God is eternal life through Jesus Christ our Lord" (Rom. 6:23).

WEDNESDAY EVENING, OCTOBER 20

Title: The God of Amos

Text: "Now therefore hear thou the word of the LORD" (**Amos 7:16**).

Scripture Reading: Amos 7–9

Introduction

The last three chapters of the book of Amos are almost impossible to arrange in logical order. They contain a series of visions and announcements of judgment upon the nation because of its wickedness, idolatry, and rebellion against God. By studying these last three chapters it is possible to gain an understanding of Amos's concept of God, which is very profitable for us today. God does not change in his nature and in his requirements of people. If the same conditions prevailed today that prevailed in Amos's day, we could be sure that God would deal with our nation and with us as individuals as he did back then.

A proper understanding of the nature of God is always important. Let us try to discover something about God's nature as Amos understood it.

I. God is personal (7:3, 6).

To Amos, God was more than just the principle behind the universe. He was more than a mechanic who had created a machine and set it in motion. Amos believed that God was active in the processes of history and that he was near and concerned.

II. God is omniscient (7:7–8).

Throughout these visions one cannot help but get the impression that God is aware of all that concerns his people Israel. He knows all about them. He has diagnosed the illness that plagues the nation. He knows both the good and the evil. He is the God from whom nothing is hidden.

III. God is omnipotent (7:9).

God is going to bring great judgment upon the house of Jeroboam. Jeroboam was the most powerful king that northern Israel had had. God's power was superior to the power of Jeroboam.

IV. God is righteous and just.

A. *The vision of the locusts (7:1–3).*
B. *The vision of the drought (7:4–6).*
C. *The vision of the wall and plumb line (7:7–9).*
D. *The vision of a basket of summer fruit (8:1–13).*
    1. The end has come for Israel (8:1–3).
    2. Fresh denunciations of sin (8:4–14).
E. *The vision of the smitten altar (9:1–6).*

V. God will ultimately accomplish his purpose of grace (9:9–15).

The message of Amos is primarily a message of doom and judgment upon a wicked, idolatrous nation. One must look closely for even a faint ray of hope in the message of the prophet.

When we come to the close of the book, there is a message of hope and promise. Some students have seriously questioned whether this is a part of the message of the prophet who preached the previous chapters. They have contended that it must have been added by some other prophet because it contains a message of hope.

Conclusion

That there was absolutely no hope would be to misunderstand the nature and character of the God of Israel. He is a God of grace and mercy. He is the God of redemption who wants to forgive and redeem. Amos preached the message of doom in the hope that the people would repent. God always responds with forgiveness and redemption when people genuinely repent.

SUNDAY MORNING, OCTOBER 24

Title: The Whole World Is Watching

Text: "For there stood by me this night the angel of God, whose I am, and whom I serve, saying, Fear not, Paul; thou must be brought before Caesar: and, lo, God hath given thee all them that sail with thee" (**Acts 27:23 – 24**).

Scripture Reading: Acts 27:21 – 26

Hymns: "We've a Story to Tell," Nichol

"Footsteps of Jesus," Slade

"Wherever He Leads I'll Go," McKinney

Offertory Prayer: (Precede offertory prayer by quoting Matthew 28:19.) Our Father, we hear again your instructions for our service. We understand this commission to be directed toward your people to bear the good news to all nations. We have heard again the assurance of your Word, "I am with you always." Here, now, we claim your presence, and with your presence let us understand the necessity of this commission for each of our lives in mission responsibilities. Receive now, O God, these gifts we bring here to you. We ask your blessing on your people wherever they are in your world. Whatever else we have to do in your kingdom service, let us always keep at a point of high priority our mission and your commission. We ask these things in Jesus' name and for his sake. Amen.

Introduction

Without question, the easiest place for the Christian to be on the Lord's Day is in the Lord's house at the time of worship. The environment and circumstances make it simple for us to lift high our voices in song, in testimony, in sermon, and in teaching.

But how does it go on Monday? And what is the witness of the Christian in the lonesome moment when he realizes that he is standing alone? This is the scene in Acts 27. Paul was on a prison ship and was apparently the only representative of Jehovah God. This is not too unusual for the average Christian. Sometimes the Christian is the only Christian in the crowd. It may be at work, in the classroom, or even in one's own family circle.

All eyes were on the apostle Paul while the ship was being tossed toward what they thought was complete destruction. Is there any word from the Lord through the witness of the Christian when he is the only Christian in the crowd? The eyes of the world are on him. Often the eyes of the world are on you, and in that moment there are some questions of basic priorities. What factors does the Christian have to have to fortify his heart and encourage him to understand Christian witness in this situation?

327

I. A lofty concept of the lordship of Jesus.

Who am I? Whom do I serve? To whom do I belong? Referring to the lordship of Jesus, Paul said, "whose I am and whom I serve."

At a moment such as this, my rights, my thoughts, mean nothing. I belong to God. I belong to God first. Nothing else can have priority!

II. A high regard for human personality.

Paul said that God had assured his heart, "I have given thee all them that sail with thee." When Christians become overaccustomed to dealing with great numbers and great multitudes, they are apt to miss individual faces in the crowd. When we stand alone, we have to understand that every face in that crowd represents a human personality whom God loved and for whom he gave himself at Calvary's cross.

III. A lofty concept of spiritual fellowship.

We find it too simple these days to be the modern Elijah who runs and hides in the cave and complains to God, "I and I only am left to serve you." We are not really alone. Somewhere in this world there are thousands who have not "bowed the knee to Baal." The early Christians faced a world infested with serious persecution and much danger. They found practical ways of relating themselves to others who had come to know God through Jesus too.

Christians must be individuals in their world, but they must also be individuals related to other individuals by the common bond of an experience of grace by faith in God through Jesus.

IV. An obligation and command to witness.

Those early Christians stood firm on the words of Jesus, "Ye shall be my witnesses." They understood that this was a command that they must take personally and individually. Why did the early Christians give themselves in a sacrificial manner to the cause of Christ and move in strange directions in his name? The answer is obvious: they felt a divine obligation; God had commanded them. They understood further that the glorious good news of God through Jesus is "the power of God unto salvation, to every one who believeth."

Conclusion

There are many things that occupy the attention of the Christian. Fundamental to one's witness are these four spiritual anchors: (1) the lordship of Jesus for one's life, (2) a high value for the human person, (3) a dedication and loyalty with others involved in a spiritual fellowship, (4) the resounding urgency of the divine command, "And ye shall be my witness."

When the doors of the church are closed behind Christians following worship on the Lord's Day, they face their finest hour. Across the days of each week are many opportunities. When we understand who we are, why we are here, what love God has for every life, and that we are frail vessels of earth entrusted with divine treasures, our witness can have a genuine uplift!

SUNDAY EVENING, OCTOBER 24

Title: A Scholar Meets the Master

Text: "Except a man be born again, he cannot see the kingdom of God" **(John 3:3)**.

Scripture Reading: John 3:1–21

Introduction

The Bible identifies Nicodemus as "a man of the Pharisees" (John 3:1). There were three prominent parties of Judaism at the time of Christ—Pharisees, Sadducees, and Essenes. The Pharisees were the most influential. They were the Separatists, Puritans, and Fundamentalists of their day. They believed in predestination, immortality, and reward for good works. They accepted the Old Testament Scriptures and believed in Jewish messianic hope. The word *legalists* best describes the Pharisees.

The Bible identifies Nicodemus as "a ruler of the Jews" (John 3:31). This means that he was a commander, chief, or leader. The word *ruler* was used to identify members of the Sanhedrin.

The Bible identifies Nicodemus as "a master of Israel" (John 3:10). Some call Nicodemus a rabbi; others call him a theological professor. The word *master* means a teacher. He was a well-known and accepted teacher of Israel.

There are many things we learn about Nicodemus from the Bible: He was a man of discernment and caution (John 3:2); a man of sincerity (3:9); a man of justice (7:51); a man of love, emotion, and a great heart (19:39); and a man of confidence (3:3).

Nicodemus was a scholar who met the Master. There are some wonderful truths in the meeting between Nicodemus and Jesus. Let us look at some of them.

I. A scholar meets the Master and understands he must be born from above.

Even though Nicodemus was highly educated, theologically trained, and a religious teacher, he did not understand that a man must be born from above. Jesus told him three times that he "must be born from above" (John 3:3, 5, 7). Nicodemus recognized Jesus as a teacher from above but could not understand the birth from above. Natural man, regardless of training, cannot understand the teachings of Jesus until he is born from above.

Every person must be born from above in order to see the kingdom of God.

II. A scholar meets the Master in order to understand spiritual truths.

There are many great spiritual truths in this passage for all of us. Consider them:

A. *One must have intellectual activity to understand spiritual truths (John 3:10).*

B. *It takes the death of Jesus to bring eternal life to a person (John 3:12–16).*

C. *The new birth is necessary for all (John 3:3).*

329

III. A scholar meets the Master and understands that light and life come to those who make a start.

Jesus gives himself to those who are honest. Nicodemus eventually found three things as a result of his visit with Jesus: revelation, illumination, and deliverance. Jesus blesses those who make a start.

IV. A scholar meets the Master and is taught the way of salvation.

So many people do not know the way of salvation. Even though Nicodemus was a rabbi, he did not know how to be saved. Hear the Master teach the scholar how to be saved: "And as Moses lifted up the serpent in the wilderness, even so must the Son of man be lifted up: that whosoever believeth in him should not perish, but have eternal life" (John 3:14–15). "He that believeth on him is not condemned: but he that believeth not is condemned already, because he hath not believed in the name of the only begotten Son of God" (John 3:18). Nicodemus had not believed in Jesus, consequently he needed to be born from above.

V. A scholar meets the Master and does his own thinking.

Someone has said that the three *R*s of traditionalism are rote, rut, and rot. Nicodemus broke with tradition and came to the truth. There are none so hard to reach as those whose minds are filled with error. We must think for ourselves when we meet the Master.

VI. A scholar meets the Master and shows his colors.

Nicodemus is mentioned in only three passages in the Bible (John 3:1–21; 7:45–52; 19:38–43). In all three references, Nicodemus relates to Jesus. Once he is talking with him, and two times he is doing something for him. I believe that Nicodemus has been too severely criticized. It is true that he was a secret disciple, and there is no premium on secret discipleship. However, there were three instances when Nicodemus did show his colors: At Olivet (John 3:1–21), at the meeting of the Sanhedrin (7:45–52), and at the cross (19:38–42).

George Pentecost used to tell of a timid little girl who came to the leader of a meeting and said, "Will you pray for me at the meeting, please, but do not mention my name." When every head was bowed and there was perfect silence, he prayed for her, saying, "O Lord, there is a little girl here who does not want her name known, but Thou dost know her; save her precious soul." There was stillness for a moment, and then way back in the congregation a little girl arose and in a pleading voice said, "Please, it's me, Jesus, it's me." She did not want to have a doubt. She wanted to be saved, and she was not ashamed to say, "Jesus, it's me" (Walter B. Knight, *Knight's Master Book of New Illustrations* [Grand Rapids: Eerdmans, 1963], 101).

Conclusion

Nicodemus said at last, "Jesus, I am your man, your follower." Every scholar and every person of every profession should make this declaration. Will you do it today?

WEDNESDAY EVENING, OCTOBER 27

Title: Can Churchgoing Be Sinful?

Text: " 'Go to Bethel and sin; go to Gilgal and sin yet more. Bring your sacrifices every morning, your tithes every three years. Burn leavened bread as a thank offering and brag about your freewill offerings—boast about them, you Israelites, for this is what you love to do,' declares the Sovereign LORD" (**Amos 4:4–5 NIV**).

Scripture Reading: Amos 4

Introduction

Regular attendance at the worship services of a church is one of the normal characteristics of one who is considered to be genuinely Christian. Is it possible that we have emphasized regular attendance at worship services at the cost of something else? Is it always wise to judge the quality of one's faith in terms of loyalty to the stated services of the congregation with which he or she worships?

Something is wrong with the emphasis that leaves the impression that regular church attendance is the hallmark of excellence as far as Christian involvement is concerned. To accept the idea that mere church attendance is a full expression of one's faith is to live under the illusion that the rest of the week is outside of the will of God and outside of his concern.

On one occasion, our Lord used irony to portray the emptiness and meaninglessness of ritualistic prayer and worship (Luke 18:10–12). A Pharisee came before the Lord and thanked the Lord that he was not like other men. A publican who was also in the temple was vividly aware of his unworthiness and made a sincere plea for pardon. He had a genuine experience with God. His experience was a transforming one with the living God, while the experience of the Pharisee but confirmed him in his pious self-righteousness.

Amos used great irony and invited the people of his day to go to church and to increase their sinfulness. Evidently there was something radically wrong with their worship activities. Is it possible that we fall into the same category?

I. When quantity is substituted for quality, a church is in great danger.

It is one thing to assemble a crowd. It is something entirely different for that crowd to become a congregation of worshipers. We must not assume that because we are a part of the crowd that we have had a genuine experience with God.

Instead of being primarily concerned with the quantity of the crowd that is worshiping together, the emphasis needs to be placed on the genuineness of the faith and commitment of those who have come together for an experience with God.

II. When form is substituted for content and when externals are accepted for spiritual realities, the church is in danger.

Amos lived in a time in which the places of worship were crowded with those who had come to bring their offerings and sacrifices. They went through the pomp and ceremony of worship. These experiences were very satisfying to the

331

people involved. However, God was not only disturbed but also displeased. The worship activities of the people were not productive of moral and ethical conduct on the part of those who went to the places of worship.

We need to question the genuineness of any experience that we consider to be a worship experience if it doesn't produce a change in our lives or in the lives of others about us.

III. When the bringing of tithes and offerings is substituted for a total commitment to the living God, a church is in danger.

One of the perils that we all face is the peril of substituting a part for the whole. There are some who labor under the erroneous idea that if they are regular in attendance at worship services and if they are faithful in bringing their tithes and offerings, then they have fulfilled their obligations to God and have met their responsibility for a lost world. The bringing of tithes and offerings is of vast importance, but this is just a part of the whole of the commitment of the genuine Christian. These should be symbols of our complete dedication to the will of God and to ministry for him in every area of life including the so-called secular part of life.

We must guard against the idea that one-seventh of our time and one-tenth of our money belongs to God and that we are free to do as we wish with the balance.

IV. A church is in great danger if it permits itself to become an end within itself.

Christ placed the church in the world to be a channel through which his redemptive work could be carried forward. He did not intend for it to become a repository into which he would bestow his blessings and upon which people would bestow their affection and energy.

The church is not to be thought of as a shrine that exists for its own purpose. Instead, it should be thought of as a force through which the people of God unite together and cooperate with each other in doing the work of God in today's world.

We need to correct our impressions concerning church work and the work of the church. There is much confusion at this point. To teach a Sunday school class, to sing in the choir, to work with a youth group probably falls in the category of church work rather than the work of the church. The work of the church is that which the people of God do during the week in the community and in the world.

Conclusion

The people during Amos's day were great as far as doing church work was concerned. They flocked to church on the Sabbath and on feast days. They brought offerings in abundance. And they probably were greatly surprised to learn that God was not pleased with these (Amos 5:21–23).

God was primarily concerned with a moral and spiritual response on the part of the people. Because God is a moral God, he was concerned about their making a moral response to his will (Amos 5:24).

332

We must beware lest our worship activities as individuals and as a church become an empty form that does not produce moral change within our lives. God would speak through Amos to us at this point.

SUNDAY MORNING, OCTOBER 31

Title: A Call to Renewal

Text: "And they shall build the old wastes, they shall raise up the former desolations, and they shall repair the waste cities, the desolations of many generations" **(Isa. 61:4).**

Scripture Reading: Isaiah 61:1–6

Hymns: "The Church's One Foundation," Stone

"A Mighty Fortress Is Our God," Luther

"Glorious Things of Thee Are Spoken," Newton

Offertory Prayer: Lord God of our fathers, who in all ages has preserved your church, we come to you now in humility and gratitude to acknowledge your goodness to us. Not according to our deserving have you blessed us but according to your grace and your infinite goodness. As we present our tithes and offerings to you, may we give ourselves in renewal to you, through Jesus Christ our Lord. Amen.

Introduction

The second half of the prophecy of Isaiah (chaps. 40–66) presents the message of the Suffering Servant and gives the people in exile a message of hope as they look toward a time of restoration. The message of each of the prophets must be approached in a threefold manner for proper interpretation: The message was always contextual—it had meaning for the time and circumstances in which it was spoken or written; it was often futuristic—it had reference to distant times in the future; and it had a timeless relevance—its principles are applicable for every age.

The context of our message today in its historical setting had to do with the time of the exile. Judah had been taken into Babylonian captivity, Persia had swallowed up the remains of ancient Chaldea, and now Cyrus had come to the Persian throne with a hospitable attitude toward the Jews. He looked with favor upon their return, and the message of Isaiah in its contextual setting was a word of admonition to return and rebuild "the old wastes," to "raise up the former desolations … [and] repair the waste cities, the desolations of many generations."

I. A time of spiritual exile.

The postapostolic years in the history of Christianity may be likened largely to the spiritual experience of Judah when she was taken into Babylonian exile. The things that Isaiah saw for Judah (chaps. 1–39) included perversion of religious

333

practices, breakdown of personal morality, malpractice in public offices (especially in the courts), and idolatry.

A. *Pagan domination.* Just as paganism became the order of the day in Isaiah's time, so in the second and third centuries of the Christian era pagan domination enslaved Christianity. Severe persecutions marked the attacks of godless leaders in the Roman Empire as attempts were made to stamp out the Christian faith. Just as in the days of Isaiah, religious truth was corrupted and emperor worship was substituted for Christianity.

B. *Development of the papacy.* During the years AD 325–1215, the Christian faith truly went into "spiritual exile." The onset of the "dark ages," with all of its accompanying ills, took the true church into a form of captivity. The human mind was enslaved in the darkness of ignorance, superstition, and false doctrine. Only a few could read; the Scriptures were not available to the common man, hence he was enslaved to whatever doctrine his spiritual "captors" might purport to impose upon him. The fall of Jerusalem, the desolation of the temple of Solomon, the breakdown of the worship of Yahweh, and the abandonment of the Mosaic law in Isaiah's time may be viewed at this point in history as symbolic of what happened to Christianity in the years AD 100–1500.

II. A message of hope.

Isaiah gave words of warning. He preached judgment. Jeremiah came along a century later with the same warnings. The people did not heed, and captivity resulted. Isaiah also preached hope. He and Ezekiel, his contemporary, assured the people that God would restore them to their former glory.

A. *Witnesses in exile.* During the post–New Testament centuries prior to the Reformation, the true witness of the gospel never really died. The Word was proclaimed in each age to the people in spiritual exile. God was never without witness, even in the catacombs!

B. *The groundwork of reform.* Just as Isaiah had said, "Hearken," "Awake," "Stand up," "Return," and "Rebuild the old wastes—raise up the former desolations—repair the waste cities—" so did Wycliffe (the "Morning Star of the Reformation") and other pre-Reformation leaders pave the way for the events that transpired under the leadership of Martin Luther and John Calvin.

C. *Principles of the Reformation.* Isaiah's call for renewal (to return and rebuild the wastes) was predicated on the fact that God would perform this work of restoration. Likewise, the Reformation was a work of God among his people, based on three famous *solas (sola gratia, sola fide,* and *sola scriptura).*

1. *Sola gratia* said that salvation was by grace alone; it was God's work.

2. *Sola fide* was the Reformation proclamation that God's work is effected in humans because of their faith.

3. *Sola scriptura* was the Lutheran principle of the *absolute supremacy of the Scriptures*. The Word and the Word alone is a person's authority for a message; it is the basis of the twin doctrine of salvation by grace and justification by faith. The Bible became the sole basis for all Reformation doctrine.

III. Truth for today.

The messages of the prophets had a timeless relevance. Isaiah called for renewal as he spoke to Judah in the exile. Luther called for renewal in his time.

A. *The Reformation message.* One might sum up the message of the Reformation to succeeding ages in the old phrases: grace alone, Christ alone, faith alone, and Scripture alone. Each of these also has its own negative connotation: no works as a plus to Christ, no saintly intercessors, no human merit as a ground for God's mercy, and no dependence on human tradition. But the thrust of the Reformation message is affirmative.

B. *The Reformation experience.* Reformation is not a static, once-for-all event. The past is there and cannot be changed, but its meaning for the present and future can change. If it is left only to the past, it becomes but a fact of history to be remembered. If, on the other hand, it becomes an experience of every believing Christian heart in this and each succeeding age, then new acts of reformation will purify and enrich the people of God. Captives will be set free — from prejudice, hatred, greed, apathy, and rebellion. "Wastes" will be rebuilt, our worship will be restored and renewed, the areas of spiritual decadence in our lives will be rebuilt, and God will be glorified.

Conclusion

The prophet Ezekiel had a vision of a valley of dry bones. No doubt this experience had its setting in some desolate area where a multitude of human lives had been lost. Abandoned bodies on the surface of the earth had mortified, and only a host of sun-parched skeletons remained. The Lord said, "Son of man, can these dry bones live?" Ezekiel said, "Lord, thou knowest." God said, "Prophesy, that these bones may live. Prophesy, and I will send my breath (spirit) into these bones, and they shall live." The prophet preached God's Word, and the valley of dry bones came alive! The primary meaning of this event related to Judah's restoration from the exile.

Our celebration of the Reformation may be admirably summed up in a brief prayer customarily used in Lutheran churches on Reformation Sunday: "Almighty God, who through the preaching of Thy servants, the blessed Reformers, has caused the light of the Gospel to shine forth: Grant, we beseech Thee, that knowing its saving power we may faithfully guard and defend it against all enemies and joyfully proclaim it to the salvation of souls and the glory of Thy holy Name."

SUNDAY EVENING, OCTOBER 31

Title: A Criminal Meets the Master

Text: "Verily I say unto thee, To-day shalt thou be with me in paradise" (**Luke 23:43**).

Scripture Reading: Luke 23:32–43

Introduction

The story of the penitent thief is one of the most surprising, significant, and instructive stories in all of the Gospels. Matthew and Mark use one Greek word to describe the thief while Luke uses another Greek word. The two words mean essentially the same thing. The thief was a robber, a plunderer, a criminal, a malefactor. What made this man a criminal we do not know, and we are not told.

There are many ways of looking at the criminal who met the Master. He was against Jesus, for Jesus, and with Jesus. He saw Jesus as King, as Savior, and as the Sinless One. He saw himself as a sinner, as one who stood in need of salvation. He saw the possibilities of faith, forgiveness, fellowship, and a future life with Jesus.

Let us look at the lessons we can learn from the criminal who met the Master.

I. A criminal meets the Master, and we understand that there are no hopeless cases.

The penitent thief was a wicked man. Only such men were usually crucified. He was being put to death for breaking the laws of man. He was paying his debt to society. Rome had pronounced him guilty, and he felt himself guilty. He said, "And we indeed justly; for we receive the due rewards of our deeds" (Luke 23:41). He was suffering the pangs of hell, and he was sensitive concerning the sins and dark deeds of his life.

II. A criminal meets the Master, and we understand that one becomes a Christian instantaneously.

The penitent thief did not have to join the catechism class to be saved. He was not put on probation and forced to attend a new members' class. He did not have time for that. He said, "Lord, remember me when thou comest into thy kingdom" (Luke 23:42). Jesus answered: "Verily I say unto thee, To-day shalt thou be with me in paradise."

You can be saved when you repent of your sins and put your faith in Jesus Christ as Lord and Savior.

III. A criminal meets the Master, and we understand that if some are saved in death, others are not.

Two thieves were crucified with Jesus. One was saved and one was not. Dr. Robert G. Lee, a great preacher from Memphis, Tennessee, says:

There were three crosses and three who died there that day on Calvary. One died for sin. That was Jesus. One died in sin. That one was the impenitent

336

thief. One died from sin. That one was the penitent thief. One died in love. That one was Jesus. One died in despair. That one was the impenitent thief. One died in faith. That one was the penitent thief. One died a Benefactor. That one was Jesus. One died a blasphemer. That one was the impenitent thief. One died a believer. That one was the penitent thief (*The Must of the Second Birth* [Westwood, N.J.: Revell, 1959], 104–5).

IV. A criminal meets the Master, and we understand that eternal life is better than earthly life.

The penitent thief had spent his life in search of the things of this life. He wanted material possessions and had probably stolen many things of value in his day, yet he was not satisfied with what he had found in life. One can spend a lifetime in pursuit of things and still be unsatisfied. On the cross, the penitent thief found life's greatest treasure—Christ.

When one finds Christ as Savior, he or she finds life's greatest treasure! You will never be satisfied in life until you find him.

V. A criminal meets the Master, and we understand that certain human teachings are false.

Dr. Russell Bradley Jones points out that the conversion of the penitent thief "struck the death-blow to some of the most dangerous and persistent heresies of the ages."

A. *The thief's conversion and death refute sacramentalism.* He could not join a church. He could not be baptized. He could not observe any rite. He could do no good works. He could not serve in any way. He had no opportunity for a period of holy living.

B. *The thief's conversion and death refute universalism.* All are not saved. The other thief was lost.

C. *The thief's conversion and death refute purgatory.* He went immediately into paradise, into heaven with the Savior.

D. *The thief's conversion and death refute soul-sleeping.* The conversion of the penitent thief is indeed instructive when it comes to the false teachings of humans.

VI. A criminal meets the Master, and we understand that believers can face eternity unafraid.

The penitent thief knew that he was going to die. After his repentance and trust in Christ there came to him a sense of serenity and eternity. "Remember me when thou comest into thy kingdom" (Luke 23:42). "To-day shalt thou be with me in paradise" (Luke 23:43).

There is a story of an old military officer who had returned from India. He had had many wonderful experiences. Audiences hung breathlessly upon his every word, but he always interrupted their expressions of wonder and amazement by quietly saying, "But I expect some day to see something more wonderful than that." He was an old man of seventy. He could never travel again. "Something more wonderful?" They asked him, "What do you expect to see that is more wonderful than that you have already seen and described to us?" There was a pause; then in a quiet voice, he replied, "I mean in the first five minutes after death!" Ah! Yes, the thrills of earth will fade away in the light of the things Christ has prepared for those whom he has bought with his blood (Russell Bradley Jones, *Gold from Golgotha* [Chicago: Moody Press, 1945], 32).

With Christ one can face eternity unafraid!

NOVEMBER

■ Sunday Mornings

The objective of the suggested Sunday morning sermons is that of meeting relevant needs in the lives of our people.

On the last Sunday of the month, as you head into the Christmas season, begin the series "Christ, the Fulfillment of Prophecy."

■ Sunday Evenings

Again this month the primary objective of the Sunday evening sermons is evangelistic. No specific theme is suggested. At times it is most helpful for a pastor to concentrate on messages designed specifically to call people to repentance and faith that they might become the children of God.

■ Wednesday Evenings

"Challenges from the Apostle Paul" is the theme for Wednesday night messages this month.

WEDNESDAY EVENING, NOVEMBER 3

Title: Develop the Habit of Prayer
Text: "Pray without ceasing" (**1 Thess. 5:17**).
Scripture Reading: 1 Thessalonians 5

Introduction

When the apostle Paul said, "Pray without ceasing," he was not encouraging his readers to assume a kneeling position and to remain in that posture permanently. Instead, he was encouraging them to develop the habit of praying regularly.

Paul believed in intercessory prayer. He prayed for the Romans (1:9), Ephesians (1:16), Philippians (1:9), Colossians (1:3), and Thessalonians (1:2). We can be sure that he prayed for others also.

I. We should pray when our hearts are filled with thanksgiving for God's blessings (Phil. 4:6).

II. We should pray when we are in need of forgiveness (I John I:9).

III. We should pray when we are in need of wisdom (James I:5–6).

339

IV. We should pray in every time of need (Heb. 4:14–16).

V. We should pray when we are tempted by evil (James 4:7–8).

Conclusion

Jesus assumed that his disciples would want to pray (Matt. 6:6). It is natural for the child of God to have a heart hunger for fellowship with God (Ps. 42:1–2). To neglect to develop the habit of prayer or to break the habit of prayer is to live in contradiction to our nature as children of God.

SUNDAY MORNING, NOVEMBER 7

Title: Christ Came to Save Sinners

Text: "When Jesus heard it, he saith unto them, They that are whole hath no need of the physician, but they that are sick: I came not to call the righteous, but sinners to repentance" **(Mark 2:17).**

Scripture Reading: Mark 2:14–17

Hymns: "He Included Me," Oatman

"The Old Rugged Cross," Bennard

"Jesus, Keep Me Near the Cross," Crosby

Offertory Prayer: Gracious Father, with abundance you have blessed us. We thank you not only for food and for the fruit of the field but also for rich spiritual blessings that come to us through Jesus Christ, your Son and our Savior. Today we offer to you the gratitude of our heart and the praise of our lips. We bring to you the fruits of our labor and dedicate them to your glory and to ministries of mercy to those who are the objects of your loving concern. Bless these tithes and offerings, and help us to give ourselves completely to you in a continuing ministry to others. Through Christ Jesus, our Lord, we pray. Amen.

Introduction

Today the sermon is for everyone. It contains some good news about God for sinners. All of us are sinners—young and old, men and women, parents and children.

I. All of us are sinners.

This may sound like strange language to some. If such should be the case, we should be reminded that our pride would cause us to deal with the problem of sin in a very superficial manner.

A. *Some of us do our best to ignore sin.*

B. *All of us try to excuse our sin. Adam and Eve began this in the Garden of Eden.*

C. *All of us want to conceal and to cover up our sin.*

D. *All of us at one time or another have denied our own sinfulness.* To recognize, to admit, and to be convicted of your sin is to receive a passport into God's presence. To be willing to admit that you are a sinner by omission or by commission or by disposition is to put yourself in a position where Jesus Christ can minister to you.

II. Jesus was the friend of sinners.

A. *Jesus was criticized by those who considered themselves to be religious because he associated with those whom they considered to be common sinners.* To this charge he pled guilty. He told three stories to illustrate his guilt. They are recorded in Luke 15. In the story of the lost sheep, he describes the shepherd's sense of loss and feeling of sorrow because one is away from the safety of the sheepfold. In the story of the lost coin, he expresses the concern of God for those who have lost values. In the story of the wayward son, he describes the waiting Father and his continuing concern for those who waste and ruin their lives. The point of these parables was to dramatize Jesus' concern and desire to save sinners from their sins.

B. *Jesus was compassionate toward sinners.* The occasion for our text was the conversion of Matthew the publican and a banquet that he gave in honor of his Savior. Matthew invited his friends, who also were sinners, to this banquet. They felt comfortable and loved in the presence of Jesus.

Jesus demonstrated this concern for sinners in the manner in which he related to the woman at the well (John 4:5–26).

Christ was compassionate toward a self-righteous Pharisee and confronted him on his way to Damascus (Acts 9:3–6).

III. Jesus grieved because of the tragic effects of sin.

A. *Sin affects us personally.* One of the words translated "sin" means to "miss the mark" or to "fall short of a standard." It is a failure to be less than what we could be.

B. *Sin affects us, as well as others, harmfully.* Sin by its very nature is destructive. It destroys that which is highest and best about us.

C. *Sin grieves and breaks the heart of God.* It was sin that separated people from God. It is sin that causes people to suffer away from God.

Christ Jesus came to save us from our sins. He came to deliver us from the power of sin. He came to save us for the glory of God. He wants to use us in a mission to others.

Conclusion

If we would let Christ work within us, we must forsake our hypocritical attitude of self-righteousness. We must take a good look at ourselves as we are and both recognize and acknowledge that we are sinners in need of his mercy, grace, and help. There is hope for the person who is willing to admit that he or she has fallen short and is in need of help. The Savior is available for those who are honest enough to admit that they are sinners.

SUNDAY EVENING, NOVEMBER 7

Title: Even So, Come, Lord Jesus

Text: "He which testifieth these things saith, Surely I come quickly. Amen. Even so, come, Lord Jesus" **(Rev. 22:20)**.

Scripture Reading: Revelation 22

Introduction

Some people contemplate the return of Jesus Christ to the earth with fear and anxiety. This is proper, for they are not prepared for his coming. Others profess to believe in him and anticipate spending eternity with him yet dread the thought of his coming during their lifetime. As far as the individual Christian is concerned, he should look forward with eager anticipation to the possibility of the Lord's coming during his lifetime. Let us contemplate some of the results of the return of the Lord.

I. At the second coming of Christ, our victory over death will be realized.

Most of us look upon death as being our archenemy. Paul spoke of death as being the last enemy of man (1 Cor. 15:26). Death will be the common fate of each of us as long as the Lord delays his coming. Our only hope of escaping physical death is for the Lord to return before death confronts us (1 Thess. 4:16–17). If you have a fear of death, you need to be informed that the only possible way by which you can escape it is for the Lord to return before the time of your death.

II. At the second coming of Christ our salvation will be complete.

We receive salvation from the penalty of sin, which is death, in the conversion experience when we first trust Jesus Christ as Savior. From the moment of conversion until death, we are in the process of being saved from the power, practice, and habit of sin. We shall be saved from the presence of sin only when the Lord Jesus Christ returns. Paul referred to this phase of our great salvation in his epistle to the Romans (13:11) and in his epistle to the Philippians (3:20–21). The writer of Hebrews says that when the Lord returns, he shall appear without sin unto salvation (9:28). This is salvation from the presence of sin. He is talking about the redeemed in heaven. There will be no sin in heaven. There will be no rebellion against God in heaven. There will be no sorrow as a result of sin in heaven. This shall be a reality for the redeemed only after the Lord has returned.

342

III. At the second coming of Christ, the devil will be cast into hell.

The Bible speaks of Satan as being the enemy of God. It also states that hell was prepared for the devil and his angels. He will be cast into the place prepared for him following the second coming of Jesus Christ. Each of us should look forward with eager anticipation to the coming of Christ, because it will bring about the end of the evil, destructive activity of the devil (Rev. 20:10; Matt. 25:41).

IV. At the second coming of Christ, the saints will be rewarded.

Throughout the Word of God we are taught that our gracious God is going to reward his children for their labors and their efforts. God must wait until the judgment day to fully reward the faithful, because their labors follow after them and continue to bear fruit. The good that a man does continues to grow and to flourish and to bless and to bear spiritual dividends. Each child of God should be faithful in anticipation of being able to enjoy heaven more wonderfully because of the rewards that will be waiting.

V. At the second coming of Christ we will discover how wonderful God is.

In our highest and most inspired moments, we begin to understand even in a small way the wonders of God's love and the lavish extent of his grace and mercy. Paul speaks of the inability of the unsaved to understand the things of God: "Eye hath not seen, nor ear heard, neither have entered into the heart of man, the things which God has prepared for them that love him" (1 Cor. 2:9). He continues by saying that God has revealed these things to us by his Spirit. However, most of us are greatly limited in our ability to understand or grasp what the Spirit would seek to reveal to us. Only when we see our Lord as he is will we begin to fully comprehend the greatness of his love for us, the lavishness of his provisions for us.

Conclusion

The big question is, Are you ready for the Lord to return? The saved can be ready if they are living a life of faithfulness in witnessing, working, serving, and being a blessing. If they are doing what their Master would have them to do, they can look forward with eager anticipation to the moment of his return.

The unsaved need to recognize that with the passing of every day we are one day closer to the return of Jesus Christ. If they are to meet him in peace, they must make peace with him now by turning from the love of sin and yielding the throne of their hearts and lives to him whom God has appointed to be Lord of all.

WEDNESDAY EVENING, NOVEMBER 10

Title: It Is Time to Awake

Text: "Wherefore he saith, Awake thou that sleepest, and arise from the dead, and Christ shall give thee light" **(Eph. 5:14)**.

Scripture Reading: Ephesians 5:1–16

Introduction

Paul's challenge to awake should arouse both those inside the church and those who have no relationship to the church.

I. Sleep is a mysterious necessity of life.

The mystery of sleep defies exact analysis. Sleep is a miracle that happens more than twenty-five thousand times in a normal life span.

A. *Sleep is a universal experience.*

B. *Sleep is a universal necessity.* Like water, food, and air, sleep is necessary for all.

C. *Sleep brings blessings for which there are no substitutes.*

II. While sleep is a necessity of life, there are times when sleep is sinful (Prov. 10:5).

A. *Eutychus had to sleep, but he should not have gone to sleep during a worship service that was being conducted by the apostle Paul (Acts 20:9).*

B. *Peter, James, and John needed sleep, but they should not have gone to sleep when the Lord had told them, "Watch and pray, that ye enter not into temptation" (Matt. 26:41).*

C. *Jonah needed sleep, but he should not have slept the sleep of indifference and disobedience on the way to Tarshish (Jonah 1:5).*

D. *Belshazzar was a man who needed sleep, but he should not have been sleeping the sleep of drunkenness and dissipation during the night that he was slain and his kingdom was taken by Darius (Dan. 5).*

III. There are times when sleep is shameful (Prov. 10:5).

A. *Sleep sometimes reveals the lack of a sense of personal responsibility.*

B. *Sleeping in the harvest time is shameful, because the harvest will not wait.*

C. *The man who is asleep is useless.* The church needs him to be awake, alert, and active.

Conclusion

It is time for everyone who claims to be a follower of Jesus Christ to awake from the sleep of indifference and disobedience. It is time for us to become alert and responsive to the command of our Lord and to the leadership of the Holy Spirit. It is time for us to be in the fields working for our Lord.

SUNDAY MORNING, NOVEMBER 14

Title: Rejoice in the Lord

Text: "Rejoice in the Lord alway: and again I say, Rejoice" (**Phil. 4:4**).

Scripture Reading: Philippians 4

Hymns: "Come, Thou Almighty King," Anonymous

"Jesus Is All the World to Me," Thompson

"Since I Have Been Redeemed," Excell

Offertory Prayer: Holy Father, we thank you for the opportunity to bring of the fruits of our labors and to dedicate them to the work of your kingdom. We thank you for the privilege of being able to speak your praises to the hearts of others. We rejoice in the opportunity of singing of your grace and mercy. We rejoice in the opportunity of joining hands and hearts with others through tithes and offerings to proclaim the goodness of your grace, love, and power to redeem to the ends of the earth. Today we would pray for your blessings upon those who serve you in difficult places, and particularly we pray for those in lonely places of obscurity. Bless those who serve on mission fields. Bless those who minister in hospitals. Bless those who minister to orphan children. Bless these offerings to that purpose in Christ's name. Amen.

Introduction

Paul's epistle to the Philippians has been called the epistle of joy. An emphasis on the joy that is available through Jesus Christ permeates and saturates the entire epistle. We see this revealed in references such as 1:4, 18, 26; 2:2, 15, 16, 17, 18, 28, 29; 3:1; and 4:22. What was the source of this wonderful joy?

I. The world needs a religion of joy.

There are many factors in today's world that contribute toward an unhappy frame of mind.

A. *The world situation is enough to make a realist sick in the pit of his stomach.*

B. *Most of us have experienced some personal failures that can contribute to a pessimistic frame of mind if we concentrate on the negative.*

C. *The competitive and materialistic spirit of our age is such as to distress the minds of many.*

D. *Personal disappointment in others can make a great contribution toward an unhappy frame of mind.*

To stand on a busy street corner and to examine the faces of those who pass by is to discover a tragic absence of joy and happiness.

II. One may search for joy in the wrong way or place.

A. *Some believe that joy is to be found in wealth.* Only a few are able to achieve a position of economic security.

B. *Some find their only joy in fame and popularity.*

C. *Some search for joy in the pleasures that the world has to offer.*

III. The source of abiding joy.

There are many legitimate sources for joy and happiness. One can find joy in worthwhile achievement, in a devoted family, and in the blessings of good health.

The apostle Paul found his source of abiding, overflowing joy in his relationship with God through Jesus Christ. We hear him say repeatedly, "Rejoice in the Lord alway: and again I say, Rejoice." The Lord does not change. Circumstances cannot remove him from us or us from him.

A. *In the Lord we can rejoice in the glad consciousness of forgiven sin (Ps. 103:3, 12; Acts 10:43; 1 John 1:7).* Guilt can be not only a disturbing thing; it can be a very destructive force. Because all of us are sinners, all of us need forgiveness.

B. *In the Lord we can rejoice in the blessed assurance of divine sonship (John 1:12; Gal. 3:26; 1 John 3:2).*

C. *In the Lord we can rejoice in the consciousness that God is at work in our lives (Phil. 1:6; 2:13).* The Christian life is not a human achievement alone. It is a cooperative achievement on the part of the one who works with God as God works within his heart.

D. *In Christ we can rejoice in the availability of the divine energy that is necessary for living a victorious Christian life (Phil. 4:13).*

E. *In the Lord we can rejoice in the hope of heavenly rewards (Phil. 4:17).*

Conclusion

Our Lord desires that we live lives that are filled with joy (John 15:11). If we will concentrate our hearts and our lives on him, we will find that joy will be the result. As we rejoice in the blessings of God, we will be equipped to bear a winning witness to those who don't know our Lord. Through the joy that will radiate from our hearts and lives, the Christ will be able to draw others unto himself (John 12:32).

SUNDAY EVENING, NOVEMBER 14

Title: Jesus Christ and Him Crucified

Text: "For I determined not to know any thing among you, save Jesus Christ, and him crucified" (**1 Cor. 2:2**).

Scripture Reading: 1 Corinthians 2

Introduction

If the apostle Paul lived in our modern world, he would preach Jesus Christ and him crucified. He would lead the secular minds of modern people into encounters with the spiritual reality of what God did in the person of Jesus Christ as he died on the cross.

Paul could have preached about the birth of Christ, his baptism, his childhood, or his life. However, he concentrated on proclaiming the significance of his death and resurrection. Tonight, by inspired imagination, let us look at Jesus Christ and him crucified.

I. Jesus Christ and him crucified reveals the depravity of sin and humankind's need for salvation.

Why should the sinless, stainless, spotless Son of God die on the cross? Was his death an accident in the plan of God? Was his death the mere martyrdom of an idealistic man? No, Scripture tells us that his death on the cross was substitutionary—he died for the sins of the world.

Each person needs to realize that it was his or her sin that put Jesus Christ on the cross. If we can see how terrible sin is, then we can see its ultimate manifestation in what it did to God's precious Son on the cross.

II. Jesus Christ and him crucified is a picture of God's inflexible justice.

Somehow in contemplating the love of God many of us have forgotten that God is just and righteous. We have gotten away from the idea of the holiness of God and the wrath of God. God's wrath is the other side of his love. It is his eternal antagonism with that which is sinful and destructive. The law of God will bring punishment on sin, for God is determined to eradicate sin from the world.

In a manner that defies complete comprehension, Jesus Christ was both the expression of God's mercy and the victim of God's justice (2 Cor. 5:21; 8:9; 1 Peter 1:18–20).

III. Jesus Christ and him crucified reveals the terrible penalty of sin (Rom. 6:23).

The law of sin and death was revealed to the first couple in the Garden of Eden (Gen. 3:3). The history of the human race bears testimony to the truthfulness of the peril against which the first pair were warned. Because of sin, physical death and spiritual death came upon the human race. Spiritual death is the separation of the soul from God. Christ Jesus took upon himself our sin and bore it to the cross. On the cross he felt the utter desolation of being forsaken by God because of the sin of a guilty race. He cried out, "My God, my God, why hast thou forsaken me?" (Matt. 27:46). He was bearing the penalty of our sin.

As individuals we must either let Christ bear the penalty of our sin or we must bear it ourselves. He has paid the penalty of our sin so that we might be forgiven and restored to fellowship with God.

IV. Jesus Christ and him crucified reveals the divine estimate of the value of man.

People need desperately to realize that in the eyes of God they are of infinite worth. In a day when people are thought of as machines and when life is depersonalized and dehumanized, we need to recognize that God looks upon each of us as being of infinite value.

God revealed the value that he places upon people by the gift of his Son Jesus Christ who came and died on the cross in our place.

V. Jesus Christ and him crucified reveals the love of God for each of us.

Nothing but love could have led Jesus Christ to the cross. Nothing but the love of God could have kept Jesus Christ on the cross when he was challenged to come down and prove his sonship.

Jesus Christ on the cross speaks with a voice that goes around the world telling people that God is for us and not against us. God loves us and does not hate us. God wants to bless us and not curse us. God wants to enrich us and not impoverish us.

Conclusion

How have you responded to Jesus Christ and him crucified? Have you ignored him, have you evaded him, or have you yielded the throne of your heart to his love? You can trust one completely who loves you to the degree that Jesus Christ loves you.

Not only did Jesus die, but he also conquered death and the grave. He came forth triumphant to dwell in the hearts of those who would trust him as a living presence. He wants to come into your heart to bestow upon you the gift of eternal life. He wants to make available to you the power that will make it possible for you to become a channel through which the love of God can reach the hearts and lives of others.

WEDNESDAY EVENING, NOVEMBER 17

Title: Are You Filled with the Spirit?

Text: "And be not drunk with wine, wherein is excess; but be filled with the Spirit" **(Eph. 5:18)**.

Scripture Reading: Ephesians 5:17–21

Introduction

In a single short statement, Paul pointed out the error of becoming intoxicated by beverages and issued a command to become intoxicated with the Holy Spirit instead. Many followers of Jesus Christ could not be compelled to become intoxicated with wine, but neither would they desire to be filled with the Spirit of God to the point that they would manifest spiritual enthusiasm that might cause someone to think of them as religious fanatics.

There are at least three conditions for being filled with the Spirit.

I. To be filled with the Spirit one must have faith.

II. To be filled with the Spirit one must pray.

Our Lord commanded his disciples to tarry in Jerusalem until the power of the Holy Spirit came upon them: "These all continued in one accord in prayer and supplication, with the women, and Mary the mother of Jesus, and with his brethren" (Acts 1:14).

III. To be filled with the Spirit the believer must be obedient.

"And we are his witnesses of these things; and so also is the Holy Ghost, whom God hath given to them that obey him" (Acts 5:32). The believer is the instrumental agent for doing God's work in the world; the Holy Spirit is the directing and enabling agent. Only when we are obedient to the loving commands of God can the Holy Spirit fill us with the power of God.

Conclusion

The Father never intended that we do his work in our strength alone. He has always intended that we do the work of the kingdom in the power of the kingdom. Zerubbabel declared, "Not by might, nor by power, but by my Spirit, saith the LORD of hosts" (Zech. 4:6).

If we are to do God's work in God's world in God's way for God's glory, we must do it in the power that comes in and through the Holy Spirit. That power is available to those who have faith, who give themselves to prayer, and who are yielded to God's loving will.

SUNDAY MORNING, NOVEMBER 21

Title: The Grace of Gratitude

Text: "Give thanks in all circumstances, for this is God's will for you in Christ Jesus" (**1 Thess. 5:18 NIV**).

Scripture Reading: Psalm 95

Hymns: "Come Ye Thankful People," Alford

"For All the Blessings of the Year," Hutchinson

"We Gather Together," Anonymous, Translated by Baker

Offertory Prayer: Almighty Father, we thank you for our land and for the faith of our fathers who came to the shores of this continent to establish here a nation of civil and religious liberty. Help us to preserve the heritage that is ours, founded on the sure foundations of justice, liberty, and true brotherhood. Grant us, we pray, your grace and wisdom in these days of peril that we may prove our gratitude for the rich blessings you have given to us through the faith, dedication, prayers, and sacrifices of our forefathers. Help us to be true to their ideals, and may our country ever be the home of freedom and human brotherhood. Defend our land, we pray, O God, against every evil from within and from without, and make it increasingly a blessing to all the world. We pray for these things as we thank you for them, through Jesus Christ, our Lord. Amen.

Introduction

When Robinson Crusoe was wrecked on his lonely island, he listed in two columns what he called the evil and the good. He was cast on a desolate island, but he was still alive — not drowned, as his ship's company were. He was divided from humankind and banished from human society, but he was not starving. He had no clothes, but he was in a hot climate where he did not need them. He was without means of defense, but he saw no wild beasts such as he had seen on the coast of Africa. He had no one to whom he could speak, but God had sent the ship so near to the shore that he could get out of it all the things necessary for his basic wants. So he concluded that there was not any condition in the world so miserable but that one could find something for which to be grateful.

I think the apostle Paul had such in mind when he wrote his first letter to the Thessalonians. He gave special reference to the grace of gratitude as suggested in our text. If ever there was a man who knew a variety of perils through which to live, suffer, and endure, it was Paul the apostle. Like Crusoe, let us then examine our text and Paul's life in a twofold manner.

I. A negative approach.

A. *Paul did not thank God for the possession of material abundance.* He did not have the affluent standard of living most of us in modern America know.

B. *Paul did not thank God for an easy time; instead, he had a "thorn" (2 Cor. 8:7ff.).* He knew the bitterness of persecution: he was stoned at Lystra; driven from Thessalonica; rejected at Athens; jailed at Philippi; apprehended at Caesarea; taken to Rome as a prisoner and shipwrecked enroute; imprisoned; released then jailed again and put in a dungeon at Rome; and finally martyred.

C. *Paul did not thank God for any superior standing among others.* He was not like the Pharisee who prayed, "God, I thank thee that I am not as other men …" (Luke 18:11; cf. Phil. 3:4–8).

There is such a thing, then, as vain gratitude. This is not a grace of the Christian spirit. It is false and unchristian — based on vanity, pride, arrogance, conceit, prejudice, and pharisaical self-righteousness — all of which calls for confession and repentance instead of expressions of praise and gratitude!

II. The positive approach.

A. *The will of God.* The text says, "This is the will of God for you." In spite of all that may have happened, you are to continue being grateful. Refuse to let any incident, circumstance, event, calamity, or other experience stifle you into the extinction of your spirit of gratitude.

B. *Take inventory.* Examine now some of the things for which Paul had (and you have) cause to be grateful:

1. Daily bread. "He took bread, and gave thanks to God in the presence of them all: and when he had broken it, he began to eat" (Acts 27:35).

2. People of faith. "First, I thank my God through Jesus Christ for you all, that your faith is spoken of throughout the whole world" (Rom. 1:8).
3. Deliverance from anxiety. "Thanks be unto God, which always causeth us to triumph in Christ" (2 Cor. 2:14).
4. Deliverance from the trials of temptation. In Romans 7 Paul speaks at length of the conflict of the two natures in him—and in all men. He talks of the warfare between the life of the flesh and the spirit, then asks in verse 24, "Who shall deliver me from the body of this death?" His reply is voiced in verse 25, "I thank God through Jesus Christ our Lord."
5. Memory of friends. "I thank my God upon every remembrance of you" (Phil. 1:3).
6. Kindness in trouble. In Acts 28 Luke records the last stages of the journey to Rome when Paul was going there for his first imprisonment. As they neared the city, friends met them at Appii Forum and Three Taverns: "Whom when Paul saw, he thanked God, and took courage" (Acts 28:15).
7. The unspeakable gift. "Thanks be unto God for his unspeakable gift" (2 Cor. 9:15). This reference is to God's gift in Christ.

Conclusion

Today we should reflect on this text, count our blessings, and try to enumerate the things for which we should be grateful. We live in a land of freedom; this is a blessing unavailable in so much of today's world.

Gratitude is an experience; it is not a theory, a formula, or a deed. It must spring from the heart, for it exists within. Paul was in prison without his cloak, his books, and his freedom, but he was never without his gratitude.

Gratitude helps us over the hills and mountains of life. It makes loads lighter, sorrow and sadness brighter. It turns grief into comfort, defeat into victory, doubt into assurance, fear into faith, hate into love, darkness into light, death into life, and mourning into joy.

Why does this grace work such wonders in the human spirit? Because gratitude grows as it is given away. If you will express it, you will see it increase.

SUNDAY EVENING, NOVEMBER 21

Title: The Invitation to Repentance

Text: "Jesus came into Galilee, preaching the gospel of the kingdom of God, and saying, The time is fulfilled, and the kingdom of God is at hand: repent ye, and believe the gospel" (**Mark 1:14–15**).

Scripture Reading: Mark 1:1–15

Introduction

Jesus came into our world, which in reality is his world, to change both the minds and the ways of people. In his opening message, he announced the keynote

351

emphasis of his mission and message. It is contained in the challenge, "Repent ye, and believe the gospel." This invitation is positive rather than negative. It is a present imperative, and yet it is a gracious invitation.

The call to repentance and faith is not a threat or a call to morbid remorseful thinking; it is a gracious invitation from Christ to prepare mentally and spiritually for participation in the wonderful work of God.

I. Repentance is emphasized throughout the New Testament.

The word *repent* occurs fifty-six times in the New Testament, which opens with a trumpet blast: "Repent ye: for the kingdom of heaven is at hand" (Matt. 3:2). Jesus began and concluded his ministry emphasizing repentance (Mark 1:15; Luke 24:46–47). When Jesus sent his apostles out to preach, the record says, "And they went out, and preached that men should repent" (Mark 6:12). Peter brought his great sermon on the day of Pentecost to a conclusion with the challenge that his listeners should repent (Acts 2:37–39). And when Paul preached the gospel in proud, sophisticated Athens, he declared that "God ... now commandeth all men everywhere to repent" (Acts 17:30).

II. Just what is repentance?

A. *Jesus was calling for something other than a fear of punishment for sin.*

B. *Jesus was calling for something other than an emotional crisis involving remorse, shame, and sorrow because of sin.*

C. *Jesus was calling for something more than acts of penitence in which effort is put forth to make restitution for the wrong done both to God and others.*

D. *Jesus was calling for something more than good resolutions and reformation of life.*

E. *By the call to repentance, Jesus was issuing an invitation and a challenge for people to completely reverse their thoughts about God.* He was stating that a complete change of mental outlook and life design is necessary if one is to participate in the kingdom of God. He was challenging the people of his day and the people of our day to experience a complete inward change of attitude and outlook concerning God, sin, life, and eternity.

The implications of this challenge would involve a basic change of attitude toward God, sin, self, and others.

III. Genuine repentance and saving faith are inseparable.

The invitation of our Lord was, "Repent ye, and believe the gospel" (Mark 1:15). The inward change of viewpoint or attitude toward God is made possible by the hearing of the gospel, the good news of God's love and mercy and grace as it is revealed in the life, death, and resurrection of Jesus Christ.

A. *The gospel tells of the God who revealed himself as infinite, with indescribable love for sinners.*

B. *The gospel tells us of the unselfishness of God who has so lavishly given of himself for us.*

C. *The gospel tells of the God who seeks the sinner.*

D. *The gospel tells of the God who forgives sin.*

E. *The gospel tells of the God who loves us individually.* God loves you as an individual as well as other people in the world.

F. *The gospel tells us of the God who wants to be our heavenly Father.* He is not only our Creator and Sustainer and he has not only provided for us abundantly in the natural world; he is the great God who wants to become our heavenly Father.

Conclusion

The gospel is good news from God to you. Jesus Christ died for your sins on the cross because of God's love for you. Jesus Christ comes into this service to speak with a still, small voice to your heart. He comes as the expression of God's love.

You would be wise to quit distrusting God. You should quit evading God and disobeying him. All of his purposes toward you are purposes of love. Now would be a good time for you to change your attitude toward him and respond to this good news of his love. That is what Jesus was talking about in his gracious invitation in which he said, "Repent ye, and believe the gospel."

WEDNESDAY EVENING, NOVEMBER 24

Title: Don't Put Out the Fire

Text: "Quench not the Spirit" (**1 Thess. 5:19**).

Scripture Reading: 1 Thessalonians 5:12–28

Introduction

In the closing section of Paul's epistle to the Thessalonians, he gave them a number of short, explicit exhortations. Among these is found our text, "Quench not the Spirit."

The word "quench" assumes the presence of the Spirit of God in the heart like a fire. The apostle is saying that it is possible to choke or to restrict the fire. It is possible to hinder the Spirit as he seeks to do God's work within us.

I. The purpose of the indwelling Spirit.

A. *The indwelling Spirit gives us assurance of sonship (Rom. 8:16–17).*

B. *The indwelling Spirit provides divine leadership (Rom. 8:14).*

C. *The indwelling Spirit wants to reproduce within us the character of Jesus Christ (Gal. 5:22–23).*

D. *The indwelling Spirit wants to equip us and lead us to be the spokespeople of God, the communicators of the good news of his love to people (Acts 2:16–18).*

E. *The indwelling Spirit wants to lead us to effectiveness in our prayer life (Rom. 8:26).*

353

II. How does one quench the Spirit?

A. *Surely we both grieve and quench the Spirit when we ignore his presence within our hearts (1 Cor. 3:16).* The Holy Spirit is hindered from doing his mightiest work when we ignore his presence. To be unaware of what he is trying to do automatically makes cooperation with him impossible.

B. *We can be confident that an attitude of disobedience to his leadership is an act of quenching the Spirit (Acts 5:32).* The Holy Spirit must have our cooperation if he is to accomplish the work for which he entered the world and the church.

C. *Living for the fleshly nature grieves the Spirit (Gal. 5:16–17).* The Holy Spirit enters the heart of each believer to lift that person above an earthly or fleshly level.

Conclusion

God has a noble plan for the life of each of us. He has bestowed the Holy Spirit within our hearts so that the fulfillment of his plan might be experienced. Each of us must recognize the presence of the Holy Spirit and respond positively. We must have confidence in his benevolent purpose. We must entrust ourselves to his power. We must cooperate with him day by day if we want to walk the high road to significant fellowship and achievement as the children of God.

SUNDAY MORNING, NOVEMBER 28

Title: Jesus, the Servant

Text: "Behold my servant, whom I uphold; mine elect, in whom my soul delighteth; I have put my spirit upon him: he shall bring forth judgment to the Gentiles. He shall not cry, nor lift up, nor cause his voice to be heard in the street. A bruised reed shall he not break, and the smoking flax shall he not quench: he shall bring forth judgment unto truth. He shall not fail nor be discouraged, till he have set judgment in the earth: and the isles shall wait for his law" **(Isa. 42:1–4)**.

Scripture Reading: Isaiah 42:1–16

Hymns: "It Came Upon the Midnight Clear," Sears

"Good Christian Men, Rejoice," German Melody

"Man of Sorrows, What a Name," Bliss

Offertory Prayer: May it be, our Father, that we will recognize that what we have in our possession is in fact not ours to hold, but rather it has been placed there for us to use for your glory. We have therefore become stewards of that which you have given us. We pray that we may use the one-tenth that is the tithe for your glory by returning it through the church to the many ministries that are ours in the world. We would also pray, just as sincerely, that the nine-tenths that we keep for ourselves be used for your glory in the building of our homes and in

354

the development of ourselves, that Jesus may be lifted and his kingdom spread. In his name. Amen.

Introduction

A prophecy is not something that a prophet is moved to say all of a sudden and after he says it writes it down and that's it. Rather, he usually speaks to a set of circumstances existing at that moment. Later it is seen to have a much greater meaning than it had at the time he said it. God, through the inspiration of the moment and the inspiration of a person, says something that will stand as a testimony not only for then but for all time to come. It becomes a "foretaste of glory divine."

I. Four facts about the servant (Isa. 42:1).

A. *First, God regards the nation of Israel as his servant.* He says that in the midst of all the nations he has a chosen people, and it is through those people that the will and purpose and fulfillment of God are going to reach the world.
   1. At first in the Old Testament God calls the whole nation Israel his chosen people.
   2. The promise is later narrowed to a remnant.
      a. Within Israel the nation there is a group that is spoken of as the remnant. They are the ones who are obedient to God, who are faithful to God (Isa. 10:20–22; 37:31–32).
      b. Not all Jewish people are chosen of God.
   3. The remnant is then narrowed to a family.
   4. The family is finally narrowed to one man.
      a. Turn to Matthew 12 and show how the Scripture was fulfilled by our living Lord (vv. 17–21).
      b. Turn to Philippians 2:5ff. and read.
      c. Here in the New Testament both Matthew and the apostle Paul, who wrote Philippians, recognized that Jesus assumed the role of God's Servant. He was one who did not exalt himself, did not wear a crown, but one who wore the sandals of a common man. He identified himself with suffering humanity and referred to himself as a servant.
B. *Second, God delights in his Servant (Isa. 42:1).*
   1. Remember the day Jesus came down to be baptized by John in the Jordan. Jesus came out of the water, then according to Matthew 3:17, there was a voice from heaven. This voice from heaven, being the voice of God, said that this man Jesus was that very one spoken of by the prophet Isaiah in 42:1.
   2. The second example is recorded in Matthew 17:5. Jesus was up on the mountain with two of the apostles, and while they were there Jesus was transfigured before them.
   3. You see, Isaiah's words are literally freighted with meaning. Though he spoke them seven hundred years before the coming of our Lord, they were only a foretaste.

C. *Third, God's Spirit is upon his Servant (Isa. 42:1).* The verse goes on to say "My spirit is upon you."
   1. We have already talked about Jesus' baptism. The heavens opened, and Jesus saw "the Spirit of God as a dove" coming upon him (Matt. 3:16).
   2. It is interesting to observe that the word "spirit" in the Old Testament is the Hebrew word *ruach,* which means breath or wind. It is speaking here particularly about the breath of God.

D. *Fourth, the servant will bring judgment (Isa. 42:1).*

   In this one verse then, we have seen that four different things are fulfilled in Jesus. That is only the beginning. I think you will agree that this is one of the most magnificent pictures of our Lord that could be seen.

II. The nature of the Servant (Isa. 42:2).

He will not cry or cause his voice to be heard in screams. Read the touching story in Luke 23. Read there how Jesus was mistreated.

III. The Servant is gentle (Isa. 42:3).

A. *The first phrase pictures a marsh where reeds are growing.* They are wind-blown; hardly a single reed stands upright. Wind, weather, weight of water, blowing together, and trampling by beast or men cause the reeds to be bent or bruised and bowed down.
   1. This refers to people. It is illustrating that there is one who comes so gently that when he comes down to the water's edge he sees every bent reed and does not break a single one.
   2. The reeds are our lives. Each of us is bruised and broken from sin.
   3. In all of the weeping and all of the hurting of humanity, Jesus came into the world so that not a single reed would be broken down.

B. *The second phrase speaks of the smoking flax that he will not quench.*
   1. This refers to the old-fashioned oil lamps, and the flax is the wick. Imagine yourself in the middle of a room and all you have is light from old oil lamps. All the lamps are burning, then one by one all of the lamps go out. They being to smolder. There is just a tiny spark of fire remaining in one of the wicks. The Bible says here of Jesus that he will not put it out; he is this gentle.
   2. This, too, is referring to people. As long as there is one little spark in a person who cries out to God, as long as there is left within that person the smallest spark of spiritual sensitivity, it is not the desire of God to put it out. Rather, Jesus came to fan it, bring it back to life, and restore that person to full fellowship with God. He is so gentle that he would not put out this last spark.
   3. These two things tell so much about our Lord that they make us love him more.

4. What a tremendous picture of how God can take the smallest spark in a human soul bent low and fan it again into full flame, that he may play the melodies of God on heartstrings of fire.
5. Alexander Maclaren has said it well: "There is no man out of hell, but has within him something that only needs to be brought to sovereign power in his life, in order to make him a light in the world."
6. That verse was surely fulfilled in our Lord. There were many who felt the tenderness of his hands and who felt the love of his life and in whose lives that little spark was brought again to full flame.

IV. The Servant is courageous in his purpose (Isa. 42:4).

He remains at God's right hand to help us (1 John 2:1). He will accomplish the purpose of God and bring righteousness to our lives.

V. Where is this Servant to be in the future?

Does the Bible show us?
A. *In the book of Revelation, Jesus is not a servant; he is a King!* The Servant has become a King!
B. *Can you imagine how that truth will dawn one day?*
  1. It will dawn upon the leper healed by Jesus in Mark 1.
  2. It will dawn upon the Gadarene demoniac whom Jesus healed.
  3. It will dawn upon that old woman whose body was doubled in pain. Jesus made her well.
    Thousands of others of us have made the same discovery.

Conclusion

The Suffering Servant has become the King of glory! Prophecy is fulfilled. Everything in heaven, everything on the earth, and everything underneath the earth will bow down and say, Jesus is Lord, to the glory of God the Father (Phil. 2:11).

Can you get a glimpse of the Servant who becomes the King? If you have never trusted him as your Savior, you have missed all of life. I invite you to come and take him as Lord of your life. Give him everything you are, everything you have. Do it now!

SUNDAY EVENING, NOVEMBER 28

Title: The Worth of Your Soul

Text: "For what shall it profit a man, if he shall gain the whole world, and lose his own soul?" (**Mark 8:36**).

Introduction

Satan appeared to Christ in the wilderness and offered him the greatest prize at his disposal to bestow. Satan had all of the kingdoms of the world with all of their glory to pass before the Christ. Then Satan made the offer that these could be Jesus' if he would but fall down before him in worship.

Some have failed to recognize the potential appeal of Satan's offer. Christ had come to die on the cross so that the kingdoms of this world might become the kingdom of God. Satan, the father of lies, promised to deliver the entire world if Christ would yield to the suggestion of evil. Satan promised Christ the fulfillment of his dreams by means of a detour around the cross. He offered a shortcut to success. This was an attempt to buy the soul of Christ and to thwart and to destroy God's great program of redemption. We can be grateful that Christ did not sell his soul for this promise of the world.

I. The promise of an impossible gain.

Satan, the prince of this world, continues to promise the world to those who are willing to fall down and worship him. He will promise whatever is necessary to secure and to maintain one's allegiance.

A. *It should be remembered that the devil pays the lowest possible wages (Rom. 6:23).*

B. *The devil promises much but gives little. No one has been able to gain the whole world.*

II. The offer of a bad bargain.

All of us are price conscious. This should be true in every area of life including the spiritual. People often fail to count the cost of neglecting their souls. They do not count the cost of buying the world with all of its glitter at the price of losing their souls.

If you could take the coin of your soul and with this currency purchase the world, and if you received the whole world, you would have made a bad bargain.

A. *The world is perishing (1 John 2:17).* Would you purchase valuable perfume if you knew that the flask contained a leak and that the perfume was certain to evaporate?

B. *The world does not satisfy.* People were made for God. Deep within human hearts there is a hunger that wealth, honor, and pleasure cannot satisfy. People are spiritual. They need God. Without God life at its best is but a fraction and will always be incomplete.

C. *The world is dangerous.* Instead of being your servant, the world would become your master. You would be possessed by the world.

D. *You cannot take it with you.* It is appointed unto people once to die. The person who has sold his soul to win the world will find himself faced with the sad destiny of having to leave it all.

III. An answered question.

The text is an unanswered question in terms of profit and loss. There is no answer concerning what a person can gain, but there is an answer to the question of what he will lose. If you sell your soul and live the life of unbelief, you lose many wonderful blessings.

A. *You lose the privilege of having eternal life (John 3:36).*
B. *You lose the privilege of becoming a child of God (John 8:44).*
C. *You deprive yourself of peace with God (Isa. 48:22).*
D. *You miss the abundant life (John 10:10).*
E. *You miss heaven (Rev. 20:15).*

IV. Count the cost.

A. *Satan offers you the world with all of its pleasures if you will serve him.* In the end he will pay off with disappointment, death, and destruction.
B. *Christ offers you life now and life hereafter.* He offers you the freedom to become all that God means for you to be.

Conclusion

You must make the decision regarding the destiny of your soul. You can let Satan have it, or you can entrust it into the care of Jesus Christ. If you lose your soul, it is your own responsibility. God has done and is doing all that he can to save you. He will not compel you, but he does invite you to be saved now and forever.

DECEMBER

■ **Sunday Mornings**

Continue the series "Christ, the Fulfillment of Prophecy" throughout the month of December.

■ **Sunday Evenings**

The sermons for this month describe the unique witness to Jesus of the writers of the four Gospels. The theme could be "The Witness to Jesus of the Gospel Writers."

■ **Wednesday Evenings**

The theme for Wednesday evenings in December is "Being a Faithful Witness for Jesus Christ."

WEDNESDAY EVENING, DECEMBER 1

Title: My Responsibility to Witness

Text: "And ye are witnesses of these things" (**Luke 24:48**).

Scripture Reading: Luke 24:36–48

Introduction

Man sinned in the Garden of Eden and was lost from God. God immediately went in search of lost man. He asked, "Where art thou?" This was not the cry of a policeman but of a brokenhearted Father. After God "found" man, it was not long before man was to hear another question: "Where is Abel thy brother?" (Gen. 4:9). Cain's response to that question provides us with an insight into man's continuing tendency to reject a sense of personal responsibility for one another. He raised the question, "Am I my brother's keeper?" (Gen. 4:9). At the beginning of human history, God affirmed that Cain did have a responsibility toward his brother.

Jesus, in the closing moments of his earthly sojourn, gave to his disciples the ringing challenge of the Great Commission. Luke sums it up as follows: "Ye are witnesses of these things" (24:48).

Our responsibility to witness stems from at least four things.

I. My responsibility to witness stems from what I have experienced.

"The love of God is shed abroad in our hearts by the Holy Ghost which is given unto us. For when we were yet without strength, in due time Christ died for the ungodly" (Rom. 5:5–6).

A. *I have experienced the joy of forgiven sins.*
B. *I have experienced the joy of fellowship with Christ.*
C. *I have experienced the joy of fellowship with other Christians.*
D. *I have experienced salvation by the mercy of God because someone cared for me.*

II. My responsibility to witness stems from what I know about humankind's condition without God.

"For all have sinned, and come short of the glory of God" (Rom. 3:23). "For the wages of sin is death; but the gift of God is eternal life through Jesus Christ our Lord" (Rom. 6:23).

A. *I know that people are lost from God and do not know the way home.*
B. *I know that people are lost and perishing away from God.*
C. *I know that perishing people have hope in Christ and in Christ alone.*

III. My responsibility to witness stems from what I have in the way of ability (Matt. 25:14–30).

A. *I have some God-given ability.*
B. *I have the responsibility of dedicating my God-given ability to the glory of God.*
C. *I have God's assurance of increasing that dedicated ability with increased capacity.*

IV. My responsibility to witness stems from what I can have in the way of help from the Holy Spirit.

"And behold, I send the promise of my Father upon you: but tarry ye in the city of Jerusalem, until ye be endued with power from on high" (Luke 24:49). "But ye shall receive power, after that the Holy Ghost is come upon you: and ye shall be witnesses unto me both in Jerusalem, and in all Judaea, and in Samaria, and unto the uttermost part of the earth" (Acts 1:8).

A. *I have Christ's promise of all the power needed for the task of witnessing.*
B. *I have the responsibility to seek that power.*
C. *I have experienced that power in the past and can experience it again.*

Conclusion

I have a responsibility to witness for Christ to a needy world, and so do you. What we do about that responsibility will largely determine the advance of the kingdom of God on earth. More than this, it will determine the eternal destiny of some soul.

SUNDAY MORNING, DECEMBER 5

Title: Jesus, the Prophet

Text: "The Lᴏʀᴅ thy God will raise up unto thee a Prophet from the midst of thee, of thy brethren, like unto me; unto him ye shall hearken" (**Deut. 18:15**).

Scripture Reading: Deuteronomy 18:15–22

Hymns: "Guide Me, O Thou Great Jehovah," Williams
"Thou Didst Leave Thy Throne," Elliott
"When I Survey the Wondrous Cross," Watts
"Hail, Thou Long-Expected Jesus," Wesley

Offertory Prayer: Our heavenly Father, your ministry to us has been so boundless that we here acknowledge as a part of our worship that all we enjoy is from your hand. May the thanksgiving of our hearts ascend to you as an offering. Likewise, may the gifts we bring bless the lives of countless others and advance the kingdom of God in the earth as they express our gratitude to you. In Jesus' name. Amen.

Introduction

Today's text is the occasion of Moses giving his farewell address to his people. He repeats to them all the things that he thinks are important to be remembered and to be preserved down through succeeding generations.

We turn from today's text, in the fifth book in the Bible, to the first book in the New Testament.

I. Matthew presents the New Moses—God's Prophet.

Matthew wrote his gospel to prove to the Jews that Jesus was that one sent from God, who is indeed the Messiah.

A. *Let us begin to notice some physical ways in which Matthew presents Jesus as the new Moses.*

1. Matthew's gospel begins by recounting the generations of the children of Israel from whose genealogy Jesus was born. This is typical of the book of Genesis.
2. Matthew's gospel is divided into five major parts, and these parts parallel the five books of the Pentateuch in the Old Testament.
3. Matthew is recounting in the first part of his gospel some things that closely parallel the life of Moses.
   a. Moses was born during a persecution; Jesus was born during a persecution.
   b. Moses was hunted by a pharaoh; Jesus was hunted by a king.
   c. Moses was in the land of Egypt; Jesus had to flee to the land of Egypt.
   d. Moses begins by giving the Law, which became the Ten Commandments, the book of Leviticus, and the book of Deuteronomy. Jesus began by giving a new law; the Sermon on the Mount.

II. Other New Testament references show parallels between the life of Moses and the life of Jesus.

There are some amazing things that we begin, then, to unravel in the New Testament.

A. *Moses was obliged to give the people water in the wilderness.* And more than once God used Moses to miraculously produce water in a bleached and sunburned land. Jesus said with a loud voice, "If any man thirst let him come unto me, and drink" (John 7:37). There is no doubt that Jesus was saying that he was the Water, the giver and sustainer of life in the wilderness.

B. *Even as Moses was supposed to lead the children of Israel into a promised land, and that responsibility had to be taken over by Joshua, even so, Jesus in the New Testament professes to lead us into the promised land of spiritual eternal life.*

III. Jesus is the Prophet prophesied in the Old Testament.

A. *The first such experience I would direct you to is in Luke 9:28–35.* It is the story of the transfiguration.

  1. The word *transfigured* literally means that the countenance, the appearance of Jesus, was suddenly changed before their very eyes.

  2. Luke 9:31 says that Jesus stood talking to Moses and Elijah about his "decease."

  3. A major point, of course, of the transfiguration is that Jesus is greater than Moses and greater than Elijah. There is something remarkable about these men and the end of their lives.

    a. Moses was buried by God, and only God knew where his body was buried.

    b. The Bible says a chariot of fire swept down and took Elijah up. He was translated. He did not die.

  4. Standing with Jesus, then, was a man who died and a man who did not die, and they were speaking to him, as Luke says, about his "decease."

  5. The point is that Jesus would lead those people who are in spiritual bondage, even as the children of Israel were in actual bondage in Egypt, out into spiritual freedom and into the Promised Land.

  6. The concept of the cloud in the Bible. This cloud is really the *shekinah* cloud of the presence and glory of God. This is, in their thought, where God dwells.

    a. When the children of Israel started out of Egypt, the living presence of God was in that pillar of fire by night and that cloud of smoke by day.

    b. When Moses went up to the top of Mount Sinai to receive the Ten Commandments, the top of the mountain was enveloped in fire and smoke.

    c. In the wilderness wandering the Israelites built a tabernacle, a tent. Everywhere they made camp they set up the tabernacle to worship God. The cloud that was the glory, that was the living presence of God, always dwelt in the tabernacle.

    d. Solomon built the temple, and on the great day of its dedication, God promised that if his people would humble themselves, pray and seek his face, and turn from their wicked ways, he would hear from heaven and heal their land (2 Chron. 7:14).

e. In the account of Jesus' transfiguration, Peter, James, and John are astounded—the cloud comes and covers Jesus and Moses and Elijah. And it was out of that cloud, where the living God dwelt, that the voice came, saying, "This is my beloved son, hear ye him."

f. The presence of God is with us in Jesus.

B. *Look at another incident.* It is no accident in Matthew's gospel that John is at the Jordan baptizing him (Matt. 3:13–17).

Through the same river that the children of Israel crossed to enter the Promised Land, Jesus, by his baptism and the announcement of his public ministry, indicated that he was leading humankind into the promised land of eternal life.

C. *Consider another New Testament description.*

1. John 5:45–47. Jesus himself announced that he was the prophet of God. He was applying the prophecy that Moses made in Deuteronomy 18:15–19 to himself. He was saying that he was the one of whom Moses spoke.

2. But do not make a break there—go on to the next chapter. Jesus teaches.

D. *Remember the Emmaus Road (Luke 24:13–31).*

Conclusion

No wonder Jesus says that when you partake of the Lord's Supper you are to take the bread and bless it and break it, remembering his body, which was broken for you. Not only is he the bread giver, he is also the Bread of Life—the new Moses! He is the prophet like unto Moses, raised up out of Israel—the promise of God come true! He leads us in the new exodus, into the spiritual promised land. He gives us the Bread and Water of Life!

I invite you now, if you are not a Christian, to go with us on this spiritual exodus out of the slavery of sin. Walk with us as Jesus feeds us the Bread and Water of Life and leads us into the spiritual promised land. Will you take him as Lord of your life?

SUNDAY EVENING, DECEMBER 5

Title: Matthew's Witness to Jesus

Text: "And as Jesus passed forth from thence, he saw a man, named Matthew, sitting at the receipt of custom: and he saith unto him, Follow me. And he arose, and followed him" (**Matt. 9:9**).

Scripture Reading: Matthew 9:9–13

Introduction

A serious study of the gospel of Matthew will reveal that the author was a quiet, meditative type of person who was seriously interested in the teachings of

Jesus. His gospel makes no attempt to give a detailed chronological account of the actions of Christ. He is primarily concerned with interpreting Jesus Christ as the fulfillment of Old Testament prophecy.

Matthew portrays Christ not as a Galilean peasant but rather as the King who has come to establish the kingdom of God in the hearts of men.

I. Christ was born of the Virgin Mary to be the King of the Jews (Matt. 2:1–2).

II. Christ was feared as a rival king by Herod (Matt. 2:16).

III. Christ was offered the kingdoms of the world by Satan (Matt. 4:8–10).

IV. Christ described the nature and the conduct of the ideal citizens in the Sermon on the Mount (Matt. 5–7).

V. Christ exercised his kingly authority and power in many areas (Matt. 8:1–9:38).

With kingly authority he manifested his power over sickness, over nature, over the demonic world, and even over death.

In spite of the manifestations of Jesus' authority there were some who refused to accept him as King.

VI. Christ as the King explains the nature of his kingdom in parables (Matt. 13).

VII. Christ made formal claims to divine kingship by his royal entry into Jerusalem (Matt. 21:1–11).

His cleansing of the temple was an act of kingship in the area of worship. His healing of blind and lame people was a manifestation of his kingly authority.

The nations of Israel rejected both Jesus' royal person and his royal purpose.

VIII. Christ was crucified because of his kingship (Matt. 27:37).

Christ was accused of pretending to be the King of the Jews. The accusation was placed on his cross, "This is Jesus the King of the Jews."

Conclusion

Christ was born to be a king. He lived like a king. He died with a kingly serenity and dignity. God declared him to be the King forever by his victorious resurrection from the dead. It was with kingly authority that Jesus commissioned his disciples to carry the good news of the love of God to the ends of the earth.

By the message of a kingship based on love, God would extend the rule of love into your heart. Matthew made Jesus the King of his heart and life. You would be exceedingly wise to make Jesus Christ your King also.

WEDNESDAY EVENING, DECEMBER 8

Title: New Testament Witnessing — Our Greatest Need

Text: "He first findeth his own brother Simon, and saith unto him, We have found the Messias, which is, being interpreted, the Christ. And he brought him to Jesus" (**John 1:41 – 42**).

Scripture Reading: John 1:31 – 49

Introduction

Dr. Robert Speer said, "A person is duty bound to propagate his religion or to change it." In other words, he was saying that unless your religion is worth passing on to others, it isn't worth anything to you.

Those of us who are disciples of Christ, claiming that his wonderful sacrifice for us at Calvary is the means of eternal salvation, surely have something to share with our fellow humans.

There are three types of witnessing or soul winning illustrated in our Scripture reading.

I. The first type of witnessing or soul winning is that done by the preacher (John 1:35 – 39).

In the pages of the New Testament, we have the witness of many preachers who followed in John's footsteps. Perhaps the outstanding example in the early days was that of Peter. We have a record of his sermon at Pentecost and of his message at the temple along with many other instances where he bore public testimony as a preacher of the gospel, spreading the Good News.

Many of us would place the apostle Paul at the top of the list of the preachers of the gospel.

God continues to use the witness of the preaching pastor or evangelist to communicate the Good News to a lost world.

II. The second type of witness or soul winner is the Bible teacher (John 1:43 – 46).

It is recorded that Philip found Nathanael and gave his personal testimony in the form of an interpretation of the Law and the Prophets (John 1:45).

Philip appears again in the New Testament record as an interpreter of the Word of God with a view to helping another person to come to know Jesus Christ as Lord and Savior (Acts 8:29 – 40). He was able to unfold the mysteries of God's Word to the eunuch in a manner that would lead him to commit himself to Jesus Christ.

There are at least three things that we should notice concerning Philip and his witnessing.

A. *Philip knew the Word of God.*

B. *Philip taught the Word of God.*

C. *Philip used the Word of God to win others to discipleship.*

Sunday school teachers have tremendous opportunity in the area of their assigned responsibility. Likewise, they also have a tremendous responsibility.

III. The third type of witness or soul winner is the layperson (John 1:40–42).

At this point, Andrew was a recent convert. By profession he was a fisherman. He was to become famous because of his simple habit of bringing people to Jesus Christ (cf. John 6:8–9; 12:20–22).

Andrew brought Peter to Jesus. Andrew brought a lad to Jesus. Andrew brought the Greeks to Jesus.

It was a simple lay preacher who was seeking to explain the Scriptures when Charles Haddon Spurgeon saw the light and trusted Jesus Christ as his Savior.

Why are there so few personal soul winners? Is it because we have decided that we can win all of the world through the preaching of the gospel from the pulpit? Is it because we feel that the church is organized to accomplish this task? Is it because of our ignorance or unawareness of the need of others for Jesus Christ? Is it because of coldhearted complacency? Is it because of a lack of genuine consecration? Is it because of a fear of failure?

Conclusion

These three types of witnesses or soul winners had something they felt they must share with others. They could not get the permission of their conscience to remain silent in the presence of the need of others. They had an inner compulsion to give voice to that which they knew about the grace, love, and mercy of God.

In Jesus Christ we have found the Water of Life. We should be as eager to share this living water with the thirsty world as Jesus was to share it with the Samaritan woman.

SUNDAY MORNING, DECEMBER 12

Title: Jesus, Our Priest

Text: "But Christ being come an high priest of good things to come, by a greater and more perfect tabernacle, not made with hands, that is to say, not of this building; neither by the blood of goats and calves, but by his own blood he entered in once into the holy place, having obtained eternal redemption for us" **(Heb. 9:11–12).**

Scripture Reading: Hebrews 9:1–14

Hymns: "All Creatures of Our God and King," Francis of Assisi

        "Praise Him! Praise Him!" Crosby

        "Once for All," Bliss

        "Angels from the Realms of Glory," Montgomery

Offertory Prayer: We would, our Father, in this moment of receiving the offering, understand that it is the heart that is won to Jesus, who in love responds openly and joyfully with a gift—to him who is our Lord. Thus may we know that it is an appropriate and meaningful part of our worship to bring gifts to Jesus. Will you, O Father, take it and use it to bless his kingdom, to multiply his glory around the earth. For Jesus' sake we pray. Amen.

Introduction

The function of a prophet is to deliver the word of God to people. The function of the priest is to provide access to God for the people. This brings us into a direct study of the Old Testament law. On Mount Sinai, God gave to Moses the law by which the children of Israel were to serve God. But God said that if they were disobedient, he would not bless them, and they would lose the joy of their relationship to him. Many did break the law, but because God knew the frailty of human nature, he made it possible for those who did break the law to make a sacrifice and once again be accepted.

For hundreds of years, God, according to the laws found in Leviticus, made a provision for the children of Israel to have access to him through the sacrifice of sheep, goats, turtledoves, and the like. This involved the setting up of certain rituals.

I. The old way.

A. *First, in the tabernacle.*

B. *When finally the children of Israel settled in the Promised Land, sacrifices were brought not to the tabernacle but to the temple.*

C. *But it was in the tabernacle and then in the temple that these sacrifices had to be offered.* Any other place was not acceptable.

D. *The people had to bring their sacrifices to the priests to be offered on the altar.*

E. *There were priests who could go farther into the temple than the laymen could, but of the priests there was one priest and only one who could go from the Holy Place into the Holy of Holies.* Only the high priest could make a sacrifice there to atone for the sins of the people, and this took place only once a year on the Day of Atonement.

F. *On the Day of Atonement the high priest purified and cleansed himself and used two goats for a ritual.*

1. The first one, called the scapegoat, had all the sins of the people laid on him through a ritual and then was turned out into the wilderness. Into the lonely wild places of the wilderness this particular goat carried away the sins of the people.

2. The other goat became the sacrifice. The Jews believed that the life was in the blood. This idea was a part of the sacrificial system. The animal had to die. Then the blood of that animal was taken and sprinkled on the altar and symbolically, at least, sprinkled on the people. The idea was this—that the life itself was in the blood. God and the people who

partook of the same life in the sacrificial animal were in this manner brought together, to be one (the "at-one-ment").

II. A new way needed.

We read all through the Old Testament that the children of Israel had a struggle trying to get right and stay right with God.

A. *The Gospels tell us that Jesus understood that his death on the cross would be the only perfect and acceptable sacrifice.*

B. *But how was this to be accomplished?* Jesus, having under his authority all the power that belonged in heaven and in earth, still made the decision to go the way of suffering, the way of dying, the way of the cross.

C. *You and I, left to our human understanding and resources, would have decided this as the last thing.*

   1. But note how Matthew tells the story of Jesus' trial.

   2. Then see Jesus finally condemned by that earthly high priest as he goes out to Calvary as our scapegoat.

   3. See the agonies of the crucifixion that Jesus suffered as the Lamb of God sacrificed for the sins of the world.

D. *In the moment that Jesus expired on the cross the veil in the temple that separated the Holy of Holies from the Holy Place was torn in two from top to bottom, signifying that people could now enter into the presence of God by a new way.* Through the sacrificial death of Jesus Christ on Calvary, people were once and for all being permitted to have access to God, a privilege previously reserved only for priests.

III. The new way had been foreshadowed.

Centuries before, Abraham's wife had given birth to a son whom he loved. The son was born late in Abraham's life, and for that reason was the more precious to him. He and Isaac went out one day to make sacrifice.

A. *The place.* Does it seem a miracle that some archaeologists and Bible scholars feel that the spot on which Abraham offered his son was the spot on Zion's hill where the temple and the Holy of Holies was?

B. *The substitute.* As God had provided a substitute hundreds of years before, he now provided access to himself through the Lamb slain from the foundation of the world, who becomes your substitute and mine.

C. *You and I deserved to die there.* Because of our sin, we had no access to God. Because of the imperfection of the sacrificial system, people had no perfect access to God until that day when Jesus died on Calvary.

IV. The new way is Jesus.

In the beginning, in order to understand what took place, we had to talk about the tabernacle, and we had to talk about the law, the temple, the altar, the Holy of Holies, and then the sacrifice.

But now the need is to point people to Jesus. He is the temple in which God dwells. He is the new law. He is the altar. He is the sacrifice. He is the Holy of

Holies. He fulfills the temple worship and the sacrificial system, and the law, and the temple, and the need for priests and go-betweens in a person's personal relationship to God.

Conclusion

All that the Bible says that the laws and the temple with all of its ritual could ever be, Jesus has become in the New Testament. So he is our High Priest "for ever, after the order of Melchizedec" (Heb. 7:17). He was a Man sent directly from God. He was of the Spirit and power of God himself. He is our eternal Priest who has given us free access to our heavenly Father.

SUNDAY EVENING, DECEMBER 12

Title: Mark's Witness to Jesus

Text: "The beginning of the gospel of Jesus Christ, the Son of God" (**Mark 1:1**).

Scripture Reading: Mark 1:1 – 14

Introduction

Each of the writers of the four Gospels portrays a different picture of Christ and his ministry in the world. Each gospel was written at a different time and to meet a specific need in the lives of the readers. Mark majors on and dramatizes the mighty actions of Jesus.

I. Mark begins his witness for Christ and closes his witness for Christ by emphasizing the gospel (Mark 1:1; 16:20).

His primary purpose in writing the second gospel was to publish the good news of God's love as it was demonstrated in the life, deeds, death, and resurrection of Jesus Christ.

II. Mark emphasizes the miraculous deeds of the Christ.

He was primarily concerned with the activity of Jesus as he sought to introduce the rule of heaven into the hearts of people. He records the miraculous actions of the Christ that demonstrate his kingly authority on the one hand and his servanthood on the other.

III. Mark gives to the world a simple, direct, dramatic record of the life, actions, and achievements of Jesus Christ.

He did not put forth a strenuous effort to interpret or explain actions or events; he merely recorded the facts and left the responsibility of decision with his readers. Perhaps this explains why Mark's gospel is the shortest of the four.

Most New Testament scholars believe that Mark's gospel was the first of the four Gospels and that it was written primarily for Gentile Christians in and

370

around Rome. Mark was led by the Spirit of God to preserve an accurate account of what Jesus had said and done.

Conclusion

Mark would encourage us to put our faith in the miracle-working Christ who lived and loved and died that he might reveal both the grace and the power of God that is available for his children.

WEDNESDAY EVENING, DECEMBER 15

Title: Witnessing—the Responsibility of Every Disciple

Text: "But ye shall receive power, after that the Holy Ghost is come upon you: and ye shall be witnesses unto me both in Jerusalem, and in all Judaea, and in Samaria, and unto the uttermost part of the earth" (**Acts 1:8**).

Scripture Reading: Acts 1:1 – 12

Introduction

When we speak about witnessing, as a rule we think about a special planned encounter with an unsaved person. Therefore, most of us feel that we are not theologically trained to successfully carry out such a mission, and we want to send the paid church staff member to do our witnessing to the unsaved. If this is your concept of carrying out the command of the Savior concerning witnessing, then you need to study what the New Testament has to say about witnessing (Luke 24:46 – 49).

I. Witnessing involves no time limitations.

There are times when it would perhaps be inappropriate to give a verbal witness, but there is never a wrong season or the wrong time for one to give his quiet, effective, and powerful witness as the salt of the earth and the light of the world. This type of living will provide many opportunities for giving a verbal witness.

II. Witnessing involves verbal expression.

Many make the sad mistake of believing that if they just live a good life, then they are fulfilling their responsibility to Christ and to a lost world. To proceed on this basis is to be "good for nothing."

If we would be obedient to Christ, and if we would have his approval, and if we would be a blessing to others, then we must communicate with them verbally concerning the grace and mercy of God.

It is interesting to note that the early disciples had an inward compulsion to speak that they could not restrain. "For we cannot but speak the things which we have seen and heard" (Acts 4:20).

371

III. Witnessing, to be effective, requires the infilling of the Holy Spirit.

On the day of Pentecost, the Holy Spirit entered the church to enable it to successfully respond to Jesus' great commission. The Holy Spirit dwells in the heart of each believer. The Holy Spirit will fill our hearts with love for Christ and a lost world if we will respond positively to his leadership.

To be effective witnesses, we must learn to cooperate with the Holy Spirit. He will lead us to those to whom God would have us to witness. He will lead us at the proper time and to the proper place. He will teach us and show us how to witness.

Conclusion

During the Christmas season, we need to face the fact that for many the true joy of Christmas is yet to be experienced. They have not let the Christ be born in their hearts and lives. They do not know the Prince of Peace. They can come to know him only as Christians share what Jesus Christ means to them personally.

SUNDAY MORNING, DECEMBER 19

Title: Jesus, Our King

Text: "For unto us a child is born, unto us a son is given: and the government shall be upon his shoulder: and his name shall be called Wonderful, Counsellor, The Mighty God, The Everlasting Father, The Prince of Peace. Of the increase of his government and peace there shall be no end, upon the throne of David, and upon his kingdom, to order it and to establish it with judgment and with justice from henceforth even for ever. The zeal of the LORD of hosts will perform it" (**Isa. 9:6–7**).

Scripture Reading: Isaiah 9:1–7

Hymns: "Holy, Holy, Holy," Heber

"O Worship the King," Grant

"All Hail the Power of Jesus' Name," Perronet

Offertory Prayer: Heavenly Father, we thank you that in years past there were those who by faithful stewardship preserved unto us the great heritage of the gospel. Help us to be as faithful. And as we give our tithes and offerings this morning, we pray that you will bless them and use them to touch lives around the world for Christ. In Jesus' name. Amen.

Introduction

The twelve tribes were scattered over Palestine and the Transjordan area. Not until David became king, in approximately 1000 BC, did all the tribes of the Hebrew nation become a kingdom under one king. David had riches and power and honor and respect among all the kings and the nations of the earth. The throne of David became almost synonymous with power and godliness. But more than that: To those who had followed historically and religiously the promise of God made to Abraham centuries ago as he came from Ur of Chaldea, this appeared to be a fulfillment of God's every promise to the Hebrew nation. It was the land that God had led them to. It was the land toward which they had journeyed forty years in the wilderness. This they thought was the fulfilled hope of Israel. However, shortly after David died at about seventy years of age, the kingdom became divided, and their hopes were dashed and broken. It appeared that God had broken his promise. It appeared that the land that God had given them would not really be theirs.

I. David's kingdom became a symbol of something greater.

In about 740 BC, God called a prophet named Isaiah. Isaiah was at ease with kings. He consorted with the elite, the intellectual, the "upper crust" of the land. Isaiah began to prophesy.

A. *The cut-down kingdom would sprout (Isa. 11:1).* The tree of the kingdom had been cut down, but there would come out a new shoot.

B. *The kingdom would have a greater king (Isa. 9:6–7).*

 1. There was going to come one from the house of David who was going to become a king of Israel. Isaiah began to roll back the scales from people's eyes.

 2. A child would be born—a son would be given, and upon his shoulders would rest the government of the world forever, of his government and his kingdom there would be no end. He would rule forever.

II. That greater kingdom was revealed in Christ (Luke 1:31–33).

A. *The angel's announcement to Mary.* And he said, "And, behold, thou shalt conceive in thy womb, and bring forth a son, and shalt call his name JESUS" (Luke 1:31).

B. *The angel referred to the prophecy of Isaiah (Isa. 9:6–7).*

 1. Listen. "He shall be great, and shall be called the son of the Highest: and the Lord God shall give unto him the throne of his father David: And he shall reign over the house of Jacob forever and of his kingdom there shall be no end" (Luke 1:32–33).

 2. Think. Miracle of miracles! Seven and a half centuries later an angel could stand in the presence of a peasant woman and say in effect, "You are going to bring forth that one who is the seed of David."

III. The disciples at first expected an earthly kingdom (Acts 1:6).

A. *The disciples asked.* In Acts 1 one of the disciples asked Jesus, "Lord, wilt thou at this time restore again the kingdom to Israel?"

B. *Jesus replied.* Repeatedly Jesus tried to get through to the apostles what they never seemed to know until after the resurrection. Jesus said, "My kingdom is not of this world."

C. *The triumphal entry showed the difference.*
1. The rejoicing. Children bearing palm branches went before Jesus in the streets and sang, "Hosanna! Hosanna!" They sang of him as a king.
2. The pathos. There was something strange and pathetic about this triumphal entry. Palms were thrown down and the people wept. They were looking for a king to come riding into the city on a white charger before legions of soldiers to take over the city of Jerusalem and return it to its rightful owners, the Jews.

IV. God intended a spiritual kingdom all along.

A. *Zechariah had foretold it (Zech. 9:9).* Prophecy fulfilled!
B. *Isaiah predicted it also (Isa. 53:3).* Jesus was a man of sorrows, lowly and acquainted with grief.
C. *Jesus confirmed it.* Jesus became what God knew he must be if the world was to be redeemed. Watch the gospel story unfold.
D. *The crucifixion illustrated it.*
1. The treatment. Jesus was taken by the cruel, abusive soldiers to the soldiers' barracks for the night, ridiculed, mocked, slapped, spat upon, and cursed.
2. The ridicule. As Jesus appeared, Pilate pointed and said, "Here is your king" (John 19:14).
3. The side events of the trial and crucifixion revealed it.
    a. You remember when Jesus stood before Pilate. Pilate said, "I just want to ask you a question—are you a king?" And Jesus quietly said, "Thou sayest it" (Luke 23:3).
    b. When he died, a sign in three different languages nailed to his cross said, "This is the King of the Jews" (Luke 23:38).
E. The resurrection proved it.
1. The tomb was empty.
2. For forty days Jesus presented himself "with many infallible proofs" (Acts 1:3).
3. His ascension to heaven from the Mount of Olives (Acts 1:9–10).
4. His promised return (Acts 1:11).
5. See in the book of Acts the strength of the persecuted early Christians who were convinced that he was their King.

V. This kingdom will be established forever.

A. *An angel declared it (Rev. 11:15).*
B. *A voice acknowledged it (Rev. 12:10–11a).*
C. *Inspired musicians repeat the glory of it!*
1. G. F. Handel received his inspiration from this heavenly scene. Handel's *Messiah* breaks out with the voices of the choir louder and louder, more forcefully, more dramatically, as they sing the "Hallelujah Chorus."

2. Do you know what the word *hallelujah* means? The *jah* ending on the word is the word for "Jehovah God." *Hallelu* means "Praise be to thee" — thus, "Praise be to God."

Conclusion

Jesus is the Root of David, the stem of Jesse, the Way, and the Lamb slain from the foundation of the world — crucified in Jerusalem, raised from the dead, ascended to the right hand of the throne of God — King of Kings and Lord of Lords.

Who is Jesus? King! Who is this King of glory? Jesus! He shall reign forever and ever. Of the increase of his government there shall be no end. He shall be called, "Wonderful, Counsellor, The Mighty God, The Everlasting Father, The Prince of Peace." Jesus is King! Is he King in your life at this moment? Have you surrendered your will as an obedient subject to the King? Have you yet done what the King said to do, by bringing your life to him? If not, I plead with you now to take him as King of your life.

SUNDAY EVENING, DECEMBER 19

Title: Luke's Witness to Jesus

Text: "That thou mightest know the certainty of those things, wherein thou hast been instructed" (**Luke 1:4**).

Scripture Reading: Luke 1:1–4

Introduction

Each of the gospel writers sought to bear a witness concerning Christ that would meet the needs in the lives of those for whom they wrote. While there are many common emphases in the four Gospels, each is unique.

Luke's gospel is perhaps the easiest of the four Gospels to read and to understand. Luke wrote to reveal the universality of Christianity. He presents his unique witness concerning Christ in order to say to the world that Christianity did not reject Judaism. Instead, Judaism rejected Christ and Christianity because Christ preached the gospel that was for all people. The gospel of Luke is the first of the two volumes that Luke wrote, for he is also the author of the book of Acts, the sequel to the gospel of Luke. These two books should be studied in relationship to each other.

I. Luke was the beloved physician (Col. 4:14).

One cannot study these two books without recognizing that Luke possessed some rather remarkable characteristics. He was an accurate and authoritative historian, and he possessed rare literary ability. He was a theologian as well as a missionary physician.

A. *Luke was the companion of the apostle Paul on his missionary journeys (2 Tim. 4:11; cf. Acts 20:5–21:17; 27:2–28:16).*
B. *The gospel of Luke was addressed to a highly esteemed Christian friend (Luke 1:3; cf. Acts 1:1).* It is believed by many that Luke's gospel was written during Paul's imprisonment at Caesarea.

II. Luke emphasizes the all-inclusive love of God for people.

The nature of this witness concerning the all-inclusive love of God is emphasized in the wording of the angelic announcement of the birth of the Savior. "Fear not: for, behold, I bring you tidings of great joy, which shall be to all people" (Luke 2:10). The last three words in this angelic announcement are not accidental or incidental. They proclaim the universality of the concern of the Savior for people. Simeon's song in the temple contains the same emphasis (Luke 2:29–32). The salvation of God is for all people. The Savior is to be a light to enlighten the Gentiles.

To emphasize again the universality of the concern of God, Luke brings his gospel to a close by quoting the Savior's commission to the effect that the Good News must be preached "among all nations, beginning at Jerusalem" (Luke 24:47).

III. Luke places more emphasis on prayer than any of the other writers.

The gospel of Luke has been called the Gospel of Prayer.

A. *Luke records seven occasions when Jesus prayed.*
1. He prayed before his baptism (3:21).
2. He prayed before his first clash with the Pharisees (5:16).
3. He prayed when he was about to choose the Twelve (6:12).
4. He prayed before questioning his disciples in a manner that brought forth the great confession (9:18).
5. He prayed in connection with the transfiguration (9:28).
6. He prayed while on the cross (23:34, 36).
7. What we call the Lord's Prayer was given to teach the disciples how to pray.
B. *Two parables in the gospel encourage persistence in prayer (Luke 11:5–8; 18:1–8).*

IV. Luke's gospel contains specific warnings concerning the dangers of wealth and the folly of a secular approach to life.

A. *The foolish farmer (Luke 12:13–21).*
B. *The rich man and Lazarus (Luke 16:19–31).*

Conclusion

Luke's gospel presents to us a picture of the Savior weeping over the city of Jerusalem (14:34–35). These were tears of compassion and concern for a city and a people who had rejected their destiny and refused to cooperate with God's great purpose for them. He yearned to be Jerusalem's Savior, Teacher, and Guide. He was eager to help the people become a part of God's great redemptive program of saving a world from sin, selfishness, and destruction. He wept because of the destiny they were bringing upon themselves.

Have you refused to hear God's gracious invitation to your heart? It is not too late for us if we will but fully and completely open ourselves up to God's Holy Spirit and become responsive to him as he seeks to lead us in the ways of God.

WEDNESDAY EVENING, DECEMBER 22

Title: Sharing Jesus with All People

Text: "Behold, three men seek thee. Arise, therefore, and get thee down, and go with them" (**Acts 10:19–20**).

Scripture Reading: Acts 10:1–20

Introduction

A dog that growls while wagging his tail is lying at one end. The same inconsistency is evident in many of our lives and churches. We believe Jesus Christ is the only Savior for all the people of the world. We send our missionaries to the furthest corners of the earth to tell people of all races about Christ. Yet we have not learned to love people of all races here at home.

I. Good grief!

We often find ourselves in Charles Schulz's popular comic strip, *Peanuts.* In one episode, Lucy is talking to Linus. The first picture presents Lucy jumping her rope while saying, "*You* a doctor! Ha! That's a laugh." Standing directly in front of him in the second picture, she says, "You can never be a doctor! You know why?" Poor Linus has not said a word. In the third picture, Lucy, nonchalantly jumping her rope again, continues, "Because you don't love mankind, that's why!"

In the last picture, thumb-sucking, blanket-carrying Linus, with about all of Lucy's advice he can endure, replies vehemently, "I love mankind! It's people I can't stand." •

II. Learning to be prejudiced.

The teacher asked a question, but no one answered. Finally, a bright-eyed little girl on the front row said to the teacher, "Mrs. Thomas, there's a boy in the class who knows the answer to that question, but he won't speak up."

The teacher asked, "Who is it?" The little girl pointed across the room to the only nonwhite student in the class and said, "That boy there in the blue sweater."

Because this child had not been taught to be prejudiced, she was more aware of the color of his sweater than the color of his skin. We learn our prejudices. We are not born with them.

Peter had a never-to-be-forgotten experience that taught him the need for world evangelism and the sin of prejudice. Cornelius, a Roman army officer, was a devout man of prayer. Even though he was a Gentile, he was quite interested in the Jewish religion. In a vision, God instructed him to seek out Peter who was staying at Joppa about thirty miles away (Acts 10:1–8).

At the same time, God was preparing Peter for his encounter with Cornelius (Acts 10:9–16). Peter had an unusual experience while praying on a rooftop. As far as Peter was concerned, salvation was not only *of* the Jews, it was also *for* the Jews. Something like a great sheet, held by its four corners, was let down from heaven to him. In this sheet were both "clean" and "unclean" animals. They were designated clean and unclean by Jewish food laws that said that only certain "clean" creatures could be eaten. A voice instructed Peter to "kill and eat." As a devout Jew, he felt he could not obey. Perhaps he had forgotten that Jesus declared all food to be clean (Mark 7:19). Perhaps he had also forgotten Jesus' declaration that a person is not defiled by what he or she eats (Mark 7:15). At any rate, Peter refused to obey the voice from heaven, saying that he had never eaten anything common or unclean. Then the voice from heaven said something that Peter must have remembered the rest of his life: "What God hath cleansed, that call not thou common" (Acts 10:15).

In the meantime, the men from Cornelius's house arrived, told Peter of their mission, and took him to Cornelius (Acts 10:17–23). A large company of people were assembled at the house of Cornelius to hear Peter (vv. 24–29). After Cornelius gave an account of his vision (vv. 30–33), Peter preached a sermon that was, in essence, almost the same sermon that he had preached at Pentecost (vv. 34–43). The Holy Spirit descended on the hearers, and they responded with commitment (vv. 43–48).

III. Learning to love.

Since we learn to be prejudicial, we must also learn to love. It often is easy to love humankind but difficult to love individuals. Our Lord teaches us to love our neighbor as ourselves (Matt. 22:39). In other words, I should love my neighbor as though I were my neighbor. It is somewhat like crawling under the other person's skin and trying to see the world as he or she feels it.

A unique school in Britain attempts to teach its students sensitivity. For a day, the children are blindfolded and taught to live without eyes. Through this experience, they learn to appreciate the blind. Their ears are stopped for a day, teaching them to understand the deaf. Likewise, everyone should learn more about love, taking on in the imagination the complexion of another race for a while.

When the Battle of Shiloh was at its peak, President Lincoln encountered the brother and sister-in-law of General Lew Wallace. The sister-in-law said to the president, "We had heard that General Wallace was among the killed, and we were afraid that it was *our* Wallace, but it wasn't." The tear-filled eyes of Abraham Lincoln looked into the happy face of the woman as he said, "Ah, but it was *somebody's* Wallace." Everybody's Wallace was his Wallace. He had learned to love his neighbor as himself.

378

IV. The greatest love act.

What better place than at the cross can this lesson be learned? The greatest act of love in history was the atoning death of the Savior on the cross. There he died for all people, assuring us that God is no respecter of persons or color.

The cross was not the Outstanding Young Citizen's Award presented to a young Jew in AD 33 by the Jerusalem Chamber of Commerce. It was the instrument of his death. Our Lord still bids us to take up our cross in repentance and faith and die to self so we may learn to love and to erase our prejudices.

In Christ, external differences among people are abolished, for Christ died for all people regardless of race or nationality (John 3:16). Christians of all races are brothers and sisters in Christ (Luke 13:29). None of God's creatures are inferior to others, because they were all created in "the image of God" (Gen. 1:27). One of the most evident truths of the Bible is "God is no respecter of persons" (Acts 10:34; Rom. 2:11; Eph. 6:9; 1 Peter 1:17). In Christ, there is neither Jew nor Greek, slave nor free, male nor female (Gal. 3:28; Col. 3:11).

V. Two lessons.

Peter learned two lessons that every Christian must always remember: "God hath shewed me that I should not call any man common or unclean" (Acts 10:28), and "Of a truth I perceive that God is no respecter of persons" (v. 34).

Plato said, "All men are by nature equal, made of the same earth by the same Creator, and however we deceive ourselves, as dear to God is the poor peasant as the mighty prince." How beautiful were the words of Harriet Beecher Stowe when she said, "In the gates of eternity the black hand and the while hold each other in an equal clasp." Billy Graham said, "When we show contempt to any creature which God has made, we insult the one who made him. Therefore, we should all be compassionate with all men — especially those who were born in situations which automatically handicap them from being accepted by the majority."

SUNDAY MORNING, DECEMBER 26

Title: Jesus, the Fulfillment

Text: "And she shall bring forth a son, and thou shalt call his name JESUS: for he shall save his people from their sins. Now all this was done, that it might be fulfilled which was spoken of the Lord by the prophet" (**Matt. 1:21–22**).

Scripture Reading: Matthew 1:18–25

Hymns: "Silent Night, Holy Night," Mohr

"Joy to the World," Watts

"While Shepherds Watched Their Flocks," Tate

"O Little Town of Bethlehem," Brooks

Offertory Prayer: Our Father, motivated by the fact that we have made a conscious, willful decision to follow Jesus, we bring you our tithes and our offerings. We believe in our hearts that what this world needs more than anything else is he whose season it is and whose birth we celebrate in these precious days. May your Spirit grant that this season of generosity may cause us to open our hearts to the needs of people around the world. May we know that we cannot adequately represent the Spirit of Jesus until we share his concern to give a cup of cold water in his name. May it be through all of this that we finally give to the world the best gift of all, Jesus himself. We pray it in his name. Amen.

Introduction

Many of you, when you were young, had the occasion to get out in the brilliant sun with a magnifying glass. Taking that magnifying glass and holding it above white paper or brown leaves, you permitted the rays of the sun, now focused, to start a flame. This flame was caused by the intensity of the heat created by the focusing of the sun's rays at a certain point. In the focusing of the sun's rays there is power to start a fire. It is in just such an example that I find in the Bible the wonderful power of the story of Jesus.

I. Let us look first at the expectation with which the world awaited this unusual event.

A. *God had revealed to the people of the Old Testament that there would be born one day a man who would be their Savior and Messiah.* He was spoken of by the prophets as being one whose birth and life were so singular that he could have been no less than God himself.

B. *It is also a well-known fact that the common folk in Israel, not only the prophets, had come to look for a Messiah who would be a Savior to them.* But between the Old and New Testaments there was a period of more than four hundred years when there was no prophet and when there was no special word from God.

C. *In the silence God was in his own way focusing the rays of his revelation on the most dramatic night the world has ever seen.*

D. *By the time of the New Testament, the expectancy was intense.*
  1. The people had begun to see the cruelty of their rulers.
  2. They had begun to feel disappointment in the faults and excesses of temple worship.

II. Thus the event took place on a solitary night in the springtime.

There was such a combination of unusual events that anyone would have to say that surely it was a spectacular night.

A. *First there is the record of some sheep farmers.*
  1. They had been sitting there as they had on a thousand other nights, when suddenly the whole night was bright and angels appeared unto them.

2. One angel said, "Glory to God in the highest, and on earth peace, good will toward men."
3. The shepherds were frightened.
4. The angel then said, "Fear not, for behold I bring you good tidings of great joy which shall be to all people."
5. Then the angel was joined with other angels as the earth and sky were filled with "a multitude of the heavenly host." (The word for heavenly host means a whole army of angels.)
6. People might have said the shepherds were out of their minds except that all the shepherds saw the whole army of angels praising God and singing, "Glory to God in the highest, and on earth peace, good will toward men."

B. *About two years later, as many authorities think, some men came from the land of Babylon.* Ancient Babylon was thought of by some to be the cradle of earth's civilization. They had seen unusual signs in the sky.
1. They might have found that Balaam the prophet, in Numbers 24:17 had said that one of these days, out of Jacob there was going to come a Star.
2. They discovered how Isaiah had said that one day the Messiah would come as a servant (Isa. 53).
3. They read Micah 5:2, which said that the place would be Bethlehem. With these clues they journeyed to Bethlehem. They asked those in authority about the young King.

C. *Add to this the "slaughter of the innocents" by Herod the tetrarch.* History records that Herod slaughtered all the boy babies two years old and younger.

D. *In addition to these events, it is clearly shown in history that the greatest Man ever born was born in that same era.*

E. *Architecture, literature, art, philosophy, and learning (from every branch and every kind in the history of the world) have been affected by the fact that there was born in Bethlehem, on this particular night, the Man who affected the history of the world more than any other man who ever lived.*

F. *The events of that time in the Middle East brought so fantastic a focus of the parallel lines of divine revelation and human experience that it cannot be denied that it was the most dramatic focal point in the history of the world.*
1. Think about what happened. In the birth of that baby in a cow stall, God took on the form of a man through his Son.
2. Out on the hillside a group of men, who were not special men, talked with angels.
3. Nature and God and man cooperated. The wise men, in seeing the star, saw a harmony like unto which the world had not seen since humankind had been in the Garden of Eden.
4. In these three revelations people discovered great things about this God who chose to reveal himself to humankind in the coming of a little baby. It was truly an unusual night in the history of the world.

III. Now look at the excitement of believing as the wise men did.

It was some months later when the wise men got there. Sometimes pictures on Christmas cards show that the wise men came to the stable. The Bible says otherwise.

A. *The wise men came not to the stable where Jesus was born but to the home of Mary and Joseph months later.*

B. *There is something unusual about that.* Can you imagine men traveling that far in those days to find a king and going to the little hovel of a home that would have been the only kind afforded by Joseph?

   1. He did not look like a king.

   2. They saw in that little baby a king. Though he was among the common people and lowly they did not waver that this was the King.

C. *Christmas may be filled with presents, laughter, and material things.* But don't forget the best! Look at the Christ child with eyes of faith, and you will go away having something happening to your heart.

Conclusion

Has this magic of Christmas happened to you? I pray to God it has. It can change your life. If you have never put your faith in this Savior, won't you please do it today?

SUNDAY EVENING, DECEMBER 26

Title: John's Witness to Jesus

Text: "And many other signs truly did Jesus in the presence of his disciples, which are not written in this book: But these are written, that ye might believe that Jesus is the Christ, the Son of God; and that believing ye might have life through his name" **(John 20:30–31).**

Scripture Reading: John 20:19–31

Introduction

One does not have to search diligently to find the controlling purpose of the writer of the fourth gospel, for John himself clearly states his purpose in providing us with his written witness concerning Jesus Christ. With all of his heart he believed that Jesus of Nazareth was the unique and divine Son of God. He was convinced that through faith in Jesus Christ people would find eternal life. He wrote to persuade his readers to respond in faith to Jesus Christ that they might experience eternal life.

John's gospel is the account of his personal firsthand experience with Jesus Christ. It takes the form of an official testimony whose purpose is that of convincing his readers that they likewise should believe that Christ is the Son of God.

John uses seven great miracles, or signs, to record his testimony that Jesus Christ is indeed the Son of God. He describes the miraculous event and then seeks to interpret the meaning of the miracle. His witness to Christ primarily centers in the meaning of these miracles or signs. By these miracles Jesus manifested his unique nature, power, and purpose as the Son of God.

I. The turning of water into wine (John 1:1–11).

II. The healing of the nobleman's son (John 4:46–54).

III. The healing of the lame man (John 5:1–16).

IV. The feeding of the five thousand (John 6:1–14).

V. His walking on the sea (John 6:15–21).

VI. The healing of the man who was born blind (John 9).

VII. The raising of Lazarus from the grave (John 11:1–14).

Conclusion

Each of these miracles could provide the occasion for a lengthy lecture or a stimulating sermon. By these miracles Jesus was manifesting the concern of God for the welfare of people. By selecting these miracles for inclusion in his gospel, John was bearing his personal testimony concerning Jesus Christ. John had his testimony, and you and I have our testimonies. John records Jesus' beatitude of congratulations upon those who believe because of the faithful testimony of those who were eyewitnesses to his redemptive life (John 20:29).

You and I should believe the testimony of John concerning Jesus. We must believe it if we are to experience the life that Jesus offers. You and I also have a witness concerning Jesus to give to others through our testimony. The Holy Spirit can impart to them the gift of faith.

WEDNESDAY EVENING, DECEMBER 29

Title: Our Greatest Debt

Text: "I am debtor both to the Greeks, and to the Barbarians; both to the wise, and to the unwise. So, as much as in me is, I am ready to preach the gospel to you that are at Rome also" (**Rom. 1:14–15**).

Scripture Reading: Romans 1:1–17

Introduction

We come to the end of the year, and we take an inventory. We find some satisfaction in knowing that we have met some financial obligations during the past year. Some of us may be disturbed over the fact that we have financial obligations hanging over us that we must meet during the new year.

As individuals we like to pay our debts; but there is a debt that many of us have without being aware of it. It is our greatest debt, because "the goods received" are priceless.

I. We are debtors to God.

A. *For the material blessings of life.* We have but to look around us to see the evidences of God's generosity.

B. *For the hope that is eternal within us.* It cost God something to bestow this eternal hope within us. It cost him the life and death of his Son, Jesus Christ.

II. We are debtors to those who have gone on before us.

A. *We are indebted to those who have suffered that we might know the way of truth.*

B. *Many people have literally given their lives that the gospel might be proclaimed in a manner that has made our civilization as Christian as it is.*

C. *We are spiritually in debt for the ministry of our immediate spiritual forefathers who brought the blessings of God into our lives.*

III. How can we meet our spiritual obligation?

A. *Paul believed that the rich blessings of God placed him under an obligation to share those blessings with others.*

B. *We can attempt to meet our spiritual obligation in a number of different ways.*

1. We should love Christ warmly and with loyalty.

2. We should put forth a persistent effort to be obedient to the Great Commission by giving our personal testimony.

3. Our talents, time, and financial resources should be dedicated to the cause of Christ and for the salvation of lost men and women.

Conclusion

We face a new year of responsibility and opportunity. We have a heavy debt to God and a continuing debt to a lost world. Let us determine tonight to be faithful. Let us determine tonight to face the new year with enthusiasm and with determination to pay our spiritual debt of love to God and to all of those, whether they be Christians or non-Christians, who cross our path during the coming year.

Miscellaneous Helps

Messages on the Lord's Supper

Title: The Master's Memorial

Text: "He took bread, gave thanks and broke it, and gave it to them, saying, "This is my body given for you; do this in remembrance of me" (**Luke 22:19 NIV**).

Scripture Reading: 1 Corinthians 11:23–29

Introduction

One may see many elaborate memorials to great people as one travels around the world, but all of them combined do not mean as much as the table spread before us. It was given to us by our Lord; it is "The Master's Memorial."

I. Remember Calvary.

It was the place of Jesus' death. Some would discount history, even debunk it. But this service of memorial speaks of the historical Jesus who visited this earth in a time-event circumstance that he might die for sinners. This memorial speaks of his death and its meaning.

A. *Its atoning power.* "*The blood of Jesus, [God's] Son, purifies us from all sin*" (1 John 1:7 NIV).

B. *Its redeeming benefit.* "*Thou wast slain, and hast redeemed us to God by thy blood*" (Rev. 5:9).

II. Remember the tomb.

There Jesus was buried. Beyond all sacrifices of the Levitical system the death of Jesus had meaning. This memorial calls us to remembrance of a span of three days following that 3:00 P.M. Good Friday event when Jesus said, "Father, into thy hands I commend my spirit." We remember now his burial.

This becomes extremely personal. It matters not how fair the garden of your life may be; somewhere therein is a grave. But remember this: Death loses its sting and terror in the redemptive work of Christ on the cross. He has gone before us. He "tasted death for every man."

III. Remember the first Easter.

This calls us to remember Jesus' resurrection. "The Master's Memorial" reminds us of the greatest single event in history. A visit to Independence Hall calls to our memory a great event that transpired at Philadelphia, but a visit to the Lord's Table reminds us of an event that transcends all monuments and memorials ever conceived by human minds or built by human hands.

A. *A great fact of history.* "Why seek ye the living among the dead? He is not here, but is risen" (Luke 24:5–6).

B. *A grand word of promise.* His word to us assures us of our ultimate triumph over death if we trust in him: "I am the resurrection, and the life: he that believeth in me, though he were dead, yet shall he live: And whosoever liveth and believeth in me shall never die" (John 11:25–26).

IV. Remember Olivet.

That was the place where by appointment Jesus met with his disciples, commissioned them to perform his world missions endeavor, and then ascended to the Father (Matt. 28:16ff.; Luke 24:49–53; Acts 1:8–12).

A. *A recorded fact of history.* "And when he had spoken these things, while they beheld, he was taken up; and a cloud received him out of their sight" (Acts 1:9).

B. *A fact that provides significant power.* Paul said, "When he ascended up on high, he led captivity captive, and gave gifts unto men" (Eph. 4:8).

C. *A fact that assured his continuing ministry.* The writer of Hebrews said, "When he had by himself purged our sins, [he] sat down on the right hand of the Majesty on high" (Heb. 1:3).

V. Remember his promised return.

Our Lord *is* coming back: he said, "I will come again...." (cf. Matt. 24:30ff.; Acts 1:11; et al.).

A. *The* parousia *(second coming of Christ) was promised.* Jesus repeatedly told his disciples that he would come again at the end of the age to climax all world history.

B. *This promise is renewed with every observance of this memorial.* "For as often as ye eat this bread, and drink this cup, ye do shew the Lord's death till he come" (1 Cor. 11:26). In all ages of Christian history this promise has been called "the blessed hope."

Conclusion

Let us come to our Lord's Table remembering all that he has done for us, and in lowliness of spirit let us contemplate the riches of all that he has done within us and will yet do for us.

Title: The Challenge of the Lord's Supper

Text: "And when he had given thanks, he brake it, and said, Take, eat: this is my body, which is broken for you: this do in remembrance of me. After the same manner also he took the cup, when he had supped, saying, This cup is the New Testament in my blood: this do ye, as oft as ye drink it, in remembrance of me" (**1 Cor. 11:24–25**).

Scripture Reading: 1 Corinthians 11:23–32

Introduction

The Lord's Supper is more than a quiet, rich, spiritual experience in which we share from time to time. Beneath the dignity of this ordinance rests some stern challenges that only the mature in spirit will dare to meet.

Only until we are strong enough to respond to the challenges of our Lord's Supper will we ever really experience the peace and closeness to God that it can impart. The Lord's Supper will be nothing more to you than a religious ritual mechanically observed unless you are willing to allow its challenges to probe deeply into your heart.

I. The challenge to see the true image of yourself.

As we read verses 24 and 25 we realize that we are not that fine upright person whom we envision ourselves to be. We are the ones responsible for that broken body and shed blood of Jesus. The Lord's Supper challenges you to see yourself as God does.

A. *A depraved sinner.* The Bible tells us that "there is none righteous, no, not one" (Rom. 3:10). At your best you are a reject in God's sight, for your righteousness is as filthy rags.

B. *Guilty of the death of Christ.* "Christ died for our sins according to the scriptures" (1 Cor. 15:3b). The fact is simply this: "The wages of sin is death." Therefore sin must be paid for by either your death or the death of Christ.

C. *Utterly dependent on God's grace.* The challenge of the Lord's Supper is for you to see yourself as you are — a depraved sinner, guilty of the death of Christ, and utterly dependent on God's grace.

II. The challenge to live up to the transformation you profess.

A woman whose husband had accepted Christ was asked, "Is it true that your husband has changed his religion?" "No," she answered, "but his religion has changed him!" The Lord's Supper reminds us that we must so live as to bear evidence of having been cleansed by the broken body and shed blood of Jesus Christ.

III. The challenge to remember the central theme of the Christian faith.

"For as often as ye eat this bread, and drink this cup, ye do shew the Lord's death till he come" (1 Cor. 11:26). The church has no new message for our time, for men are still lost sinners and the way of salvation is still through Christ.

IV. The challenge to partake in the right attitude.

"Wherefore whosoever shall eat this bread, and drink this cup of the Lord, unworthily, shall be guilty of the body and blood of the Lord" (1 Cor. 11:27). Our belief that Scripture calls us to partake in a right attitude is based upon the adverb "unworthily." Paul is not saying that any of us are worthy to touch even a symbol of the body or blood of Christ, but he does say we can partake of it in a worthy manner. This word modifies not the man who partakes of the Lord's Supper but the manner in which he partakes.

A. *The right manner acknowledges the wrong committed. As we gather around the table of our Lord we should be willing to confess our sins, knowing that he is faithful and just to forgive us our sins.*

387

B. *The right attitude forgives our offenders.*
  1. God's forgiveness of you is dependent on your forgiveness of others, for Jesus reminds us, "But if ye do not forgive, neither will your Father which is in heaven forgive your trespasses" (Mark 11:26).
  2. Failure to forgive makes mockery of the supper of our Lord.

V. The challenge to make a self-examination.

"But let a man examine himself, and so let him eat of that bread, and drink of that cup" (1 Cor. 11:28).
  A. *Self-examination will spare you divine judgment.* "For if we would judge ourselves, we would not be judged" (1 Cor. 11:31). Divine judgment comes only as God's last resort.
  B. *Self-examination will lead to an understanding of present trials.* "But when we are judged, we are chastened of the Lord, that we should not be condemned with the world" (1 Cor. 11:32).

Conclusion

> *In this broken bread we claim thee,*
> *Bruised for us and put to shame;*
> *And this cup, O Lord, we thank thee,*
> *Speaks our pardon through thy name.*
>
> *—J. R. McBride*

MESSAGES FOR CHILDREN AND YOUNG PEOPLE

Title: Life's Great Choices

Text: "And if it seem evil unto you to serve the LORD, choose you this day whom ye will serve; whether the gods which your fathers served that were on the other side of the flood, or the gods of the Amorites, in whose land ye dwell: but as for me and my house, we will serve the LORD" **(Josh. 24:15)**.

Scripture Reading: Joshua 24:14–25

Introduction

Our lives are made up of choices. You chose whether you would get up this morning or whether you would sleep through breakfast. You chose whether you would go to school or not. You choose whether you will study or not. You choose what clothes you will wear, what friends you will have, and what activities you will pursue.

The Bible places great emphasis on this matter of choice. Joshua said, "Choose ye this day whom ye will serve." Elijah said, "How long halt ye between two opinions?" Moses said, "I have set before you life and death. Choose life and live."

Out of the many choices in life, there are three that are of paramount importance — three that will determine your happiness here and in eternity.

I. First, there is the choice of a Master of life.

A. *Jesus said, "No man can serve two masters."* You serve either God or Satan. You serve righteousness or sin. There is no middle ground. Jesus said, "You are either for me or against me." Look at these two masters and see what they offer.

B. *Look at the man who serves Satan and sin.*
   1. Paul said, "He that commits sin is the slave of sin." Sin has become his master.
   2. Romans 6:23 reads, "The wages of sin is death." Satan offers happiness but gives misery. He promises peace but gives turmoil. He offers life but gives death.

C. *When Christ is Master he gives:*
   1. A new life. "If any man be in Christ, he is a new creation; old things are passed away; behold, all things are become new" (2 Cor. 5:17).
   2. A new power. "I can do all things through Christ who strengthens me" (Phil. 4:13).
   3. A new happiness. Life takes on new meaning and purpose when one is in Christ. It is a life of joy.
   4. A new destiny. "In my father's house are many mansions" (John 14:1). Your name is written in the Lamb's Book of Life.

II. Second, there is the choice of a mate.

A. *One's happiness in all areas of life is determined by the choice of a companion.*

B. *You determine the kind of person you marry by the kind of person you date.*

C. *You may have standards that are too high mentally, socially, or physically, but your moral standards can never be too high.*

D. *Because of its importance, you should seek God's guidance in your selection.*

E. *Your choice should certainly be a Christian person.*

III. Third, there is the choice of a mission in life.

A. *This question constantly reoccurs to a young person.* Where shall I invest my life? What vocation shall I follow? Whatever your choice, it must be within the context of God's will for your life.

B. *God may lead you to be a doctor or lawyer, a butcher or baker; but whatever it is, you must determine to be the best Christian possible.*

C. *God may call you to a church-related vocation — full-time Christian service.*
   1. There are many avenues of service open here — pastoral, ministerial, education, music, secretarial, children's work, etc.
   2. The need is great. Jesus said, "Lift up your eyes unto the fields. They are white already unto harvest." God needs you.

D. *Your happiness and usefulness depend on the proper choice here.* Many would testify in their unhappiness: "How I wish I had done God's will when he called. Now I have only regrets."

Conclusion

The choice is yours. You may drift and delay, but time will make the choice for you. Today is the time to decide. "Remember now thy creator in the days of thy youth."

Title: The Needs of Youth

Text: "Remember now thy Creator in the days of thy youth, while the evil days come not, nor the years draw near, when thou shalt say, I have no pleasure in them" **(Eccl. 12:1).**

Scripture Reading: Ecclesiastes 12

Introduction

Physically and intellectually, youth never had it so good! Teenagers have more money to spend, more places to go, more things to do, and more opportunities for success in life than ever before. Yet teens still have some basic needs, which, if unmet, will cause them to miss out on the rich and full life God wants them to have.

I. Youth need someone who cares.

Some of the saddest words recorded in sacred Scripture were spoken by David (Ps. 142:4).

A. *Youth need someone in the home who cares.*
1. In the home the fiber of character is woven. The Bible assures us, "Train up a child in the way he should go: and when he is old, he will not depart from it" (Prov. 22:6).
2. In the home God's truths are to be taught. "And he said unto them, Set your hearts unto all the words which I testify among you this day, which you shall command your children to observe to do, all the words of this law" (Deut. 32:46).
B. *Youth need someone in the church who cares.*
1. In the church a *personal* interest must be shown.
2. In the church a proper program must be offered.
3. In the church God's Word must be taught.

II. Youth need an example.

Wendell Phillips said, "If I had a great idea to give the world, I would put it in boots and send it across the continent." And Jesus Christ said, "Let your light so shine before men that they may *see* your good works, and glorify your Father which is in heaven" (Matt. 5:16; emphasis added).

A. *Youth need an example of consistent Christianity.*

390

1. Youth need an example of consistent Christianity that acts as good at home as at church. Some adults act like children in front of their own families and consequently call into question the faith of Jesus Christ.
2. Youth need an example of consistent Christianity that applies one's faith to all areas of life.
3. Youth need an example of consistent Christianity that expresses as much interest during the week as on Sunday.

B. *Youth need an example of loyalty to the church.*
C. *Youth need an example of high goals and ambitions.*

III. Youth need knowledge.

God's Word admonishes us that "wisdom is the principal thing; therefore get wisdom: and with all thy getting get understanding" (Prov. 4:7).

A. *Youth need a knowledge of youth's potentialities.*
B. *Youth need a knowledge of youth's dangers.* Peter reminds us, "Be sober, be vigilant; because your adversary the devil, as a roaring lion, walketh about, seeking whom he may devour" (1 Peter 5:8).

   Some of the dangers of which youth need a knowledge are the dangers of:
   1. Following the crowd (Prov. 1:10).
   2. The tragedy of lost virtue (Prov. 7:6–10, 26–27).
   3. Pride (1 Cor. 10:12).
   4. Slothfulness (Prov. 15:19; 19:15).

IV. Youth need a Savior.

Our text reads, "Remember now thy Creator in the days of thy youth" (Eccl. 12:1a).

A. *Youth need a Savior because they may be lost.* The Scripture states that all have sinned.
B. *Youth need a Savior because life is complicated (Ps. 107:19).*
C. *Youth need a Savior because there is a life beyond for all.*

Conclusion

> *He stood at the crossroads all alone,*
> *The sunlight in his face;*
> *He had no thought for a world unknown,*
> *He was out for a manly race.*
> *But the road stretched east, and the road stretched west,*
> *And the boy did not know which road was best;*
> *So he took the wrong road and went down,*
> *And lost his race and the victor's crown;*
> *He was caught at last in an angry snare*
> *Because no one stood at the crossroads there*

To show him the better road.
Another day at the same place
A boy with high hopes stood.
He, too, was set for a manly race;
He was seeking the things that were good.
And one was there who the roads did know,
And that one showed him which way to go;
And he turned away from the road that led down
And he won the race and the victor's crown;
Because one stood at the crossroads there
To show him the better road.

—Author Unknown

FUNERAL MEDITATIONS

Title: My Help Cometh from the Lord

Text: "My help cometh from the LORD, which made heaven and earth" (**Ps. 121:2**).

Scripture Reading: Psalm 121

Introduction

There are times when each of us stands in need of help. In many respects, humans are helpless creatures in need of the help of others. We are born in a state of helplessness, and as we approach death, we find ourselves in a helpless condition. There are many points along the journey between birth and death when we must have the help of others.

When death comes to take a loved one from our midst, there are many resources for help through a difficult time.

I. We can receive help from memory.

By some miracle, death can cause us to forget many unpleasant things, and we have a tendency to remember only that which was good. If there is an abundance of pleasant memories, this can help us greatly.

II. We can receive help from friends.

Those who have experienced grief in the presence of a great host of Christian friends are indeed fortunate, for Christian compassion brings these friends to our side to help us in our time of need. They bring flowers. They bring food to the home. They bring the strength of their presence to relieve suffering and to encourage us. We can thank God for friends in the time of sorrow.

III. We can receive help from the Scriptures.

The precious promises of God's Word can give us assurance concerning our beloved dead who died in the Lord (Rev. 14:13). The apostle Paul sought to bring comfort to the hearts of those who were distressed concerning those who died in the hope that the Lord would return before death came to them (1 Thess. 5:13–18). He assured these believers that the dead in Christ would be raised from the dead to die no more.

Fortunate indeed is the person who, along the journey of life, has filled his or her mind and heart with the precious promises of God concerning immortality and the life eternal. These great promises from the Scriptures will come marching to the rescue in the time of need.

IV. Our greatest help comes from the Lord.

As wonderful as pleasant memories and as gratifying as the presence of friends and as valuable as are the promises of the Scriptures, our real source of strength and help is to be found in the Lord himself.

God has been gracious and good to us in the past. He has blessed us beyond what we deserve. And he is with us today to sustain, to strengthen, and to impart wisdom. He is as near to us as the breath that we breathe.

The living Lord who conquered death and the grave and who walked and talked with his disciples will meet those who grieve as they walk the road of life. He will speak words of comfort and strength and help to them.

Conclusion

I pray that you will have eyes that can see, ears that can hear, and a heart that can recognize and respond to God not only during this day of sorrow but for all of the future days when you are called on to work and worship and witness.

Death is no dead-end street to those who trust Christ. It is instead the doorway into the eternal home. In this faith let us face the future with courage and hope and determination to live a full life for the glory of God and for the welfare of others.

Title: Christ's Word of Comfort

Text: "Let not your heart be troubled: ye believe in God, believe also in me. In my Father's house are many mansions: if it were not so, I would have told you. I go to prepare a place for you" **(John 14:1–2)**.

Introduction

Jesus was about to leave his disciples, and their hearts were heavy with sorrow. Their dearest Friend was no longer to be physically present. This was more than they could bear. Jesus, sensing this, said, "Let not your hearts be troubled." This was what they needed for their hour of crisis.

We stand much in the same position today. Our friend, our loved one, has been removed from our midst, and our hearts are breaking with sorrow.

I believe that the same message that Jesus gave two thousand years ago to those sorrowing disciples, he gives to us in this hour. Basically, Jesus said three things that speak comfort to us.

I. Jesus was saying that your faith in God is sufficient.

"You believe in God, believe also in me."

A. *Our loved one embodied this faith.* Early in life he placed his trust in Jesus. Every step of his life was lived in this faith. Like Enoch, he "walked with God and he was not, for God took him." God simply said, "I've left you on earth long enough. Now I want you home with me."

B. *This same faith sustains us today.* It helps us to see that God is working for good in all things for those who love him and are called according to his purpose (Rom. 8:28).

C. *Our faith tells us that God's grace is sufficient for our every need in the hour of crisis.*

II. Jesus was saying that death is not the end.

It is the beginning of a richer, fuller, more abundant life than we have ever known. "I will come again and receive you unto myself."

A. *It means that our loved one is today with Christ.*

B. *He is in heaven with all of its glories.*

C. *There is no more sorrow or heartache for him.* There is no more suffering. He is now released from all this. Instead, there is joy and happiness and peace.

D. *For our loved one it is a time of reward.* Jesus will say to him, "Well done, thou good and faithful servant."

III. Jesus was saying that we can see our loved one again.

"Where I am, there ye may be also."

A. *One day Jesus shall come for us also.*

B. *We, too, shall be with our Savior and with those whom "we have loved and lost for a while."* That husband or wife, that father or mother, that sister or brother will be seen and known before the throne of God.

Conclusion

This is our Christian faith. This is why we do not come to this hour with unrestrained sorrow and grief. This is why we can even rejoice in the victory our loved one has experienced. This is what Christ does for his own!

WEDDINGS

Title: Marriage Ceremony

We are gathered together in this holy and happy sacred hour in which two devoted hearts are joined in the bonds of matrimony. This noblest of human contracts was first celebrated in the Garden of Eden when God the Father placed the stamp of his approval thereupon by uniting the first man and the first woman in enduring wedlock. Centuries later when a wedding was celebrated in Cana of Galilee, it was sanctioned by the blessed presence of our Lord. And that noblest of all his apostles, the beloved Paul, writes in his epistles that marriage is honorable in all.

Both of you, in the sweet and quiet hours of your loving communion, have thought of the duties and obligations that grow out of your relationship. Now you present yourselves before me, a minister of God's Holy Word and an officer of this state, to pledge your love and to take upon you wedlock's holy vows.

Who gives this woman to be married to this man?

(Response.)

If anyone knows of any reason why this ceremony should not go forward, let him speak now or forever hold his peace.

Let us pray. *(Pastor prays.)*

And now if you come to me, having the real desire in your hearts to be joined in the indissoluble bonds of abiding wedlock, and if you know of no legal, moral, or religious barriers to such a union between yourselves, please signify such by joining your right hands.

Do you, _____, take _____ to be your lawful wedded wife (husband), promising before God, with your friends as witnesses, that you will be to her (him) a faithful, loving, and devoted husband (wife); that you will provide for her (him) and encourage her (him); that you will honor her (him) and remain with her (him) in sickness and in health, in prosperity and adversity; and that, forsaking all others, you will keep yourself to her (him), and to her (him) only, as long as you both shall live?

(I do.)

Are there tokens of this union?

From time immemorial the ring has been used to seal important covenants. When the race was young and the state was new the great seal was fixed upon a ring worn by the reigning monarch and the simple band of gold was often exchanged by friends as a sign of enduring good will. But in recent times the ring has been devoted to the more beautiful purpose of sealing the engagement and the holy covenant of marriage, the purity of which is symbolized by its circle, having neither beginning nor end.

Take this ring, _____, and place it on the third finger of the bride's left hand, and repeat after me:

With this ring I do thee wed, and with all my earthly goods and love I do thee endow.

(Same for bride.)

Please rejoin your right hands.

Having pledged your faith and love to each other and having sealed your solemn marital vows by giving and receiving the rings, by the authority vested in me and by the laws of this state and by divine sanction I pronounce you husband and wife in the presence of God and these witnesses. Therefore, let all men take care in the sight of God that this holy covenant shall ever remain sacred, and what God hath joined together let no one put asunder.

Let us pray.

Ladies and gentlemen may I present to you Mr. and Mrs. _____.

Title: Wedding Ceremony

It is a happy and dedicated hour that we now observe to unite two Christians in the highest, most virtuous, and most perfect of the human expressions of love.

It has always been known among those who know Jehovah as God and live for him that no greater declaration can be found than that which has resounded upon the ancient cliffs of the old world and now is echoed as the prayer of these two as they face each other at the marriage altar.

Entreat me not to leave thee,
and to return from following after thee,
for whither thou goest, I will go,
and where thou lodgest, I will lodge:
Thy people shall be my people
and thy God my God,
where thou diest, will I die,
and there will I be buried.

Such a loyalty and such a devotion is naught but natural when the heart from which it flows is first dedicated to the Author of love himself. Then I charge you both in the presence of God and this company and in this dedicated hour always to draw whatever affection God's grace might grant you from him who is its Creator. I charge you to make him the center of your home and the Father who meets your greatest and smallest needs. I charge you to make this union the completion of your personality, your spirit and your flesh. Upon these charges rests your future usefulness to the kingdom of God. I charge you to dedicate this hour, its memories, and its results to God. _____, wilt thou have this woman (man) to be thy wedded wife (husband), to live together after God's ordinance in the holy estate of matrimony? Wilt thou love her (him) comfort her (him), honor and keep her (him), in sickness and in health; and, forsaking all others, keep thee only unto her (him), as long as ye both shall live? (I will.)

Who giveth this woman to be married to this man?

(Response.)

Do you, _____, take_____ to be your wedded wife (husband), to have and to hold from this day forward, for better, for worse, for richer, for poorer, in sickness and in health, to love and to cherish, till death do you part, according to God's holy ordinance; and thereto pledge your love? (I do.)

Ring Ceremony

(Take bride's ring from best man and hold in hand.)

The ring has been used for centuries to seal important covenants. When the race was young and parliaments unknown, the great seal of a state was fixed upon a ring that was worn by the reigning monarch or ruler. This was to denote his imperial authority.

Now friends exchange the simple band as an enduring evidence of goodwill. It stands as a seal for the covenant between two hearts that unite as one. It stands as a symbol of purity as it gives testimony of a pledge of faith and trust in your companion.

(Hands ring to groom [bride] to be placed on the third finger of the left hand of the bride [groom]. He [she] holds hand. Groom [bride] repeats, "This ring I give in token and pledge of my constant faith and abiding love." They then join right hands.)

Having pledged your faith in and love to each other, and having sealed your solemn vows by giving and receiving the rings, acting in the authority granted me by the laws of this state and looking to heaven for divine sanction, I now pronounce you husband and wife, in the presence of God and these assembled witnesses. Therefore, let all take care in the sight of God that this holy covenant shall ever remain sacred.

Let us pray.

Sentence Sermonettes

Do unto others as though you were the others.
If God is your partner, make your plans big.
Hope is life and life is hope.
The worldly hope people set their hearts upon turns to ashes.
The Bible is to be trusted and not just dusted.
Christ makes no compromises with anything that is wrong.
If one aims at nothing, he will hit it every time.
The light that shines the farthest shines brightest at its base.
Foul-mouthed people fill the air with the smog of bitterness.
In our social life we have to know in order to love, but in our spiritual life we
    have to love in order to know.
For the Christian, death is but an inevitable interlude that has to be passed
    through on the way to life.
Good work rendered for the Lord, however humble, never dies.
Death is not the end; it is only "the gate on the skyline" leading to the
    presence of Jesus Christ.
The soul would have no rainbow if the eyes had no tears.
To take time to pray is to save time for work.
We pray not to change God's mind but to understand his mind.
God's wisdom is eternal.
With Jesus, prayer always preceded service.
God's wisdom is both timely and timeless.
Prayer is the heart of worship.
God does not share his greatest riches with those who cultivate him for what
    they hope to get for themselves.
Any talent, however simple, can be used to minister for God to man.
The supreme treasure in life is service.
Kindness is a language understood by all.
One does not really give until he gives his all.
You never truly test the power of God until you attempt the impossible.
God works with both hands.
Prayer is private conversation between God and one of his children.
Prayer is the most necessary action of a Christian.
Stewardship is like the beating of your heart; either you do it, or it isn't done
    for you.
Success has many fathers, but defeat is an orphan.
Nothing lies beyond the reach of prayer except those things that lie outside
    the will of God.

Impatience is a thief.

Trouble is only opportunity in work clothes.

Better to be poisoned in one's blood than to be poisoned in one's principles.

He who would be a mover of the world must not be moved by the world.

Subject Index

Index of Scripture Texts

Axiom

Powerful Leadership Proverbs

Author: Bill Hybels,
author of Courageous Leadership

The best leaders not only lead well but also reflect on their leadership long enough and thoughtfully enough to articulate the philosophies that enable them to lead. Whether serving in the marketplace or in ministry, as executives or rank-and-file employees, as salaried staff or volunteer servants, good leaders can pinpoint the rationale for their actions and decisions with the ease of reciting their home address.

In *Axiom* author Bill Hybels divulges the God-given convictions that have dictated his leadership strategy for more than three decades as senior pastor of Willow Creek Community Church.

Axiom brokers accessible wisdom from one leader's journey and emboldens you to nail down the reasons why you lead the way you lead.

Axiom is available in:

Hardcover, Jacketed: 978-0-310-27236-6   Audio CD: 978-0-310-28540-3

Or as an ebook in various reader formats:

Adobe, ePub, Microsoft, Mobipocket , Palm, Sony

Pick up a copy today at your favorite bookstore!

The Power of Multisensory Preaching and Teaching

Increase Attention, Comprehension, and Retention

Author: Rick Blackwood

Most preaching and teaching in the church engage only one of the senses—hearing. In *The Power of Multisensory Preaching and Teaching*, Rick Blackwood shows how recognizing and engaging the multiple senses of your congregation can lead to greater impact.

Blackwood presents both biblical evidence and scientific research showing that the more senses we stimulate in teaching and preaching, the greater the levels of learner attention, comprehension, and retention. Blackwood addresses both the "why" and the "how" of multisensory communication. Regardless of a person's current skill level, this practical book can help anyone add multisensory elements to messages in order to take communication to the next level—more compelling, clear, and memorable. As a result of reading this book readers can be more effective as a communicator and teacher. The book includes tools, examples, and worksheets.

Hardcover, Jacketed: 978-0-310-28097-2

Pick up a copy today at your favorite bookstore!

Mad Church Disease

Overcoming the Burnout Epidemic

Author: Anne Jackson

Growing up as the daughter of a pastor, Anne Jackson experienced firsthand the conflict, stress, and struggle church leaders often face. She vowed her life in ministry would be different.

Yet, years later, as a church leader, she was hospitalized because stress began wreaking havoc on her body. After being released from the hospital, an associate pastor asked her, "Does working at this church interfere with your communion with Christ?" The question was paramount in turning her life around.

Thinking she wasn't alone, Anne developed a website that allows church leaders to share their struggles. Within a few days she was flooded with over a thousand responses from people pouring out their stories of burnout.

Using anecdotal parallels between Mad Cow Disease and leadership trends in the church, Anne writes not only to help us realize what church leaders are facing, but also to provide practical and positive treatment plans.

Mad Church Disease is a lively, informative, and potentially life-saving resource for anyone in ministry—vocational or volunteer—who would like to understand, prevent, or treat the epidemic of burnout in church culture.

Hardcover, Printed: 978-0-310-28755-1

Pick up a copy today at your favorite bookstore!

What Women Wish Pastors Knew

Understanding the Hopes, Hurts, Needs, and Dreams of Women in the Church

Author: Denise George

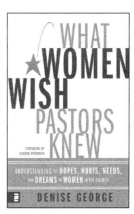

This book will open your eyes to the needs, frustrations, dreams, and potential of your church's greatest resource—the 60 percent of its members who provide far more than 60 percent of what keeps it going. The women of your church think the world of you, pastor. But they deeply wish you understood a few things about them that can make an enormous difference to their well-being and that of your church.

From the findings of her personal survey of hundreds of Christian women, Denise George shares unique, long-overdue insights about things that have left you scratching your head. Better still, you'll find out what you can actually do about

- The tiredness and the hurts of women
- Their longing for friends, fellowship, and spiritual growth
- Their concerns for their marriages and their children
- Your impact on them
- Respecting the ways women differ from men
- Helping women fulfill their need to give to the church ... and much more.

Hardcover, Jacketed: 978-0-310-26930-4

Pick up a copy today at your favorite bookstore!

Joshua

The NIV Application Commentary

Author: Robert L. Hubbard Jr.

Most Bible commentaries take us on a one-way trip from our world to the world of the Bible. They focus on the original meaning of the passage but don't discuss its contemporary application. The information they offer is valuable — but the job is only half done! The NIV Application Commentary Series helps draw both halves of the interpretive task together. This unique, award-winning series shows readers how to bring an ancient message into our present-day context.

Renowned Old Testament scholar Robert L. Hubbard brings the text of Joshua to life with this latest installment in The NIV Application Commentary series. Joshua is often unsettling reading for any church congregation, but it is still the Word of God and can have the same powerful impact today as it did when it was first written. Robert Hubbard's thoughtful work will be a boon to pastors who wish to guide their congregations through the entirety of Scripture.

Hardcover, Printed: 978-0-310-20934-8

Pick up a copy today at your favorite bookstore!

The Zondervan Greek and English Interlinear: New Testament (TNIV/NLT)

Author: William D. Mounce and Robert H. Mounce, General Editors

Edited by two foremost scholars of biblical languages, this Zondervan interlinear Bible offers the following features:

- Word-for-word (NLT) and dynamic equivalency (TNIV) translation approaches side by side
- Interlinear text as a third translation
- Parsing and Goodrich/Kohlenberger numbers for each word
- Greek/English dictionary accessible by G/K number
- Clear, easy-to-use interior design

Printed Caseside: 978-0-310-29082-7

Pick up a copy today at your favorite bookstore!

ZONDERVAN ACADEMIC

Rick Warren's Bible Study Methods

Twelve Ways You Can Unlock God's Word

Author: Rick Warren

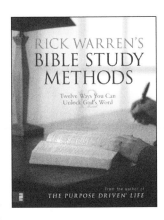

Get Your Congregation into Deeper Study

Your church members were created to become like Christ. This is one of the five God-ordained purposes for your life described in *The Purpose Driven® Life* by Rick Warren, and it is why studying the Bible is so important. This easy-to-understand book shows readers how to study the Bible Rick Warren's way. It gives them not just one, but twelve methods for exploring the riches of God's Word. At least one of them is exactly what each of your church members is looking for—an approach that's right for them, right where they're at.

Simple step-by-step instructions will guide your congregation through the how-tos of the following methods:

- Devotional
- Chapter Summary
- Character Quality
- Thematic
- Biographical
- Topical
- Word Study
- Book Background
- Book Survey
- Chapter Analysis
- Book Synthesis
- Verse Analysis

Thousands of individuals, small groups, churches, and seminary classes have used this practical manual to unlock the wonderful truths of Scripture.

Softcover: 978-0-310-27300-4

Pick up a copy today at your favorite bookstore!

Share Your Thoughts

With the Author: Your comments will be forwarded to the author when you send them to *zauthor@zondervan.com*.

With Zondervan: Submit your review of this book by writing to *zreview@zondervan.com*.

Free Online Resources at

www.zondervan.com

Zondervan AuthorTracker: Be notified whenever your favorite authors publish new books, go on tour, or post an update about what's happening in their lives.

Daily Bible Verses and Devotions: Enrich your life with daily Bible verses or devotions that help you start every morning focused on God.

Free Email Publications: Sign up for newsletters on fiction, Christian living, church ministry, parenting, and more.

Zondervan Bible Search: Find and compare Bible passages in a variety of translations at www.zondervanbiblesearch.com.

Other Benefits: Register yourself to receive online benefits like coupons and special offers, or to participate in research.